Mastering Elastic Kubernetes Service on AWS

Deploy and manage EKS clusters to support cloud-native applications in AWS

Malcolm Orr

Yang-Xin Cao (Eason)

BIRMINGHAM   MUMBAI

Mastering Elastic Kubernetes Service on AWS

Group Product Manager: Preet Ahuja

Publishing Product Manager: Niranjan Naikwadi

Senior Editor: Sayali Pingale

Technical Editor: Nithik Cheruvakodan

Copy Editor: Safis Editing

Project Coordinator: Deeksha Thakkar

Proofreader: Safis Editing

Indexer: Pratik Shirodkar

Production Designer: Shankar Kalbhor

Marketing Coordinator: Rohan Dobhal

First published: July 2023

Production reference: 1220623

Published by Packt Publishing Ltd.
Livery Place
35 Livery Street
Birmingham
B3 2PB, UK.

ISBN 978-1-80323-121-1

www.packtpub.com

Contributors

About the authors

Malcolm Orr is a principal engineer at AWS, who has spent close to two decades designing, building, and deploying systems and applications at telcos, banks, and media companies. He has published a number of books, with topics ranging from automating virtual data centers to site reliability engineering on AWS, and he works extensively with AWS customers, helping them adopt modern development practices for cloud-native applications.

I want to thank the people who have been close to me and supported me, especially my wife, Alison.

Yang-Xin Cao (Eason) has over five years of experience in AWS DevOps and the container field. He holds multiple accreditations, including AWS Professional Solution Architect, AWS Professional DevOps Engineer, and CNCF Certified Kubernetes Administrator. Fascinated by cloud technology, Eason joined AWS even before graduating from college in 2017. During his time at AWS, he successfully handled numerous critical troubleshooting issues and implemented various product improvements. His expertise and contributions have earned him the title of SME in AWS services, such as ECS, EKS, and CodePipeline. Additionally, he is the creator of `EasonTechTalk.com`, a platform dedicated to disseminating tech knowledge to a wider audience. You can find out more about him at `EasonCao.com`.

I am deeply grateful to the key individuals behind this book – Malcolm, Niranjan, Tanya, Deeksha, Sangeeta, Nihar, Shagun, and everyone in the Packt team. Their efforts have made this book possible and helped spread this fascinating technology to the world.

About the reviewers

Andres Sacco has worked as a developer since 2007 in different languages, including Java, PHP, Node.js, and Android. Most of his background is in Java and the libraries or frameworks associated with this language. In most of the companies that he has worked for, he has researched new technologies to improve the performance, stability, and quality of the applications of each company. He has dictated some internal courses to different audiences, such as developers, business analysts, and commercial people.

Werner Dijkerman is a freelance platform, Kubernetes (certified), and Dev(Sec)Ops engineer. He currently focuses on, and works with, cloud-native solutions and tools, including AWS, Ansible, Kubernetes, and Terraform. He focuses on infrastructure as code and monitoring the correct "thing," with tools such as Zabbix, Prometheus, and the ELK Stack. He has a passion for automating everything and avoiding doing anything that resembles manual work. He is an active reader of comics and self-care/psychology and IT-related books, and he is a technical reviewer of various books about DevOps, CI/CD, and Kubernetes.

Table of Contents

3

Building Your First EKS Cluster 27

4

Running Your First Application on EKS 49

5

Using Helm to Manage a Kubernetes Application 69

Part 2: Deep Dive into EKS

6

Securing and Accessing Clusters on EKS 83

7

Networking in EKS 93

Part 3: Deploying an Application on EKS

11

12

13

Part 5: Overcoming Common EKS Challenges

Preface

Welcome! This is a handy book on using **Elastic Kubernetes Service (EKS)** to effortlessly deploy and manage your Kubernetes clusters on AWS. With EKS, running Kubernetes on AWS becomes a breeze as you no longer have to worry about the complexity of managing the underlying infrastructure. **Kubernetes (K8s)** is one the fastest-growing open source projects in the world and is rapidly becoming the de facto container orchestration platform for cloud-native applications.

But for those not familiar with AWS, you might be wondering, *"Why is running Kubernetes on AWS challenging?"* There are a few factors that can make it difficult. One of the primary issues is configuring and managing the foundational AWS infrastructure, including virtual networks and security groups. Additionally, managing the resources required for a Kubernetes cluster can pose its own set of challenges. Integrating with other AWS services, such as load balancers and storage, can also introduce complexities. However, EKS has enabled many features to make these things easier, so rest assured that with time and effort, you can become proficient in managing a Kubernetes cluster on AWS – and the rewards will be well worth it.

This book looks at the AWS managed EKS service in detail, from its basic architecture and configuration through to advanced use cases such as GitOps or Service Mesh. The book aims to take the reader from a basic understanding of K8s and the AWS platform to being able to create EKS clusters and build and deploy production workloads on them.

Throughout the book, we will dive into various techniques that enable you to optimize your EKS clusters. The coverage spans a wide range of topics, including networking, security, storage, scaling, observability, service mesh, and cluster upgrade strategies. We have structured this book to provide you with a step-by-step guide to mastering EKS on AWS. Each chapter covers a specific topic and includes practical examples, tips, and best practices to help you understand and apply the concepts in real-world scenarios.

Our intention is not only to equip you with the technical skills required for success, but also to foster a deeper understanding of the underlying concepts so that you can apply them to your own unique situations.

Who this book is for

This book is aimed at engineers and developers with minimal experience of the AWS platform and K8s, who want to understand how to use EKS to run containerized workloads in their environments and integrate them with other AWS services. It's a practical guide with plenty of code examples, so familiarization with Linux, Python, Terraform, and YAML is recommended.

Overall, there are three main roles as the target audience who will gain practical insights from this book:

- **Developers and DevOps engineers**: They will understand the Kubernetes environment on AWS, know how to configure the cluster to run cloud-native applications by using EKS, and learn CI/CD practices.
- **Cloud architects**: They will gain a comprehensive understanding of how to design well-architected cloud infrastructure when running Kubernetes on AWS.
- **Kubernetes administrators**: Cluster administrators will learn the practical operation methods for managing Kubernetes workloads on AWS. Additionally, they will gain a complete understanding of EKS features to enhance cluster scalability, availability, and observability.

Whether you are just getting started with cloud computing or are looking to expand your knowledge and skills, this book has something for everyone who owns an AWS account and wants to start their EKS journey.

What this book covers

Chapter 1, The Fundamentals of Kubernetes and Containers, covers an introduction to Kubernetes and container technology. It will also deep dive into the elements that constitute a container, the concept of the container orchestrator, and the Kubernetes architecture.

Chapter 2, Introducing Amazon EKS, provides a comprehensive guide to explain what Amazon EKS is, its architecture behind the scenes, its pricing model, and the common mistakes that users may have. This chapter also gives you a brief overview to compare the options for running workloads on AWS: using EKS or a self-managed Kubernetes cluster.

Chapter 3, Building Your First EKS Cluster, explores different options to create your first EKS cluster step by step and gives an overview of the automation process when building your workflow, including the AWS console, AWS CLI, eksctl, AWS CDK, and Terraform.

Chapter 4, Running Your First Application on EKS, covers the different ways you can deploy and operate a simple application on EKS, including how to implement and expose your application to make it accessible externally. It also touches on tools to visualize your workload.

Chapter 5, Using Helm to Manage a Kubernetes Application, focuses on how to install and use Helm to simplify your Kubernetes deployment experience. This chapter also covers the details of Helm charts, their architecture, and common scenarios for their use.

Chapter 6, Securing and Accessing Clusters on EKS, dives into the essential aspects of authentication and authorization in Kubernetes and how they apply to EKS. The chapter explains the significance of configuring client tools and accessing your EKS cluster securely.

Chapter 7, Networking in EKS, explains Kubernetes networking and demonstrates how EKS can be seamlessly integrated with AWS **Virtual Private Cloud** (**VPC**).

Chapter 8, Managing Worker Nodes on EKS, explores the configuration and effective management of EKS worker nodes. It highlights the benefits of using EKS-optimized images (AMIs) and managed node groups, offering insights into their advantages over self-managed alternatives.

Chapter 9, Advanced Networking with EKS, delves into advanced networking scenarios in EKS. It covers topics such as managing Pod IP addresses with IPv6, implementing network policies for traffic control, and utilizing complex network-based information systems such as Multus CNI.

Chapter 10, Upgrading EKS Clusters, focuses on the strategies for upgrading EKS clusters to leverage new features and ensure continued support. It provides guidance on key areas to consider, including in-place and blue/green upgrades of the control plane, critical components, node groups, and migrating workloads to new clusters.

Chapter 11, Building Applications and Pushing Them to Amazon ECR, examines the process of building and storing container images on Amazon ECR for EKS deployments. It covers topics such as repository authentication, pushing container images, utilizing advanced ECR features, and integrating ECR into EKS clusters.

Chapter 12, Deploying Pods with Amazon Storage, explains Kubernetes volumes, **Container Storage Interface** (**CSI**), and the need for persistent storage in Kubernetes Pods, and demonstrates the usage of EBS and EFS on EKS. It also covers the details for installing and configuring AWS CSI drivers for utilizing EBS and EFS volumes with your application.

Chapter 13, Using IAM for Granting Access to Applications, discusses Pod security with a scenario on integrating IAM with your containerized applications. It includes defining IAM permissions for Pods, utilizing **IAM Roles for Service Accounts** (**IRSA**), and troubleshooting IAM issues specific to EKS deployments.

Chapter 14, Setting Load Balancing for Applications on EKS, explores the concept of load balancing for EKS applications. It also expands the discussion of scalability and resilience and provides insights into the **Elastic Load Balancer** (**ELB**) options available in AWS.

Chapter 15, Working with AWS Fargate, introduces AWS Fargate as an alternative serverless option for hosting Pods in EKS. It examines the benefits of using Fargate, provides guidance on creating Fargate profiles, deploying Pods to Fargate environments seamlessly, and troubleshooting common issues that may arise.

Chapter 16, Working with a Service Mesh, explores the use of service mesh technology to enhance control, visibility, and security in microservices-based ecosystems on EKS. The chapter covers the installation of the AWS App Mesh Controller, integration with Pods, leveraging AWS Cloud Map, and troubleshooting the Envoy proxy.

Chapter 17, EKS Observability, describes the importance of observability in EKS deployments and provides insights into monitoring, logging, and tracing techniques. The chapter covers native AWS tools for monitoring EKS clusters and Pods, building dashboards with Managed Prometheus and Grafana, leveraging OpenTelemetry, and utilizing machine learning capabilities to capture cluster status with DevOps Guru.

Chapter 18, Scaling Your EKS Cluster, discusses the challenges of capacity planning in EKS and explores various strategies and tools for scaling your cluster to meet application demands while optimizing cost. The chapter walks through topics such as scaling node groups with Cluster Autoscaler and Karpenter, scaling applications with **Horizontal Pod Autoscaler** (HPA), describing the use case of custom metrics, and utilizing KEDA to optimize event-driven autoscaling.

Chapter 19, Developing on EKS, explores ways to improve efficiency for developers and DevOps engineers when building EKS clusters. The chapter focuses on different automation tools and CI/CD practices to streamline these activities, including Cloud9, EKS Blueprints, Terraform, CodePipeline, CodeBuild, ArgoCD, and GitOps for workload deployment.

Chapter 20, Troubleshooting Common Issues, provides an EKS troubleshooting checklist and discusses common problems and their solutions.

To get the most out of this book

You will need an AWS Account and an operating system to run applications as listed in the table below. To ensure a smooth reading experience, knowledge of basic AWS concepts such **Virtual Private Cloud (VPC)**, **Elastic Block Storage (EBS)**, EC2, **Elastic Load Balancer (ELB)**, **Identity and Access Management (IAM)**, and Kubernetes are recommended.

Software covered in the book	Prequisite
Amazon Elastic Kubernetes Service (EKS)	An AWS Account
Amazon Command Line Interface (AWS CLI)	Linux/macOS/Linux
kubectl	Linux/macOS/Linux
eksctl	Linux/macOS/Linux
Helm	Linux/macOS/Linux
Lens (Kubernetes IDE)	Linux/macOS/Linux

In this book, we will explore various tools and learn how to manage Kubernetes clusters on AWS. You can find the latest version and download the required software by following the following guides:

- AWS CLI: https://docs.aws.amazon.com/cli/latest/userguide/getting-started-install.html
- kubectl: https://docs.aws.amazon.com/eks/latest/userguide/install-kubectl.html

- eksctl: `https://docs.aws.amazon.com/eks/latest/userguide/eksctl.html`
- Helm: `https://docs.aws.amazon.com/eks/latest/userguide/helm.html`
- Lens: `https://k8slens.dev/`

We have tried to make this a practical book with plenty of code examples. To get the most out of this book, you should have basic familiarity with AWS, Linux, YAML, and K8s architecture.

Download the color images

We also provide a PDF file that has color images of the screenshots and diagrams used in this book. You can download it here: `https://packt.link/g2oZN`.

Conventions used

There are a number of text conventions used throughout this book.

`Code in text`: Indicates code words in text, database table names, folder names, filenames, file extensions, pathnames, dummy URLs, user input, and Twitter handles. Here is an example: "The `MAINTAINER` and `CMD` commands don't generate layers."

A block of code is set as follows:

```
apiVersion: v1
kind: Pod
metadata:
  name: nginx
spec:
  containers:
```

Any command-line input or output is written as follows:

```
$ docker run hello-world
```

Bold: Indicates a new term, an important word, or words that you see onscreen. For instance, words in menus or dialog boxes appear in **bold**. Here is an example: "The most common example of this is **OverlayFS**, which is included in the Linux kernel and used by default by Docker."

> **Tips or important notes**
> Appear like this.

Get in touch

Feedback from our readers is always welcome.

General feedback: If you have questions about any aspect of this book, email us at customercare@packtpub.com and mention the book title in the subject of your message.

Errata: Although we have taken every care to ensure the accuracy of our content, mistakes do happen. If you have found a mistake in this book, we would be grateful if you would report this to us. Please visit www.packtpub.com/support/errata and fill in the form.

Piracy: If you come across any illegal copies of our works in any form on the internet, we would be grateful if you would provide us with the location address or website name. Please contact us at copyright@packt.com with a link to the material.

If you are interested in becoming an author: If there is a topic that you have expertise in and you are interested in either writing or contributing to a book, please visit authors.packtpub.com.

Share Your Thoughts

Once you've read *Mastering Elastic Kubernetes Service on AWS*, we'd love to hear your thoughts! Scan the QR code below to go straight to the Amazon review page for this book and share your feedback.

https://packt.link/r/1803231211

Your review is important to us and the tech community and will help us make sure we're delivering excellent quality content.

Download a free PDF copy of this book

Thanks for purchasing this book!

Do you like to read on the go but are unable to carry your print books everywhere?

Is your eBook purchase not compatible with the device of your choice?

Don't worry, now with every Packt book you get a DRM-free PDF version of that book at no cost.

Read anywhere, any place, on any device. Search, copy, and paste code from your favorite technical books directly into your application.

The perks don't stop there, you can get exclusive access to discounts, newsletters, and great free content in your inbox daily

Follow these simple steps to get the benefits:

1. Scan the QR code or visit the link below

https://packt.link/free-ebook/9781803231211

2. Submit your proof of purchase
3. That's it! We'll send your free PDF and other benefits to your email directly

Part 1:
Getting Started with
Amazon EKS

In this part, you will gain a comprehensive overview of Kubernetes and containers, along with insights into Amazon EKS and its architecture. You will also get your EKS cluster ready by following a step-by-step guide. By the end of this section, you will have learned the basics of deploying and operating an application on EKS, and will know how to utilize Helm to simplify your Kubernetes application deployments.

This section contains the following chapters:

- *Chapter 1, The Fundamentals of Kubernetes and Containers*
- *Chapter 2, Introducing Amazon EKS*
- *Chapter 3, Building Your First EKS Cluster*
- *Chapter 4, Running Your First Application on EKS*
- *Chapter 5, Using Helm to Manage a Kubernetes Application*

1
The Fundamentals of Kubernetes and Containers

As more organizations adopt agile development and modern (cloud-native) application architectures, the need for a platform that can deploy, scale, and provide reliable container services has become critical for many medium-sized and large companies. Kubernetes has become the de facto platform for hosting container workloads but can be complex to install, configure, and manage.

Elastic Kubernetes Service (**EKS**) is a managed service that enables users of the AWS platform to focus on using a Kubernetes cluster rather than spending time on installation and maintenance.

In this chapter, we will review the basic building blocks of Kubernetes. Specifically, however, we will be covering the following topics:

- A brief history of Docker, containerd, and runc

- A deeper dive into containers

- What is container orchestration?

- What is Kubernetes?

- Understanding Kubernetes deployment architectures

For a deeper understanding of the chapter, it is recommended that you have some familiarity with Linux commands and architectures.

> **Important note**
> The content in this book is intended for IT professionals that have experience building and/or running Kubernetes on-premises or on other cloud platforms. We recognize that not everyone with the prerequisite experience is aware of the background of Kubernetes so this first chapter is included (but optional) to provide a consistent view of where Kubernetes has come from and the supporting technology it leverages. If you think you already have a clear understanding of the topics discussed in this chapter, feel free to skip this one and move on to the next chapter.

A brief history of Docker, containerd, and runc

The IT industry has gone through a number of changes: from large, dedicated mainframes and UNIX systems in the 1970s-80s, to the virtualization movement with Solaris Zones, VMware, and the development of **cgroups** and **namespaces** in the Linux kernel in the early 2000s. In 2008, LXC was released. It provided a way to manage cgroups and namespaces in a consistent way to allow virtualization natively in the Linux kernel. The host system has no concept of a *container* so LXC orchestrates the underlying technology to create an isolated set of processes, that is, the container.

Docker, launched in 2013, was initially built on top of LXC and introduced a whole ecosystem around container management including a packaging format (the **Dockerfile**), which leverages a union filesystem to allow developers to build lightweight container images, and a runtime environment that manages Docker containers, container storage and CPU, RAM limits, and so on, while managing and transferring images (the **Docker daemon**) and provides an **Application Programming Interface** (**API**) that can be consumed by the Docker CLI. Docker also provides a set of registries (**Docker Hub**) that allows operating systems, middleware, and application vendors to build and distribute their code in containers.

In 2016, Docker extracted these runtime capabilities into a separate engine called **containerd** and donated it to the **Cloud Native Compute Foundation** (**CNCF**), allowing other container ecosystems such as Kubernetes to deploy and manage containers. Kubernetes initially used Docker as its container runtime, but in Kubernetes 1.15, the **Container Runtime Interface** (**CRI**) was introduced, which allows Kubernetes to use different runtimes such as containerd.

The **Open Container Initiative** (**OCI**) was founded by Docker and the container industry to help provide a lower-level interface to manage containers. One of the first standards they developed was the OCI Runtime Specification, which adopted the Docker image format as the basis for all of its image specifications. The **runc** tool was developed by the OCI to implement its Runtime Specification and has been adopted by most runtime engines, such as containerd, as a low-level interface to manage containers and images.

The following diagram illustrates how all the concepts we have discussed in this section fit together:

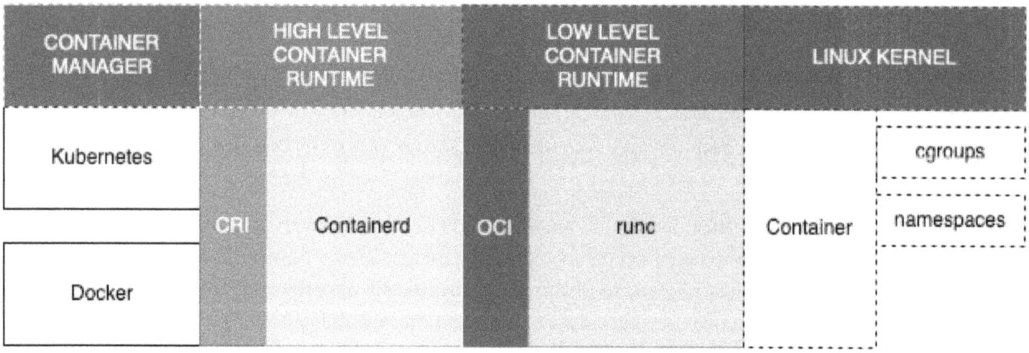

Figure 1.1 – Container runtimes

In this section, we discussed the history of containers and the various technologies used to create and manage them. In the next section, we will dive deeper into what a container actually consists of.

A deeper dive into containers

The container is a purely logical construction and consists of a set of technologies *glued* together by the container runtime. This section will provide a more detailed view of the technologies used in a Linux kernel to create and manage containers. The two foundational Linux services are namespaces and control groups:

- **Namespaces (in the context of Linux)**: A namespace is a feature of the Linux kernel used to partition kernel resources, allowing processes running within the namespace to be isolated from other processes. Each namespace will have its own **process IDs** (**PIDs**), hostname, network access, and so on.
- **Control groups**: A control group (cgroup) is used to limit the usage by a process or set of processes of resources such as CPU, RAM, disk I/O, or network I/O. Originally developed by Google, this technology has been incorporated into the Linux kernel.

The combination of namespaces and control groups in Linux allows a container to be defined as a set of isolated processes (namespace) with resource limits (cgroups):

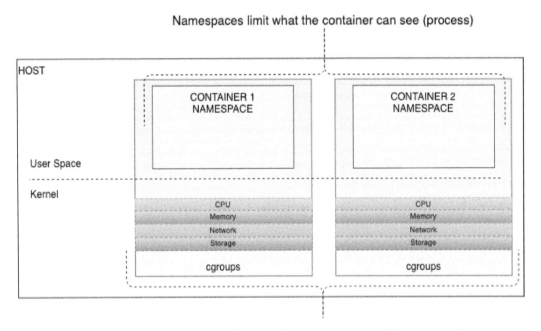

Figure 1.2 – The container as a combination of cgroup and namespace

The way the container runtime image is created is important as it has a direct bearing on how that container works and is secured. A **union filesystem** (**UFS**) is a special filesystem used in container images and will be discussed next.

Getting to know union filesystems

A UFS is a type of filesystem that can merge/overlay multiple directories/files into a single view. It also gives the appearance of a single writable filesystem, but is read-only and does allow the modification of the original content. The most common example of this is **OverlayFS**, which is included in the Linux kernel and used by default by Docker.

A UFS is a very efficient way to merge content for a container image. Each set of discreet content is considered a layer, and layers can be reused between container images. Docker, for example, will use the Dockerfile to create a layered file based on a base image. An example is shown in the following diagram:

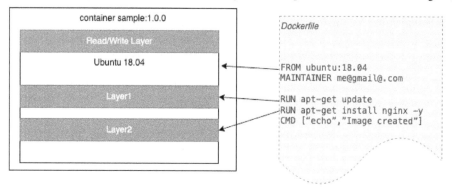

Figure 1.3 – Sample Docker image

In *Figure 1.3*, the FROM command creates an initial layer from the ubuntu 18.04 image. The output from the two RUN commands creates discreet layers while the final step is for Docker to add a thin read/write layer where all changes to the running container are written. The MAINTAINER and CMD commands don't generate layers.

Docker is the most prevalent container runtime environment and can be used on Windows, macOS, and Linux so it provides an easy way to learn how to build and run containers (although please note that the Windows and Linux operating systems are fundamentally different so, at present, you can't run Windows containers on Linux). While the Docker binaries have been removed from the current version of Kubernetes, the concepts and techniques in the next section will help you understand how containers work at a fundamental level.

How to use Docker

The simplest way to get started with containers is to use Docker on your development machine. As the OCI has developed standardization for Docker images, images created locally can be used anywhere. If you have already installed Docker, the following command will run a simple container with the official `hello-world` sample image and show its output:

```
$ docker run hello-world
Unable to find image 'hello-world:latest' locally
latest: Pulling from library/hello-world
2db29710123e: Pull complete
...
Status: Downloaded newer image for hello-world:latest
Hello from Docker!
```

This preceding message shows that your installation appears to be working correctly. You can see that the `hello-world` image is "pulled" from a repository. This defaults to the public Docker Hub repositories at `https://hub.docker.com/`. We will discuss repositories, and in particular, AWS **Elastic Container Registry** (**ECR**) in *Chapter 11, Building Applications and Pushing Them to Amazon ECR*.

> **Important note**
>
> If you would like to know how to install and run with Docker, you can refer to the *Get Started* guide in the Docker official documentation: `https://docs.docker.com/get-started/`.

Meanwhile, you can use the following command to list containers on your host:

```
$ docker ps -a
CONTAINER ID    IMAGE
  COMMAND         CREATED         STATUS
  PORTS       NAMES
39bad0810900    hello-world
  "/hello"                  10 minutes ago    Exited (0) 10
minutes ago               distracted_tereshkova
...
```

Although the preceding commands are simple, they demonstrate how easy it is to build and run containers. When you use the Docker CLI (client), it will interact with the runtime engine, which is the Docker daemon. When the daemon receives the request from the CLI, the Docker daemon proceeds with the corresponding action. In the `docker run` example, this means creating a container from the `hello-world` image. If the image is stored on your machine, it will use that; otherwise, it will try and *pull* the image from a public Docker repository such as *Docker Hub*.

As discussed in the previous section, Docker now leverages containerd and runc. You can use the `docker info` command to view the versions of these components:

```
$ docker info
...
   buildx: Docker Buildx (Docker Inc., v0.8.1)
   compose: Docker Compose (Docker Inc., v2.3.3)
   scan: Docker Scan (Docker Inc., v0.17.0)
.......
containerd version: 2a1d4dbdb2a1030dc5b01e96fb110a9d9f150ecc
 runc version: v1.0.3-0-gf46b6ba
 init version: de40ad0
 . . .
```

In this section, we looked at the underlying technology used in Linux to support containers. In the following sections, we will look at container orchestration and Kubernetes in more detail.

What is container orchestration?

Docker works well on a single machine, but what if you need to deploy thousands of containers across many different machines? This is what container orchestration aims to do: to schedule, deploy, and manage hundreds or thousands of containers across your environment. There are several platforms that attempt to do this:

- **Docker Swarm**: A cluster management and orchestration solution from Docker (`https://docs.docker.com/engine/swarm/`).

- **Kubernetes** (**K8s**): An open source container orchestration system, originally designed by Google and now maintained by CNCF. Thanks to active contributions from the open source community, Kubernetes has a strong ecosystem for a series of solutions regarding deployment, scheduling, scaling, monitoring, and so on (`https://kubernetes.io/`).

- **Amazon Elastic Container Service** (**ECS**): A highly secure, reliable, and scalable container orchestration solution provided by AWS. With a similar concept as many other orchestration systems, ECS also makes it easy to run, stop, and manage containers and is integrated with other AWS services such as CloudFormation, IAM, and ELB, among others (see more at `https://ecs.aws/`).

The control/data plane, a common architecture for container orchestrators, is shown in the following diagram:

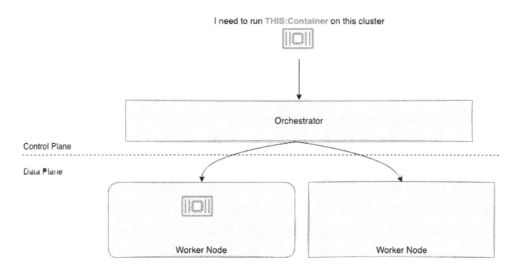

Figure 1.4 – An overview of container orchestration

Container orchestration usually consists of the *brain* or scheduler/orchestrator that decides where to put the containers (control plane), while the *worker* runs the actual containers (data plane). The orchestrator offers a number of additional features:

- Maintains the desired state for the entire cluster system

- Provisions and schedules containers

- Reschedules containers when a worker becomes unavailable

- Recovery from failure

- Scales containers in or out based on workload metrics, time, or some external event

We've spoken about container orchestration at the conceptual level, now let's take a look at Kubernetes to make this concept *real*.

What is Kubernetes?

Kubernetes is an open source container orchestrator originally developed by Google but now seen as the de facto container platform for many organizations. Kubernetes is deployed as clusters containing a control plane that provides an API that exposes the Kubernetes operations, a scheduler that schedules containers (Pods are discussed next) across the worker nodes, a datastore to store all cluster data and state (**etcd**), and a controller that manages jobs, failures, and restarts.

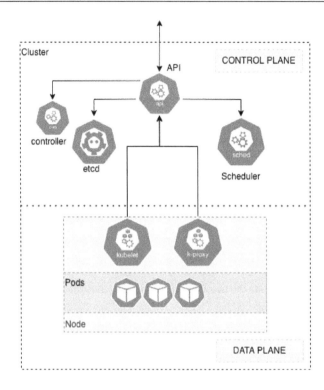

Figure 1.5 – An overview of Kubernetes

The cluster is also composed of many worker nodes that make up the data plane. Each node runs the **kubelet** agent, which makes sure that containers are running on a specific node, and **kube-proxy**, which manages the networking for the node.

One of the major advantages of Kubernetes is that all the resources are defined as objects that can be created, read, updated, and deleted. The next section will review the major K8s objects, or "**kinds**" as they are called, that you will typically be working with.

Key Kubernetes API resources

Containerized applications will be deployed and launched on a worker node(s) using the API. The API provides an abstract object called a **Pod**, which is defined as one or more containers sharing the same Linux namespace, cgroups, network, and storage resources. Let's look at a simple example of a Pod:

```
apiVersion: v1
kind: Pod
metadata:
  name: nginx
```

```
spec:
  containers:
  - name: nginx
    image: nginx:1.14.2
    ports:
    - containerPort: 80
```

In this example, `kind` defines the API object, a single Pod, and `metadata` contains the name of the Pod, in this case, `nginx`. The `spec` section contains one container, which will use the nginx `1.14.2` image and expose a port (80).

In most cases, you want to deploy multiple Pods across multiple nodes and maintain that number of Pods even if you have node failures. To do this, you use a Deployment, which will keep your Pods running. A Deployment is a Kubernetes `kind` that allows you to define the number of replicas or Pods you want, along with the Pod specification we saw previously. Let's look at an example that builds on the `nginx` Pod we discussed previously:

```
ApiVersion: apps/v1
kind: Deployment
metadata:
  name: nginx-deployment
  labels:
    app: nginx
spec:
  replicas: 3
  selector:
    matchLabels:
      app: nginx
  template:
    metadata:
      labels:
        app: nginx
    spec:
      containers:
      - name: nginx
        image: nginx:1.14.2
        ports:
        - containerPort: 80
```

Finally, you want to expose your Pods outside the clusters! This is because, by default, Pods and Deployments are only accessible from inside the cluster's other Pods. There are various services, but let's discuss the `NodePort` service here, which exposes a dynamic port on all nodes in the cluster.

To do this, you will use the `kind` of `Service`, an example of which is shown here:

```
kind: Service
apiVersion: v1
metadata:
  name: nginx-service
spec:
  type: NodePort
  selector:
    app: nginx
  ports:
  port: 80
  nodePort: 30163
```

In the preceding example, `Service` exposes port `30163` on any host in the cluster and maps it back to any Pod that has `label app=nginx` (set in the Deployment), even if a host is not running on that Pod. It translates the `port` value to port `80`, which is what the `nginx` Pod is listening on.

In this section, we've looked at the basic Kubernetes architecture and some basic API objects. In the final section, we will review some standard deployment architectures.

Understanding Kubernetes deployment architectures

There are a multitude of ways to deploy Kubernetes, depending on whether you are developing on your laptop/workstation, deploying to non-production or productions, or whether you are building it yourself or using a managed service such as EKS.

The following sections will discuss how Kubernetes can be deployed for different development environments such as locally on your laptop for testing or for production workloads.

Developer deployment

For local development, you may want to use a simple deployment such as minikube or Kind. These deploy a full control plane on a virtual machine (minikube) or Docker container (Kind) and allow you to deploy API resources on your local machine, which acts as both the control plane and data plane. The advantages of this approach are that everything is run on your development machine, you can easily build and test your app, and your Deployment manifests . However, you only have one worker node, which means that complex, multi-node application scenarios are not possible.

Non-production deployments

In most cases, non-production deployments have a non-resilient control plane. This typically means having a single master node hosting the control plane components (API server, etcd, and so on) and multiple worker nodes. This helps test multi-node application architectures but without the overhead of a complex control plane.

The one exception is integration and/or operational non-production environments where you want to test cluster or application operations in the case of a control plane failure. In this case, you may want to have at least two master nodes.

Self-built production environments

In production environments, you will need a resilient control plane, typically following the *rule of 3*, where you deploy 3, 6, or 9 control nodes to ensure an odd number of nodes are used to gain a majority during a failure event. The control plane components are mainly stateless, while configuration is stored in etcd. A load balancer can be deployed across the API controllers to provide resilience for K8s API requests; however, a key design decision is how to provide a resilient **etcd** layer.

In the first model, *stacked* etcd, etcd is deployed directly on the master nodes making the etcd and Kubernetes topologies tightly coupled (see `https://d33wubrfki0168.cloudfront.net/d1411cded83856552f37911eb4522d9887ca4e83/b94b2/images/kubeadm/kubeadm-ha-topology-stacked-etcd.svg`).

This means if one node fails, both the API layer and data persistence (etcd) layers are affected. A solution to this problem is to use an external etcd cluster hosted on separate machines than the other Kubernetes components, effectively decoupling them (see `https://d33wubrfki0168.cloudfront.net/ad49fffce42d5a35ae0d0cc1186b97209d86b99c/5a6ae/images/kubeadm/kubeadm-ha-topology-external-etcd.svg`).

In the case of the external etcd model, failure in either the API or etcd clusters will not impact the other. It does mean, however, that you will have twice as many machines (virtual or physical) to manage and maintain.

Managed service environments

AWS EKS is a managed service where AWS provides the control plane and you connect worker nodes to it using either self-managed or AWS-managed node groups (see *Chapter 8, Managing Worker Nodes on EKS*). You simply create a cluster and AWS will provision and manage at least two API servers (in two distinct Availability Zones) and a separate etcd autoscaling group spread over three Availability Zones.

The cluster supports a service level of 99.95% uptime and AWS will fix any issues with your control plane. This model means that you don't have any flexibility in the control plane architecture but, at the same time, you won't be required to manage it. EKS can be used for test, non-production, and production workloads, but remember there is a cost associated with each cluster (this will be discussed in *Chapter 2, Introducing Amazon EKS*).

Now you've learned about several architectures that can be implemented when building a Kubernetes cluster from development to production. In this book, you don't have to know how to build an entire Kubernetes cluster by yourself, as we will be using EKS.

Summary

In this chapter, we explored the basic concepts of containers and Kubernetes. We discussed the core technical concepts used by Docker, containerd, and runc on Linux systems, as well as scaling deployments using a container orchestration system such as Kubernetes.

We also looked at what Kubernetes is, reviewed several components and API resources, and discussed different deployment architectures for development and production.

In the next chapter, let's talk about the managed Kubernetes service, **Amazon Elastic Kubernetes Service** (**Amazon EKS**), in more detail and learn what its key benefits are.

Further reading

- *Understanding the EKS SLA*

  ```
  https://aws.amazon.com/eks/sla/
  ```

- *Understanding the Kubernetes API*

  ```
  https://kubernetes.io/docs/concepts/overview/kubernetes-api/
  ```

- *Getting started with minikube*

  ```
  https://minikube.sigs.k8s.io/docs/start/
  ```

- *Getting started with Kind*

  ```
  https://kind.sigs.k8s.io/docs/user/quick-start/
  ```

- *EKS control plane best practice*

  ```
  https://aws.github.io/aws-eks-best-practices/reliability/docs/controlplane/
  ```

- *Open Container Initiative document*

  ```
  https://opencontainers.org/
  ```

2

Introducing Amazon EKS

In the previous chapter, we talked about the basic concepts of a container, container orchestration, and Kubernetes. Building and managing a Kubernetes cluster by yourself can be a very complex and time-consuming task, but using a managed Kubernetes service can remove all that heavy lifting and allow users to focus on application development and deployment.

In this chapter, we are going to explore **Elastic Kubernetes Service** (**EKS**) and its technical architecture at a high level to get a good understanding of its benefits and drawbacks.

To sum up, this chapter covers the following topics:

- What is Amazon EKS?
- Understanding the EKS architecture
- Investigating the Amazon EKS pricing model
- Common mistakes when using EKS

Technical requirements

You should have some familiarity with the following:

- What Kubernetes is and how it works (refer to *Chapter 1, The Fundamentals of Kubernetes and Containers*)
- AWS foundational services including **Virtual Private Cloud** (**VPC**), **Elastic Computing Cloud** (**EC2**), **Elastic Block Storage** (**EBS**), and **Elastic Load Balancer** (**ELB**)
- A general appreciation of standard Kubernetes deployment tools

What is Amazon EKS?

According to data from **Cloud Native Computing Foundation** (CNCF), at the end of 2017, nearly 57% of Kubernetes environments were running on AWS. Initially, if you wanted to run Kubernetes on AWS, you had to build the cluster by using tools such as Rancher or Kops on top of EC2 instances. You would also be required to constantly monitor and manage the cluster, deploying open source tools such as Prometheus or Grafana, and have a team of operational staff making sure the cluster was available and managing the upgrade process. Kubernetes also has a regular release cadence: three releases per year as of June 2021! This also leads to a constant operational pressure to upgrade the cluster.

As the AWS service roadmap is predominately driven by customer requirements, the effort needed to build and run Kubernetes on AWS led to the AWS service teams releasing EKS in June 2018.

Amazon EKS is Kubernetes! AWS takes the open source code, adds AWS-specific plugins for identity and networking (discussed later in this book), and allows you to deploy it in your AWS account. AWS will then manage the control plane and allow you to connect compute and storage resources to it, allowing you to run Pods and store Pod data.

Today, Amazon EKS has been adopted by many leading organizations worldwide – Snap Inc., HSBC, Delivery Hero, Fidelity Investments, and more. It simplifies the Kubernetes management process of building, securing, and following best practices on AWS, which brings benefits for organizations so they can focus on building container-based applications instead of creating Kubernetes clusters from scratch.

> Cloud Native Computing Foundation
>
> CNCF is a Linux Foundation project that was founded in 2015 and is responsible for driving Kubernetes development along with other cloud-native projects. CNCF has over 600 members including AWS, Google, Microsoft, Red Hat, SAP, Huawei, Intel, Cisco, IBM, Apple, and VMware.

Why use Amazon EKS?

The main advantage of using EKS is that you no longer have to manage the control plane; even upgrades are a single-click operation. As simple as this sounds, the operational savings of having AWS deploy, scale, fix, and upgrade your control plane cannot be underestimated for production environments or when you have many clusters.

As EKS is a managed service, it is also heavily integrated into the AWS ecosystem. This means the following:

- Pods are first-class network citizens, have VPC network addresses, and can be managed and controlled like any other AWS resources
- Pods can be allocated specific **Identity and Access Management** (IAM) roles, simplifying how Kubernetes-based applications connect and use AWS services such as DynamoDB

- Kubernetes' control and data plane logs and metrics can be sent to AWS CloudWatch where they can be reported on, managed, and visualized without any additional servers or software required

- Operational and development teams can mix compute (EC2 and/or Fargate) and storage services (EBS and/or EFS) to support a variety of performance, cost, and security requirements

> **Important note**
> It's important to understand that EKS is predominantly a managed control plane. The data plane uses standard AWS services such EC2 and Fargate to provide the runtime environment for Pods. The data plane is, in most cases, managed by the operational or development teams.

In subsequent chapters, we will dive deep into these areas and illustrate how they are used and configured. But for now, let's move on to the differences between a self-managed K8s cluster and EKS.

Self-managed Kubernetes clusters versus Amazon EKS

The following table compares the two approaches of self-built clusters versus EKS:

	Self-managed Kubernetes cluster	EKS
Full control	Yes	Mostly (no direct access to underlying control plane servers)
Kubernetes Version	Community release	Community release
Version Support	The Kubernetes project maintains release branches for the most recent three minor releases. From Kubernetes 1.19 onward, releases receive approximately 1 year of patch support. Kubernetes 1.18 and older received approximately 9 months of patch support.	A Kubernetes version is supported for 14 months after first being available on Amazon EKS, even if it is no longer supported by the Kubernetes project/community.
Network Access Control	Manually set up and configure VPC controls	EKS creates standard security groups and supports public IP whitelisting.
Authentication	Manually set up and configure Kubernetes RBAC controls	Integrated with AWS IAM
Scalability	Manually setup and configure scaling	Managed control plane and standard compute/storage scaling
Security	Manually patched	Control plane patching is done by AWS

	Self-managed Kubernetes cluster	**EKS**
Upgrade	Manually update and replace components	Upgrade with a single click for the control plane, while managed node groups support simpler upgrades
Monitoring	Need to monitor by yourself and support the monitoring platform	EKS will do monitoring and replace unhealthy master nodes, integrated with CloudWatch

Table 2.1 – Comparing self-managed Kubernetes and EKS

In the next section, we will dive deeper into the EKS architecture so you can begin to really understand the differences between a self-managed cluster and EKS.

Understanding the EKS architecture

Every EKS cluster will have a single endpoint URL used by tools such as kubectl, the main Kubernetes client. This URL hides all the control plane servers deployed on an AWS-managed VPC across multiple Availability Zones in the region you have selected to deploy the cluster to, and the servers that make up the control plane are not accessible to the cluster users or administrators.

The data plane is typically composed of EC2 workers that are deployed across multiple Availability Zones and have the **kubelet** and **kube-proxy** agents configured to point to the cluster endpoint. The following diagram illustrates the standard EKS architecture:

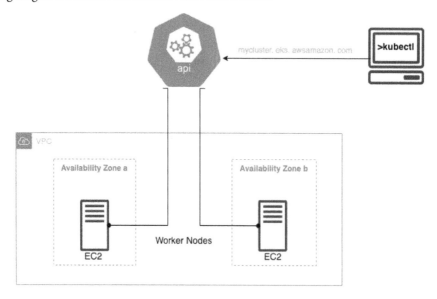

Figure 2.1 – High-level overview of EKS architecture

The next sections will look into how AWS configures and secures the EKS control plane along with specific commands you can use to interact with it.

Understanding the EKS control plane

When a new cluster is created, a new control plane is created in an AWS-owned VPC in a separate account. There are a minimum of two API servers per control plane, spread across two Availability Zones for resilience, which are then exposed through a public **network load balancer** (**NLB**). The etcd servers are spread across three Availability Zones and configured in an autoscaling group, again for resilience.

The clusters administrators and/or users have no direct access to the cluster's servers; they can only access the K8s API through the load balancer. The API servers are integrated with the worker nodes running under a different account/VPC owned by the customer by creating **Elastic Network Interfaces** (**ENIs**) in two Availability Zones. The kubelet agent running on the worker nodes uses a Route 53 private hosted zone, attached to the worker node VPC, to resolve the IP addresses associated with the ENIs. The following diagram illustrates this architecture:

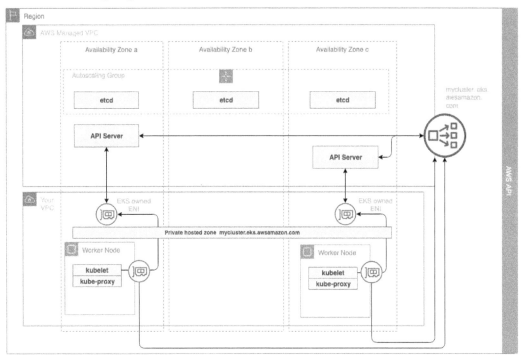

Figure 2.2 – Detailed EKS architecture

> **Important note**
>
> One key *gotcha* with this architecture, as there is currently no private EKS endpoint, is that worker nodes need internet access to be able to get the cluster details through the AWS EKS DescribeCluster API. This generally means that subnets with worker nodes need either an internet/NAT gateway or a route to the internet.

Understanding cluster security

When a new cluster is created, a new security group is also created and controls access to the API server ENIs. The cluster security group must be configured to allow any network addresses that need to access the API servers. In the case of a public cluster (discussed in *Chapter 7, Networking in EKS*), these ENIs are only used by the worker nodes. When the cluster is private, these ENIs are also used for client (kubectl) access to the API servers; otherwise, all API connectivity is through the public endpoint.

Typically, separate security groups are configured for the worker nodes and allow access to and from the nodes that make up the data plane. AWS has a feature called *security group referencing*, with which you can reference an existing security group from another security group. This simplifies the process of connecting worker nodes to cluster ENIs by referencing any worker node security groups in the cluster security group. The minimum you will need to allow from the worker node security group is HTTPS (TCP 443), DNS (TCP/UDP 53), and kubelet commands and logs (TCP 10250). The following diagram illustrates this architecture.

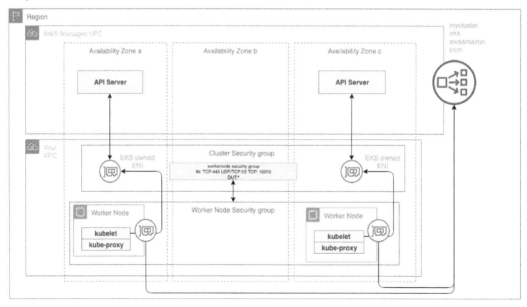

Figure 2.3 – EKS security groups

Understanding your cluster through the command line

Let's use the AWS and kubectl **Command Line Interpreters** (**CLIs**) to explore a newly created cluster. We can begin by discovering which clusters are available in a specific region using the AWS CLI aws eks list-clusters command:

```
$ aws eks list-clusters
{
    "clusters": [
        "mycluster13DCA0395 "
    ]}
```

In the preceding output, we can see one cluster listed. We can get more details using the aws eks describe-cluster –name command:

```
$ aws eks describe-cluster --name mycluster13DCA0395
{
    "cluster": {
        "status": "ACTIVE",
        "endpoint": "https://12.gr7.eu-central-1.eks.amazonaws.
com",
.......... . .
        "name": "mycluster13DCA0395 ",
.......
            "endpointPublicAccess": true,
            "endpointPrivateAccess": true
............}
```

The preceding output has been truncated but shows the endpoint located in the eu-central-1 region. We can see the name of the cluster and that the endpoint is set to allow PublicAccess (internet) and also PrivateAccess (VPC). This means your client (kubectl, for example) can access the cluster through the internet or from anything connected that can route to the VPC hosting the cluster ENIs (assuming access lists, firewall rules, and security groups allow access).

One further step is needed before we can use kubectl, which is to use the aws eks update-kubeconfig command to set up the relevant certificates and contexts in the config file to allow **kubectl** to communicate with the cluster. This can be done manually, but it's much easier to use the AWS CLI command:

```
$ aws eks update-kubeconfig --name mycluster13DCA03950b0
Updated context arn:aws:eks:eu-central-1:676687:cluster/
mycluster13DCA0395 in /../.kube/config
```

> **Important note**
> You will need IAM privileges to the AWS EKS to perform these commands, along with K8s RBAC privilege to perform the kubectl commands, even if you have network access to the cluster endpoint.

If you use the `kubectl cluster-info` and `kubectl version` commands, you'll see similar information displayed to the `aws eks describe-cluster` command. Cluster node, storage, and Pod details can be determined using the kubectl commands, `get nodes`, `get pv`, and `get po`, as shown here. Namespace and sort command modifiers can be used to help with the output:

```
$ kubectl get nodes
NAME            STATUS    ROLES     AGE    VERSION
ip-x.x.x.x.     Ready     <none>    25d    v1.21.5-eks-9017834
ip-x.x.x.x.     Ready     <none>    25d    v1.21.5-eks-9017834
$kubectl get pv --sort-by=.spec.capacity.storage
No resources found
$ kubectl get po --all-namespaces
NAMESPACE       NAME        READY    STATUS     RESTARTS    AGE
kube-system     aws-node-d2vpk    1/1       Running    0   1d
kube-system     aws-node-ljdz6   1/1      Running    0  1d
kube-system     coredns-12    1/1       Running    0  1d
kube-system     coredns-12    1/1       Running    0    1d
kube-system     kube-proxy-bhw6p 1/1 Running    0    1d
kube-system     kube-proxy-fdqlb  1/1 Running    0            1d
```

The previous output tells us that the cluster has two worker nodes with no physical volumes configured, and is just hosting the key cluster services of `coredns` (cluster DNS services), `kube-proxy` (cluster networking), and `aws-node` (AWS VPC CNI).

Now that we have reviewed what EKS is, let's look at how it's priced in AWS.

Investigating the Amazon EKS pricing model

In this section, we will have a brief overview of the Amazon EKS pricing model. As the pricing model for AWS changes from time to time, it is always recommended to check out the latest updates on the Amazon EKS pricing page to get more detail:

- Amazon EKS pricing: `https://aws.amazon.com/eks/pricing/`
- AWS Pricing Calculator: `https://calculator.aws`

A single cluster will incur two types of costs:

- Fixed monthly costs for the EKS control plane
- Variable costs from your computing, networking, and storage resources

Fixed control plane costs

Control plane pricing is fixed at $0.10 per hour, which equates to $73 (USD) per month per cluster, as shown in the following calculation. This is irrespective of any scaling or failure recovery activities that happen in the control plane managed by AWS.

1 cluster x 0.10 USD per hour x 730 hours per month = 73.00 USD

Variable costs

By itself, the control plane cannot really work. It needs compute resources so it can actually schedule and host Pods. In turn, the compute platform needs storage and networking to function, but these resources are very much based on a variable cost model that will fluctuate depending on how much is used.

There are two compute options for EKS workers, which will be discussed in detail later when we talk about worker nodes (EC2) and Fargate:

- When using EC2, costs will fluctuate based on the following:

  - The size and number of EC2 instances

  - The amount of storage attached to an instance

  - The region they are deployed into

  - The type of pricing model, on-demand, reserve instances, spot instances, or any saving plans you have

- When using Fargate, costs will fluctuate based on the following:

  - The number of Fargate instances

  - The instance operating system/CPU processor

  - The region they are deployed into

  - The per CPU/RAM per instance/hour used

  - The amount of GB storage/per instance

EC2 workers will communicate with each other and the control plane and Pods will do the same, communicating across worker nodes with each other and, in some cases, outside the VPC. AWS charges for egress traffic, cross-AZ traffic, and network services such as transit or NAT Gateway. Estimating costs for network traffic can be one of the most difficult activities as, in most cases, you have very little knowledge of how traffic will be routed in the application, nor technical aspects such as packet sizes, packets per second, and so on. Network traffic estimation is outside the scope of this book but there are some best practices you should try and observe:

- Design and deploy applications such that as much traffic as possible can be kept *inside* the worker node. For example, if two services need to communicate with each other, then use Pod **affinity** labels (EC2 only) to make sure they coexist on the same node/nodes.

- Design your AWS VPC to keep traffic in the same Availability Zones; for example, if your worker nodes are spread over two AZs for resilience, deploy two NAT gateway (one per AZ) to reduce cross-AZ network charges. This, of course, could be more expensive if you have very little internet traffic, so again, a full understanding of your application network profile is needed.

- When communicating with AWS services that have an AWS API, such as DynamoDB for example, use private endpoints to reduce the network egress costs.

We've looked at the theory, the next section will use some concrete examples to make it a bit clearer.

Estimating costs for an EKS cluster

To better help you understand how to estimate the cost when running an EKS cluster, here are a couple of examples of measuring expenses on AWS.

Example 1 – Running an EKS cluster with worker nodes by launching an EC2 instance

Assume that you choose to create an EKS cluster in the AWS US East Region (N. Virginia, us-east-1) with the following:

- 3 on-demand Linux EC2 instances with **m5.large** as the worker, each with a 20 GB EBS storage gp2 volume attached (General Purpose SSD)

- A cluster that's available all month (30 days, 730 hours)

The monthly expense can be estimated with the following formula:

1 cluster x 0.10 USD per hour x 730 hours per month = 73.00 USD

3 instances x 0.096 USD x 730 hours in a month = 210.24 USD (monthly on-demand cost)

30 GB x 0.10 USD x 3 instances = 9.00 USD (EBS cost)

Totaling all these costs results in a cost per month of $292.24.

> **Important note**
> This is just a simple example; in reality, these costs can be (and should be) significantly reduced using saving plans or reserved instances and storage options such as gp3.

Example 2 – Running an EKS cluster with AWS Fargate

In the previous example, each **m5.large** instance supports 8GB of RAM and 2 vCPUs and, therefore, we can deploy many Pods to each worker node. If we now choose to use Fargate as the compute layer, we now need to think in terms of how many Pods we need to support, as one Fargate instance supports one Pod.

Assume that we have the same cluster control plane/region but with the following:

- 15 Pods running and supported by 15 Fargate instances, each with 1 vCPU and 2 GB memory, and 20GB of ephemeral storage
- 15 tasks or Pods per day (730 hours in a month / 24 hours in a day) = 456.25 tasks per month

The monthly expense can be estimated with the following formula:

1 cluster x 0.10 USD per hour x 730 hours per month = 73.00 USD

456.25 tasks x 1 vCPU x 1 hours x 0.04048 USD per hour = 18.47 USD for vCPU hours

456.25 tasks x 2.00 GB x 1 hours x 0.004445 USD per GB per hour = 4.06 USD for GB hours

20 GB - 20 GB (no additional charge) = 0.00 GB billable ephemeral storage per task

Totaling all these costs results in a cost per month of $95.53.

As you can see, the costs between EC2 and Fargate are significantly different ($292.24 versus $95.53). However, in the Fargate example, there are 15 Pods/instances and the Pods are only executing for 1 hour a day. If your applications do not behave like this, then the costs will change and could be higher. On EC2, on the other hand, you are paying for the compute nodes and so the number of Pods and how long they execute for doesn't matter. In practice, you may see a mixed compute environment with EC2 providing compute for long-running Pods and Fargate used for more batch-type operations or where you need enhanced security.

Common mistakes when using EKS

Finally, let's round off this chapter by discussing how to configure and manage EKS in an efficient way, applying best practices when possible. Here are some of the common mistakes that we see often when people first begin to use EKS:

- **Leaving clusters running**: If you don't need your EKS cluster, shut it down or at least remove or scale in the node groups. Creating a cluster for dev or test environments (or even just to try the code in the book) will cost you real money, so if you're not using it, shut it down.

- **Not having access**: The AWS user account used to create the cluster is the only user account that will have access initially. To allow other users, groups, or roles access to the cluster (e.g., using kubectl) you need to add them to the `aws-auth` ConfigMap. Please read *Chapter 6, Securing and Accessing Clusters on EKS*, for more information.

- **Running out of Pod IP addresses**: With the AWS CNI, every Pod is assigned a VPC IP address. If you don't configure your VPC and EKS cluster correctly, you will run out of IP addresses and your cluster will not be able to schedule any more. Please read *Chapter 7, Networking in EKS*, for more information.

- **My cluster IP address is not accessible from my workstation**: Clusters can be private (only accessible from the AWS and connected private networks) or public (accessible from the internet), so depending on how the cluster is configured, as well as the firewalls between your client and the API servers, you may not have access to the API servers.

Summary

In this chapter, we described how EKS is just a managed version of Kubernetes, with the main difference that AWS will manage and scale the control plane (API servers, etcd) for you, while the cluster users/administrators are responsible for deploying compute and storage resources to host Pods on the cluster.

We also looked at the technical architecture of the AWS-managed control plane and how you can interact with it. However, we pointed out that's as it is an AWS Managed Service, you have very little ability to modify the servers that make up the control plane.

We then looked at a couple of EKS cost models to help you understand that while the control plane costs are mostly fixed, the costs for compute and storage will vary depending on how many Pods or EC2 worker nodes you have. Finally, we discussed a few common mistakes made by first-time EKS users.

In the next chapter, we will learn how to create an EKS cluster and set up the environment. We will also cover how you can create your own Amazon EKS cluster using different tools.

Further reading

- EKS price reductions: `https://aws.amazon.com/about-aws/whats-new/2020/01/amazon-eks-announces-price-reduction/`

- A deep dive into Amazon EKS: `https://www.youtube.com/watch?v=cipDJwDWWbY`

- AWS EKS SLA: `https://aws.amazon.com/eks/sla/`

3

Building Your First EKS Cluster

In the previous chapters, we talked about Kubernetes and EKS in detail. In this chapter, we will begin to explore how to configure and build a basic cluster.

Although EKS is a managed service from AWS, there are a number of ways you can create the cluster, using the console, **Command-Line Interface (CLI)**, and **Infrastructure as Code (IaC)**. There are also different configurations that can be applied to a cluster, including networking, storage, and application configurations. This chapter will focus on the prerequisites for building a cluster along with the basic configuration you need to build a cluster. Specifically, we will cover the following topics:

- Understanding the prerequisites for building an EKS cluster
- Understanding the different configuration options for an EKS cluster
- Enumerating the automation options
- Creating your first EKS cluster

Let's begin by looking at what needs to be done before creating your first cluster.

Technical requirements

You should have a familiarity with cloud automation, ideally CloudFormation, and some experience with programming languages or software development.

In order to follow along, you will also need an AWS account to be able to launch EKS resources. If you don't have an account, please go to AWS and create one: `https://aws.amazon.com/`.

> **Important note**
> These activities will result in AWS charges, so please make sure to delete all resources after you have built them.

Understanding the prerequisites for building an EKS cluster

By default, the email address and password used to create the AWS account are the root user's, and they have privileges to do everything in the AWS Account. AWS best practice is to enable **Multi-Factor Authentication (MFA)** on this account and *never* use this account other than in an emergency.

The following list of activities need to be performed once you have an AWS account and the root user access credentials prior to creating an EKS cluster:

1. Configure your AWS CLI environment with temporary root credentials.

2. As the root user, you should:

   A. Create an EKS admin policy, using the least privileges that can be used to deploy and manage EKS clusters

   B. Create an EKS cluster Admin group and assign the EKS Admin role to that group

   C. Create a new user and add them to the EKS cluster Admin group

   D. Create the access credentials and add them to your AWS CLI configuration

3. Install kubectl on your workstation using the following guide: `https://docs.aws.amazon.com/eks/latest/userguide/install-kubectl.html`.

Configure your AWS CLI environment with temporary root credentials

Normally you would simply run the `$ aws configure` command, which will ask you for the default access credentials, region, and output format, but we don't want to persist the root credentials, so we will use environment variables to hold them temporarily:

```
export AWS_ACCESS_KEY_ID=<root access key>
export AWS_SECRET_ACCESS_KEY=<root secret access key>
export AWS_DEFAULT_REGION=<working region>
```

Create the EKS Admin policy

The easiest way to provide the right permissions to the EKS administrator is to grant them access to the AWS-managed `AdministratorAccess` managed role. You can get the unique identity for the role **AWS Resource Name (ARN)** using the following command:

```
$ export EKSARN=$(aws iam list-policies --query
'Policies[?PolicyName==`AdministratorAccess`].{ARN:Arn}'
--output text)
```

The `AdministratorAccess` role is very broad and allows the resource assigned the permission, the principal, with a lot of privileges that are not needed. Ideally, the EKS admin role that is created has reduced permissions, defined in the least-privilege security model. Creating this role is quite complex as it requires multiple resource permissions. The following table lists the minimum permissions you need for EC2, EKS, KMS, and IAM. However, you may need to add permissions to this role if you need to create a VPC/subnets, for example.

AWS Resource	Minimal Permission Set
EC2 API	`"ec2:RunInstances"`, `"ec2:RevokeSecurityGroupIngress"`, `"ec2:RevokeSecurityGroupEgress"`, `"ec2:DescribeRegions"`, `"ec2:DescribeVpcs"`, `"ec2:DescribeTags"`, `"ec2:DescribeSubnets"`, `"ec2:DescribeSecurityGroups"`, `"ec2:DescribeRouteTables"`,`"ec2:DescribeLaunchTemplateVersions"`, `"ec2:DescribeLaunchTemplates"`, `"ec2:DescribeKeyPairs"`, `"ec2:DescribeInternetGateways"`, `"ec2:DescribeImages"`, `"ec2:DescribeAvailabilityZones"`, `"ec2:DescribeAccountAttributes"`, `"ec2:DeleteTags"`, `"ec2:DeleteSecurityGroup"`, `"ec2:DeleteKeyPair"`, `"ec2:CreateTags"`, `"ec2:CreateSecurityGroup"`, `"ec2:CreateLaunchTemplateVersion"`, `"ec2:CreateLaunchTemplate"`, `"ec2:CreateKeyPair"`, `"ec2:AuthorizeSecurityGroupIngress"`, `"ec2:AuthorizeSecurityGroupEgress"`
EKS API	`"eks:UpdateNodegroupVersion"`, `"eks:UpdateNodegroupConfig"`, `"eks:UpdateClusterVersion"`, `"eks:UpdateClusterConfig"`, `"eks:UntagResource"`, `"eks:TagResource"`, `"eks:ListUpdates"`, `"eks:ListTagsForResource"`, `"eks:ListNodegroups"`, `"eks:ListFargateProfiles"`, `"eks:ListClusters"`, `"eks:DescribeUpdate"`, `"eks:DescribeNodegroup"`, `"eks:DescribeFargateProfile"`, `"eks:DescribeCluster"`, `"eks:DeleteNodegroup"`, `"eks:DeleteFargateProfile"`, `"eks:DeleteCluster"`, `"eks:CreateNodegroup"`, `"eks:CreateFargateProfile"`, `"eks:CreateCluster"`
KMS API	`"kms:ListKeys"`

AWS Resource	Minimal Permission Set
IAM API	`"iam:PassRole"`, `"iam:ListRoles"`, `"iam:ListRoleTags"`, `"iam:ListInstanceProfilesForRole"`, `"iam:ListInstanceProfiles"`, `"iam:ListAttachedRolePolicies"`, `"iam:GetRole"`, `"iam:GetInstanceProfile"`, `"iam:DetachRolePolicy"`, `"iam:DeleteRole"`, `"iam:CreateRole"`, `"iam:AttachRolePolicy"`

Table 3.1 – EKS Admin example privileges

Once you have the desired permissions set, you can create a policy document. A JSON example is shown in the following snippet with just the KMS permission included for simplicity:

```
{       "Version": "2012-10-17",
    "Statement": [
        {"Sid": "KMSPermisssions",
            "Effect": "Allow",
            "Action": ["kms:ListKeys"],
            "Resource": "*"
        }]}
```

Using the aws iam create-policy --policy-name bespoke-eks-policy --policy-document file://<mypolicyfile.json> command to create the IAM policy based on the JSON file you have created, you can then retrieve the ARN using the following command:

```
$ export EKSARN=$(aws iam list-policies --query
'Policies[?PolicyName==`bespoke-eks-policy`].{ARN:Arn}'
--output text)
```

Create the EKS Admin group

Creating the group using the CLI is pretty straightforward, using this:

```
$ aws iam create-group --group-name EKS-Admins.
```

You then need to attach the policy created in the previous step using this:

```
$ aws iam attach-group-policy --policy-arn $EKSARN --group-name
EKS-Admins.
```

Create a new user

Now we have the permissions, and the group has been created, we can create a new user and assign it to the group using the following command:

```
$ aws iam create-user --user-name <MYUSERNAME>
```

You can then add the user you just created to the group using this:

```
$ aws iam add-user-to-group --user-name <MYUSERNAME> --group-
name EKS-Admins
```

You will also need to create a password using this:

```
$ aws iam update-login-profile --user-name <MYUSERNAME>
--password <password>
```

You now need to create access credentials and store them using the following:

```
$ aws iam create-access-key --user-name <MYUSERNAME>
{ "AccessKey": {
        "UserName": "<MYUSERNAME>",
        "Status": "Active",
        "CreateDate": "2022-08-19T11:01:07Z",
        "SecretAccessKey": "67ghjghjhjihk",
        "AccessKeyId": "hgjgjgjhgjhgj"}}
```

You should copy the credentials (`SecretAccessKey` and `AccessKeyId`) output from this command, add them to your CLI configuration using the `$aws configure` command, and use this account/credentials for the remainder of the examples.

> **Important note**
>
> You still need to grant console access. Please refer to this link: `https://docs.aws.amazon.com/IAM/latest/UserGuide/console_controlling-access.html`.
>
> You should also enable MFA. Please refer to this link: `https://docs.aws.amazon.com/IAM/latest/UserGuide/id_credentials_mfa.html`.

Now that we have all the prerequisites in place, we need to consider how we configure the EKS cluster.

Understanding the different configuration options for an EKS cluster

Kubernetes is extensible by default, which is one of the reasons it has become so popular. As well as the standard API objects we've already discussed such as **Pods** and **Services**, you can extend the API to support custom resources, controllers, operators, and standard plugins for networking and storage. All of these elements can be added to an EKS cluster as part of the cluster creation process; however, in this chapter, we will cover the basic configuration to get a simple cluster up and running. The following table defines what will be configured as well as providing a map to other chapters that show additional configuration steps:

EKS Configuration Domain	Description
Control plane	As we have mentioned, EKS is really a managed control plane, so this must always be done, and the next sections will focus on creating this.
Basic networking	We will cover this briefly in this section using the default AWS EKS VPC plugin (CNI), but it's covered in more detail in *Chapter 7*.
Base node group	In the next section, we will create a small node group on EC2 resources to host key cluster resources such as the VPC network plugin.
Pod storage services	We won't cover this in this section but will go into more detail in *Chapter 12*.
Additional node groups	We won't cover this in this section but will go into more detail in *Chapter 8*.
Fargate profiles	We won't cover this in this section but will go into more detail in *Chapter 15*.
Kubernetes applications	We won't cover this in this section but will go into more detail in *Chapters 11, 13*, and *14*.
Advanced networking concepts	We won't cover this in this section but will go into more detail in *Chapter 8*.
Service mesh	We won't cover this in this section but will go into more detail in *Chapter 16*.

Table 3.2 – EKS configuration areas

Before we actually create a cluster that is composed of a managed control plane, basic networking, and a base node group, let's review the different ways we can approach deploying and automating it and why you would choose one over the others.

Enumerating the automation options

The following diagram (*Figure 3.1*) illustrates the evolution of infrastructure automation in AWS. Most users start off with manual configuration using playbooks or wikis and the AWS console. The challenge with this is it's difficult to repeat, and if you need to change or add something, you need to do it manually.

The next step is to then use shell scripts to automate the deployment of AWS resources using, for example, the AWS CLI. This is not perfect because if you run the same command twice you can get different results. Thus, the AWS CLI is not (necessarily) idempotent. So, in 2011, AWS released CloudFormation, an IaC framework that can safely create infrastructure resources.

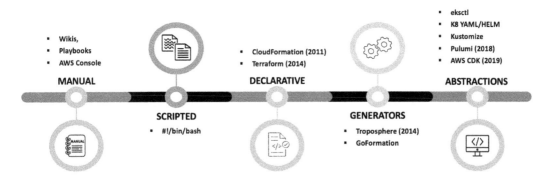

Figure 3.1 – Automation options

IaC has become best practice for deploying AWS resources, and in 2014 HashiCorp released Terraform, which has become very popular and again allows you to automate and deploy AWS resources safely. The challenge with both CloudFormation and Terraform is they have their own markup language that must be learned and can be complex.

Over the years, various generators have been produced that allow you to create CloudFormation and Terraform scripts without needing to understand how to write them. This concept has further been extended with abstractions such as AWS **Cloud Development Kit** (**CDK**), which allows you to generate and deploy CloudFormation using regular programming languages such as Python, Typeset, and so on.

In Kubernetes, this additional layer abstraction is part of the cluster with manifest, Helm charts, and Kustomize being used to abstract Kubernetes resources, and tools such as eksctl providing a simple interface for provisioning EKS clusters.

Which automation tool/framework should I use?

A general rule of thumb for any automation is **Don't Repeat Yourself** (**DRY**), so if you are going to create or delete clusters on a regular basis, use automation and use the highest level of abstraction you can. Tools such as the CDK and eksctl mean you don't have to learn CloudFormation but can still rely on *safe* deployment practices such as declarative configurations and idempotent operations.

Terraform supports these *safe* operations, which in addition means you can support other clouds such as Microsoft Azure and Google Cloud Platform, as well as other on-premises resources.

In the next section, we will show you how you can create a basic cluster using the console and AWS CLI and then simplify the operation using the following IaC Tools: Terraform, eksctl, and the AWS CDK.

Creating your first EKS cluster

Please verify you are using the credentials for the username you created as part of the prerequisites using the following command:

```
$ aws sts get-caller-identity
{
    "UserId": <MYUSERNAME>",
   "Account": "11112222333",
   "Arn": "arn:aws:sts::11112222333<MYUSERNAME>/IAM_ROLE>"}
```

Option 1: Creating your EKS cluster with the AWS console

To start this exercise, open a browser, go to the URL https://aws.amazon.com/, and sign in to your account using the username/credentials you created as part of the prerequisites.

Once you have logged in, complete the following steps:

1. Type IAM in the search bar and select **IAM | Roles** from the resulting search results.

2. You should now create a cluster Service role by clicking on the **Create Role** button, which will allow the cluster to make calls to other AWS Services. It's a simple policy, is defined at https://docs.aws.amazon.com/eks/latest/userguide/service_IAM_role.html, and should be linked to the AmazonEKSClusterPolicy managed policy.

3. Once the Service role has been created, select the region that you would like to launch the Amazon EKS cluster in, type EKS in the search bar, and select **Elastic Kubernetes Service**.

Figure 3.2 – Select EKS

4. On the EKS launch screen, click on the **Add cluster | Create** button.

Figure 3.3 – Add cluster

5. On the resulting screen, enter the cluster name in the **Name** field, select the version of Kubernetes you want to deploy from the **Kubernetes version** field, select the Service role created in *step 2*, and click **Next**.

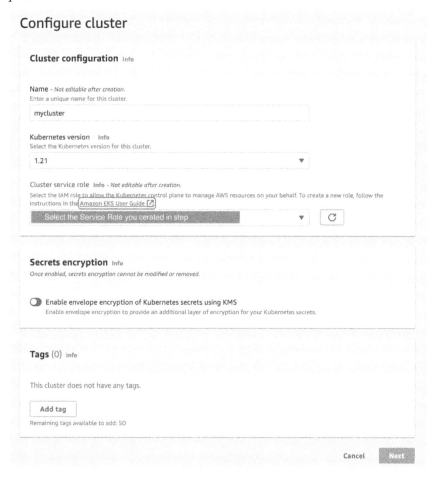

Figure 3.3 – Configure cluster

6. In the first panel of the EKS networking screen, you need to select the VPC and subnets that the control plane will use as well as the security group used by any worker nodes. If these resources don't exist, you can add them using the VPC console link (make sure you open the link in a browser tab or window).

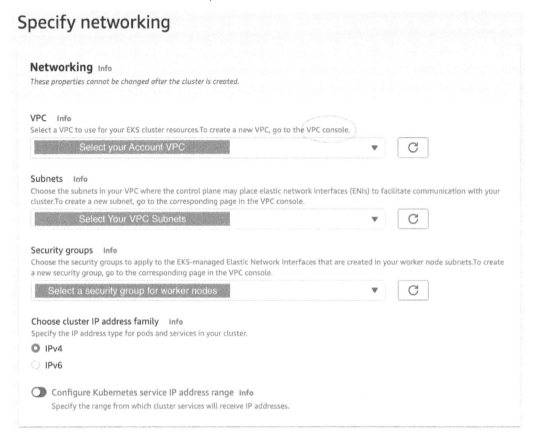

Figure 3.4 – Enter VPC and security group details

7. In the next panel, select the type of cluster endpoint. In this example, we will keep the **Public** default, which means the cluster API is accessible from the internet.

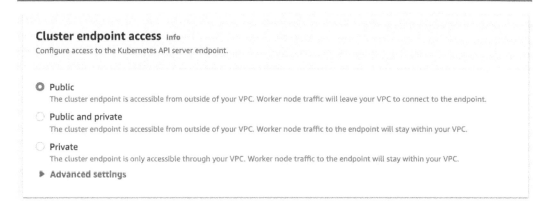

Figure 3.5 – Cluster endpoints

8. In the final networking panel, you can leave the defaults, which relate to the Kubernetes version chosen in *step 5* and click **Next**.

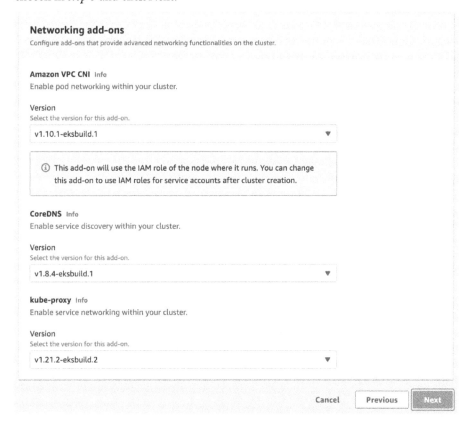

Figure 3.6 – Complete networking section

9. Enable **Audit** logging to CloudWatch logs by selecting the button and clicking **Next**.

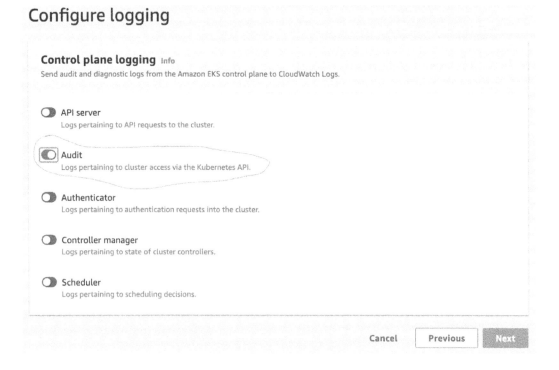

Figure 3.7 – Control plane logging

10. Review your cluster settings and click the **Create** button. This will now take 20-30 minutes to complete and involves setting up the control plane (API and etcd servers) in an AWS-owned VPC and connecting it through **Elastic Network Interfaces** (**ENIs**) to your VPC. When it completes, you will see a new cluster with a status of **Active**, as shown in the following screenshot:

Figure 3.8 – An active cluster

11. As this is a public cluster, you can run the `aws eks update-kubeconfig --cluster <CLUSTERNAME> --region <YOURREGION>` command to update your `kubeconfig` file. We have created an EKS control plane and set up networking but currently, we don't have any nodes attached to it. We can validate this by using the `kubectl get nodes` command. You should get a **No resources found** message.

12. If you click on the name link of your cluster (this is **mycluster** in *step 10*), you will be taken to the cluster configuration screen shown in the following screenshot. Click the **Compute** tab, and then click on the **Add node group** button.

Figure 3.9 – Compute

13. In the first **Node group configuration** panel, enter a name for the node group and an EC2 worker IAM role. If this role doesn't exist, you can add it using the VPC console link (make sure you open the link in a browser tab or window). The role should be created in line with this link: `https://docs.aws.amazon.com/eks/latest/userguide/create-node-role.html`.

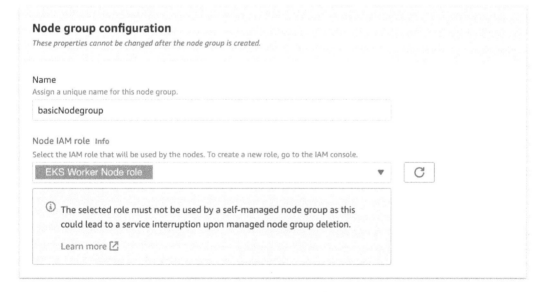

Figure 3.10 – Node group configuration

14. You can accept all the defaults in the **Set compute and scaling configuration** window, which will create two `t3.medium` EC2 instances in an autoscaling group using an EKS-optimized Amazon Linux **operating system** (**OS**) image. Click on **Next**.

15. Select the subnets you will use for the EC2 worker nodes in your VPC; you should select at least two subnets/availability zones. Click **Next**.

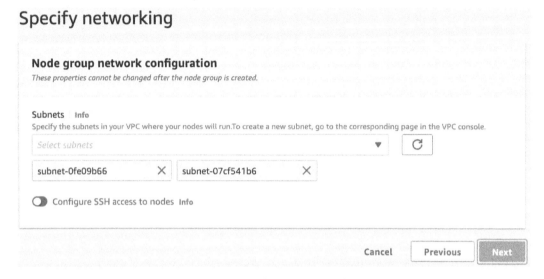

Figure 3.11 – Node group networking

16. Review your node group settings and click the **Create** button. This will now take 10-20 minutes and will create two EC2 instances and configure the Kubernetes agents (`kubelet` and `kubeproxy`) and connect back to the control plane. Once the job completes, the node group should be **Active** and the two EC2 instances should be **Ready**.

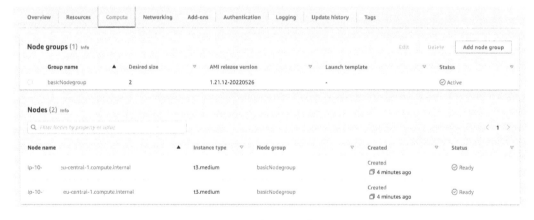

Figure 3.12 — Active node group

17. We can validate this by using the kubectl get nodes command. The output should now show the two nodes you have just created.

18. Once you have finished with the cluster, delete the node group, and then you can delete the cluster.

> **Important note**
>
> As the AWS console interface may be changed, if you have questions, you can always check the AWS documentation for creating the EKS cluster (https://docs.aws.amazon.com/eks/latest/userguide/create-cluster.html) and for creating managed node groups (https://docs.aws.amazon.com/eks/latest/userguide/create-managed-node-group.html) to get the latest updated steps.

In this subsection, we have created a basic cluster with a managed control plane, an AWS VPC network, and a basic node group with two EC2 workers. In the next subsection, we will see how we can create the same cluster using the AWS CLI.

Option 2: Creating your EKS cluster with the AWS CLI

The AWS CLI is a tool for managing your AWS resources. It can be installed using this link: https://docs.aws.amazon.com/cli/latest/userguide/getting-started-install.html.

To create an EKS cluster using the AWS CLI, you should follow the steps detailed here:

1. We will reuse the cluster Service role and the same subnets used in *Option 1*. If they don't exist, create them using the steps in *Option 1*.

2. You can then create the managed control plane in your account using the following commands with the username/credentials you created as part of the prerequisites. The subnets and security group can be the same ones used in *Option 1*:

```
$ aws eks create-cluster --region <MYREGION>
--name mycluster --kubernetes-version 1.22 --role-
arn <MYSERVICEROLEARN> --resources-vpc-config
subnetIds=subnet-1,subnet-2,securityGroupIds=sg-a
```

3. This will now take 20-30 minutes to complete and involves setting up the control plane (API and etcd servers) in an AWS-owned VPC and connecting it through ENIs to your VPC. When it completes, you will see a new cluster with a status of **Active, as** shown in the following screenshot.

Cluster name	▲	Status	▽	Kubernetes version	▽	Provider	▽
○ mycluster		⊘ Active		1.21 Update now		EKS	

Figure 3.13 – Active cluster

4. Again, we have created an EKS control plane and set up networking but currently, we don't have any nodes attached to it. We can validate this by using the `kubectl get nodes` command, after updating the `kubeconfig` file. You should get a **No resources found** message.

5. You can create the basic node group using the following command, which will create two t3.medium EC2 instances in an autoscaling group using an EKS-optimized Amazon Linux OS image using the EC2 role created in *Option 1*.

```
$ aws eks create-nodegroup --region
<MYREGION>    --cluster-name mycluster
--nodegroup-name basicCLI --scaling-config
minSize=2,maxSize=2,desiredSize=2 --subnets subnet-
1  subnet-2 --ami-type AL2_x86_64 --node-role
<EKSWORKERNODEROLEARN>
```

6. This will now take 10-20 minutes and will create two EC2 instances and configure the Kubernetes agents (`kubelet` and `kubeproxy`) and connect back to the control plane. Once the job completes, the node group should be **Active** and the two EC2 instances should be **Ready**.

Figure 3.14 – A CLI node group

7. We can validate this by using the `kubectl get nodes` command. The output should now show the two nodes you have just created.

8. Once you have finished with the cluster, delete the node group, and then you can delete the cluster using the following commands:

```
$ aws eks delete-nodegroup --cluster-name <CLUSTER_NAME>
--nodegroup-name <NODEGROUP_NAME> --region <REGION>
$aws eks delete-cluster --name <CLUSTER_NAME> --region
<REGION>
```

As you can see, this process is much simpler than clicking through the AWS console. These commands can be placed in a shell script, and you can use environment variables to parameterize the input, changing the cluster name, for example. However, it's not guaranteed that every command is *safe* to run repeatedly, and script execution can be problematic if there are any failures. A better way is to use IaC and we will explore that over the next subsections.

Option 3: Creating your EKS cluster with Terraform

Terraform is an open source project created by HashiCorp and is composed of a single binary that can be used to validate, deploy, and delete (destroy) AWS infrastructure resources. You can install Terraform by following the instructions shown at `https://learn.hashicorp.com/tutorials/terraform/install-cli`.

To create your first EKS cluster using Terraform, we will clone the official example containing the configuration file for creating an EKS cluster provided by HashiCorp. This is a very complete solution (creating 53 resources) and will create a new VPC, two managed worker node groups, and all the associated roles and permissions. Use the following commands to clone and change into the cloned directory:

```
$ git clone https://github.com/hashicorp/learn-terraform-
provision-eks-cluster
$ cd learn-terraform-provision-eks-cluster
```

Terraform works by aggregating all `.tf` files into a single configuration and then deploying it to AWS using your local credentials. You will need to modify certain `.tf` files for your AWS account; the following table explains which ones:

Terraform (.tf) file	Changes

`./vpc.tf`	Change the region variable to the region you want to use, for example:
	
	`variable "region" {`
	
	`    default      = "eu-central-1"`
	
	`    description = "AWS region"`
	
	`}`

`./eks-cluster.tf`	Change the EKS version to the desired version, for example:
	
	`module "eks" {`
	
	`        cluster_version = "1.22" }`

Table 3.3 – Terraform changes

Now that you have made the changes to the Terraform files, you can create an EKS cluster and environment using Terraform. You should follow the steps detailed here:

1. Run the $ `terraform init` command to create the local state and download all the remote module files such as the VPC module used to create the new VPC. It can take some time to download all the module files. If this command is successful, you will see the **Terraform has been successfully initialized!** message.

2. Run the $ `terraform plan` command to see what resources will be created before actually deploying them. This is a major advantage over the console and CLI methods, as you can also use this to see what will change when you make a change to the `.tf` files.

3. Run the $ `terraform apply -auto-approve` command to create/deploy the resources. This will take 20-30 minutes to complete (so take a seat). At the end of it, you will have a new IAM role, an EKS cluster in a new VPC, new internet and NAT gateways, and two managed node groups with three EC2 instances.

4. In this option, we have actually created managed node groups, which we can validate by using the $ `kubectl get nodes` command. After updating the `kubeconfig` file, you will see three worker nodes.

5. Once you have finished with the cluster, use the $ `terraform destroy -auto-approve` command to delete all resources. Terraform will automatically figure out the order of deletion.

As you can see, Terraform is a very powerful tool and simplifies the way you configure and deploy resources. You still have to configure or create the Terraform modules, which in turn requires you to learn the Terraform syntax and markup language.

In the next subsection, we will see how you can use eksctl to create an EKS cluster using CloudFormation under the covers without learning any CloudFormation syntax.

Option 4: Creating your EKS cluster with eksctl

eksctl is an open source project on GitHub (`https://github.com/weaveworks/eksctl`) co-developed between Weaveworks and AWS. It's similar to Terraform in that it runs as a single binary and creates AWS resources; however, it can only be used to create, update, and manage EKS clusters (and any associated resources).

You can install eksctl by following the instructions shown at `https://docs.aws.amazon.com/eks/latest/userguide/eksctl.html`. After you install the binary on your workstation, you can test the install using the `eksctl info` command. The easiest way to create a cluster is to run the following command:

```
$ eksctl create cluster --name mycluster --region eu-central-1
```

This works in a similar way to Terraform in that it will create the VPC, EKS cluster, a node group, and all the associated resources, such as IAM roles. In the background, eksctl uses CloudFormation and will create two CloudFormation stacks that will create (29+) AWS resources. If you run the $ aws cloudformation list-stacks command, you will see stacks called *eksctl-xx*, which deploy all the EKS resources: one for the main resources, including the VPC, and one specifically for the node group. The CloudFormation stacks manage the state of the resources and can also be used to detect drift and make changes.

Again, using this option, we have created managed node groups, which we can validate by using the kubectl get nodes command. After updating the kubeconfig file, you will see two worker nodes.

You can also modify the default configuration by adding command-line options. The following command will change the type and number of instances that are being deployed as part of the default node group:

```
$ eksctl create cluster --name mycluster --instance-types
m5.xlarge --nodes 2 --region eu-central-1
```

eksctl supports different options for your cluster creation. You can list other supported options by using the flag --help to get more details.

Once you have finished with the cluster, you can use the $ eksctl delete cluster --name mycluster --region eu-central-1 command to remove all the resources. As eksctl is a specific EKS provisioning tool, it does have some built-in features, such as node draining.

As you can see, eksctl provides a higher level of abstraction to Terraform, but it is not as versatile as it is an EKS tool. In the next subsection, we will briefly look at the AWS CDK, which uses programming languages such as Python to move completely away from any IaC markup languages.

Option 5: Creating your EKS cluster with the CDK

The AWS CDK is similar to Terraform and eksctl in that you end up with a set of binaries that can deploy AWS infrastructures. It uses CloudFormation under the cover, but it has four main advantages over eksctl:

- The IaC code is written in standard programming languages such as Python, TypeScript, Golang, and so on, so developers can build code without learning Terraform or CloudFormation markup.
- You can leverage existing language control constructs, IF-THEN-ELSE, FOR loops, and so on, as well as existing libraries to build complex logic into your IaC scripts.
- You can create non-EKS-related resources such as DynamoDB.
- Templates can be tested and linted using standard language tools such as pylint or pytest.

A detailed exploration of the CDK is out of the scope of this book (in fact, it could be a whole new book). If you want to really get to grips with the CDK, `https://cdkworkshop.com/` is a great resource. Instead, the following table shows the basic commands needed to create an EKS cluster:

Python Line	Description
`my_vpc = ec2.Vpc.from_lookup(self,"clusterVPC",vpc_id=params['VPC'])`	This line uses the CDK `ec2.Vpc` object to retrieve VPC details from your AWS account using the `params['VPC']` dictionary.
`eks_master_role = iam.Role.from_role_arn(self,"iderole",params['IDEROLE'])`	This line uses the CDK `iam.Role` object to retrieve role details from your AWS account using the `params['IDEROLE']` dictionary, used as the main admin role for the cluster.
`security_group = ec2.SecurityGroup.from_lookup_by_id(self,"idesg",params['IDESG'])`	This line uses the CDK `iam.SecurityGroup` object to retrieve an existing security group from your AWS account using the `params['IDESG']` dictionary, used as an additional security group for the cluster.

`my_subnets=[]`
 	
`for subnet in params['SUBID']:`
 	
`my_subnets.append(ec2.Subnet.from_subnet_id(self,f"1{subnet.split('-')[1]}",subnet_id=subnet))`
	These lines create a blank subnet list, then use a standard `FOR` loop to iterate over a list or subnet IDs stored in `params['SUBID']`, create a subnet object using the CDK `ec2.Subnet` object, and append it to the subnet list.

`eks.Cluster(self,params['CLUSTERNAME'],`
 	
`masters_role=eks_master_role,`
 	
`security_group=security_group,`
 	
`version=eval(f"eks.KubernetesVersion.{params['VERSION']}"),vpc=my_vpc,`
 	
`vpc_subnets=my_subnets,`
 	
`endpoint_access=eval(f"eks.EndpointAccess.{params['CLUSTERTYPE']}"))`
	This line will create a cluster using the role, VPC, and subnets retrieved in the previous lines and also set the endpoint type and version from the params Python dictionary, which has all the configuration information.

Table 3.4 – Python EKS CDK example

Once the code has been written, the CDK binary can be used to do the following:

- Initialize the AWS region for CDK deployments using the cdk bootstrap command
- Create CloudFormation templates using the cdk synth command
- Understand what will be deployed or changed using the cdk diff command
- Create and deploy CloudFormation templates using the cdk deploy command

The CDK provides the highest level of abstraction of all the deployment tools and, as such, should be considered a good starting point for EKS automation and deployment, but tools such as eksctl and Terraform (Terraform also has a CDK variant) provide good options as well. This section has given an overview of the different ways a basic EKS cluster can be deployed.

Summary

In this chapter, we examined the prerequisites needed before the configuration and deployment of a basic Amazon EKS cluster, such as setting up a deployment user . We reviewed the different EKS configuration and automation options that need configuring in EKS and what frameworks and tools are available to you.

We then stepped through five options, from using the AWS console and CLI to different IaC frameworks to create a basic EKS cluster.

After completing this lesson, you learned how to provision your EKS cluster and have a running cluster under your AWS account, as well as have kubectl and the AWS CLI installed to enable interaction with your EKS cluster.

In the next chapter, we are going to move on to the topic of learning how to deploy and run your containerized application on Amazon EKS.

Further reading

- Making AWS API calls safely: https://docs.aws.amazon.com/AWSEC2/latest/APIReference/Run_Instance_Idempotency.html
- CDK deep dive: https://cdkworkshop.com/
- CloudFormation overview: https://docs.aws.amazon.com/AWSCloudFormation/latest/UserGuide/Welcome.html
- Terraform overview: https://www.terraform.io/intro
- Getting started with eksctl: https://eksctl.io/

4

Running Your First Application on EKS

In the previous chapters, we talked about how to configure and build a basic cluster. In this chapter, we will explore how we deploy our first application on that cluster.

Kubernetes has grown in popularity due in part to the flexible way you can build and deploy services and applications and how you can use key Kubernetes features to recover from failure and scale your application in and out. In the CNCF Annual Survey in 2021, 96% of respondents said they were either using or evaluating Kubernetes.

In this chapter, we cover the different ways you can deploy a simple application on EKS and tools to visualize your workloads. Specifically, we will cover the following:

- Understanding the different configuration options for your application
- Creating your first EKS application
- Visualizing your workloads using the AWS Management Console and third-party tools, such as Lens

You should be familiar with YAML, basic networking, and EKS architecture. Let's begin by determining what needs to be done prior to deploying your first application.

Technical requirements

Before getting started with this chapter, please ensure the following:

- You have an EKS cluster and are able to perform administrative tasks
- You have at least two worker nodes connected to your cluster
- You have network connectivity to your EKS API endpoint
- The AWS CLI and the kubectl binary are installed on your workstation

Understanding the different configuration options for your application

An application on Kubernetes is made up of one or more containers, spread across the worker nodes and exposed outside the cluster using different methods. The following table defines what will be configured and provides a map to other chapters that show additional configuration steps:

Application Configuration Domain	Description
Single Pod	In this example, a single Pod can be pulled from a supported repository image and deployed to a specific namespace.
Resilient deployment	In this example, a Kubernetes Deployment will be used to deploy multiple Pods across different worker nodes, and the scheduler will maintain the desired number.
Updating your Deployment	In this example, the Deployment container image is updated, and the new image is rolled out across the Deployment.
External service	In this example, the Deployment will be exposed as a simple node-port service.
Ingress controller	In this example, the Deployment will be exposed using an NGINX Ingress controller that provides more access control.
Multi-container Pod	Typically using a sidecar for a health check or service mesh. This is discussed in detail in *Chapter 16*.
Load balancer	This is discussed in detail in *Chapter 14*.
Auto-scaling Pods	This is discussed in *Chapter 18*.
Storage for Pods	This is discussed in *Chapter 12*.

Table 4.1 – Application configuration areas

Let's now look at what you need to deploy your first application to EKS.

Introducing kubectl configuration

kubectl is a Kubernetes command-line management client tool that allows a user to interact with the Kubernetes API server and perform any administrative task, including deploying, updating, or deleting an application (as long as they have permission to do so).

In order to communicate with the cluster, the cluster details, such as the API endpoint DNS name and server certificates, all need to be added to the kubeconfig file. The following command can be used (you will need to have the AWS CLI installed) to update the config file, which will normally be stored in the config file in $HOME/.kube:

```
$ aws eks update-kubeconfig --name mycluster  --region
eu-central-1
```

> **Important note**
> The AWS user that is being used to run the CLI command will need IAM permissions to the AWS EKS API to successfully perform this operation.

The file will now contain a reference to the new cluster, in the cluster section, with the certificate data, API endpoint (*server*), and name. An example is shown here:

```
clusters:
- cluster:
    certificate-authority-data: xxxxxx
    server: https://hfjhf.gr7.eu-central-1.eks.amazonaws.com
    name: arn:aws:eks:eu-central-1:334:cluster/mycluster
```

It will also contain a user section. By default, EKS will use an IAM identity, so there is no actual user data. Instead, the CLI command aws eks get-token (with supporting parameters) is used to get the identity token that's used by EKS to map the IAM user to a Kubernetes identity (see *Chapter 6* for more information). An example of the configuration seen in the configuration file is shown here:

```
users:
- name: arn:aws:eks:eu-central-1:334:cluster/mycluster
  user:
    exec:
      apiVersion: client.authentication.k8s.io/v1beta1
      args:
      - --region
      - eu-central-1
      - eks
      - get-token
      - --cluster-name
      - education-eks-D20eNmiw
```

```
        command: aws
        env: null
        provideClusterInfo: false
```

Finally, a Kubernetes `context` is also created, which will link the `cluster` and `user` configuration together. An example of this is shown next:

```
contexts:
- context:
    cluster: arn:aws:eks:eu-central-1:334:cluster/mycluster
    user: arn:aws:eks:eu-central-1:334:cluster/mycluster
    name: arn:aws:eks:eu-central-1:334:cluster/mycluster
```

Contexts allow multiple clusters and identities to be configured in the config file and for a user to switch between them. Switching between contexts can be done using the `kubectl config --kubeconfig=<CONFIGDIR> use-context <CONTEXT>` command or using an open source tool, such as `https://github.com/ahmetb/kubectx`.

Now we have set up the basic configuration needed to communicate with our cluster. In the next section, we will do some basic cluster connectivity verification with `kubectl` and deploy our first Pod.

Verifying connectivity with kubectl

The easiest way to verify whether you have connectivity to your cluster is to use the `kubectl version` command. You should see something similar to the output shown here:

```
$ kubectl version
Client Version: version.Info{Major:"1",
Minor:"22+", GitVersion:"v1.22.6-eks-7d68063",
GitCommit:"f24e667e49fb137336f7b064dba897beed639bad",
GitTreeState:"clean", BuildDate:"2022-02-23T19:32:14Z",
GoVersion:"go1.16.12", Compiler:"gc", Platform:"linux/amd64"}
Server Version: version.Info{Major:"1",
Minor:"20+", GitVersion:"v1.20.15-eks-18ef993",
GitCommit:"77b5697130c2dea4087e1009638e21cc93f5c5b6",
GitTreeState:"clean", BuildDate:"2022-07-06T18:04:29Z",
GoVersion:"go1.15.15", Compiler:"gc", Platform:"linux/amd64"}
```

The following table indicates some errors you may see when running this command and how to resolve them:

Error output	Description
Unable to connect to the server: getting credentials: exec: executable aws failed with exit code 253	In this case, `kubectl` can't retrieve AWS IAM credentials to request a token from the EKS API; update or add your AWS credentials to the workstation.
Unable to connect to the server: dial tcp 10.1.3.51:443: i/o timeout	In this case, the IP address is a private address, and the `kubectl` client has no route to it. This error typically indicates a network issue such as IP routing or some sort of firewall/IP whitelisting issue with the client IP.
error: You must be logged in to the server (the server has asked for the client to provide credentials)	In this case, `kubectl` has credentials and can connect to the server endpoint, but the credentials don't have permission to retrieve version information. This is an RBAC issue and typically means that the IAM user being used doesnt have the right Kubernetes permissions.

Table 4.2 – Typical kubectl connectivity error examples

> **kubectl cheat sheet**
>
> The kubectl cheat sheet contains very useful content that can help you quickly learn which `kubectl` command to use. You can study commonly used `kubectl` commands and flags in the official Kubernetes documentation: `https://kubernetes.io/docs/reference/kubectl/cheatsheet/`.

Now that we've validated connectivity to the cluster from kubectl, we deploy our first application.

Creating your first EKS application

The lowest level of abstraction in Kubernetes is the Pod, which represents one or more containers that share the same namespace. You may choose to have additional containers in your Pod to provide additional functionality, such as a service mesh or cache. So, while many Pods only contain one single container, you are not restricted to one.

In the following sections, we will deploy a Pod and then build on this using more advanced Kubernetes objects. As a developer or DevOps engineer, you will spend a lot of time building and deploying applications, so it's really important to understand what you need to do.

Deploying your first Pod on Amazon EKS using the kubectl command

You can use the kubectl run command to quickly deploy and attach your CLI session to a Pod using the following command:

```
$ kubectl run -it busybox --image=busybox --restart=Never
```

There are several things that happen when you execute this command, but before we review them, let's look at the manifest being created with the kubectl run busybox --image=busybox --restart=Never **--dry-run=client -o yaml** command, which shows the API object/kind being created *but* will not send it to the Kubernetes API. The output of the command is shown next:

```
apiVersion: v1
kind: Pod
metadata:
  creationTimestamp: null
  labels:
    run: busybox
  name: busybox
spec:
  containers:
  - image: busybox
    name: busybox
    resources: {}
  dnsPolicy: ClusterFirst
  restartPolicy: Never
status: {}
```

As we can see, the manifest defines a Pod specification, with a name, the busybox image (which will be pulled from a public repository), and a restartPolicy, which means once it finishes, the scheduler won't try to restart it.

The deployment process is as follows:

1. The kubectl run command will create the manifest for the Pod and submit it to the Kubernetes API.

2. The API server will persist the Pod specification.

3. The scheduler will pick up the new Pod specification, review it, and through a process of filtering and scoring, select a worker node to deploy the resource onto and mark the Pod spec for this node.

4. On the node, the kubelet agent is monitoring the cluster datastore, etcd, and if a new Pod specification is found, the specification is used to create the Pod on the node.

5. Once the Pod has started, your kubectl session will attach to the Pod (as we specified with the -it flag). You will now be able to use Linux commands to interact with your Pod. You can leave the session by typing exit.

Once you exit the session, you can verify the Pod status as follows:

```
$ kubectl get pods
NAME        READY    STATUS        RESTARTS    AGE
busybox     0/1      Completed     0           20s
```

> **Important note**
>
> The Pod status is Completed, because we specified restartPolicy: Never, so once the interactive session has terminated, the container is no longer accessible. You can delete the Pod using the $ kubectl delete pod busybox command.

In the next section, we will see how to extend this concept of a Pod into a Deployment.

Deploying a Pod using a Kubernetes Deployment

A Deployment adds a further layer of abstraction on top of a Pod; it allows you to deploy a Pod specification and supports scaling those Pods and updating the Pod images. A Deployment will allow you to manage the life cycle of your application much more efficiently than the basic Pod specifications. The following Deployment manifest will be used to deploy two Pods running version 1.34.1 of BusyBox. We also include a simple command to execute sleep 3600, which keeps the container *alive* for 3,600 seconds:

chapter4-deployment.yaml

```
---
apiVersion: apps/v1
kind: Deployment
metadata:
  name: simple-deployment
spec:
  replicas: 2
  selector:
    matchLabels:
      app: simple-deployment-app
```

```
template:
  metadata:
    labels:
      app: simple-deployment-app
  spec:
    containers:
    - name: busybox
      image: busybox:1.34.1
      command:
        - sleep
        - "3600"
```

You can use the $ kubectl create -f chapter4-deployment.yaml command to create the Deployment. You will also see the deployment.apps/busybox-deployment created message in response.

You can verify the Deployment by using the $ kubectl get deployment simple-deployment command; an example output is shown next:

```
NAME                READY   UP-TO-DATE   AVAILABLE   AGE
simple-deployment   2/2     2            2           106m
```

The Deployment is a composite type, and it contains the Deployment itself, the Pods, and a *ReplicaSet*, which is used to maintain the desired state of two Pods per Deployment. You can use the kubectl get all command to retrieve all the resources in the current namespace. An example output is shown next:

```
$ kukectl get all
..........
NAME                            READY   STATUS    RESTARTS   AGE
pod/simple-deployment-123-
5mbpb   1/1     Running   1          108m
pod/simple-deployment-432-
74kxf   1/1     Running   1          108m
NAME                            READY   UP-TO-DATE   AVAILABLE   AGE
deployment.apps/simple-deployment   2/2     2            2           108m
NAME                            DESIRED   CURRENT   READY   AGE
replicaset.apps/simple-deployment-6995f6966   2   2 2   108m
```

A Deployment provides an easy way to make changes. Let's look at how we can modify this Deployment.

Modifying your Deployment

Now that we have a Deployment, we can scale it with the `kubectl scale deployment simple-deployment --replicas=3` command, which will increase the desired number of Pods to three, which, in turn, will add another Pod.

We can also update the Deployment image with the `kubectl set image deployment simple-deployment busybox=busybox:1.35.0` command, which will trigger a rolling update (the default mechanism).

You can validate the rollout using the `kubectl rollout status` command:

```
$ kubectl rollout status deployment/simple-deployment
deployment "simple-deployment" successfully rolled out
```

You will see that the Pods are all replaced with the new version, which you can attach to the Pod shell (`/bin/sh`) using the `$ kubectl exec --stdin --tty <POD ID>    -- /bin/sh` command and then, once in the Pod shell, run the `busybox |head -1` command.

Next, let's look at how we make this Deployment visible to users outside the cluster.

Exposing your Deployment

While we have deployed the pods using a Deployment, in order for other Pods/Deployments to communicate with these Pods, they must use the Pods IP address. A better way to expose these Pods is by using a service, which means other cluster Pods or external systems can use the service, and Kubernetes will load balance the requests over all the available Pods. An example of a service is shown next:

chapter4-basic-service.yaml

```
---
apiVersion: v1
kind: Service
metadata:
    name: myapp
spec:
    type: ClusterIP
```

```
    ports:
      - protocol: TCP
        port: 80
        targetPort: 9376
    selector:
      app: simple-deployment-app
```

The service we create is a `ClusterIP` service, which means it is only visible from inside the cluster. It will expose port 80 and map that to port 9376 on any Pod that has a label of app=simple-deployment-app (the Pods we created previously with the Deployment).

We can validate the service using the kubectl get service command:

```
$ kubectl get svc -o wide
NAME    TYPE       CLUSTER-IP     EXTERNAL-IP    PORT(S)    AGE      SELECTOR
myapp   ClusterIP   172.20.124.66   <none>      80/
TCP     16m     app=simple-deployment-app
```

If we look deeper at the service using the kubectl describe service myappcommand, we can see the Endpoints configuration item, which contains the IP addresses of the Pods that have the label app=simple-deployment-app. We verify this with the kubectl get po -o wide command, illustrated as follows:

```
$ kubectl describe service myapp
Name:               myapp
Namespace:          default
.....................
Selector:           app=simple-deployment-app
Type:               ClusterIP
IP Family Policy:   SingleStack
IP Families:        IPv4
IP:                 172.20.124.66
.................. . .
Endpoints:   10.1.3.27:9376,10.1.30.176:9376,10.1.30.38:9376
Session Affinity:   None
Events:             <none>
$ k get po -o wide
```

```
NAME    READY     STATUS      RESTARTS    AGE    IP    NODE    NOMINATED
NODE     READINESS GATES
simple-deployment-111-
5gq92    1/1      Running    0    52m    10.1.30.38 ip-3.
eu-central-1.compute.internal    <none>       <none>
simple-deployment-222-
8chg8    1/1      Running    0          52m    10.1.30.176 ip-1.
eu-central-1.compute.internal    <none>            <none>
simple-deployment-333-
wpdwl    1/1      Running    0          52m    10.1.3.27 ip-2.
eu-central-1.compute.internal    <none>            <none>
```

This service is visible in the cluster using the cluster DNS, so myapp.default.svc.cluster. local will resolve to 172.20.124.66, which is the IP address assigned to the clusterIP. To expose the service outside of the cluster, we need to use either a different service, an Ingress or Ingress controller, or a load balancer. We will discuss these next.

Using a NodePort service

A NodePort service exposes a static port, between 30000-32768 by default on each worker node in the cluster, and then maps traffic back to port 80 (in the configuration shown next, only one port is defined, so the target port and the service have the same value) on any Pod that matches the selector.

chapter4-basic-nodeport-service.yaml

```yaml
---
apiVersion: v1
kind: Service
metadata:
  name: myapp-ext
spec:
  type: NodePort
  ports:
    - protocol: TCP
      port: 80
  selector:
    app: simple-nginx-app
```

The service we create is a `NodePort` service that selects a Pod that has a label of `app=simple-nginx-app`, which is another Deployment of NGINX Pods. We can see that `NodePort` has been created successfully using the `kubectl get service` command:

```
$ kubectl get service
NAME    TYPE   CLUSTER-IP           EXTERNAL-IP   PORT(S)       AGE
myapp-ext NodePort 172.20.225.210 <none>   80:30496/TCP   12m
```

If you use **curl** to browse the service endpoint, you will see the NGINX standard page (assuming all worker node security groups are configured to allow traffic).

Using an Ingress

An Ingress builds on top of services by providing a mechanism to expose HTTP/HTTPS routes, such as `/login` or `/order`, outside of the cluster. An Ingress is independent of the underlying services, so a typical use case is to use a single Ingress to provide a central entry point for multiple (micro) services. To use an Ingress, you need an Ingress controller; this is not provided by Kubernetes, so it must be installed. We will use the NGINX Ingress controller.

To install the NGINX Ingress controller with no cloud/AWS extensions, you can use the following command to deploy the bare-metal controller:

```
$ kubectl apply -f https://raw.githubusercontent.com/
kubernetes/ingress-nginx/controller-v1.2.0/deploy/static/
provider/baremetal/deploy.yaml
```

We can verify the new Ingress controller with the following command:

```
$ kubectl get service ingress-nginx-controller
--namespace=ingress-nginx
NAME    TYPE    CLUSTER-IP      EXTERNAL-IP   PORT(S)   AGE
ingress-nginx-controller   NodePort    172.20.150.207   <none>
        80:31371/TCP,443:31159/TCP   5m27s
```

We can see the Ingress controller is exposed as a `NodePort` service listening on `31371` for HTTP connections and `31159` for HTTPS connections. Normally, we would place a load balancer in front of this `NodePort` service (which we will explore in the next example), but for the time being, we will just use the simple `NodePort` service.

We can use the previous service and simply expose a URL on top of the service using the following manifest with the $ kubectl create -f chapter4-@ingress.yaml command:

chapter4-ingress.yaml

```
---
apiVersion: networking.k8s.io/v1
kind: Ingress
metadata:
  name: myapp-web
  annotations:
      kubernetes.io/ingress.class: nginx
      nginx.ingress.kubernetes.io/rewrite-target: /
spec:
  rules:
    - host: "myweb.packt.com"
      http:
      paths:
      - pathType: Prefix
        path: "/login"
        backend:
          service:
            name: myapp-ext
            port:
              number: 80
```

The Ingress we create uses annotations to configure the Ingress controller we created previously with the path rules in the spec section. The rule states when a request arrives for myweb.packt.com/login, you need to send it to the myapp-ext service on port 80 and rewrite /login to just /.

We can test this with the following command, which should return the NGINX welcome page:

```
curl -H 'Host: myweb.packt.com' http://<WORKERNODEIP>:31371/
login
```

Using an AWS Load Balancer

As we have an Ingress controller, exposed as a `NodePort`, and the underlying service, we could simply create a load balancer and create a target group for the worker nodes and the Ingress controller `NodePort` port. However, we want to integrate the Ingress controller and `loadbalancer` so that as the Ingress controller scales and changes, the `loadbalancer` configuration will also change.

> **Important note**
>
> Make sure you have removed the Ingress (`$ kubectl delete -f chapter4-ingress.yaml`) and the Ingress controller (`$ kubectl delete -f https://raw.githubusercontent.com/kubernetes/ingress-nginx/controller-v1.2.0/deploy/static/provider/baremetal/deploy.yaml`) from the previous section.

We will now redeploy the NGINX Ingress controller that is integrated with AWS load balancers using the following command:

```
$ kubectl apply -f https://raw.githubusercontent.com/
kubernetes/ingress-nginx/controller-v1.2.0/deploy/static/
provider/aws/deploy.yaml
```

After we have deployed the controller, we can review the Ingress controller with the following command. From the output, we can see the annotations that will create an AWS **Network Load Balancer** (**NLB**) and also the target group for the Ingress controller running in EKS:

```
$ kubectl describe service ingress-nginx-controller
--namespace=ingress-nginx
Name:                    ingress-nginx-controller
Namespace:               ingress-nginx
......... .
Annotations:
service.beta.kubernetes.io/aws-load-balancer-backend-protocol:
tcp
service.beta.kubernetes.io/aws-load-balancer-cross-zone-load-
balancing-enabled: true
service.beta.kubernetes.io/aws-load-balancer-type: nlb
.........
LoadBalancer Ingress: 111-22.elb.eu-central-1.amazonaws.com
Port:                    http   80/TCP
TargetPort:              http/TCP
NodePort:                http   32163/TCP
```

```
Endpoints:                    10.1.30.38:80
Port:                         https   443/TCP
TargetPort:                   https/TCP
NodePort:                     https   31484/TCP
Endpoints:                    10.1.30.38:443
Session Affinity:             None
External Traffic Policy:      Local
HealthCheck NodePort:         31086
..........
```

We can see the load balancer that we have created using the AWS CLI command shown next:

```
$ aws elbv2 describe-load-balancers
{"LoadBalancers": [{
  IpAddressType": "ipv4",
  "VpcId": "vpc-56567",
 "LoadBalancerArn": "arn:aws:elasticloadbalancing:eu-central-
1:11223:loadbalancer/net/111/22",
          "State": {"Code": "active"},
          "DNSName": "111-22.elb.eu-central-1.amazonaws.com",
          "LoadBalancerName": "111-22",
          "CreatedTime": "2022-06-19T07:31:52.901Z",
          "Scheme": "internet-facing",
          "Type": "network",
          "CanonicalHostedZoneId": "Z3F0SRJ5LGBH90",
 ........
}]}
```

This is a public load balancer (internet-facing), so the service is now reachable (through the Ingress controller) from the internet. You can access the link using the DNSName of the load balancer. We can now redeploy the Ingress manifest (without any changes as we've just added an NLB on top of the Ingress controller) using the $ kubectl create -f chapter4-ingress.yaml command to enable access through the NLB to our service.

You can now test access to your service by using the following command from any workstation with internet access. This will display the NGINX welcome screen:

```
$ curl -H 'Host: myweb.packt.com' http://111-22.elb.
eu-central-1.amazonaws.com/login
```

> **Important note**
>
> Make sure you have removed the Ingress (`$ kubectl delete -f chapter4-ingress.yaml`) and the Ingress controller (`$ kubectl delete -f https://raw.githubusercontent.com/kubernetes/ingress-nginx/controller-v1.2.0/deploy/static/provider/aws/deploy.yaml`).

In this section, we have looked at the different ways you can deploy Pods and expose them through services, an Ingress, and a load balancer. So far, all the examples have been using the command line. In the next section, we will look at how you can visualize your workloads and applications using the AWS console and a third-party tool.

Visualizing your workloads

Throughout the book and in the real world, you will mainly interact with EKS through the command line or a CI/CD pipeline. It is, however, sometimes useful to be able to view what you have running on a cluster in a visual form. Kubernetes provides a web dashboard, but with EKS, you can see most of the cluster configuration through the main EKS and using CloudWatch (discussed more in *Chapter 19, Developing on EKS*), which has removed the need to deploy a separate dashboard. To access the console, sign in to `http://aws.amazon.com` and log in with credentials that are allowed to view the cluster (see *Chapter 3, Building Your First EKS Cluster*). You can then select Amazon **Elastic Kubernetes Service | Clusters** and you will be presented with a list of clusters running in the region (you can now add on-premise clusters as well). From the main view, you can see clusters, their version, and whether they need updating (discussed more in *Chapter 10, Upgrading EKS Cluster*).

Figure 4.1 – The main cluster panel

You can select a cluster by clicking on the name hyperlink, and you will be taken to a more detailed view, where you can do the following:

- Upgrade the cluster control plane with a single click
- Delete the cluster (you may have to delete the node groups first)
- View and modify the cluster configuration

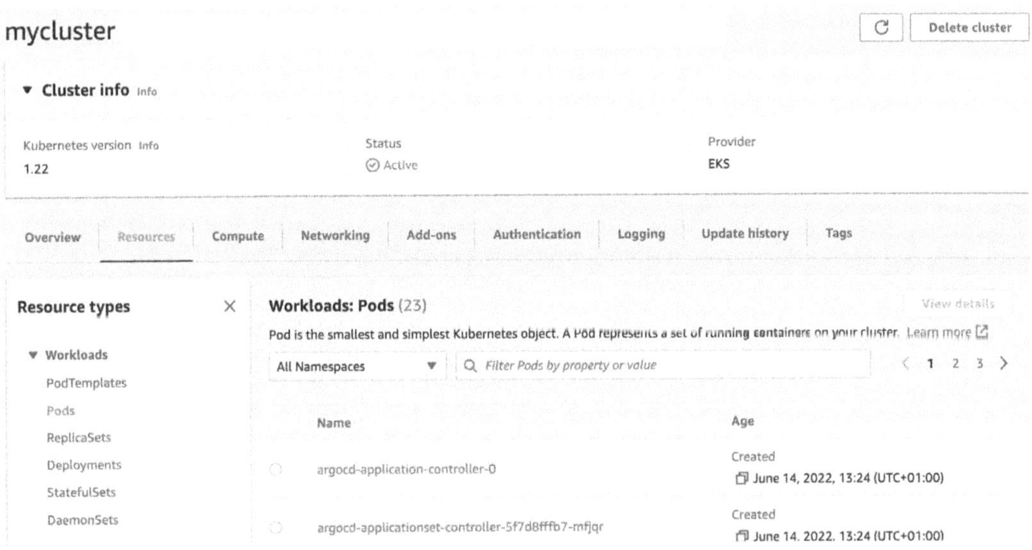

mycluster

Figure 4.2 – mycluster details panel

The preceding figure shows the **mycluster | Resources** window, which can be used to get a list of currently running Pods, Deployments, and Services, but remember the IAM User/Role you use in the console must have cluster (RBAC) permissions to at least read/get the resources. It's also possible to create node groups from here and manage configuration items such as **Public Endpoint** IP whitelists, and add-ons.

Generally, it's better to make changes using infrastructure as code or through a CI/CD pipeline, but you can also manage the cluster through the console. There are a host of other tools you can run from your workstation that are useful if you're trying to troubleshoot an issue. I often use `https://k8slens.dev/`, but other options are available!

All these tools will need a network route/path to the EKS API endpoint (public or private) and AWS IAM credentials that have permission to manage the EKS cluster (`system:masters` if you want to make changes).

In your `.kube/config` file, you will need to make changes to the `users` section to include the `AWS_PROFILE` environment variable to point to the AWS credentials profile that has access to the cluster itself. An example is shown next:

```
users:
- name: arn:aws:eks:eu-central-1:11222:cluster/mycluster
..................
    env:
    - name: AWS_PROFILE
      value: eksprofile
```

Once your workstation is configured, you install and launch Lens. If you are using temporary credentials, then you might find it easier to launch Lens from the command line on macOS. I would recommend using the $ open -a lens command, following which you will have a workstation environment so you can visualize your cluster/clusters from your workstation. The next screenshot shows the cluster view presented by Lens:

Figure 4.3 – A Lens cluster view

One of the things I really like about Lens is the ability to add extensions; for example, if you install the Resource Map Extension (https://github.com/nevalla/lens-resource-map-extension) from Lauri Nevala, you can get a visualization of the resources of your cluster and how they link together. For a complete list of extensions, take a look at https://github.com/lensapp/lens-extensions/blob/main/README.md.

The following screenshot shows an example of a Resource Map:

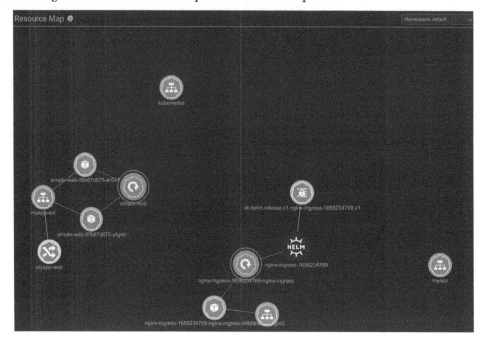

Figure 4.4 – An example Resource Map

You are now familiar with how you can visualize the workloads in your cluster using the AWS console and a third-party tool such as Lens.

In all, we have looked at how to verify connectivity to your cluster, and deploy and visualize Pods in the cluster. Let's now revisit the key learning points from this chapter.

Summary

In this chapter, we examined the different ways you can deploy applications, starting with creating a simple Pod and building on top of this concept with deployments, services, an Ingress, and finally deploying an AWS NLB and NGINX Ingress controller to expose the service to the internet. We discussed how a Deployment and Service can provide greater resilience and abstraction on top of a Pod and how services, Ingresses, and load balancers can be used to expose a service in a secure/resilient manner outside of the cluster/VPC.

Throughout this chapter, we used a Kubernetes YAML manifest to illustrate how to build and deploy these objects using kubectl. You now have the ability to deploy applications in EKS using the basic YAML manifests and kubectl. In the next chapter, we will look at how Helm can be used to create flexible manifests that can be parametrized at deployment time to support different requirements and/or environments.

Further reading

- Understanding Deployments:

  `https://kubernetes.io/docs/concepts/workloads/controllers/deployment/`

- Understanding Services:

  `https://kubernetes.io/docs/concepts/services-networking/service/`

- Using NGINX Ingress Controller and AWS NLB:

  `https://aws.amazon.com/blogs/opensource/network-load-balancer-nginx-ingress-controller-eks/`

- NGINX Ingress Controller:

  `https://kubernetes.github.io/ingress-nginx/examples/`

- Kubernetes Lens:

  `https://k8slens.dev/`

- Deploying and using the Kubernetes Dashboard:

  `https://kubernetes.io/docs/tasks/access-application-cluster/web-ui-dashboard/`

5

Using Helm to Manage a Kubernetes Application

In the previous chapter, we described how you can deploy a simple application using kubectl and a standard Kubernetes manifest. The challenge with using this approach is the manifest files are fixed. If you wanted to change the tag for a web server in a manifest for different environments (development, test, production, etc.) you would need to have multiple manifests or alter the manifest content every time you deploy it.

In this chapter, we introduce **Helm**, a tool that can be used to define, install, and upgrade complex applications and allows you to easily customize deployments for different environments. Specifically, we will cover the following topics:

- Understanding Helm and its architecture
- Installing the Helm binary
- Deploying a sample Kubernetes application with Helm
- Creating, deploying, updating, and rolling back a Helm chart
- Deleting an application via Helm
- Deploying a Helm chart with Lens

> **Important note**
> Helm is an abstraction on top of Kubernetes, and, as such, there is no difference between using Helm on EKS or another Kubernetes distribution or Deployment. We will focus on the basic functionality of Helm in this chapter. More advanced operations/configurations can be found by following the link in the *Further reading* section.

Technical requirements

Before starting this chapter, please ensure that the following is in place:

- You have a working EKS cluster and are able to perform administrative tasks
- kubectl is installed and properly configured on your workstation
- You have network connectivity to your EKS API endpoint
- You are familiar with YAML, basic networking, and EKS architecture

Understanding Helm and its architecture

As we saw in the previous chapters, Kubernetes YAML templates are fine for simple applications. However, as you try and cope with complex applications where you have multiple components, several dependencies between these components, and the need to deploy and update these components frequently using techniques such as blue/green deployments, you need something more; you need a package manager.

Package management is not a new idea; you can see a similar concept and critical software package management tools in software such as APT/YUM on Linux, Homebrew on Mac, or Chocolatey on Windows. Similarly, Helm can be considered the package management tool for Kubernetes.

Helm is composed of the following:

- **Charts**: A package of pre-configured Kubernetes resources
- **Releases**: A specific instance of a chart that has been deployed to the cluster using Helm
- **Repositories**: A group of published charts that can be made available to others
- **Helm binary**: A tool used to deploy a chart/release

In the next few sections, we will explore these components in more detail.

The benefit of Helm

The primary benefit of using Helm is to simplify the way Kubernetes resources are created and deployed. Helm allows developers to adopt a **don't repeat yourself** (**DRY**) approach, allows default attributes to be set but still allows them to be modified (overridden) to support different use cases or environments.

Developers also can easily share the template through a *Helm Chart Repository*. For example, if you want to install Prometheus (an open source monitoring system on Kubernetes) in development, you can manually create the manifests, specify the standard images, set up any supporting resources – such as ingress, deployment, and service – configure any environment variables, and repeat the process for production.

Instead of all this work, you can simply add the Helm Chart Repository for Prometheus using the following commands and then deploy it:

```
$ helm repo add prometheus-community https://prometheus-
community.github.io/helm-charts
$ helm install stable/prometheus
```

There are some alternatives to Helm, namely Kustomize (https://kustomize.io/), which builds on layers of YAML while also creating a custom operator for your application to manage its life cycle; an example of this is the Kafka operator. Helm, however, remains the simplest way to customize and deploy applications.

Getting to know Helm charts

The basic configuration item in Helm is the chart. A template that consists of a Kubernetes application that is used by Helm, is called a **chart**. The chart has a standard file and directory structure, shown next. You can use the $ helm create <mychartname> command to create this structure:

```
mychartname/
|
|- .helmignore
|
|- Chart.yaml
|
|- values.yaml
|
|- charts/
|
|- templates/
```

Let's look at each of the components of a chart:

- The .helmignore file works like a .gitignore file and specifies files or directories to be ignored by the Helm command.
- The Chart.yaml file holds metadata about the chart you are packaging, such as your version of the chart itself.
- The values.yaml file stores any values used for the deployment. You will normally see one file, the default values, but multiple value files can be used for different environments.
- The charts directory is used to store other charts that your chart may depend on.

- The `templates` directory holds the actual manifest you have created to support the deployment of your application. This may consist of multiple YAML files to deploy pods, config maps, secrets, and so on.

Values are transposed into the chart using the `{{ define }}` directive, which means the templates are significantly more flexible than standard Kubernetes manifests. What follows is an example of Helm manifest that shows a resource, in this case, a ConfigMap can be modified:

```
apiVersion: v1
kind: ConfigMap
metadata:
  name: {{ .Release.Name }}-configmap
data:
  myvalue: "Hello World"
```

In this example, the name of the ConfigMap will be a combination of `Release.Name` and the `-configmap` string. For example, if your chart name is *CM1*, the resulting ConfigMap will be named `CM1-configmap`.

Now that we have discussed the basic configuration, let's look at how we actually install and use Helm.

Installing the Helm binary

Helm can be easily installed and can be compliable with many different operating systems. You can refer to the following instruction to set up Helm on your system:

`https://helm.sh/docs/intro/install/`

You must configure kubectl to work for Amazon EKS. If you have not already done this, please refer to *Chapter 3, Building Your First EKS Cluster*, to help you configure kubectl properly.

On Linux, you can use the following command to download and install the Helm binary:

```
$ curl -L https://git.io/get_helm.sh | bash -s -- --version
v3.8.2
```

At the time of writing this book, Helm 3.9.x had some issues using the AWS authenticator plugin, so v3.8.2 is used. You will need to make sure that the `/usr/local/bin/` directory is in your PATH.

Deploying a sample Kubernetes application with Helm

In the previous chapter, we deployed the NGINX ingress controller using the following command:

```
$ kubectl create -f https://raw.githubusercontent.com/
kubernetes/ingress-nginx/I
```

If we want to install it using Helm, we need to perform the following tasks:

1. Add the public stable repository to your Helm configuration:

    ```
    $ helm repo add nginx-stable https://helm.nginx.com/
    stable
    ```

2. Refresh the repository information:

    ```
    $ helm repo update
    ```

3. We can then show the charts in the repository:

    ```
    $ helm search repo nginx-stable
    ```

4. One of the charts will be nginx-ingress, which can be installed using the following command:

    ```
    $ helm install my-release nginx-stable/nginx-ingress
    ```

5. The chart release can be viewed using either of these commands:

    ```
    $ helm list
    $ helm history my-release
    ```

6. You can also view the Kubernetes resources using the following command:

    ```
    $ kubectl api-resources --verbs=list -o name | xargs -n 1
    kubectl get --show-kind -l app.kubernetes.io/instance=my-
    release --ignore-not-found -o name
    ```

Let's look at how we create a new Helm chart from scratch.

Creating, deploying, updating, and rolling back a Helm chart

As you can see from the previous example, deploying pre-packaged applications with Helm is pretty simple. Deploying your own application is also easy. We start with the following command, which will create a directory in your current directory called myhelmchart and populate it with the relevant files and templates:

```
$ helm create myhelmchart
```

By default, the `values.yaml` file created by this command contains references to a single NGINX pod and creates a `ClusterIP` service, which is only accessible from within the cluster. The key values from the default file are shown next:

```
replicaCount: 1
image:
  repository: nginx
service:
  type: ClusterIP
```

We can easily deploy this new Helm chart using the following command:

```
$ helm install example ./myhelmchart --set service.
type=NodePort
```

This will override the `service.type` value seen in the `values.yaml` file with a `NodePort` service, so it is now exposed outside of the cluster. We can then validate the chart deployment with the following command and see the name of the `NodePort` service that was created, along with the other Kubernetes resources:

```
$ kubectl api-resources --verbs=list -o name | xargs -n 1
kubectl get --show-kind -l app.kubernetes.io/instance=example
--ignore-not-found -o name
endpoints/example-myhelmchart
pod/example-myhelmchart-cb76665d4-sq41k
serviceaccount/example-myhelmchart
service/example-myhelmchart
deployment.apps/example-myhelmchart
replicaset.apps/example-myhelmchart-cb76665d4
endpointslice.discovery.k8s.io/example-myhelmchart-8kw8t
```

If you run the following command using the service name from the previous step, you will be able to extract the IP address and port of the service and curl the `NodePort` service:

```
$ export NODE_PORT=$(kubectl get --namespace default -o
jsonpath="{.spec.ports[0].nodePort}" services example-
myhelmchart) | curl http://$NODE_IP:$NODE_PORT
```

To update the Helm deployment, we are going to perform the following steps:

1. Modify the `values.yaml` file and increase `replicaCount:` to 2. We can also change the `service.type` value to `NodePort`.

2. Modify the `Chart.yaml` file and update `version` to `0.2.0`.

3. Validate the changes:

    ```
    $ helm lint
    ```

4. Then roll out the changes:

    ```
    $ helm upgrade example ./myhelmchart
    ```

5. We can then validate the deployment:

    ```
    $ helm history example
    ```

    You will notice the revision number shown next when you run the preceding command:

    ```
    $ helm history example
    REVISION   UPDATED STATUS   CHART     APP
    VERSION        DESCRIPTION
    1 Sat xx superseded  myhelmchart-0.1.0 1.16.0 Install
    complete
    2 Sat xx deployed  myhelmchart-0.2.0   1.16.0 Upgrade
    complete
    ```

6. We can also validate that two Pods exist for the Deployment:

    ```
    kubectl get pod | grep example
    ```

You can easily roll back to a previous revision using the `helm rollback example 1` command, where 1 represents the revision you want to return to. This is one of the major advantages of Helm over basic Kubernetes manifests, each change to the manifest can be versioned and deployed as a new revision, and if issues occur, you can easily roll back to a previous version/revision.

The `helm list` command can show all the revisions in the cluster, which are stored as Kubernetes Secrets in the namespace where the release is deployed. Next, let's look at how we remove our Helm application.

Deleting an application via the Helm command

Helm provides a simple `uninstall` command to delete the application release. The first step is to determine which Helm deployment you want to remove using the `helm list` command:

```
$ helm list --all-namespaces
NAME    NAMESPACE REVISION  UPDATED        STATUS        CHART
                  APP VERSION
cm1               default         1              2022-
deployed          myhelmchart-0.1.0      1.16.0
example           default         4              2022-
deployed          myhelmchart-0.2.0      1.16.0
my-release        default         1              2022-
deployed          nginx-ingress-0.13.2   2.2.2
```

In this example, we want to remove the example deployment, so we can simply run the `$ helm uninstall example` command and all the resources created by the chart or charts will be removed.

> **Important note**
>
> This will remove all deployment history as well. Please also make sure you have removed all the Helm charts using the `$ helm uninstall` command.

In this section, we reviewed using the Helm binary to deploy public charts and create, update, roll back, and delete your own charts. In the next section, we will show you how to use Lens to deploy charts.

Deploying a Helm chart with Lens

In the previous chapter, we discussed how to visualize your Kubernetes resources using Lens. However, you can also use Lens to manage Helm charts. Please refer to *Chapter 4, Running Your First Application on EKS* (the *Visualizing your workloads* section), for guidance on the setup of Lens.

By default, Lens will fetch available Helm repositories from the public Artifact Hub (`https://artifacthub.io/`) and Bitnami. As we are going to redeploy the NGINX ingress controller we deployed using the Helm **Command Line Interface (CLI)**, we need to add a custom repository. To do this, follow these steps while referring to *Figure 5.1*:

1. Choose **Lens | Preferences** from the main toolbar.

2. Then select **Kubernetes**.

3. Select **Add custom Helm Repo** from the Kubernetes panel.

4. This will display a pop-up box, which works in the same way as the `helm repo add` command. Here, we are going to add the NGINX repository we used in a previous example: `https://helm.nginx.com/stable`.

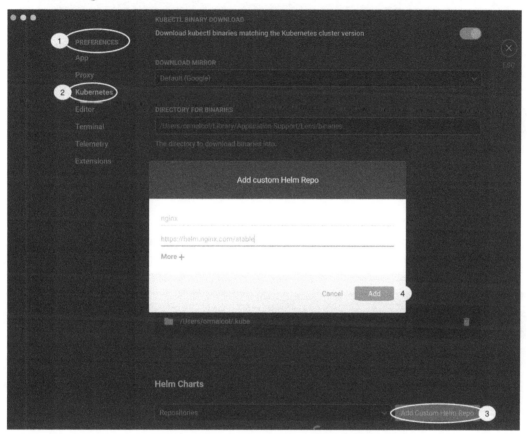

Figure 5.1 – Adding a custom Helm repository in Lens

Once the repository has been added, we can now deploy charts from it. To do this, follow these steps while referring to *Figure 5.2*:

1. Select your cluster.

2. Choose **Helm | Charts**. This will show all the charts available to you based on the repositories you've added.

3. Filter out NGINX as we have done in the following screenshot, and you will see two NGINX ingress controller charts: one from Bitnami and the other from NGINX.

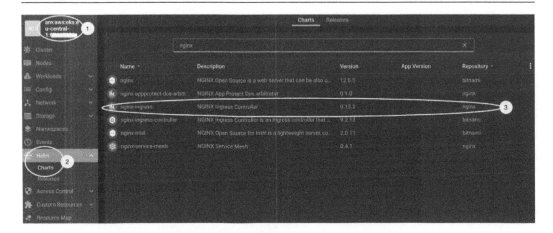

Figure 5.2 – Finding the required chart in Lens

4. Click on the NGINX chart.

5. This will bring up another panel where you must click on **Install**. Fill in the details (or leave them unchanged) and click **Install** again. The chart will be deployed, as shown in the following screenshot:

Figure 5.3 – Installing a chart in Lens

6. You can now click on the **Releases** tab, and you will see all the deployed Helm charts. In the following example, we only have the NGINX ingress controller deployed. From the **Releases** tab, you can also upgrade and delete the release by clicking on the three dots (the kebab menu) on the right of the chart:

Figure 5.4 – Viewing Releases in Lens

As you can see, Lens performs the same functions that the Helm binary does but just provides it in a graphical view. As discussed in the previous chapter, Lens also allows you to review the running workloads, something we had to do with Kubectl. Hence, Lens helps bring together these tools, but it is still recommended that you know how to use both Kubectl and Helm if you're going to work with multiple clusters in production.

Summary

In this chapter, we learned how to use Helm to accelerate application deployment on Kubernetes and improve the efficiency of template creation. This included how to install the Helm CLI and use it to deploy applications (charts) hosted in a public repository. We then created our own chart, customized it, deployed it, modified the configuration, deployed the new revision, rolled back to a previous revision, and finally deleted it from our cluster.

We then discussed how we could perform similar activities using a third-party tool, Lens, and how it achieves the same things but provides a graphical user interface while also integrating multiple views such as Kubernetes resources (kubectl) and Helm releases.

In the next chapter, we will look deeper into how you access and secure your EKS cluster, focusing on how you access the EKS cluster endpoints and authenticate users.

Further reading

- An example operator: `https://docs.confluent.io/5.5.1/installation/operator/index.html`

- Understanding Helm in more detail: `https://helm.sh/docs/`

Part 2:
Deep Dive into EKS

In this section, we will dive deeper into EKS and its various components. This part aims to demystify key aspects such as security, networking, and node groups, providing you with a comprehensive understanding of each feature. Finally, you will take away strategies regarding how to upgrade your EKS cluster version and follow the upstream Kubernetes release cadence.

This part contains the following topics:

- *Chapter 6, Securing and Accessing Clusters on EKS*
- *Chapter 7, Networking in EKS*
- *Chapter 8, Managing Worker Nodes on EKS*
- *Chapter 9, Advanced Networking with EKS*
- *Chapter 10, Upgrading EKS Clusters*

6

Securing and Accessing Clusters on EKS

This chapter will introduce the general concepts for authentication and authorization in Kubernetes, and will also discuss the differences between these concepts and **Elastic Kubernetes Service** (**EKS**). We will also look at how to configure EKS and client tools to securely communicate.

Authentication verifies the identity of a user or service, and authorization manages what they can do. In this chapter, we will review the mechanism used in EKS to implement authentication and authorization so you to use them to build secure clusters. Specifically, we will cover the following topics:

- Understanding key Kubernetes concepts
- Configuring EKS cluster access

Understanding key Kubernetes concepts

Kubernetes clusters have two categories of users: service accounts managed by Kubernetes, and normal users (administrators, developers, etc.). **Kubernetes** (**K8s**) is extensible by design and supports multiple authentication plugins. We will focus on the most common one, client certificates, while discussing generic user authentication/authorization in Kubernetes.

Using the client certificates' plugin, users are considered authenticated when they furnish a valid certificate signed by the cluster's **certificate authority** (**CA**).

With a valid certificate, Kubernetes determines the username from the common name field in the **Subject** of the certificate (e.g., /CN=bob) while the group information is provided in the **Organization** field (e.g., /O=dev). From this point onwards, the **role-based access control** (**RBAC**) sub-system will determine whether the user is authorized to perform a particular operation on a resource.

The following diagram illustrates this concept. Please note that service accounts will be discussed in *Chapter 13, Using IAM for Granting Access to Applications*.

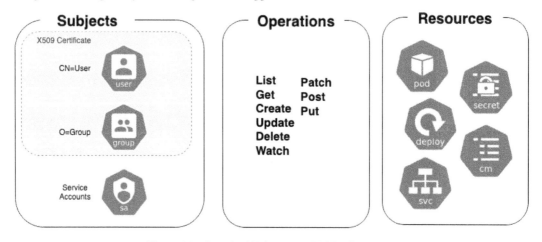

Figure 6.1 – Standard Kubernetes RBAC sub-system

In order to generate the certificate for a normal user, you need to generate a PKI private key and CSR using an operating system tool such as OpenSSL (see the following example) and then export the CSR request in base64 encoding for signing by the cluster CA:

```
$ openssl genrsa -out myuser.key 2048
$ openssl req -new -key myuser.key -out myuser.csr
$ cat myuser.csr | base64 | tr -d "\n"
```

The resulting encoded string can be submitted to the K8s cluster for signing using the CertificateSigningRequest kind. An example is shown here:

```
apiVersion: certificates.k8s.io/v1
kind: CertificateSigningRequest
metadata:
  name: myuser
spec:
  request: <BASE64.csr>
  signerName: kubernetes.io/kube-apiserver-client
  expirationSeconds: 86400  # one day
  usages:
  - client auth
```

Now that we understand how standard K8s authentication works, let's move on to how it works in EKS by default.

Understanding the default EKS authentication method

Managing users, groups, and certificates for one or more K8s clusters can be an operational challenge. Thankfully, EKS offloads this by default to the AWS **Identity and Access Management (IAM)** service. IAM is a globally distributed service that allows you to create users and groups, as well as assign AWS permissions including the AWS EKS API.

By default, when you create an EKS cluster, the IAM entity that creates that cluster is automatically granted `system:masters` permissions, effectively making it the system administrator role for the EKS cluster. This means that without additional configuration, the IAM identity used for cluster creation is the only identity that can perform any functions on the EKS cluster.

This is a typical error when starting out with EKS, as a CI/CD pipeline may be used to create your cluster, but its IAM identity is different to that of the regular users. Therefore, when they go to interact with the cluster, they have no K8s privileges. The EKS cluster comes pre-integrated with AWS IAM. The following diagram illustrates how the user and the EKS cluster interact with the IAM service.

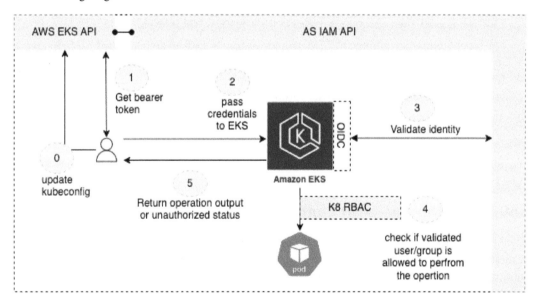

Figure 6.2 – EKS authentication flow

We will now discuss in detail each of the steps in the EKS authentication flow shown in *Figure 6.2*:

0. The starting point is for the client to retrieve the cluster configuration and update your **kubeconfig** file with the clusters' TLS certificate and context. The update-kubeconfig CLI command is the simplest way to do this and will use the DescribeCluster API operation. Any user using this API call must have an IAM identity and the privilege to use this API to automatically update the config file. An example is shown here for the cluster called mycluster:

```
$ aws eks update-kubeconfig --name mycluster
```

1. A bearer token now needs to be generated and used in each EKS API (**kubectl**) request. This is based on the kubeconfig context and can be fetched manually using the get-token CLI command or automatically using the AWS IAM Authenticator:

```
$ aws eks get-token --cluster-name mycluster
```

2. The bearer token is added to the request either manually (on the kubectl command line for example) or automatically by the IAM authenticator/kubectl command.

3. This bearer token is now validated against the AWS IAM service using a token—authentication-webhook—which is being used by the IAM authenticator service in EKS. If it is valid, then a request is passed to the K8s RBAC sub-system.

4. The set of permissions granted by IAM policies associated with an authenticated IAM identity has no bearing EKS cluster permissions. The bridge between the IAM and RBAC sub-systems is the aws-auth ConfigMap that provides the mappings between IAM principals (roles/users/groups) and Kubernetes subjects (users/groups).

5. The operation (in the case of authorization) is returned to the client, or alternatively they receive a "not authorized" response.

So far, we've discussed how user identities are authenticated. The next section describes how the request from an authenticated user is authorized.

Configuring the aws-auth ConfigMap for authorization

We will see how to configure and maintain the aws-auth ConfigMap later on in this section, but it's important to understand that this ConfigMap manages the relationship between the AWS IAM identity, and the Kubernetes identity and permissions. Without a corresponding entry in the aws-auth ConfigMap, IAM users or groups won't have any permissions to perform any K8s operations, regardless of what permissions are assigned through the IAM role or policy.

EKS uses **OpenID Connect** (**OIDC**) identity providers as a method to authenticate/authorize users to your cluster. This means that each cluster is given a unique OIDC identity that can be used as a trusted entity in the AWS IAM policy. You can validate the identity of the cluster using the following command:

```
$ aws eks describe-cluster --name my-cluster --query "cluster.
identity.oidc.issuer" --output text
```

OIDC identity providers can be used with AWS IAM or with other OIDC-compliant providers. This means you can manage users/passwords and permissions in a platform such as GitHub Enterprise or GitLab instead of AWS IAM, and use the OIDC provider to authenticate/authorize users. You can associate one OIDC identity provider to your cluster so you cannot use IAM and another identity provider.

Accessing the cluster endpoint

So far, we have talked about the ability to authenticate and authorize operations on an EKS cluster; however, to do so you will need to be able to communicate with the cluster's endpoint over HTTPS. Once you've updated your **kubeconfig** file for a given cluster/context, you will have the DNS name (server) and TLS certificate (`certificate-authority-data`). How you access that endpoint will depend on how you have configured your EKS endpoint, either as public only, private only, or both.

As discussed previously, EKS is a managed service, so the control plane (API/etcd) servers run in a VPC managed by AWS. The worker nodes (typically EC2) run in the customer's VPC and communicate with the control plane using whatever IP address is returned through the DNS lookup of the server. The following diagram illustrates how the user accesses public or private EKS endpoints:

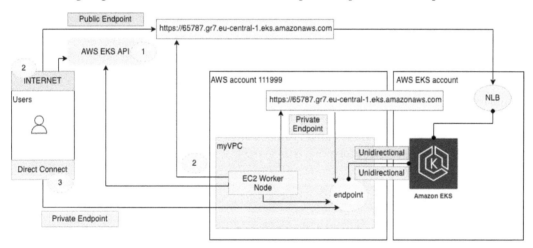

Figure 6.3 – EKS endpoint access

The steps needed to access EKS endpoint, as shown in the preceding diagram, are as follows:

1. The initial requirement is to obtain the EKS cluster's DNS name. In most user access scenarios, this step has already been done using the `update-kubeconfig` CLI command but when worker nodes are created, they will make a call to the AWS EKS API to get the cluster configuration and DNS information. At time of writing, the AWS EKS API is a public API only (no private endpoint) so all worker nodes need access to the public API through a NAT, internet, and/or transit gateway.

2. For public endpoints, the DNS name resolves to a public **Network Load Balancer** (**NLB**) hosted in the AWS-managed VPC. This means all user and worker node communication goes through this public endpoint (although worker node traffic doesn't leave the AWS backbone).

3. For a private endpoint, the DNS name resolves to the private endpoint attached to the customer's VPC (this uses a privately hosted Route 53 zone managed by AWS). More specifically, it resolves to a VPC private IP address, meaning it is only accessible in the VPC or through a private connection using a transit gateway, a VPN, and/or Direct Connect. In this case, the private connection between the customer's VPC and the VPC managed by AWS is bidirectional, being used by the control plane and the users/worker nodes.

It is possible to enable both public and private endpoints, in which case users can access the K8s API through the public NLB, and also through the private endpoint. In this model, all API server/worker node communication occurs through the private endpoint.

Configuring EKS cluster access

In this section, we will look in more detail at the configuration of the two key files needed to securely access your cluster, `kubeconfig` and `aws-auth`, along with the use of IP controls to secure EKS endpoints.

Configuring .kube/config

The **kubeconfig** file is central to providing access to the cluster. The `clusters` list has an entry for each cluster you want to access, containing both the DNS name and the TLS certificate to allow communication to take place. These entries can be added manually or through the `update-kubeconfig` CLI command. The following is an example `kubeconfig` file:

```
clusters:
- cluster:
  certificate-authority-data: xx==
  server: https://65787.gr7.eu-central-1.eks.amazonaws.com
  name: arn:aws:eks:eu-central-1:111999:cluster/mycluster
```

The `context` section in the `kubeconfig` file is used to group access parameters together for a client tool such as kubectl. You can have different contexts to access a single cluster. In the following example, we are grouping the `myuser` user and `mycluster` cluster together in the `mycontext` context:

```
contexts:
- context:
    cluster: arn:aws:eks:eu-central-1:111999:cluster/mycluster
    user:  arn:aws:eks:eu-central-1:111999:cluster/myuser
    name:  arn:aws:eks:eu-central-1:111999:cluster/mycontext
```

Finally, the users section in the kubeconfig file holds the specific parameters for the user (associated with the context). In the following example, the user uses the aws eks get-token command to automatically provide the bearer token for authentication based on the IAM identity configured for the caller of the mycluster cluster, which is in the eu-central-1 Region in account 111999:

```
users:
- name: arn:aws:eks:eu-central-1:111999:cluster/myuser
  user:
    exec:
      apiVersion: client.authentication.k8s.io/v1alpha1
      args:
      - --region
      - eu-central-1
      - eks
      - get-token
      - --cluster-name
      - mycluster
      command: aws
```

Configuring your kubeconfig file is a critical part of establishing communication with the EKS cluster and the following commands can be used to validate/view the configuration:

```
$ kubectl config view
$ kubectl config view -o template --template='{{ index .
"current-context" }}'
```

So far, we've reviewed the way a K8s client, such as kubectl, can provide the identity of a user to the API servers. The next section reviews how that user's identity is authorized using the aws-auth Config Map.

Configuring the aws-auth Config Map

A correctly configured client's kubeconfig file provides the bearer token that allows EKS to identify and validate the user. Once their identity has been validated, the RBAC subsystem and aws-auth ConfigMap will then validate whether they have the correct permissions. We add users' permissions via role details in the ConfigMap, under the data section. Each entry supports the following parameters:

- groups: A list of Kubernetes groups to which the role is mapped.

- rolearn: The ARN of the IAM role associated with the user bearer token.

- username: A username within Kubernetes to map to the IAM role. As discussed previously, this is something that is not used and need not be mapped to an existing user.

In the following example, the myIAMRole IAM role in account 111999 is mapped to the system:masters group and assigned the K8s username of creator-account. This is an example of the default configuration you will see in the aws-auth ConfigMap:

```
- groups:
  - system:masters
  rolearn: arn:aws:iam::111999:role/myIAMrole
  username: creatorAccount
```

You can modify the ConfigMap directly using either kubectl or an IAC tool such as eksctl as follows:

```
$ kubectl edit cm aws-auth -n kube-system
eksctl create iamidentitymapping --cluster  mycluster
--region=eu-central-1 --arn arn:aws:iam::111999:role/myIAMrole
--group system:masters --username creatorAccount
```

This approach is not advised as there is no version/change control. A better approach is to place the ConfigMap manifest into a Git repository and then use a CI/CD pipeline to push/pull changes. You can still use kubectl or eksctl to make the changes, but it's done using a file under version control and managed through an audited pipeline that could have any number of build checks or tests. Typically, the following steps will be followed for the deployment of the EKS cluster and the incremental management of ConfigMap:

1.   Deploy the EKS cluster using your preferred infrastructure-as-code tool and/or pipeline.

2.   Export the default aws-auth ConfigMap into a separate version-controlled repository/manifest with its own deployment pipeline. This can be done by running the following command:

```
kubectl get cm aws-auth -n kube-system -o yaml > xx.yaml
```

3.   Leverage a suitable code review process, to add new groups/users and role mappings. Please note, the IAM role referenced in the configuration must exist, due to which it must be created first in the AWS IAM service.

4.   Update your cluster using a push (CI/CD) or pull (GitOps) method using the following command:

```
kubectl patch configmap/aws-auth -n kube-system –patch
"$(cat /tmp/xx.yml)"
```

5.   Steps 3 and 4 need to be repeated on an ongoing basis as you add and delete users/groups to and from the aws-auth file.

So far, we've discussed how users are authenticated/authorized when a request arrives at the K8s API server endpoint. In the next section, we consider how you can secure access to the API endpoint.

Protecting EKS endpoints

On the whole, it is generally better to use private EKS endpoints. While accessing any EKS endpoint requires a valid TLS certificate (if using client certificates) and the appropriate IAM/RBAC permissions, if these were compromised and you had a public endpoint, then your cluster would be accessible from anywhere in the world. If you need to use a public endpoint, then make sure to configure public access CIDR ranges to restrict which public IP addresses have access. In the following example, access to the mycluster public cluster has been restricted to a single /32 IP address:

```
$ aws eks describe-cluster --name mycluster
{    "cluster": {
.......
            "endpointPublicAccess": true,
            "publicAccessCidrs": ["203.0.113.5/32 "]}}
```

The EKS API network interfaces are protected by a separate security group that provides stateful IP ingress protection. So, while EKS private endpoints can only be accessed from the VPC or connected private networks, the security groups associated with the API endpoint (shown as securityGroupIds in the following example) can be used as an additional control to restrict access to any specific IP addresses:

```
$ aws eks describe-cluster --name mycluster
{"cluster": {
........ . .
            "securityGroupIds": ["sg-5656576d"],
            "clusterSecurityGroupId": "sg-5657657s"}}
```

Please note that the API security groups are different from the clusterSecurityGroupId security group, which is used to protect worker nodes.

With that, you have now understood or have at least gained familiarity with how EKS performs authentication and authorization and how to protect your API endpoints. We'll now revisit the key learning points from this chapter.

Summary

In this chapter, we explored the basic concepts of authentication and authorization in native Kubernetes and how EKS differs. We described how EKS, by default, is integrated with AWS IAM and that a bearer code needs to be generated by a client tool such as kubectl in order for EKS to authenticate the user. This bearer code can be generated manually using the get-token CLI action or automatically using the kubeconfig file and will be submitted on every API request and be automatically validated by EKS.

We also described how the `aws-auth` ConfigMap is used by the Kubernetes RBAC sub-system to accept or deny any API request. It is important to place this file under version control and manage changes using a CI/CD pipeline as, by default, only the cluster creator has permission to do anything on the cluster.

Finally, we talked about how you can secure access to the API endpoints using IP whitelisting and/or security groups and how it is typically better to use private clusters.

In the next chapter, we will discuss Kubernetes networking and how EKS can be configured to use an **AWS Virtual Private Cloud** (**VPC**).

Further readings

- Overview of the AWS IAM authenticator:

  `https://docs.aws.amazon.com/eks/latest/userguide/install-aws-iam-authenticator.html`

- Overview of webhook authentication in K8s:

  `https://kubernetes.io/docs/reference/access-authn-autWhz/authentication/#webhook-token-authentication`

- Overview of the AWS OIDC Provider Integration:

  `https://github.com/awsdocs/amazon-eks-user-guide/blob/master/doc_source/authenticate-oidc-identity-provider.md`

7

Networking in EKS

Kubernetes (**K8s**) isn't prescriptive about external networking. This means it is possible to use multiple network plugins and configurations in Kubernetes to meet security, latency, and operational requirements.

In this chapter, we will focus on how standard K8s Pod and cluster networking works and then discuss the similarities and differences in an AWS **Virtual Private Cloud** (**VPC**). Specifically, we will cover the following:

- Understanding networking in Kubernetes
- Getting to grips with basic AWS networking
- Understanding EKS networking
- Configuring EKS networking using the VPC CNI
- Common networking issues

The reader should have a familiarity with TCP/IP networking, how networks work in AWS, and the concepts of NAT. This chapter is intended to give the reader the skills to configure and manage EKS networking for one or more clusters.

Understanding networking in Kubernetes

Kubernetes is designed to be extensible, and as such it supports multiple network implementations, all of which meet a clearly defined networking model. K8s has some basic networking rules that all network plugins must follow:

- Every Pod gets its own IP address
- Containers within a Pod share the Pod IP address
- Pods can communicate with all other Pods in the cluster using Pod IP addresses (without NAT)
- Isolation of Pods at the network level is performed using network policies

For compliance reasons, any K8s network implementation must be built to support the **Container Network Interface (CNI)** specification, which is a **Cloud Native Computing Foundation (CNCF)** project. The CNI specification consists of guides and libraries for writing plugins to configure network interfaces in containers. While it is possible to have multiple CNIs in a single cluster, by default, a single K8s cluster will be configured to support only a single CNI. There are many types and providers of CNI plugins, but they all allow Pods to connect to an external network and/or the allocation of Pod IP addresses.

Before we dive into networking specifically for EKS, it's important to understand how networking generally works in K8s as most CNI implementations follow this pattern.

Network implementation in Kubernetes

A Pod is the smallest unit that can be deployed and managed by Kubernetes. A Pod can contain more than one container. Containers in a Pod share a network namespace, which means they share the same IP address, network port space, and Ethernet interface. The following diagram illustrates Pod-to-Pod connectivity within a node and across nodes in the same cluster.

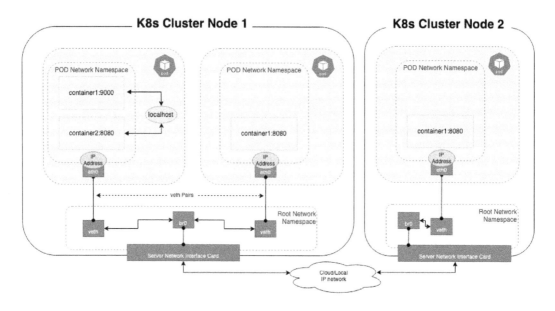

Figure 7.1 – Basic Pod networking

K8s network communication happens in several ways, depending on the sources and destinations:

- As the containers in a Pod share the same network namespace and port space, they can communicate with each other using a localhost (127.0.0.1) address.

- Each Pod has a corresponding interface (veth) in the root network namespace of the host, as well as its own interface in its network namespace. This is known as a veth pair, which acts as a virtual network cable between the Pod network namespace and the host networking, which has the actual Ethernet interface. Pods that want to talk to each other use the cluster DNS to resolve a service name to an IP address, and the ARP protocol to map the IP address to a Pod Ethernet address.

- If the Pod is on another node, the cluster DNS resolves the IP address. In cases where the ARP request fails, the packet is routed out of the host to the network where it hopefully finds a route to the target IP address.

The CNI integrates with kubelet, which is the primary K8s agent that runs on all worker nodes. When a new Pod is created, it doesn't have a network interface. The kubelet will send an ADD command to the CNI, which is then responsible for the following:

1. Inserting a network interface into the container network namespace (eth0)

2. Making any necessary changes on the host such as creating the veth interface and attaching it to the Bridge0 and the eth0 interfaces

3. Assigning an IP address to the interface and setting up the relevant routes

Kubernetes adds further abstraction on top of the basic Pod networking. A Kubernetes cluster allows multiple replicas of the same Pod to be deployed across multiple hosts and allows ingress traffic to be routed to any one of those hosts. There are different types of service; we will focus on a NodePort service for this example. When a service is created, it will select (typically) Pods based on a label. It creates a new DNS name, virtual IP, assigns a dynamic port on each node, and keeps a map of which nodes are hosting which Pods with the label defined in the service specifcation. This is shown in the following diagram.

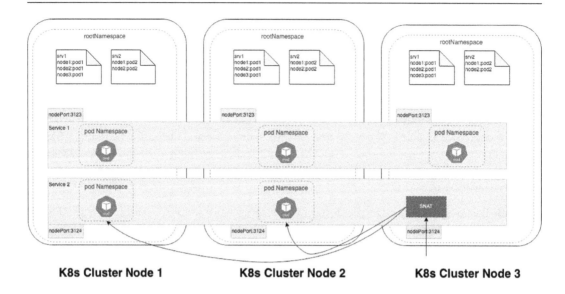

Figure 7.2 – Nodeport services

As traffic arrives at the service (using the service DNS name or *host:dynamic port* combination), iptables or IP Virtual Server (IPVS) are used to rewrite the request service address to a relevant Pod address (under the control of kube-proxy) and then the basic Pod networking rules are applied as described previously. In the case of service 1 (*Figure 7.2*), traffic can be sent to each node and the destination will be rewritten to the Pod running on that node. In the case of service 2, traffic arriving at node 3 has no local Pod, so traffic will be sent to either node 1 or node 2.

By default, traffic will be source NAT'd from node 3, so traffic always flows in and out of node 3 irrespective of where the Pods are located. The Kubernetes network proxy (kube-proxy) runs on each node and is responsible for managing services and the requests (including SNAT) and load balancing for the Pods.

SNAT means replacing the source IP address of the IP packet with another address. In most cases, this will be the IP address of the node's Ethernet address. **Destination NAT** (**DNAT**) is where the destination IP address is replaced with another address, generally the IP address of a Pod. The following diagram illustrates these concepts.

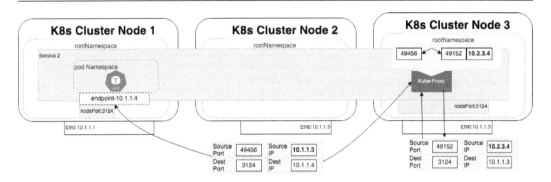

Figure 7.3 – K8s source/destination NAT

In *Figure 7.3*, using a nodePort service as the example:

1. The traffic is received on node 3 from the client (10.2.3.4) for the service exposed on nodeport service port 3124.

2. kube-proxy will perform the SNAT, mapping the source IP to the local node's Ethernet address and using DNAT to map a service address to a Pod IP address (on node 1).

3. The packet is sent to node 1 (as this will respond to the ARP request for the Pod IP address). The K8s endpoint, which contains the IP addresses of any Pods that match the service selector, is used to send the packet to the Pod.

4. The Pod response is set back to node 3 (based on the source IP address) and then mapped back to the client based on the source port mapping maintained by kube-proxy.

AWS networking is prescriptive, it configures K8s networking to work in conjunction with AWS VPC networking, and it has a big impact on how EKS networking works by default. The next section will quickly review how AWS VPC networking works and some of the concepts you need to understand as we dive deeper in EKS networking.

Getting to grips with basic AWS networking

Before we discuss EKS networking, we will quickly review basic VPC networking in AWS. When you sign up to AWS, you are provided with an AWS account that can deploy services across multiple Regions, and multiple **Availability Zones (AZ)** in each Region. A Region is a geographic location, such as London, Frankfurt, or Oregon, and consists of multiple AZs, which in turn each consist of two or more AWS data centers connected to each other over high-speed networks. An AZ is the basic unit of network reliability in AWS.

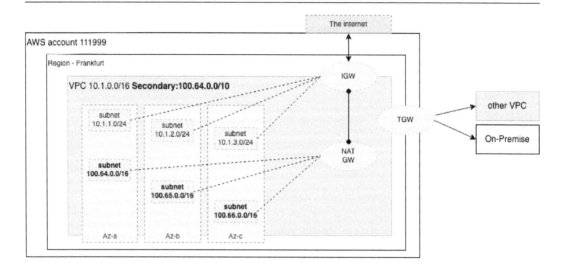

Figure 7.4 – Basic VPC structure

A VPC is a regional construct that is defined by an IP **Classless Inter-Domain Routing** (**CIDR**) range such as 10.1.0.0/16. Subnets are assigned from a VPC and map to one AZ. Services that have an IP address, such as EKS, are assigned to a subnet (or group of subnets) and the AWS platform will assign an available IP address from the subnet range and create an **Elastic Network Interface** (**ENI**) in that subnet. In most AWS VPCs, RFC1918, that is, private, addressing is used, which means VPC CIDR ranges are drawn from the following subnets:

- 10.0.0.0 – 10.255.255.255 (10/8 prefix)

- 172.16.0.0 – 172.31.255.255 (172.16/12 prefix)

- 192.168.0.0 – 192.168.255.255 (192.168/16 prefix)

In addition, the VPC can now use non-RFC1918 addresses, those in the 100.64.0.0/10 and 198.19.0.0/16 ranges, which EKS supports. In large enterprises, these ranges are shared across the existing data centers and offices, so a small range of addresses are typically given to the AWS platform, which is then shared across multiple VPCs and AWS services including EKS. It is possible to add additional IP ranges to a VPC, that is, secondary addressing, but not to change the ranges once they have been set. In the preceding example, an additional range, 100.64.0.0/10, has been added and three additional subnets created from that range in three separate AZs. Within a VPC, any IP range, primary or secondary, is routable. In the preceding example, a host on subnet 10.1.1.0/24 can route to any other subnet including 100.64.0.0/16; however, AWS **Security Groups** (**SGs**) and/or **Network Access Control List** (**NACLs**) control which systems can communicate with which other systems.

Three additional services are needed to allow access to and from the internet. An **Internet Gateway** (**IGW**) allows mapping between public IP addresses and the VPC addresses (ingress and egress traffic).

A **NAT Gateway** (**NATGW**) can use an IGW to provide outbound access only and is used when applications/systems need to access public AWS APIs (such as the EKS API) or public services such as Docker Hub to pull container images, but don't want to be accessed by anything on the internet. Private NATGWs are also possible, which simply involves a NAT of a private subnet to a private address without any relationship to an IGW. This is used to translate between a range that is being reused elsewhere (on-premises or in another part of the AWS cloud) or is not being routed on premises.

A **Transit Gateway** (**TGW**) is used to route between other VPCs (in the same or other AWS accounts) and connects to on-premises workloads and services (through a VPN or a Direct Connect private connection).

Understanding EKS networking

Now that we understand the basic K8s network models, what a CNI is, and how VPC networking works, we can explore how EKS networking works. The VPC CNI has several configuration options; we will not cover all possible configurations in this section, only the most common ones.

EKS is a managed service, and the control plane is managed by AWS in a separate VPC. The two main networking questions you need to ask when configuring your cluster are: how do I access the API endpoint from kubectl (and other) clients? And how are my Pods accessed or access other systems? We covered public and private endpoints in *Chapter 6*, so for the remainder of this chapter, we will focus on Pod networking. Let's start with a basic EKS deployment, a private cluster with two EC2 instances in a node group. The cluster has been configured to connect to two private VPC subnets; the node group is also deployed to the same two subnets.

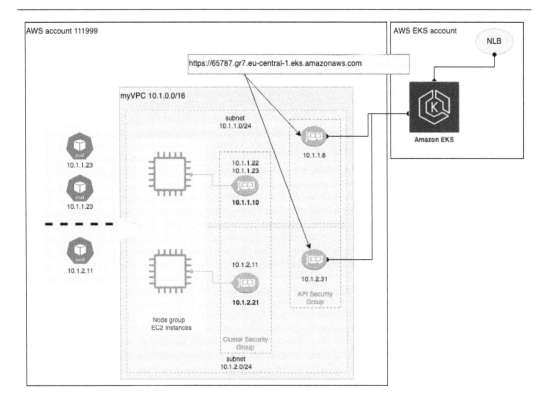

Figure 7.5 – EKS networking (basic)

If you look at the VPC in *Figure 7.5*, you can see four interfaces (ENIs) – one for each of the worker nodes and two (typically) for the EKS cluster – along with a private hosted zone that maps the server's name to those two cluster ENIs. There are also two security groups, one for the worker nodes and one for EKS control plane/APIs. Currently, this is all default AWS platform behavior. Each of the ENIs has been assigned an IP address from the subnet it is attached to. The security groups will reference each other and allow access between the worker nodes and API.

EKS is deployed with the AWS VPC CNI as the default CNI for the cluster. Other CNIs can be used, some of which are described in *Chapter 9, Advanced Networking with EKS*. The **vpc-cni** works in conjunction with the kubelet agent to request and map an IP address from the VPC to the ENI used by the host and then assign it to the Pod. The number of EC2 ENIs and therefore the number of IP addresses that can be assigned to Pods is limited per EC2 instance type. For example, a **m4.4xlarge** node can have up to 8 ENIs, and each ENI can have up to 30 IP addresses, which means you can theoretically support up to 120 addresses per worker node (as we'll see later, there are some limits to this).

The advantage of this approach is that the Pod is a first-class citizen in an AWS VPC. There is no difference between the Pod and an EC2 instance; Pod networking behaves exactly as described in this chapter. Another benefit is when traffic leaves the node: traffic can be routed to and controlled through the same AWS network gateways and controls, used by all the other services in AWS.

The disadvantage to this approach is that the EKS cluster, given the ephemeral nature of Pods/containers, can quickly *eat* all your available subnet addresses, preventing you from deploying new Pods and/or other AWS services such as databases (RDS). This is particularly problematic if you have small VPC or subnet IP (CIDR) ranges. There are several approaches to mitigate this issue.

Non-routable secondary addresses

The concept of *non-routable* is to use an existing range used on premises, or ideally one of the new non-RFC1918 ranges that is not routed on premises for AWS for Pod addresses, allowing a large range to be used. This is shown in *Figure 7.6*.

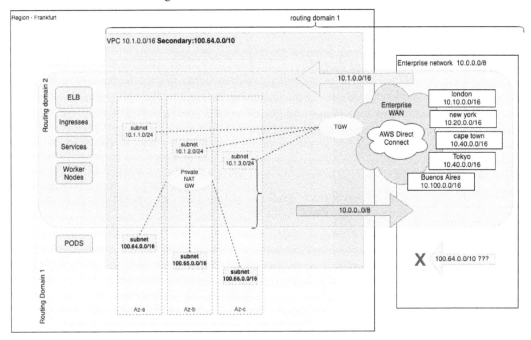

Figure 7.6 – Non-routable Pod networking

In *Figure 7.6*, two different IP zones or routing domains are shown. In **Routing Domain 1**, the VPC itself, all IP ranges are routable, so the primary range, 10.1.0.0/16, and the secondary range, 100.64.0.0/10, can both communicate with the enterprise network on 10.0.0.0/8.

In **Routing Domain 2**, the secondary ranges in the VPC subnets using the 100.64.0.0/10 range are private and not routable. They use a NATGW, which means that all outbound traffic undergoes NAT based on the source address as it leaves the 100.64.0.0 subnets, so these IP addresses are never seen outside the VPC.

Any Pods assigned an address from the 100.64.x.x range (**Routing Domain 2**) are not reachable from the enterprise network and the TGW doesn't advertise ten routes.

Prefix addressing

The default behavior with EC2 worker nodes involves allocating the number of addresses available to assign to Pods based on the number of IP addresses assigned to ENIs as well as the number of network interfaces attached to your Amazon EC2 node. For example, the **m5.large** node can have up to 3 ENIs, and each ENI can have up to 10 IP addresses, so with some limits, it can support 29 Pods based on the following calculation:

*3 ENIs * (10 IP addresses -1) + 2 (AWS CNI and kube-proxy Pods per node) = 29 Pods per node*

Version 1.9.0 or later of the Amazon VPC CNI supports *prefix assignment mode*, enabling you to run more Pods per node on **AWS Nitro-based EC2** instance types. This is done by assigning /28 IPv4 address prefixes to each of the host ENIs as long as you have enough space in your VPC CIDR range:

*3 ENIs * (9 prefixes per ENI * 16 IPs per prefix) + 2 = 434 Pods per node*

However, please note that the Kubernetes scalability guide recommends a maximum number of 110 Pods per node, and in most cases this will be the maximum enforced by the CNI. Prefix addressing can be used in conjunction with non-routable addresses as it will only work if the VPC CIDR is able to allocate contiguous /28 subnets from the VPC CIDR.

IPv6

Another option is to use IPv6 instead of IPv4. A full discussion of the differences between IPv6 and IPv4 is out of scope here, but in a VPC, if you enable IPv6, you automatically get a public /56 IPv6 CIDR block and each subnet is allocated a /64 range. This provides 2^{64} (approximately 18 quintillion) IPv6 addresses per subnet, so you will never exhaust the IP range. If the cluster is configured with IPv6, each Pod is assigned a native IPv6 address, which is used for Pod-to-Pod communication and an IPv6 IGW (egress only) is used for IPv6 internet access.

As most environments will support a mix of IPv6 and IPv4, EKS implements a **host-local CNI** plugin that is paired with the **VPC CNI**, which supports Pods with only an IPv6 address connecting to IPv4 endpoints outside the cluster (egress only). IPv6 definitively solves IP allocation issues but introduces more complexity as you need to manage IPv4 NAT and needs to be considered carefully. IPv6 is discussed in more detail in described in *Chapter 9, Advanced Networking with EKS*.

In this section, we've reviewed at a high level how native K8s networking works and how EKS/VPC networking is different. In the next section, we will review in detail how to configure and manage EKS networking.

Configuring EKS networking using the VPC CNI

As discussed previously, the AWS VPC CNI is installed by default, but you may need to upgrade the CNI to use prefix assignment mode, for example, or change a configuration parameter. The following sections will take you through configuration steps for common tasks.

Managing the CNI plugin

The simplest way to carry out an upgrade of the CNI for a new cluster is to apply the new Kubernetes manifest. The following code snippet will install version v1.9.1 onto your cluster and change the version as desired. Be aware, however, that downgrading the CNI version can be very tricky and, in some cases, will not work!

In a script or CI/CD pipeline, it's often a good idea to be able to export the version of the currently running CNI (as long as it is deployed). The following code snippet will allow you to do that:

```
$ export CNI_VER=$(kubectl describe daemonset aws-node
--namespace kube-system | grep Image | cut -d "/" -f 2 | sed -e
's/amazon-k8s-cni-init:\(.*\)-eksbuild.1/\1/')
$ echo $CNI_VER
v1.11.3 amazon-k8s-cni:v1.11.3-eksbuild.1
```

We can now deploy the CNI using the following command:

```
$ kubectl apply -f https://raw.githubusercontent.com/aws/
amazon-vpc-cni-k8s/v1.9.1/config/v1.9/aws-k8s-cni.yaml
```

To enable prefix assignment in the CNI configuration, you can use the following command (this will work for any of the CNI configuration parameters):

```
$ kubectl set env daemonset aws-n
ode                          -n kube-system ENABLE_PREFIX_
DELEGATION=true
```

The EKS cluster also supports the use of add-ons, which allow you to configure, deploy, and update the operational software, or provide key functionality to support your Kubernetes applications such as the VPC CNI. Add-ons are the preferred way to manage your cluster after the initial build and when you have running workloads. The easiest way to create an add-on is to use the eksctl tool, as follows:

```
$ eksctl create addon --name vpc-cni --version $CNI_VER
--cluster $CLUSTERNAME -force
```

This will create an add-on (visible in the AWS console). You can see the managed fields if you run the kubectl get command as follows:

```
$ kubectl get daemonset/aws-node --namespace kube-system
--show-managed-fields -o yaml
```

You should be able to see the fields managed by the EKS control plane in the YAML, that is, the output under the managedFields key, as follows:

```
. .
managedFields:
  - apiVersion: apps/v1
    fieldsType: FieldsV1
    fieldsV1:
```

A simpler way to look at the plugin is to use the eksctl command:

```
$ eksctl get addons --cluster $CLUSTERNAME --region $AWS_REGION
```

This will output something similar to the following code:

```
vpc-cni v1.9.1-
eksbuild.1        ACTIVE   0           arn:aws:iam::119991111:role/
eksctl-mycluster-addon-vpc-cni-Role1-4454          v1.10.2-
eksbuild.1,v1.10.1-eksbuild.1,v1.9.3-eksbuild.1
```

This tells us there are updates available: v1.10.2, v1.10.1, and v1.9.3. So, if we want to upgrade the CNI, we issue the following command:

```
$ eksctl update addon --name vpc-cni --version 1.9.3 --cluster
$CLUSTERNAME --region $AWS_REGION --force
```

Disabling CNI source NAT

When Pod network traffic is destined for an IPv4 address outside of the VPC, by default, **vpc-cni** translates the address of each Pod to the IP address of the EC2 node that the Pod is running on based on the Pod's source address (SNAT). This behavior is controlled by the AWS_VPC_K8S_CNI_EXTERNALSNAT variable, which is set to **false** by default.

If you want to use an external NAT device such as the AWS NATGW, you need to disable this behavior using the following command:

```
$ kubectl set env daemonset aws-node -n kube-system AWS_VPC_
K8S_CNI_EXTERNALSNAT=true
```

Configuring custom networking

When Pods are created, their ENI will use the security groups and subnet of the node's primary network interface. Custom networking allows the use of a different security group or subnet within the same VPC, and we've already described a use case (non-routable secondary addresses) that requires this configuration. To enable custom networking, you first need to have configured the required security groups and subnets in your VPC. Then you can run the following command:

```
$ kubectl set env daemonset aws-node -n kube-system AWS_VPC_
K8S_CNI_CUSTOM_NETWORK_CFG=true
```

You will need to create an ENIConfig file that defines the required subnets and security groups; an example is shown next. Note that the name is set to the AZ the subnet is in; this is a best practice and allows EKS to automatically assign the right subnet based on the node/AZ combination a Pod is deployed to:

```
apiVersion: crd.k8s.amazonaws.com/v1alpha1
kind: ENIConfig
metadata:
  name: eu-central-1a
spec:
  securityGroups:
    - sg-67346437643864389
  subnet: subnet-7847489798437
```

This configuration is applied using the kubectl apply -f eu-central-1a.yaml command (assuming you have given the file the same name as the resource in the metadata section of the file). You can then apply the following command to automatically map to the right **ENIConfig** based on the AZ (topology.kubernetes.io/zone) label:

```
$ kubectl set env daemonset aws-node -n kube-system ENI_CONFIG_
LABEL_DEF=topology.kubernetes.io/zone
```

Let's look at some common EKS networking issues and how to troubleshoot them.

Common networking issues

Networking is generally a complex issue, and although K8s defines a standard model, each CNI introduces different issues. We will look at how to solve some of the more common issues associated with the VPC CNI next.

Issue	Solution
My worker nodes cannot join the cluster.	Check that the worker nodes subnets have IP access to the internet (through an IGW or NATGW) as well as access to the EKS API ENIs. Check the route tables and associated security groups to make sure.
My Pods cannot be assigned an IP address from the VPC.	Check that the VPC has enough IP addresses free, if not assign a secondary CIDR range. Enable prefix addressing once you have IP addresses or make the EC2 instance size bigger (more ENIs).
Pods are unable to resolve K8S DNS names.	Ensure all worker node subnets do not have any security groups or network ACLS that block outbound or inbound UDP port 53 and ensure your VPC has enableDNSHostnames and enableDNSSupport set to true.
AWS load balancers cannot be deployed.	Ensure the worker node subnets are tagged with either kubernetes.io/role/elb or kubernetes.io/role/internal-elb.

In this section, we have looked at the detailed commands needed to configure and manage the VPC CNI. We'll now revisit the key learning points from this chapter.

Summary

In this chapter, we explored the basic concept of networking and the network model in native Kubernetes and how EKS differs. We described how EKS comes configured with the AWS VPC CNI, which integrates with the AWS VPC to assign ENIs and IP addresses to Pods from the VPC.

We also learned that Pods in EKS are native VPC citizens and traffic can use VPC network devices such as Internet Gateway, Transit Gateway, and NAT Gateway, and can be controlled using VPC network controls such as SGs and/or NACLs. However, this can come with some challenges such as VPC IP exhaustion. We discussed a few ways to handle IP exhaustion, including non-routable subnets, prefix addressing, and IPv6.

Finally, we talked about performing common tasks such as managing and upgrading the CNI, disabling CNI source NAT so you can use external NAT devices such as the AWS NATGW, and configuring custom networking so Pods can use other SGs or subnets to the main worker node to help with security or IP exhaustion.

In the next chapter, we will discuss EKS managed node groups, what they are, and how they are configured and managed.

Further reading

- AWS VPC CNI repository: `https://github.com/aws/amazon-vpc-cni-k8s`

- What is an EC2 ENI?: `https://docs.aws.amazon.com/AWSEC2/latest/UserGuide/using-eni.html`

- Overview of EKS and IPv6: `https://aws.amazon.com/blogs/containers/amazon-eks-launches-ipv6-support/`

- Supported CNIs on EKS: `https://docs.aws.amazon.com/eks/latest/userguide/alternate-cni-plugins.html`

- Private NAT Gateways: `https://aws.amazon.com/about-aws/whats-new/2021/06/aws-removes-nat-gateways-dependence-on-internet-gateway-for-private-communications/`

- Using Transit Gateway: `https://docs.aws.amazon.com/whitepapers/latest/building-scalable-secure-multi-vpc-network-infrastructure/transit-gateway.html`

- EC2 Max Pods Details by instance type: `https://github.com/awslabs/amazon-eks-ami/blob/master/files/eni-max-pods.txt`

- Kubernetes scaling limits: `https://github.com/kubernetes/community/blob/master/sig-scalability/configs-and-limits/thresholds.md`

- Overview of EKS add-ons: `https://aws.amazon.com/blogs/containers/introducing-amazon-eks-add-ons/`

8
Managing Worker Nodes on EKS

In previous chapters, we have focused on **Elastic Kubernetes Service** (**EKS**) architecture and APIs, deploying workloads with both kubectl and Helm. EKS can use both EC2 and Fargate to host these workloads. In this chapter, we will focus on how to configure, deploy, and manage the different **Elastic Compute Cloud** (**EC2**) configurations you will see in EKS. We will also discuss the benefits of using EKS-optimized images and managed node groups over self-managed images and instances. Fargate configuration will be discussed in more detail in *Chapter 15*.

But for now, we will cover the following topics:

- Launching a node with Amazon Linux
- Launching self-managed Amazon Linux nodes with CloudFormation
- Launching self-managed Bottlerocket nodes with eksctl
- Understanding managed nodes with eksctl
- Building a custom **Amazon Machine Image** (**AMI**) for EKS

Technical requirements

The reader should have a familiarity with YAML, basic networking, and EKS architecture. Before getting started with this chapter, please ensure the following:

- You have an EKS cluster and are able to perform administrative tasks
- You have network connectivity to your EKS API endpoint
- The **Amazon Web Services** (**AWS**) CLI and **kubectl** binary are installed on your workstation

Launching a node with Amazon Linux

In this section, we will discuss what is needed to launch a single EC2 instance and connect it to a cluster. We will then build on this as we discuss managed node groups.

Prerequisites for launching a node with Amazon Linux

A worker node is simply an EC2 instance that is used by EKS to actually host the Pods deployed on the cluster. Any EC2 instance will need the following:

- An **Identity and Access Management** (**IAM**) role that allows it to talk to the AWS API (EKS, EC2, and so on)

- A security group that, at a minimum, allows communication to the EKS control plane

- An operating system image that has the Kubernetes agents (kubelet, and so on) installed

- An init/boot script to register with a specific EKS cluster

IAM role and permissions

Each worker node and EC2 instance requires an IAM role to be attached to it that allows communication with the AWS EKS API, **Elastic Container Registry** (**ECR**), and the EC2 API. There are three AWS managed policies that need to be applied:

- `AmazonEKSWorkerNodePolicy`

- `AmazonEKS_CNI_Policy`

- `AmazonEC2ContainerRegistryReadOnly`

In addition, if you want to SSH into your worker nodes using Systems Manager, you should also add the following policy:

- `AmazonSSMManagedInstanceCore`

> **Important note**
> The worker node role must be added to the `aws-auth` ConfigMap to allow the instances to register with the cluster. If you are creating self-managed nodes, you will need to modify the ConfigMap yourself; tools such as eksctl or the AWS Console will make these changes for you.

Security groups

Every EC2 **elastic network interface** (**ENI**) needs to be associated with at least one security group. Worker nodes are normally given their own security group, which ensures network access to those nodes can be controlled.

Typically the EC2 worker node, a security group is referenced in the main EKS cluster security group that controls access to the control plane ENIs and allows the **kubelet** agent to register the node with the API servers, send updates, and receive instructions— for example, `create Pod`.

AWS AMIs

An EC2 AMI is the base image any EC2 instance uses and contains the operating system (Windows- or Linux-based) and, typically, a set of utilities to enable the EC2 instance to work in AWS. EKS supports multiple AMIs, but in this section, we will discuss two: **Amazon Linux** and **Bottlerocket**.

Amazon EKS-optimized Amazon Linux AMIs

The Amazon EKS-optimized Amazon Linux AMI is built on top of Amazon Linux 2 and is configured to work with Amazon EKS including Docker (this is replaced with containerd in later versions of the AMI), kubelet, and the AWS IAM authenticator.

You need to align the AMI with the version of Kubernetes; the following URL can be used to find the right image ID: `https://docs.aws.amazon.com/eks/latest/userguide/eks-optimized-ami.html`. For example, for x86, Kubernetes 1.21 in the `eu-central-1` region, the AMI ID is `ami-03fa8a7508f8f3ccc`.

Amazon EKS-optimized Bottlerocket AMIs

Bottlerocket is an open source Linux-based operating system that is purpose-built by AWS for running containers. As with a container, it only includes the bare-minimum packages required to run containers, reducing the attack surface of the node itself. EKS-optimized Bottlerocket is configured to work with Amazon EKS, and it includes containerd and **kubelet** as part of the image. As with Amazon Linux, you need to align the AMI with the version of Kubernetes; the following URL can be used to find the right image ID: `https://docs.aws.amazon.com/eks/latest/userguide/eks-optimized-ami-bottlerocket.html`. For example, for x86, Kubernetes 1.21 in the `eu-central-1` region, the AMI ID is `ami-0674d57b3d6b6ef14`.

Bootstrap scripts

A bootstrap script is needed to configure the various agents and EC2 metadata and needs to be run once. The bootstrap script is published by AWS and can be found at the following link: `https://github.com/awslabs/amazon-eks-ami/blob/master/files/bootstrap.sh`. It needs to be integrated into the EC2 boot process or run manually.

Putting it all together and creating a standalone worker node

It's possible to just create a single EC2 worker node, but in practice, you will always want to use EC2 Auto Scaling to recover from failure and scale your worker nodes. The following steps are used only to illustrate the activities you need to go through to get a worker node up and running and should only be used as an example:

1. Assuming we have a running cluster with some worker nodes already (if not, see *Chapter 3*), note down the security group, IAM role, VPC, and subnet used by the existing node group/EC2 instances.

2. Run the following command, replacing the attributes with the values you collected in *step 1*, to create the EC2 worker node. Please note that the `image-id` value is region- and Kubernetes version-specific, so you may need to modify it as well:

```
$ aws ec2 run-instances --image-id ami-03fa8a7508f8f3ccc
--count 1 --instance-type t3.large --key-name <my-key> \
--security-group-ids <worker-node-sg-id> \
--subnet-id <subnet-id> --iam-instance-profile
Name=<instance-profile-name> \
--tag-specifications \
 'ResourceType=instance,Tags=[{Key=Name,Value=standalone-
worker}]'
```

3. Once the instance has booted and is available, you can SSH to it using AWS Session Manager or using the SSH key you specified in *step 2*. You should then verify whether you have permission to get the cluster description using the following commands:

```
$ export AWS_DEFAULT_REGION=<myregion>
$ aws eks describe-cluster --name <clustername>
```

> **Important note**
>
> It may be easier to run the `aws configure` command and specify the default region (only) so that changes are preserved across different shells or logins.

4. As root, you can now download and run the bootstrap script to configure the worker node using the following commands:

```
$ curl -o bootstrap.sh https://raw.githubusercontent.com/
awslabs/amazon-eks-ami/master/files/bootstrap.sh
$ chmod +x bootstrap.sh
$ ./bootstrap.sh <clustername>
```

5. Exit the SSH session, go back onto the Kubernetes admin machine, and run the `kubectl get nodes --watch` command. What you should see are the original worker nodes and *NOT* the new worker node you just created.

6. On the Kubernetes admin machine, verify that the role assigned to the newly created worker node is configured in the `aws-auth` ConfigMap using the following command:

```
$ kubectl get cm aws-auth -n kube-system -o json
```

7. In order to allow a specific EKS cluster to claim a worker node and monitor things such as auto scaling events, you need to add a `kubernetes.io/cluster/<clustername>` instance tag to the EC2 instance. In the AWS Console, navigate to your instance by going to **EC2 | Instances | myinstance** and then click on the **Instance ID** value and select **Tags**. You can then add the `kubernetes.io/cluster/...` tag with a value of owned to the instance, click **Save**, and then return to the Kubernetes admin machine where the `--watch` command should now show the new worker node registering and becoming ready.

Please refer to `https://docs.aws.amazon.com/eks/latest/userguide/worker.html` for more details on self managed worker nodes and how to configure them. You will normally use an auto scaling group to support your worker nodes, so the next example will use a pre-created CloudFormation template to configure this using the Amazon Linux AMI we used in this example.

Launching self-managed Amazon Linux nodes with CloudFormation

AWS provides a CloudFormation script hosted at `https://s3.us-west-2.amazonaws.com/amazon-eks/cloudformation/2020-10-29/amazon-eks-nodegroup.yaml` that can also be used to create a self-managed node group. Let's take a look at how that works!

1. From the AWS Console, select the **CloudFormation** service and click on the **Create stack** button, as shown in the following screenshot:

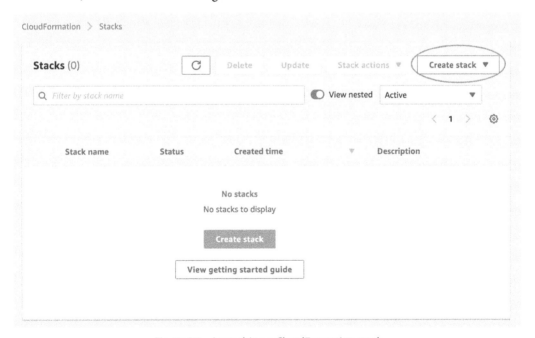

Figure 8.1 – Launching a CloudFormation stack

2. In the **Create stack** window, paste the URL, shown previously, for the `nodegroup.yaml` file in the **Amazon S3 URL** box and click **Next**:

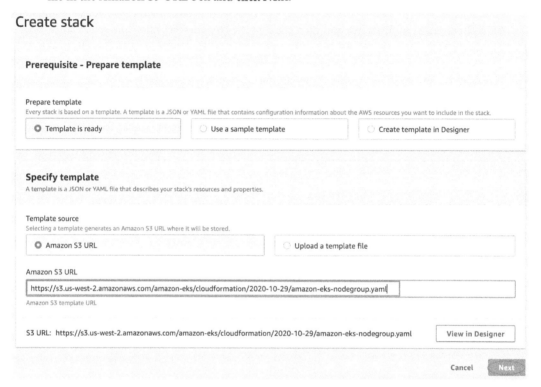

Figure 8.2 – The Create stack window

3. You will now be asked to configure the stack properties; most of these are the same as in the previous example. A subset of the parameters typically used is shown next:

Parameter name	Description
ClusterName	The name of the existing cluster. If it is incorrect, nodes will not be able to join the cluster.
ClusterControlPlaneSecurityGroup	The security group used by the cluster control plane.
NodeGroupName	A unique name for the node group.
NodeAutoScalingGroupMinSize	The minimum number of nodes in the auto scaling group.
Desired capacity of Node Group ASG.	The desired number of nodes in the auto scaling group.
NodeAutoScalingGroupMaxSize	The maximum number of nodes in the auto scaling group. Set to at least 1 greater than desired capacity.
NodeInstanceType	The EC2 instance type for the worker nodes.
NodeVolumeSize	The worker node **Elastic Block Store** (**EBS**) volume size.
KeyName	The EC2 key pair to allow SSH access to the instances.
DisableIMDSv1	Set to true or false.
VpcId	The VPC of the worker instances.
Subnets	The subnets where workers can be created.

Table 8.1 – CloudFormation parameter list

As this template uses an auto scaling group, you need to specify the minimum, maximum, and desired capacity of the auto scaling group (refer to https://docs.aws.amazon.com/autoscaling/ec2/userguide/asg-capacity-limits.html for more details). Please also note that the security group is the one defined for the cluster API, as the template creates a new security group for the instances in the auto scaling group.

4. Enter the parameters (use the ones from the previous example) and click through the stack workflow until the stack starts to be deployed. Once the stack has been deployed, you can use the kubectl get nodes command to verify whether the node/s have been registered. Again, the node/s should *NOT* be visible, but this time it's a different problem.

5. This template creates a new IAM role that needs to be added to the `aws-auth` file. You can use the `kubectl edit cm aws-auth -n kube-system` command from the Kubernetes admin workstation to edit the ConfigMap and add the following entry to the `mapRoles` key, where `<rolearn>` is the role assigned to the EC2 instances:

```
mapRoles: |
- groups:
  - system:bootstrappers
  - system:nodes
  rolearn: arn:aws:iam::<ACCOUNTID>:role/<instanceROLE>
  username: system:node:{{EC2PrivateDNSName}}
```

6. Once you have added the role and deployed the ConfigMap, you can use the following command to see the node register and become ready for the scheduler:

```
$ kubectl get nodes --watch
```

Amazon Linux is based on a standard Linux kernel, while Bottlerocket has been built from the ground up to support containers. In the next section, we will look at how you can deploy self-managed nodes based on the Bottlerocket operating system, which provides better support for containers.

Launching self-managed Bottlerocket nodes with eksctl

Bottlerocket is gaining momentum as a secure platform for running container workloads. One of the key benefits is that it runs two operating system partitions, which means that it is simpler to upgrade with minimal downtime. This is discussed in more detail in *Chapter 10, Upgrading EKS Clusters*.

So far, we have created a managed node using the AWS CLI, the console, and a pre-made CloudFormation template. **eksctl** is a tool jointly developed by *Weaveworks* and AWS and will generate and deploy CloudFormation stacks based on a configuration file or CLI options. You can install it using the following URL: `https://docs.aws.amazon.com/eks/latest/userguide/eksctl.html`.

Prior to version 0.40.0 of eksctl, you could only modify clusters that had been created using eksctl. However, later versions allow a subset of operations on clusters not created by eksctl—this includes adding node groups.

We are going to use an existing cluster (see *Chapter 3, Building Your First EKS Cluster*) and add two self-managed Bottlerocket nodes. The following configuration file is used; please note it is split into multiple sections to make it more readable:

```
---
apiVersion: eksctl.io/v1alpha5
kind: ClusterConfig
```

```
metadata:
  name: myclusterName
  region: eu-central-1
  version: '1.21'

vpc:
  id: "vpc-123454"
  subnets:
    private:
      private1:
        id:   "subnet-11222"
      private2:
        id:   "subnet-11333"
  securityGroup: "sg-4444444"
```

In the preceding section, we define the cluster `name`, `region`, and `version` values, along with the VPC details as we will reuse an existing VPC. In the following section, we define a node group. Make sure the `privateNetworking` key is set to `true` if you are using a set of private subnets (without an **internet gateway (IGW)**); otherwise, the deployment will fail!

```
iam:
   withOIDC: true
nodeGroups:
   - name: ng-bottlerocket
     instanceType: m5.large
     privateNetworking: true
     desiredCapacity: 2
     amiFamily: Bottlerocket
     ami: auto-ssm
     iam:
        attachPolicyARNs:
           - arn:aws:iam::aws:policy/AmazonEKSWorkerNodePolicy
           - arn:aws:iam::aws:policy/
AmazonEC2ContainerRegistryReadOnly
           - arn:aws:iam::aws:policy/
AmazonSSMManagedInstanceCore
           - arn:aws:iam::aws:policy/AmazonEKS_CNI_Policy
```

```
ssh:
    allow: true
    publicKeyName: mykeypair
subnets:
  - subnet-11222
  - subnet-11333
```

> **Important note**
>
> As this is using an existing cluster, the `vpc:` section must be included. The `securityGroup` key refers to the cluster security group, not the worker node one. As this is also a private cluster, the `privateNetworking: true` key-value pair needs to be included. The `nodegroups` keyword is used for self-managed nodes. Please adjust the configuration file (keys in `code style`) and save it as `bottlerocket.yaml`.

Once eksctl has been installed and the configuration file saved, you can run the following command to create a cluster using the configuration file:

```
$ eksctl create nodegroup --config-file=bottlerocket.yaml
```

Then, use the following command to see the nodes be registered and become ready for the scheduler:

```
$ kubectl get nodes --watch
```

Please note that eksctl will tag nodes and modify the `aws-auth` ConfigMap, so as long as the `eksctl` command is successful, the nodes will automatically register and become available.

Self-managed node groups are useful if you have a lot of custom operating system configurations or you need a specific AMI. If you need to do any node updates, you will be responsible for draining nodes, moving Pods, adjusting scheduler logic, and replacing nodes. Managed node groups allow you to do this at the click of a button (or with an API call) and so generally should be preferred over self-managed nodes. In the next section, we will see how you can use managed node groups instead.

Understanding managed nodes with eksctl

A managed node group leverages auto scaling groups to provide the basic functionality used to do upgrades and modifications to worker nodes. Each auto scaling group specifies a launch template, which specifies the configuration options.

If you replace the launch configuration—changing the EKS AMI ID, for example—any new instances that are created use the new launch template and, therefore, the new AMI. You can then terminate old instances, and the auto scaling group will automatically replace them using the new launch template. This process is automated for managed node groups, and the EKS control plane performs the following steps for a managed node group:

1. It randomly selects a node and drains the Pods from the node.

2. It ordons the node after every Pod is evicted so that the Kubernetes scheduler doesn't send any new requests to this node and removes this node from its list of active nodes.

3. It sends a termination request to the Auto Scaling group for the cordoned node. This in turn will trigger a new node deployment with the new launch template/AMI.

4. It repeats *steps 1-3* until there are no nodes in the node group that are deployed with the earlier version of the launch template.

Let's deploy a new managed node group using the following command:

```
$ eksctl create nodegroup --config-file=managed-ng.yaml
```

Then, use the following command to see the nodes be registered and become ready for the scheduler:

```
$ kubectl get nodes --watch
```

The following configuration file should be used; again, this is split into multiple sections for readability:

> **Important note**
>
> You can use the previous template, but make sure you change the nodeGroups: key to managedNodeGroups:. You also need to remove the Bottlerocket-specific amiFamily: and ami: keys and (optionally) add the labels: key.

```
---
apiVersion: eksctl.io/v1alpha5
kind: ClusterConfig

metadata:
  name: myclusterName
  region: eu-central-1
  version: '1.21'
vpc:
  id: "vpc-123454"
  subnets:
```

```
        private:
            private1:
                id:  "subnet-11222"
            private2:
                id:  "subnet-11333"
      securityGroup: "sg-4444444"


  iam:
    withOIDC: true
```

The preceding section is no different from the unmanaged node group; we define the cluster and VPC information (using an existing VPC). In the following section, we replace the nodeGroups key with the managedNodeGroups key and also add a label:

```
managedNodeGroups:
  - name: managed-ng
    labels: { role: workers }
    instanceType: m5.large
    privateNetworking: true
    desiredCapacity: 2
    iam:
        attachPolicyARNs:
            - arn:aws:iam::aws:policy/AmazonEKSWorkerNodePolicy
            - arn:aws:iam::aws:policy/
AmazonEC2ContainerRegistryReadOnly
            - arn:aws:iam::aws:policy/
AmazonSSMManagedInstanceCore
            - arn:aws:iam::aws:policy/AmazonEKS_CNI_Policy
    ssh:
        allow: true
        publicKeyName: mykeypair
    subnets:
      - subnet-11222
      - subnet-11333
```

Once the nodes have been registered, if you go into the AWS Console and select **EKS | Clusters | mycluster** and the **Compute** tab, you will see the managed node group registered and showing an **Active** status. In the following screenshot, you can see the new node group along with the old node group, which is at an older AMI version:

Figure 8.3 – Node groups window

This can now be automatically upgraded (with kubelet, containerd, and so on) by clicking the **Update now** link. This process is discussed in more detail in *Chapter 10, Upgrading EKS Clusters*.

So far, we have used standard AMIs without any customization. In the final section of this chapter, we will look at how you can build a custom AMI for use with EKS, which might be needed if you want to harden the operating system or make some kernel changes.

Building a custom AMI for EKS

There are a number of reasons why you may want to use a custom AMI—for example, security hardening, updates to Kubernetes agent binaries, and so on. There are also many ways you can do this, but we are going to look at using Packer from HashiCorp (`https://learn.hashicorp.com/packer`), which is an open source tool that can be used to create a number of different types of operating system images. Here are the steps:

1. In the first step, we need to install Packer on our workstation using the following link: `https://learn.hashicorp.com/collections/packer/aws-get-started`. This will then allow us to create a custom AMI.

2. You can then clone the following Git repository and change into the new `amazon-eks-ami` directory: `https://github.com/awslabs/amazon-eks-ami`. This is the same process used to create official AMIs.

3. From the root of the cloned repository, you can now run the `make` command shown next to create a basic `1.21` AMI (ensure the region you are using has a default VPC configured):

    ```
    $ make 1.21 aws_region=<yourRegion>
    ```

4. It will take 15-20 minutes to spin up a new EC2 instance. Connect to from the Packer machine using SSH and then configure the instance using the scripts in the `/scripts` directory. Once configured, the EBS volume is converted into an AMI and the instance is terminated.

5. You can validate that the image exists using the following command:

    ```
    $ aws ec2 describe-images --owners self --output json
    --region <yourRegion>
    ```

In order to customize the build, you can make changes to the makefile, the Packer build file (`eks-worker-al2.json`), and/or add/modify the scripts in the `/scripts` directory. This requires detailed knowledge of Packer and Linux and so is out of the scope of this book, but there is a useful post on the following link that describes some of this customization in more detail (you will need an AWS login to access this): `https://aws.amazon.com/premiumsupport/knowledge-center/eks-custom-linux-ami/`.

Now that we have looked at the variety of ways you can configure and deploy EC2 worker nodes, we'll revisit the key learning points from this chapter.

Summary

In this chapter, we explored the basic requirements for any EC2-based worker node, including the need to configure an IAM role, the Kubernetes agents (kubelet, and so on), and security groups to allow communication with the EKS control plane endpoint.

We then learned how you can use Amazon Linux and Bottlerocket (a secure container operating system developed by AWS) AMIs to create self-managed node groups using the AWS Console/CLI, CloudFormation, and eksctl. It's important to understand there are several options when it comes to choosing operating systems, from Amazon EKS-optimized Linux and Bottlerocket through to the completely customized operating systems you define. Amazon Linux is the easiest operating system choice as images are created and managed by AWS, and it will also allow access to the standard Linux kernel if you want to make changes. Bottlerocket is more secure but is quite a different architecture from standard Linux kernels, so requires a lot more investment in training and design. If you have some very specific hardening requirements or particular management tools you use, then you will need to use custom AMIs. We then talked about how managed node groups simplify the operation burden of updating worker node operating systems and Kubernetes agents and showed how, with some simple changes, we can use eksctl to deploy them.

Finally, we briefly explored how you can use HashiCorp's Packer and an AWS repository to create custom AMIs that could support a more customized EC2-based worker node.

In the next chapter, we will look at the overall process of upgrading your cluster and build on some of the concepts discussed in the previous chapters.

Further reading

- Deeper dive into Amazon Linux EKS-optimized AMIs: `https://docs.aws.amazon.com/eks/latest/userguide/eks-optimized-ami.html`

- Deeper dive into Bottlerocket EKS-optimized AMIs: `https://docs.aws.amazon.com/eks/latest/userguide/eks-optimized-ami-bottlerocket.html`

- eksctl user guide: `https://eksctl.io/`

- Deeper dive into EC2 auto scaling: `https://docs.aws.amazon.com/autoscaling/ec2/userguide/what-is-amazon-ec2-auto-scaling.html`

9

Advanced Networking with EKS

In previous chapters, we reviewed standard AWS and EKS networking (*Chapter 7*). However, there are certain situations where you will need to use some of the more advanced networking features we will describe in this chapter.

This chapter looks at use cases such as how you can manage Pod address exhaustion with **Internet Protocol version 6 (IPv6)** and how you can enforce Layer 3 network controls for Pod traffic using network policies. We also look at how you can use different **complex network-based information systems (CNIs)** in EKS to support multiple Pod network interfaces using the Multus CNI and how you can support overlay networks for encryption and network acceleration, such as the **Data Plane Development Kit (DPDK)** or **Extended BerkeleyPacket Filter (eBPF)**. These are complex topics, and the aim of this chapter is to provide the base knowledge for a cluster administrator to be able to assess whether these solutions need to be configured and the impact they will have on the EKS deployment.

Specifically, we will cover the following topics in this chapter:

- Using IPv6 in your EKS cluster
- Installing and using Calico network policies
- Choosing and using different CNIs in EKS

Technical requirements

You should be familiar with YAML, basic networking, and EKS architecture. Before getting started with this chapter, please ensure that you have the following in place:

- Network connectivity to your EKS API endpoint
- The AWS CLI and the kubectl binary are installed on your workstation
- A basic understanding of IPv6 addressing and usage
- A good understanding of **virtual private cloud (VPC)** networking and how to create network objects such as **elastic network interfaces (ENIs)**, and so on

Using IPv6 in your EKS cluster

IPv6 has some distinct advantages over IPv4, namely, it provides a much larger address space (this includes public IP addresses), reduces some latency by removing **Network Address Translation (NAT)** hops, and can simplify the overall routing network configuration. It does have some limitations (not only for EKS but other AWS services as well) so care must be taken when adopting IPv6. Please review https://aws.amazon.com/vpc/ipv6/ and https://docs.aws.amazon.com/eks/latest/userguide/cni-ipv6.html before implementing it in production.

IPv6 cannot currently be enabled on an existing cluster, so the first thing we need to do is create a new cluster with the IPv6 address family, which is at least running Kubernetes 1.21. We will use eksctl with the following configuration file, myipv6cluster.yaml:

```
---
apiVersion: eksctl.io/v1alpha5
kind: ClusterConfig

metadata:
  name: myipv6cluster
  region: "eu-central-1"
  version: "1.21"
kubernetesNetworkConfig:
  ipFamily: IPv6
addons:
  - name: vpc-cni
    version: latest
  - name: coredns
    version: latest
  - name: kube-proxy
    version: latest
iam:
  withOIDC: true
managedNodeGroups:
  - name: ipv6mng
    instanceType: t3.medium
```

We can then run the following eksctl command to create and deploy the cluster:

```
$ eksctl create cluster -f myipv6cluster.yaml
```

> **Important note**
> This process may take 15–25 minutes to complete.

As we haven't specified an existing VPC, `eksctl` will create one for us and assign it an additional IPv6 **Classless Inter-Domain Routing** (**CIDR**) range from the Amazon pool (every VPC needs an IPv4 CIDR range), illustrated next:

Figure 9.1 – eksctl VPC

If we look at the subnets assigned to this VPC, we can see `eksctl` has created six subnets, three public, and three private (two per **Availability Zone** (**AZ**)) subnets. It has also allocated an IPv4 (required) CIDR range and an IPv6 CIDR range from the main ranges allocated to the VPC:

Figure 9.2 – eksctl IPv4/v6 subnets

The cluster will be created with the two worker nodes (on the public subnets by default). Each worker node has both an IPv4 and IPv6 IP address, as IPv4 is required by the VPC:

```
$ kubectl get nodes -o wide
```

This will output something similar to the following:

```
NAME    STATUS    ROLES    AGE    VERSION    INTERNAL-IP EXTERNAL-IP
ip-192-168-3-11.eu-central-1.compute.
internal Ready <none>    27h    v1.21.12-eks-
5308cf7    2a05:d014:ec6:2f00:4e36:b47b:c13f:cb1f    52.58.98.70
ip-192-168-90-100.eu-central-1.compute.
internal    Ready    <none>    27h    v1.21.12-eks-
5308cf7    2a05:d014:ec6:2f02:2d4c:d5df:4eb5:cb86    18.195.1.196
```

IPv6 prefix assignment occurs on each worker node at startup. A single `IPv6 /80` prefix is assigned (the `/80 => ~10^14` addresses) per worker node ENI and is big enough to support large clusters with millions of Pods although the current Kubernetes recommendation is no more than 110 Pods per host.

You can see the prefix assignment by looking at the EC2 instance and clicking on the network tab. In the following example, a `2a05:d014:ec6:2f00:8207::/80` prefix has been assigned, and no IPv4 prefix is assigned:

Figure 9.3 – IPv6 prefix assignment

Once you have enabled IPv6 at the cluster level, you can't assign IPv4 addresses to your Pods; only IPv6 addresses can be assigned as EKS doesn't currently support Pods with both an IPv4 and IPv6 address (as they do with worker nodes). However, if we use the `kubectl get pods` command to list the system Pods in the `kube-system` namespace, we can see that the Pods are assigned IPv6 addresses:

```
$ kubectl get pods -n kube-system -o wide
NAME         READY    STATUS     RESTARTS    AGE    IP        ...
aws-node-qvqpx   1/1      Running    0    15h    2a05:d014:ec6:2f00:
4e36:b47b:c13f:cc1f
aws-node-wkr9g   1/1      Running    1    15h    2a05:d014:ec6:2f02:
2d4c:d5df:4eb5:c686
coredns-745979c988-7qqmr 1/1 Running   0    15h    2a05:d014:ec6:
2f00:8207::
coredns-745979c988-hzxx8 1/1 Running   0    15h    2a05:d014:ec6:
2f00:8207::1
kube-proxy-2rh47         1/1 Running   0    15h    2a05:d014:ec6:
2f02:2d4c:d5df:4eb5:c686
kube-proxy-vwzp9         1/1
Running   0    15h    2a05:d014:ec6:2f00:
4e36:b47b:c13f:cc1f
```

We can deploy a simple web app using the deployment .yaml files from *Chapter 4, Running Your First Application on EKS*. If we look at the resulting Pods, we can see they also have an IPv6 address. An example output is shown next:

```
NAME        READY    STATUS      RESTARTS    AGE
simple-web-99b67d675-4t68q    1/1    Running    0    11s
2a05:d014:ec6:2f00:8207::2
simple-web-99b67d675-vl6hk    1/1    Running    0    11s
2a05:d014:ec6:2f02:b49c::
```

We've looked at how to create a cluster with an IPv6 IP address family and how to deploy Pods. However, there are some basic differences in how the Pods can communicate in and outside the VPC with IPv6. The next sections describe these networking scenarios in more detail, focusing on how traffic is routed.

> **Important note**
> Security group configuration is needed to *allow* traffic as a minimum. Therefore, we will only discuss the VPC routing table configuration in the next section.

Pod to external IPv6 address

An IPv6 address is so large they are globally unique, so no NAT is performed. Any Pods running on worker nodes in public subnets, which are assigned an IP address from a prefix in the subnet, will be able to route directly to the internet through an **internet gateway** (**IGW**) without any address translation. This also means that they are accessible from the internet (access is controlled through security groups). If the subnet is private, an **egress-only IGW** (**EIGW**) can be used to provide access to external IPv6 addresses but not allow any direct inbound IPv6 traffic (unlike the regular IGW).

VPC routing

As any IPv6 Pod always uses its IPv6 address as its source IP address, standard Kubernetes service discovery and routing mechanisms and VPC routing tables can be used to reach another Pod. Any intra-VPC IPv6 traffic is not source NATed (unlike IPv4 by default), so the destination Pod always sees the source Pod's *real VPC* IPv6 address.

As a Pod only has an IPv6 stack, it can only communicate with other elements running an IPv6 stack that have entries in the VPC routing tables. This includes the following:

- Other Pods with IPv6 addresses
- An EC2 host with an IPv6 address (single or dual stack)
- ASW services that support IPv6 endpoints (refer to https://docs.aws.amazon.com/general/latest/gr/aws-ipv6-support.html)

To communicate with IPv4 endpoints, a translation service is required; this can be achieved in a number of ways:

- Using a host-local CNI plugin
- Using NAT64 (AWS NAT Gateway)
- Using DNS64 (AWS Route 53)

We will review these options in detail next.

Using host-local CNI plugin

The approach, still used today, is to extend the VPC CNI to support an internal IPV4 address range, `169.254.172.0/22`, allocated to every worker node and used to create a secondary IPv4 interface in each Pod. This configuration is included in the IPv6 cluster we created and can be viewed by SSHing into a worker node and running the `cat /etc/cni/net.d/10-aws.conflist` command as *root*.

As this IPv4 `169.254.172.0/22` range is not visible in the VPC and is reused by each worker node, all IPv4 egress traffic is **source NAT**ed (**SNAT**) to the IPv4 ENI allocated to the worker node; otherwise, there will be IP address conflicts. The following diagram illustrates this solution:

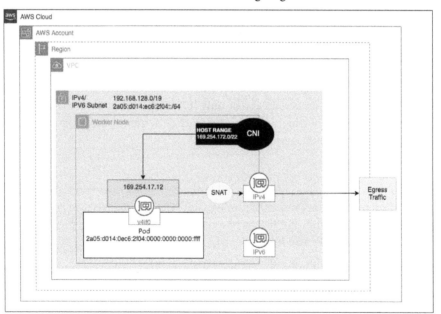

Figure 9.4 – host-local solution

To see how this works, let's create a new container and shell into it using the following command:

```
$ kubectl run -i --tty busybox --image=busybox --restart=Never
-- sh
```

Once in the container shell, you can see the secondary interface and route tables in the container with the `iptables` and `netstat` commands. This will output something similar to the block shown here:

```
$ ifconfig
eth0
Link encap:Ethernet  HWaddr AA:1D:5F:F0:B6:C7
inet6 addr: 2a05:d014:ec6:2f02:b49c::2/128 Scope:Global

......

v4if0
Link encap:Ethernet  HWaddr 5A:FE:0E:46:EC:D9
inet
addr:169.254.172.4  Bcast:169.254.175.255  Mask:255.255.252.0
$ netstat -rn
Kernel IP routing table
Destination      Gateway          Genmask          ... Iface
0.0.0.0          169.254.172.1    0.0.0.0          ... v4if0
169.254.172.0    169.254.172.1    255.255.252.0    ... v4if0
169.254.172.1    0.0.0.0          255.255.255.255 ... v4if0
```

This means when a Pod tries to communicate with an IPv4 address, it will use the `v4if0` interface, which will SNATed to the Host IPv4 ENI. We will now look at some enhancements that AWS has announced in 2021 that can simplify this configuration and remove the need for the host SNAT.

Using DNS64 with AWS Route 53

Each VPC has its own DNS resolver built into the subnet (normally residing at the second IP address of the subnet CIDR). Normally this resolves on IPv4 DNS requests, but you can now add DNS64 to the subnet, and it applies to all the AWS resources within that subnet.

With DNS64, the AWS Route 53 Resolver looks up the DNS entry based on the client request and, based on the response, does one of the two following things:

- If the DNS response contains an IPv6 address, the resolver responds to the client with the IPV6 address, and then the client establishes an IPv6 networking session directly using the IPv6 address.

- If there is no IPv6 address in the response, only an IPv4 address, then the Resolver responds to the client by adding the well-known /96 prefix, defined in RFC6052 (64:ff9b::/96), to the IPv4 address in the record to enable it to work with NAT64 (described next).

This diagram illustrates this:

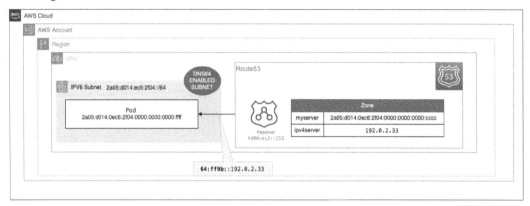

Figure 9.5 – DNS64 on your VPC

Let's look at how the well-known 64:ff9b::/96 prefix is used to communicate with the IPv4 endpoint.

Using NAT64 with a NATGW

In *Chapter 7, Networking in EKS*, we discussed how a **NAT Gateway** (**NATGW**) could be used to allow outbound network access from private subnets. It does this by mapping private addresses (IPv4) to a public IP address assigned to the NATGW.

NAT64 is automatically available on any existing or new NATGW. Once you have enabled DNS64 for the subnet and added a route for the 64:ff9b::/96 prefix to the NATGW, the following steps happen:

1. As described previously, if there is no matching IPv6 record, the VPC DNS resolver will respond with the IPv4 address and the RFC6052 prefix, which is used by the client to establish an IPv6 session. The VPC routing table will send the traffic to the NAT64 gateway, which translates the IPv6 packets to IPv4 by replacing the IPv6 (Pod) address with the NATGW IPV4 address.

2. The NAT64 gateway forwards the IPv4 packets to the destination using the route table associated with its subnet.

3. The IPv4 destination sends back IPv4 response packets to the NATGW. The response IPv4 packets are translated back to IPv6 by the NATGW by replacing its IP (destination IPv4) with the Pod's IPv6 address and prepending 64:ff9b::/96 to the source IPv4 address. The packet then flows to the Pod following the local route statement in the route table:

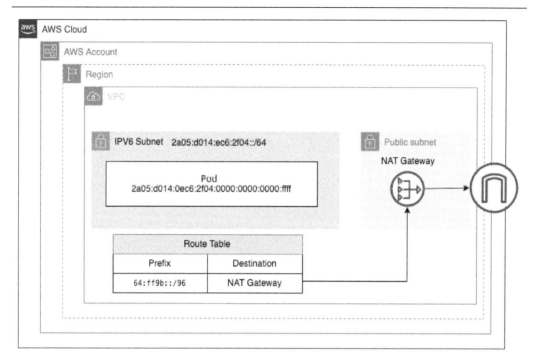

Figure 9.6 – NAT64 on your VPC

> **Important note**
>
> Don't forget to delete your IPv6 cluster using the `eksctl delete cluster myipv6cluster`
> command unless you want to use it for the next sections.

Now let's look at how we can control traffic inside the cluster using network policies.

Installing and using Calico network policies

By default, all Pods in all namespaces in a cluster can communicate with each other. This might be desirable, but, in many cases, you want to take a *least privilege* approach to network access. Fortunately, Kubernetes provides network policies to restrict access between Pods (west-to-east communication). A network policy operates at Layer 3 and Layer 4 of the OSI model and, as such, is equivalent to a traditional on-premises firewall or AWS security group. More details can be found at `https://kubernetes.io/docs/concepts/services-networking/network-policies/`.

The EKS VPC CNI doesn't support network policies, so a network plugin or different CNI is required. In this section, we use the **Calico** (https://www.projectcalico.org/) policy engine, which is the simplest way to add network policies while still using the AWS VPC CNI. We will create a new IPv4 cluster using eksctl with the following configuration file, myipv4cluster.yaml:

```
---
apiVersion: eksctl.io/v1alpha5
kind: ClusterConfig
metadata:
  name: myipv4cluster
  region: "eu-central-1"
  version: "1.19"
kubernetesNetworkConfig:
  ipFamily: IPv4
addons:
  - name: vpc-cni
    version: latest
  - name: coredns
    version: latest
  - name: kube-proxy
    version: latest
iam:
  withOIDC: true
managedNodeGroups:
  - name: ipv4mng
    instanceType: t3.medium
```

> **Important note**
> We noticed some challenges with getting this solution working with IPv6 clusters and the newer Tigera Operator, so care should be taken when using either.

We can then run the following eksctl command to create and deploy the cluster:

```
$ eksctl create cluster -f myipv4cluster.yaml
```

Once the cluster is active, add the cluster to your local admin machine if needed:

```
$ aws eks update-kubeconfig --name myipv4cluster
```

Then add `calico-operator` to the cluster using the following command:

```
$ kubectl apply -f https://raw.githubusercontent.com/aws/
amazon-vpc-cni-k8s/master/config/master/calico-operator.yaml
```

We can then configure the Calico plugin using `kubectl` to deploy the `calico-install.yaml` configuration file:

```
apiVersion: operator.tigera.io/v1
kind: Installation
metadata:
  name: default
  annotations:
    "helm.sh/hook": post-install
spec:
  cni:
    type: AmazonVPC
```

We can verify that the plugin is installed using the following command:

```
$ kubectl get tigerastatus/calico
NAME       AVAILABLE   PROGRESSING   DEGRADED   SINCE
calico     True        False         False      11m
```

We have all the prerequisites to support network policies, let's now deploy two simple deployments using the `simple-deployments.yaml` manifest. This section of the file will create the two namespaces:

```
---
apiVersion: v1
kind: Namespace
metadata:
  name: deploy1
---
apiVersion: v1
kind: Namespace
metadata:
  name: deploy2
```

The following code section will create the deployment, deploy1, in the deploy1 namespace:

```
---
apiVersion: apps/v1
kind: Deployment
metadata:
  name: deploy1
  namespace: deploy1
spec:
  replicas: 1
  selector:
    matchLabels:
      app: deploy1
  template:
    metadata:
      labels:
        app: deploy1
    spec:
      containers:
        - name: busybox
          image: busybox
          imagePullPolicy: IfNotPresent
          command: ['sh', '-c', 'echo Running ; sleep 3600']
```

The next code section will create the second deployment, deploy2, in the deploy2 namespace:

```
---
apiVersion: apps/v1
kind: Deployment
metadata:
  name: deploy2
  namespace: deploy2
spec:
  replicas: 1
  selector:
    matchLabels:
      app: deploy2
```

```
    template:
      metadata:
        labels:
          app: deploy2
      spec:
        containers:
          - name: busybox
            image: busybox
            imagePullPolicy: IfNotPresent
            command: ['sh', '-c', 'echo Running ; sleep 3600']
```

Once the deployment completes, make a note of the IP address of the Pod in the deploy1 namespace using the following command (in the example, it is 192.168.42.16):

```
$ kubectl get po -o wide -n deploy1
NAME       READY    STATUS     RESTARTS    AGE    IP        ...
deploy1-111  1/1   Running    0 69s      192.168.42.16 ....
```

You can now shell into the Pod in the deploy2 namespace using the following command:

```
$ kubectl exec --stdin --tty <pod-name> -n deploy2 -- sh
```

If you run the following command in the shell, it will succeed (change the IP address to the one for the Pod in the deploy1 namespace):

```
$ ping -c 5 192.168.42.16
PING 192.168.42.16 (192.168.42.16): 56 data bytes
64 bytes from 192.168.42.16: seq=0 ttl=254 time=0.110 ms
.....
```

Once the ping has finished, we can deploy the deny-all.yaml network policy, which denies all outbound traffic (egress) of the deploy2 namespace:

```
---
apiVersion: networking.k8s.io/v1
kind: NetworkPolicy
metadata:
  name: default-deny-ingress
  namespace: deploy2
spec:
```

```
    podSelector:
      matchLabels: {}
    policyTypes:
    - Egress
```

If you run the following command in the `deploy2` Pod namespace, it will *fail* due to the network policy:

```
$ ping -c 5 192.168.42.16
PING 192.168.42.16 (192.168.42.16): 56 data bytes
```

We've now seen how to extend EKS using the Calico policy engine to support network policies. In the next section, let's look at how we can make more changes to the CNI and even replace it completely.

Choosing and using different CNIs in EKS

We have seen how AWS CNI integrates with the VPC to offer **IP address management** (**IPAM**) services and the creation and management of the Pod network interface. The following are some of the reasons why you might want to replace the default AWS VPC CNI:

- If you want to have multiple Pod interfaces
- If you want to use an overlay network for encryption
- If you want to use network acceleration, such as DPDK or eBPF

As the EKS control plane is managed by AWS, there are a limited number of CNIs supported today; please refer to `https://docs.aws.amazon.com/eks/latest/userguide/alternate-cni-plugins.html` for the most up-to-date list.

The most important decision you need to make is whether you can extend the existing VPC CNI as we did with Calico but continue to use the VPC CNI to manage IP addresses and Pod interfaces. This is referred to as CNI plugin chaining, where a primary CNI is enhanced with additional capabilities. Therefore, if we look at the default CNI configuration file on an `/etc/cni/net.d/10-aws.conflist` EC2 host, we can see three plugins are enabled by default:

```
{"cniVersion": "0.4.0",
  "name": "aws-cni",
  "disableCheck": true,
  "plugins": [
    {
```

```
      "name":  "aws-cni",
      "type":  "aws-cni",
 ...
 pluginLogFile":  "/var/log/aws-routed-eni/plugin.log",
 ...},
     {
      "name":  "egress-v4-cni",
      "type":  "egress-v4-cni",
      ...},
     {
      "type":  "portmap",
      "capabilities":  {"portMappings":  true},
      "snat":  true }]
```

Kubernetes will call the aws-cni plugin first as it's listed first when it wants to add or remove a Pod network interface. It will then call the next plugin in the chain; in the default case, this is egress-v4-cni (which is the IPv4 host-local allocator discussed in the *Using IPv6 in your EKS cluster* section), passing it the command and the parameters passed to the first CNI plugin plus the result from the last plugin and so on until the chain is complete. This allows different functions to be configured by the CNI plugins, so in the default case in EKS, the first plugin configures the Pod interface and provides a VPC routable IP address. The second is used to do the IPv6-to-IPv4 conversion or source NAT.

Let's look at how we can use Multus, one of the supported EKS CNIs, to have multiple Pod network interfaces without losing VPC connectivity. In this case, Multus will act as a *meta plugin* and call other CNIs to do the Pod networking.

This is very useful as we don't have to replace the standard VPC-CNI, so IP addressing and routing is set up in the VPC using the VPC API by the AWS CNI. We can use Multus to create a second Pod interface that could be used as a management interface or to exchange heartbeat information if the Pods want to act as a cluster.

Configuring multiple network interfaces for Pods

As you can see from the following diagram, we normally attach other ENIs to the worker nodes to be managed by Multus, whereas the primary (master) EC2 interface is always managed by the VPC CNI:

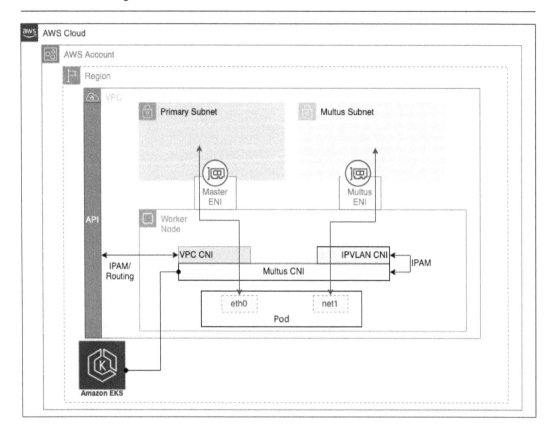

Figure 9.7 – Multus CNI integration with EKS

The first thing we should do is install Multus on the cluster we used for the network policies using the following command:

```
$ kubectl apply -f https://raw.githubusercontent.com/aws/
amazon-vpc-cni-k8s/master/config/multus/v3.7.2-eksbuild.1/
aws-k8s-multus.yaml
```

This will create a kube-multus-ds DaemonSet that runs across your worker nodes in this case, 2. This can be viewed using the following command:

```
$ kubectl get ds kube-multus-ds -n kube-system
NAME                DESIRED    CURRENT    READY     ...
kube-multus-ds      2          2          2         ...
```

If we look in the host's /etc/cni/net.d/ CNI configuration directory, we see there is a new 00-multus.conf configuration file. This file will be used first by Kubernetes as it starts with a lower numeric value (00).

Looking in more detail at the new CNI configuration file, we can see Multus is now the primary CNI (defined by the type keyword). It also used the delegates keyword to call other CNIs; in this case, just the AWS VPC CNI, which behaves as it did before as the plugin list is the same. The following output shows a truncated view of the new configuration file that, with the exception of the initial block, is the same as the default AWS VPC CNI:

```
{
        "cniVersion": "0.3.1",
        "name": "multus-cni-network",
        "type": "multus",
        "capabilities": {
            "portMappings": true},
...

        "delegates": [{
            "cniVersion": "0.4.0",
            "name": "aws-cni",
            "disableCheck": true,
             "plugins": [{
                 "name": "aws-cni",
                 "type": "aws-cni",
                 ....
         }, {
                 "name": "egress-v4-cni",
                 "type": "egress-v4-cni",
             ...
         }, {
                 "type": "portmap",
...
             },
             "snat": true }]}]}
```

If you remember, when we used `eksctl` to create our cluster, it also created a VPC and some private subnets, examples are shown next. We will use these to host the Multus-managed ENIs:

Name		Subnet ID		State		VPC		IPv4 CIDR
eksctl-myipv4cluster-cluster/SubnetPrivateEUCENTRAL1A				⊘ Available		vpc-06f8d68340929a7f6 | eks...		192.168.96.0/19
eksctl-myipv4cluster-cluster/SubnetPrivateEUCENTRAL1B				⊘ Available		vpc-06f8d68340929a7f6 | eks...		192.168.128.0/19
eksctl-myipv4cluster-cluster/SubnetPrivateEUCENTRAL1C				⊘ Available		vpc-06f8d68340929a7f6 | eks...		192.168.160.0/19

Figure 9.8 – Private subnets created by eksctl

There is some network *plumbing* we need to do before Multus works properly after we have enabled it in the cluster. We will need to do the following:

- Create some ENIs for Multus to use, tagging them so EKS ignores them
- Attach them to our worker nodes and sort out the IP address allocation and routing so the VPC can route traffic to and from the Pod's secondary interface

Creating the Multus ENIs

The first thing we need to do is create ENIs in the various private subnets. The CloudFormation script shown next provides an example of how to do it programmatically, but you can do it other ways. You should pay special attention to the tags; we explicitly state the cluster and zone (availability) that the interface is connected to and the fact it should *not be managed* by the EKS control plane. We also create a security group, as this is a mandatory parameter for an ENI:

```
AWSTemplateFormatVersion: "2010-09-09"
Resources:
    multusSec:
        Type: AWS::EC2::SecurityGroup
        Properties:
            GroupDescription: Multus security group
            GroupName: multus
            VpcId: <MYVPC>
```

In the following section, we create the first ENI in the first subnet:

```
    private1:
        Type: AWS::EC2::NetworkInterface
        Properties:
            Description: Interface 1 in az-a.
            Tags:
              - Key: multus
```

```
         Value: true
       - Key: Zone
         Value: <AZ-a>
       - Key:  node.k8s.amazonaws.com/no_manage
         Value: true
       - Key: cluster
         Value: <myclustername>
     SourceDestCheck: 'false'
     GroupSet:
     - !Ref multusSec
     SubnetId: <private subnet ID>
```

In the next section, we create the second ENI in the second subnet:

```
  private2:
      Type: AWS::EC2::NetworkInterface
      Properties:
         Description: Interface 1 in az-b.
         Tags:
         - Key: multus
           Value: true
         - Key: Zone
           Value: <AZ-b>
         - Key:  node.k8s.amazonaws.com/no_manage
           Value: true
         - Key: cluster
           Value: <myclustername>
         SourceDestCheck: 'false'
         GroupSet:
         - !Ref multusSec
         SubnetId: <private subnet ID>
```

In the final section, we create the last ENI in the third subnet:

```
  private3:
      Type: AWS::EC2::NetworkInterface
      Properties:
         Description: Interface 1 in az-c.
```

```
            Tags:
              - Key: multus
                Value: true
              - Key: Zone
                Value: <AZ-c>
              - Key:  node.k8s.amazonaws.com/no_manage
                Value: true
              - Key: cluster
                Value: <myclustername>
            SourceDestCheck: 'false'
            GroupSet:
            - !Ref multusSec
            SubnetId: <private subnet ID>
```

Successfully deploying this script should result in three new interfaces being created; an example is shown here:

Name	Network interface ID	Subnet ID	VPC ID	Availability Zone	Security group names	Interface Type	Description
-	eni-08165637:	subnet-08f457c2	vpc-06f8d683	eu-central-1c	multus	Elastic network interface	Interface 1 in az-c.
-	eni-080f5ffa6:	subnet-064d481	vpc-06f8d685	eu-central-1b	multus	Elastic network interface	Interface 1 in az-b.
-	eni-0a04f24ef	subnet-0ac57d9(	vpc-06f8d683	eu-central-1a	multus	Elastic network interface	Interface 1 in az-a.

Figure 9.9 – New ENIs for Multus

Attaching the ENIs to your worker nodes and configuring VPC routing

You will now need to attach the interfaces to the worker nodes that your EC2 instances are using. You can do this through the console by selecting the worker node and selecting **Actions** | **Networking** | **Attach network interface**, or you can attach them automatically (more on this later).

As we have only created one interface by AZ, you will only see the interface that corresponds to the AZ the instance is in. This will create a new Ethernet interface on your worker nodes with an address assigned from the private subnets. You can review the configuration by connecting to the host and running the following command:

```
$ ifconfig -a
```

This will output something similar to the block shown next, where we can see a second ENI (eth1 in this example), but depending on how many interfaces are already allocated to the worker node, the interface number may vary:

```
eth0: flags=4163<UP,BROADCAST,RUNNING,MULTICAST>  mtu 9001
inet 192.168.27.63  netmask 255.255.224.0  broadcast
```

```
192.168.31.255
.....
eth1: flags=4098<BROADCAST,MULTICAST>  mtu 1500
ether 02:4f:d3:c2:fb:0e  txqueuelen 1000  (Ethernet)
.......
lo: flags=73<UP,LOOPBACK,RUNNING>  mtu 65536
inet 127.0.0.1  netmask 255.0.0.0
.....
```

As the interface name could vary per worker node, we need to normalize them so we can rename them using the ip link command. Again this can be done per host using the following command:

```
$ sudo ip link set eth1 name multus
```

This may seem like a lot of work so far, but we still have to solve the major issue of how we route traffic to and from this secondary interface. Multus uses NetworkAttachmentDefinition to define the network used by the secondary interface:

```
apiVersion: "k8s.cni.cncf.io/v1"
kind: NetworkAttachmentDefinition
metadata:
  name: ipvlan-private-a
spec:
  config: '{
      "cniVersion": "0.3.0",
      "type": "ipvlan",
      "master": "multus",
      "mode": "l3",
      "ipam": {
        "type": "host-local",
        "subnet": "192.168.96.0/19",
        "rangeStart": "192.168.96.20",
        "rangeEnd": "192.168.96.40",
        "gateway": "192.168.96.1"
      }
    }'
```

NetworkAttachmentDefinition is referenced in the Pod or Deployment; an example is shown next. The Pod will have a second interface attached by Multus with an IP address allocated between 192.168.96.20 and 192.168.96.40, as defined in the config section of the NetworkAttachmentDefinition file, shown previously.

> **Important note**
> The range used here is just a subset of the subnet CIDR that will be used by Multus.

We will use the nodeSelector tag to allocate an IP address based on the AZ defined in NetworkAttachmentDefinition:

```
apiVersion: v1
kind: Pod
metadata:
  name: multus-pod
  annotations:
      k8s.v1.cni.cncf.io/networks: ipvlan-private-a
spec:
  nodeSelector:
    topology.kubernetes.io/zone: eu-central-1a
  containers:
        - name: busybox
          image: busybox
          imagePullPolicy: IfNotPresent
          command: ['sh', '-c', 'echo Container 1 is Running ;
sleep 3600']
```

If you run the following command, you can see the Pod is hosted on the worker node that is hosted in the eu-central-1a AZ:

```
$ kubectl get pod -o=custom-columns=NODE:.spec.nodeName,NAME:.
metadata.name
```

If we shell into the Pod using the following commands, you can see the Pod has two interfaces:

```
$ kubectl exec --stdin --tty multus-pod  -- sh
# ip addr
1: lo: <LOOPBACK,UP,LOWER_UP> mtu 65536 qdisc noqueue qlen 1000
```

```
        link/loopback 00:00:00:00:00:00 brd 00:00:00:00:00:00
        inet 127.0.0.1/8 scope host lo
3: eth0@if23: <BROADCAST,MULTICAST,UP,LOWER_UP,M-DOWN> mtu 9001
qdisc noqueue
        link/ether 96:f4:8f:ef:82:92 brd ff:ff:ff:ff:ff:ff
        inet 192.168.14.60/32 scope global eth0
4: net1@if15: <BROADCAST,MULTICAST,NOARP,UP,LOWER_UP,M-DOWN>
mtu 1500 qdisc noqueue
        link/ether 02:4f:d3:c2:fb:0e brd ff:ff:ff:ff:ff:ff
        inet 192.168.96.20/19 brd 192.168.127.255 scope global net1
```

Now to the meat of the problem! A VPC is a Layer 3 networking construct, everything needs an IP address to communicate, and the VPC maintains routes to all IP addresses/ranges in route tables. The VPC also maintains MAC address mapping to map IP addresses to the right ENI to make sure traffic keys to the right interfaces.

This all works as the IP addresses are requested from the VPC. But in the case of Multus, it is assigning the IP address, and as it is creating an ipvlan-based interface, the MAC address is actually the one assigned to the Multus interface (eth2 in NetworkAttachmentDefinition). So, the VPC doesn't know that the IP addresses have been allocated or which ENI it needs to map them to. You need to associate the IP address assigned to the Pod with the Multus ENI using the following command:

```
$ aws ec2 assign-private-ip-addresses --network-interface-id
<multus ENI-ID> --private-ip-addresses 192.168.96.30
```

There are a few ways you can automate some of this:

- The AWS-managed repository, https://github.com/aws-samples/eks-automated-ipmgmt-multus-pods, suggests using either an init container or a sidecar to make calls to the AssignPrivateIpAddresses EC2 API (or the equivalent IPv6 API call)

- There's a great blog by Joe Alford, https://joealford.medium.com/deploying-multus-into-amazons-eks-42269146f421, that looks to address some of the shortcomings of the AWS scripts, which we recommend

- Roll your own solution using tools such as AWS Lambda and auto-scaling events to create, attach interfaces, and configure prefixes that can be used by a deployment

Deploying these solutions is outside the scope of this book, but hopefully, you can see that the VPC CNI is the simplest way to get native AWS networking in your cluster, both for IPv4 and IPv6.

A different CNI may still be required if you want to do the following:

- Use an overlay network based on IPsec, VXLAN, or IP in IP
- Support enhanced networking use cases such as source IP address preservation, direct server return, and low latency networking using eBPF
- Support for Windows **Host Networking Services** (**HNS**)
- BGP Integration

One of the major reasons for using another CNI, VPC address exhaustion, is still a use case, but prefix addressing, discussed in *Chapter 7*, *Networking in EKS*, solves this issue as long as you can allocate prefixes to interfaces. If you truly don't have VPC addresses, then this still could be a reason to use another CNI.

In this section, we looked at how you can extend and replace the VPC CNI. We'll now revisit the key learning points from this chapter.

Summary

We started by describing how IPv6 can be configured in a new cluster to provide almost limitless IP addresses that don't require NATing. We also discussed that IPv6 does have limits in terms of what it can communicate with and how techniques such as the host-local plugin, DNS64, and NAT64 can be used to provide IPv6 to IPv4 translation.

We then looked at how the Calico policy engine can be used to enhance the capabilities of EKS by providing IPv4 L3/L4 network policies (just like a traditional firewall) that can be used to limit access between Pods and external IP addresses.

Finally, we looked at how a CNI works with plugins and chaining and using Multus as an example, how the AWS VPC CNI can be replaced and the advantages that brings, but also the complexity it can add. We also briefly discussed that there are some valid use cases where a different CNI will be required but that the one that used to be the main driver, VPC IP exhaustion, can now be solved using prefix addresses.

In the next chapter, we will look at the overall process of upgrading your cluster and build on some of the concepts discussed in the previous chapters.

Further reading

- Configuring Multus CNI: `https://aws.amazon.com/blogs/containers/amazon-eks-now-supports-multus-cni/`
- CNI Chaining: `https://karampok.me/posts/chained-plugins-cni/`
- IPv6 on AWS: `https://aws.amazon.com/vpc/ipv6/`

10

Upgrading EKS Clusters

The Kubernetes community will release a new version of Kubernetes approximately three times a year, as well as maintain release branches for the three most recent minor releases. In addition, AWS will maintain at least four production-ready versions of Kubernetes at any given time; at the time of writing, they are versions 1.24, 1.23, 1.22, and 1.21. Given these two different release schedules, at some point, you will need to upgrade your EKS clusters either because you want to use a new feature developed by the Kubernetes community or because AWS is no longer supporting the version you are using. The good news is that as EKS is a managed service, AWS does most of the upgrade work for you!

This chapter looks at the best way to do this and the impact it can have on running workloads. Specifically, we will cover the following:

- Reasons for upgrading EKS and key areas to focus on
- How to do in-place upgrades of the control plane
- Upgrading nodes and their critical components
- Creating a new cluster and migrating workloads

Technical requirements

The reader should have a familiarity with YAML, basic networking, and EKS architecture. Before getting started with this chapter, please ensure you have the following:

- Network connectivity to your EKS API endpoint
- The AWS CLI and kubectl binary installed on your workstation
- A good understanding of VPC networking and how to create network objects such as ENIs

Reasons for upgrading EKS and key areas to focus on

EKS is a community project and, as such, it is constantly evolving; big releases currently happen approximately three times per year and normally contain at least one major change. For example, 1.21, released in April 2021, deprecated Pod security policies in favor of external admission control. This means that you will need to take advantage of newer Kubernetes features at some point. In addition, the Kubernetes community only supports the most recent three minor releases (for example, 1.25, 1.24, and 1.23), with older releases normally getting 1 year of patch releases, after which you are on your own!

Amazon takes the upstream Kubernetes release, tests and validates it with the AWS platform and components such as the AWS VPC CNI, and so on, and packages and releases it as an EKS release. This process takes roughly 6 months after the Kubernetes community release and will normally be supported for 14 months. This is illustrated in the following diagram:

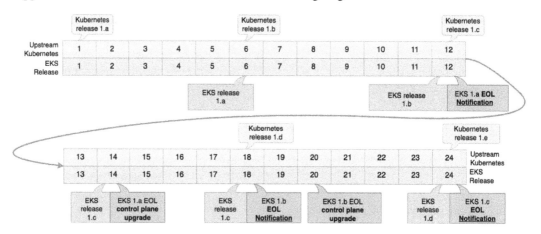

Figure 10.1 – Example Kubernetes release schedule

After 12 months, AWS will notify customers, using the console and AWS Health Dashboard, that a release is approaching the **end-of-life** (EOL)—sometimes called **end-of-support** (EOS)—date, and after 14 months they will automatically upgrade the control plane to the earliest supported version through a gradual deployment process after the EOS date.

As the cluster owner, you can choose to upgrade the control plane at any time before the EOS date, but you will always be responsible for upgrading worker nodes, add-ons, and any core components such as kube-proxy.

There are certain key areas to consider when upgrading as you cannot roll back a version. If you want to roll back, you must deploy a new cluster with a previous version. Key considerations are as follows:

- Are Kubernetes APIs or key functionality being deprecated that may require changes to the deployment manifest or Kubernetes component upgrades such as replacing kubelet?

- Do add-ons, third-party DaemonSets, and so on need upgrading to support the new release?

- Is there a new functionality that needs designing, such as the use of **Open Policy Agent** (**OPA**) to replace Pod policies?

- Are there security patches that need to be applied?

On the whole, there should be little impact on running workloads unless they are *aware* or interact with the Kubernetes control plane, but it is always worth reading the release notes and upgrading in lower environments first before you modify your production environment.

Now that we have discussed *why* you will need to upgrade, let's discuss *how* you do a cluster upgrade.

How to do in-place upgrades of the control plane

If you do nothing, eventually, AWS will upgrade your control plane, but as discussed previously, this might have an impact on other components. It is, therefore, best to take a proactive approach. Upgrading the control plane is literally a *single-click* operation, and AWS will progressively upgrade the API and etcd servers. In most cases, this will be fine, but as discussed in the previous section, it can break *services*

A structured approach is, therefore, recommended. In the following example, the team responsible for the **Infrastructure as Code** (**IaC**) used by the other team or organization will create a new template. This could be as simple as updating the version string in Terraform, CDK, or an `eksctl` configuration file, or it may be a more detailed development for add-ons such as Argo CD, Flux, and so on. In the following diagram, this is illustrated as the responsibility of a platform engineering team, but in smaller companies, this might be a DevOps or **site reliability engineering** (**SRE**) team's or application development team's responsibility:

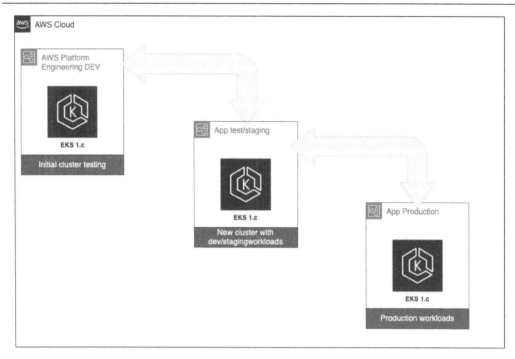

Figure 10.2 – Structured upgrade approach

Once the master IaC template has been created, this can be used by the development teams to test their workloads in lower environments (testing/staging) and, ultimately, in production.

Assuming you have used eksctl to create your cluster, you can upgrade the control plane with a simple one-line command. If we use the IPv4 cluster from the previous chapter, we can upgrade it using the following command:

```
$ eksctl upgrade cluster myipv4cluster --version=1.20 --approve
```

> **Important note**
> If you leave out the --approve keyword, eksctl will not make changes. It's also worth noting that normally you can't jump directly from a minor release such as 1.19 to 1.22 without upgrading to 1.20 and then 1.21 first!

This process can take up to 20 minutes, so it's worth planning a change window as Kubernetes API access may be intermittent during the upgrade (no existing workloads should be affected). Once the control plane has been upgraded, you should upgrade your worker nodes to match the cluster version prior to moving to the next version (eksctl enforces this requirement). Let's look at how we do this upgrade next.

Upgrading nodes and their critical components

Simplifying the upgrade process is one of the key reasons for using managed node groups. If we want to upgrade a single worker node in an active cluster manually, we would need to perform the following actions:

1. Add a new worker that can run the Pods that will be evicted from the node running the old version of the Kubernetes agents (kubelet, and so on) we are upgrading, if we want to maintain the overall cluster capacity (the overall number of worker nodes that can run active Pods) during the upgrade.

2. Drain the Pods from the node we are working on and remove them from the scheduling process so that no new Pods are allocated.

3. Upgrade the operating system binaries and apply patches if needed.

4. Update and configure the Kubernetes agents (kubelet, and so on).

5. Once the upgraded node has registered and is ready, add it back to the scheduler.

6. Update any critical components such as `kube-proxy`, `coreDNS`, and so on.

If we have node groups with 10 or 20 nodes, you will see how this can become painful very quickly.

Let's look at how we upgrade the worker nodes now that the cluster control plane is upgraded.

Upgrading managed node groups

Once you have upgraded the cluster, if you look at the managed node groups for that cluster, you will see the **Update now** link. This can be used to automatically upgrade the node group using the autoscaling launch template process described in *Chapter 8, Managing Worker Nodes on EKS*. An example is shown next:

Figure 10.3 – Node group updates

Using the link will automatically replace all EC2 workers in the node group; you will be presented with a pop-up window (an example is shown next) that provides a few more options:

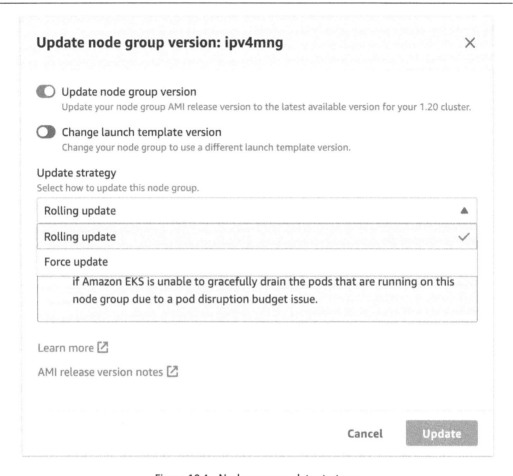

Figure 10.4 – Node group update strategy

The upgrade node dialog box shown previously allows you to do the following:

- Replace the nodes with the latest AMI by setting the **Update node group version** switch.

- Replace the current autoscaling launch template with a different one using the **Change launch template version** switch.

- Use the **Rolling update** strategy (default) to drain the Pods from the running node. This strategy will respect any Pod disruption budgets defined, and so the update will fail if the Pods cannot be drained gracefully. Alternatively, the **Force update** strategy will try to drain the Pods as per a rolling update, but if it fails, it will simply terminate the node rather than fail the update.

Clicking the **Update** button will initiate the node group update/replacement. You can also do the operation programmatically using your IaC tool of choice. The next example shows how you can do the same operation with `eksctl`:

```
$ eksctl upgrade nodegroup   --name=ipv4mng   --cluster=myipv
4cluster  --kubernetes-version=1.20
```

You can watch the status of the replacement using the following command. In the following example, you can see the older 1.19 AMI has `SchedulingDisabled` set:

```
$ kubectl get nodes --watch
NAME            STATUS          ROLES     AGE     VERSION
ipx.eu-central-1.compute.internal    Ready
<none>    15m    v1.20.15-eks-ba74326
ip-192-168-40-12.eu-central-1.compute.
internal    Ready,SchedulingDisabled    <none>    26d    v1.19.
15-eks-9c63c4
ipy.eu-central-1.compute.internal    Ready
<none>    15m    v1.20.15-eks-ba74326
ipz.eu-central-1.compute.internal    Ready
<none>    15m    v1.20.15-eks-ba74326
```

Upgrading self-managed node groups

Upgrading self-managed nodes will depend on how you want to perform the upgrade (draining Pods first, replacing nodes, or in-place upgrades), and which additional components are installed.

Generally, node groups should be viewed as immutable; so, as unmanaged node groups may be part of an autoscaling group, you can change the AMI and use a new launch template to force replacement, but as the operator you will be responsible for removing the nodes from the scheduler (`SchedulingDisabled`), draining the Pods, and then scaling out and scaling in (effectively, everything a managed group does for you).

A simpler way may be to simply create a new node group, move the Pods onto the new node group, and delete the old one.

Updating core components

The node group will have an updated kubelet agent, but key components such as `kube-proxy`, `coreDNS`, and `vpc-cni` will typically need to be upgraded to work with a specific Kubernetes release.

If you look at the current version of kube-proxy on the upgraded cluster and node groups using the following command, we can see this is still at the previous cluster's versions (v1.19.16):

```
$ kubectl get daemonset kube-proxy --namespace kube-system
-o=jsonpath='{$.spec.template.spec.containers[:1].image}'
1122334.dkr.ecr.eu-central-1.amazonaws.com/eks/kube-
proxy:v1.19.16-eksbuild.2
```

We can do an upgrade using eksctl or another IaC tool. The next example shows how to use eksctl utils to update kube-proxy:

```
$ eksctl utils update-kube-proxy --cluster=myipv4cluster -
approve
2022-09-11 10:27:07 "kube-proxy" is now up-to-date
$ kubectl get daemonset kube-proxy --namespace kube-system
-o=jsonpath='{$.spec.template.spec.containers[:1].image}'
1122334.dkr.ecr.eu-central-1.amazonaws.com/eks/kube-
proxy:v1.20.15-eksbuild.2
```

To simplify this process, AWS introduced EKS add-ons, which allow the update of operational software such as kube-proxy or monitoring daemons such as **AWS Distro for OpenTelemetry (ADOT)**.

If we use the AWS console and click on the **Add-ons** tab, we can see, in the next example, that we have three add-ons configured that reflect the three core components we need to update on every cluster upgrade. Clicking on the **Update now** link and choosing the desired versions will allow the vpc-cni add-on to upgrade the aws-node DaemonSet that implements the CNI:

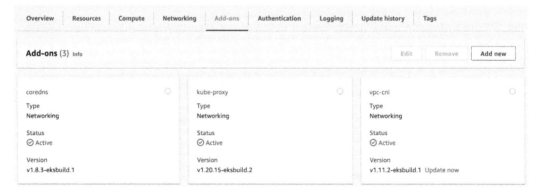

Figure 10.5 – Cluster add-ons

You can also do the operation programmatically using your IaC tool of choice. The next example shows how you can do the same operation with `eksctl`:

```
$ eksctl update addon --name vpc-cni --cluster myipv4cluster
--version 1.11.3 --force
2022-09-11 10:47:40 []  Kubernetes version "1.20" in use by
cluster "myipv4cluster"
2022-09-11 10:47:41 []  new version provided v1.11.3-eksbuild.1
2022-09-11 10:47:41 []  updating addon
2022-09-11 10:50:50 []  addon "vpc-cni" active
```

> **Important note**
> The use of `--force` will force the configuration onto the cluster. These actions should all be tested on lower environments to ensure they don't cause an outage prior to being run on production.

Let's look at using an alternative cluster and/or node group to provide a blue/green deployment approach at the cluster level.

Creating a new cluster and migrating workloads

As you can see, a typical upgrade will involve at least three steps:

1. Upgrading the control plane
2. Upgrading/replacing the worker nodes with more up-to-date AMIs and the kubelet
3. At least upgrading the core components, `kube-proxy`, `coreDNS`, and `vpc-cni`

In this approach, the Pods must first be drained and reallocated to worker nodes as they are replaced. This can lead to interruptions if not managed well. An alternative is to deploy a new cluster and then migrate workloads; this is sometimes referred to as blue/green cluster deployment.

> **Important note**
> This will be the least cost-effective approach as you will be paying for two control planes but may be suitable if you want to try to minimize disruption. We will only discuss this approach at a high level in this book as the most common approach is to upgrade the EKS control plane and then the worker nodes using managed worker nodes, greatly reducing cost and complexity.

A multi-cluster solution presents some different challenges: How do you move workloads? Have any manual changes been applied to the cluster? How do you provide ingress and egress connectivity? How do you manage state? The following diagram illustrates the solutions to these challenges:

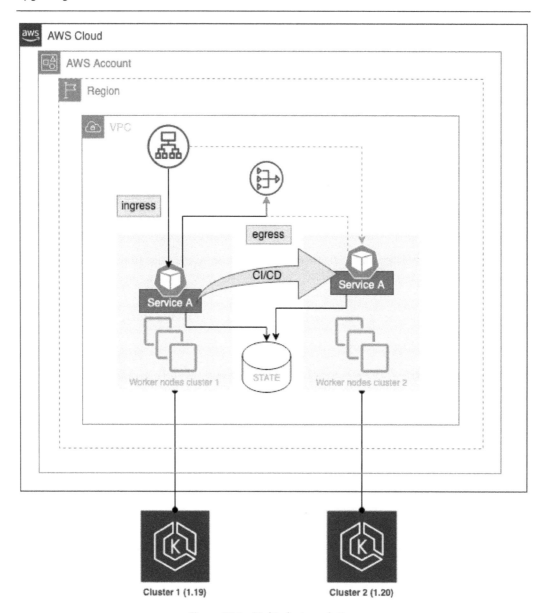

Figure 10.6 – Multi-cluster solution

Now, to understand some of the challenges, let's look at one approach to migrating workloads between two clusters.

How do you move workloads?

When using kubectl or Helm, the current context defines which cluster you will use. By switching context, the same manifest can be deployed on either cluster. In *Figure 10.6*, a CI/CD pipeline can automate the provisioning of the service on either cluster. For example, **Cluster 1** (v1.19) is running **Service A**; **Cluster 2** can be created with v1.20, and this can trigger a deployment of **Service A** on **Cluster 2**.

How do you provide consistent ingress and egress network access?

Egress (Pod initiating connections out) can use either an internal or external VPC NAT gateway to mask the IP address of the Pods from both clusters, masking any Pod IP address changes.

An **elastic load balancer (ELB)**, **application load balancer (ALB)**, or **network load balancer (NLB)** can be used to mask the IP addresses of the Pod or the different worker nodes for incoming connections (ingress). Typically, you would use the AWS Load Balancer Controller, which would create a new load balancer for each service, one per cluster. However, you can configure a TargetGroupBinding instance, which will reuse an existing ALB or NLB target group for both clusters configured outside the EKS cluster using IaC. An example is shown next and references the testapp service on port 80:

```
apiVersion: elbv2.k8s.aws/v1beta1
kind: TargetGroupBinding
metadata:
  name: testappt
  namespace: mynamespace
spec:
  serviceRef:
    name: testapp
    port: 80
  targetGroupARN: arn:aws:elasticloadbalancing:eu-west-
1:1122224:targetgroup/example/fc3409bc5e613beb
```

Now, let's look at how applications typically manage state.

How do you manage state?

Your application may need to maintain state in a database or on a filesystem. As long as these services are configured outside the cluster using an AWS service such as **Relational Database Service** (RDS) or **Elastic File System** (EFS), they can be referenced by either cluster.

With these solutions in place, you can easily flip between clusters. By deploying to the new cluster first and making sure the service is registered with the ELB, you can make the transition almost seamless; however, you will pay more for this type of configuration.

In this section, we have looked at how to upgrade key EKS components and the different approaches required for managed and unmanaged node groups. We'll now revisit the key learning points from this chapter.

Summary

In this chapter, we explored why you will need to upgrade your cluster: either you want to use a new Kubernetes feature or a bug fix or AWS is deprecating the version you are using. We identified you will need to perform three actions for each cluster: upgrade the control plane, upgrade the worker nodes, and upgrade the core components such as `kube-proxy` and `coreDNS`.

We also discussed how the control plane upgrade is pretty straightforward as it's a managed service, but node group and component upgrades can be more challenging. Using managed node groups and add-ons simplifies this, but you could also use a second cluster and move the workload between them, upgrading the non-active cluster. This approach—sometimes referred to as blue/green cluster deployments—will add cost and complexity, so it is not recommended, but it can minimize application outages due to upgrades.

In the next chapter, we will look at how you can use AWS **Elastic Container Repository (ECR)** as a source of your applications and Pods.

Further reading

- Pod disruption budgets: `https://kubernetes.io/docs/concepts/workloads/pods/disruptions/`
- Managed node group update process: `https://docs.aws.amazon.com/eks/latest/userguide/managed-node-update-behavior.html`
- AWS Load Balancer Controller TargetGroupBinding: `https://kubernetes-sigs.github.io/aws-load-balancer-controller/v2.1/guide/targetgroupbinding/targetgroupbinding/`
- EKS add-ons: `https://docs.aws.amazon.com/eks/latest/userguide/eks-add-ons.html`
- Kubernetes upgrades: `https://kubernetes.io/docs/tasks/administer-cluster/cluster-upgrade/`

Part 3: Deploying an Application on EKS

This part will cover topics related to features that help you deploy your application on EKS. This section includes a complete guide for storing container images on Amazon ECR, providing persistent volumes for your application with AWS storage services such as EBS and EFS, defining the Pod security and granting permissions with IAM, and exposing and load balancing your Kubernetes application. In the last two chapters, we will look at more advanced topics such as using AWS Fargate, and how to use App Mesh to control and monitor our deployments

This section contains the following chapters:

- *Chapter 11, Building Applications and Pushing Them to Amazon ECR*
- *Chapter 12, Deploying Pods with Amazon Storage*
- *Chapter 13, Using IAM for Granting Access to Applications*
- *Chapter 14, Setting Load Balancing for Applications on EKS*
- *Chapter 15, Working with AWS Fargate*
- *Chapter 16, Working with a Service Mesh*

11

Building Applications and Pushing Them to Amazon ECR

A Kubernetes Pod consists of at least one container. These containers are stored in a public or private repository and pulled by a worker node when it receives a Pod specification and needs to deploy a container. This chapter looks at how you can use AWS **Elastic Container Registry** (**ECR**) to securely store container images using multiple repositories and allow EKS to use them when it deploys Pods.

Specifically, we will cover the following topics:

- Introducing Amazon ECR
- Understanding repository authentication
- Building and pushing a container image to ECR
- Using advanced ECR features
- Using an ECR image in your EKS cluster

Technical requirements

The reader should have a familiarity with YAML, basic networking, and EKS architecture. Before getting started with this chapter, please ensure the following:

- You have network connectivity to your EKS cluster API endpoint
- The AWS CLI, Docker, and kubectl binary are installed on your workstation
- You have a basic understanding of Docker and Dockerfiles

Introducing Amazon ECR

In *Chapter 1*, we talked about the general structure of a container and how it uses a union filesystem to create a layered image. This image format has become the **Open Container Initiative** (**OCI**) image specification, and various open source build tools such as Podman or BuildKit support this format.

When you build an image using the `docker build` command, an image is created locally, which is fine for the local machine, but when you need to use that image in EKS or another Kubernetes distribution/service, you need to push it to a repository that can be accessed by other systems that make up your EKS cluster.

If you browse Docker Hub at `https://hub.docker.com/` and log in, you can see multiple container images for Postgres, Redis, Python, and so on. Each image is tagged with a version tag such as 13.8 as well as potentially the latest tag, which will often (but not always) denote the latest version of a container image. Docker Hub is a public repository, which means it can be accessed from the internet. These are considered public repositories and can be accessed by anyone with a Docker Hub ID.

ECR hosts multiple repositories that in turn host multiple versions of a container image (as well as other OCI-compliant artifacts) in the same way Docker Hub does, but access is controlled through IAM and repository controls that you control and are often used to host containers that contain private code or configurations.

The easiest way to understand ECR is to create a repository. The next example shows a simple Terraform configuration that will create a private repository called `myapp` in the current AWS account/region:

```
resource "aws_ecr_repository" "myapp" {
  name                   = "myapp"
  image_tag_mutability = "MUTABLE"
  image_scanning_configuration {
    scan_on_push = true }}
output "repo-url" {
  value = aws_ecr_repository.myapp.repository_url}
```

Two key attributes in the ECR configuration are `image_tag_mutability` (which allows an image with an existing tag to upload, replacing the existing one) and `scan_on_push`, which will scan the image for basic vulnerabilities after it is uploaded (pushed).

The Terraform code will output the newly created repository URL (for example, `1122334.dkr.ecr.eu-central-1.amazonaws.com/myapp`), which we will use later to push a local image to ECR.

ECR is charged based on the size of the images that are stored in the registry as well as any data transfer costs for data leaving AWS. For example, assuming you are storing a total of 60 GB of software images, you will be charged for storage at $0.10 per GB equaling a total of $6/month, but charged nothing for data transfer in. Any EKS cluster within the same region pulling the images will not be charged for data transfer out. So, the total cost will equal $6/month.

In reality, your costs will probably be lower as there is a Free Tier discount in the first year for private repositories and some free storage and transfer-out limits as well. Please refer to https://aws. amazon.com/ecr/pricing/ for more information.

Let's look at how ECR provides secure access to the repositories.

Understanding repository authentication

As we discussed, ECR repositories can be private or public, and the security credentials you use to access these repositories will vary depending on the type of repository you create.

Accessing ECR private repositories

Access to private repositories is controlled through AWS IAM and repository permissions. If you are using the native AWS API, then you can use the standard Signature Version 4 signing process used by API clients such as the AWS CLI or the Python boto3 library.

In this chapter, we will use Docker commands to interact with the ECR repository, so we need to convert the AWS access and secret keys into something Docker will understand. This is done with the aws ecr get-login-password command and passing the output into the docker login command. An example is shown next:

```
$ aws ecr get-login-password --region eu-central-1 | docker
login --username AWS --password-stdin 1122334.dkr.ecr.
eu-central-1.amazonaws.com/myapp
WARNING! Your password will be stored unencrypted in /home/
ec2-user/.docker/config.json.
......
Login Succeeded
```

> **Important note**
> Please note that credentials are valid for 12 hours, after which time the docker login command needs to be rerun.

This now means Docker commands such as docker pull or docker push will have an authentication token that will allow them to interact with the ECR. In order to use the aws ecr get-login-password command, the user account being used must have the appropriate IAM permissions.

The following IAM policy is the default one used by EKS worker nodes to both access and pull images, as well as retrieve an authorization token (`GetAuthorizationToken` is the underlying API call the `get-login-password` command calls):

```
{ "Version": "2012-10-17",
    "Statement": [
        {
            "Effect": "Allow",
            "Action": [
                "ecr:BatchCheckLayerAvailability",
                "ecr:BatchGetImage",
                "ecr:GetDownloadUrlForLayer",
                "ecr:GetAuthorizationToken"
            ],
            "Resource": "*"}]}
```

As well as the IAM permissions, every registry has the ability to apply individual policies. Typically, an IAM role such as the one shown previously is used to give broad access to the ECR service, and repository policies are used to restrict access to specific repositories. For example, the following Terraform resource adds a policy that would allow account 22334455 to push images to our repository:

```
resource "aws_ecr_repository_policy" "apppolicy" {
  repository = aws_ecr_repository.myapp.name
  policy = <<EOF
{
    "Version": "2012-10-17",
    "Statement": [
        {
            "Sid": "AllowCrossAccountPush",
            "Effect": "Allow",
            "Principal": {
                "AWS": "arn:aws:iam::22334455:root"
            },
            "Action": [
                "ecr:BatchCheckLayerAvailability",
                "ecr:CompleteLayerUpload",
                "ecr:InitiateLayerUpload",
                "ecr:PutImage",
```

```
                        "ecr:UploadLayerPart"
             ]}]}
EOF
}
```

> **Important note**
>
> There are also registry-wide permissions you can apply that are used to scope access to the replication and pull through cache features, which will be discussed later in this chapter.
>
> Also, note that `aws_ecr_repository.myapp.name` references the repository created previously and would need to be changed if you structure your Terraform repository or code differently.
>
> One final note—there is no real difference between private and public ECR repositories as they are managed and costed in the same way. The key difference is public repositories allow anonymous users to pull images from them and are visible on the Amazon ECR Public Gallery. This means anyone can pull images and, as repositories have a cost element based on data transfer, *anonymous users pulling your images will contribute to your overall bill!*
>
> We will use private ECR repositories only for EKS, so please refer to `https://docs.aws.amazon.com/AmazonECR/latest/public/what-is-ecr.html` if you want further information on public repositories.

Now we understand how to authenticate with a private repository, let's see how we build and push an image to our ECR repository.

Building and pushing a container image to ECR

If we consider a simple API using Python and FastAPI, shown next, we need to first package that up into a Docker image locally. We can then test if it is working locally before we push it to ECR. I've chosen Python and FastAPI as they are very simple to get up and running, but you can create the container using any language or framework.

The Python code in the `main.py` file is shown next:

```
#!/usr/bin/env python3
'''simple API server that returns Hello World'''
from fastapi import FastAPI
app = FastAPI()
@app.get("/")
async def root():
    return {"message": "Hello World"}
```

We will also need a `requirements.txt` file, which will have the following entries:

```
nyio==3.6.1
click==8.1.3
fastapi==0.83.0
h11==0.13.0
httptools==0.5.0
idna==3.3
importlib-metadata==4.12.0
pydantic==1.10.2
python-dotenv==0.21.0
PyYAML==6.0
sniffio==1.3.0
starlette==0.19.1
typing-extensions==4.3.0
uvicorn==0.18.3
uvloop==0.16.0
watchfiles==0.17.0
websockets==10.3
zipp==3.8.1
```

We will use a simple Dockerfile (shown next) that creates an image using a non-root user, installs the necessary libraries through `pip` (in this case, FastAPI and Uvicorn), and then runs the server using the Docker CMD key:

```
FROM python:3.9
RUN pip install --upgrade pip
RUN adduser worker
USER worker
WORKDIR /home/worker
ENV PATH="/home/worker/.local/bin:${PATH}"
COPY ./requirements.txt /home/worker/requirements.txt
RUN pip install --no-cache-dir --upgrade -r /home/worker/
requirements.txt
COPY ./main.py /home/worker/main.py
CMD ["uvicorn", "main:app", "--host", "0.0.0.0", "--port",
"8080", "--reload"]
```

We can then build and run the container using the following Docker commands:

```
$ docker build -t myapi:0.0.1 .
$ docker run -p 8080:8080 --rm myapi:0.0.1

......

INFO:       Uvicorn running on http://0.0.0.0:8080
INFO:       Application startup complete.
```

You now be able to curl http://127.0.0.1:8080 to get a reply or http://127.0.0.1:8080/docs to get the API definition. Now that we have a working application, we can use the following commands to log in, tag, and push the image to our ECR repository we created in the previous section:

```
$ aws ecr get-login-password --region eu-central-1 | docker login
--username AWS --password-stdin 1122334.dkr.ecr.eu-central-1.amazonaws.
com/myapp
WARNING! Your password will be stored unencrypted in /home/ec2-user/.
docker/config.json.

......

$ docker tag myapi:0.0.1 1122334.dkr.ecr.eu-central-1.amazonaws.com/
myapp:0.0.1
$ docker images
REPOSITORY  TAG IMAGE ID        CREATED         SIZE
1122334.dkr.ecr.eu-central-1.amazonaws.com/
myapp    0.0.1          c163cea7a037    9 hours ago     1.01GB
$ docker push 1122334.dkr.ecr.eu-central-1.amazonaws.com/myapp    :0.0.1
The push refers to repository [1122334.dkr.ecr.eu-central-1.amazonaws.
com/myapp]
e6aadc5ffa3e: Pushed

......

54b354c15c5a: Pushed
0.0.1: digest: sha256:193687f5606a46e61634b1020edaea6e347281ea
ba8ff41d328371982a533efc size: 3264
```

If we now go into the AWS console, we will be able to view the image in our repository. As we enabled scan_on_push, we will also get a view of any vulnerabilities that the basic scanning has detected. This scanning uses the open source Clair project to perform the scan:

Figure 11.1 – Initial image details in ECR

If we click on the **details** link in the bottom-right corner, we get a more detailed view of the issues, complete with a link to the **Common Vulnerabilities and Exposures (CVE)** number. An example is shown next that references the two critical issues identified in my image:

Figure 11.2 – Initial image scan output

In most companies I have worked with, all the **CRITICAL** issues need to be removed, as a minimum, before the image can be considered *safe*. This might be the developers', DevOps', or platform engineers' responsibility, but in reality, it's everyone's responsibility to make the image as secure as possible. Image remediation can be a time-consuming practice, but there are some simple things you can do!

By simply changing the base image from `python:3.9` to `python:3.10-slim-bullseye` in the Dockerfile and tagging it as version 0.0.2, I have removed all the critical vulnerabilities, reduced the overall vulnerability count, *and* reduced the size of the image to nearly a quarter, which will really improve download time and save costs. This is shown next:

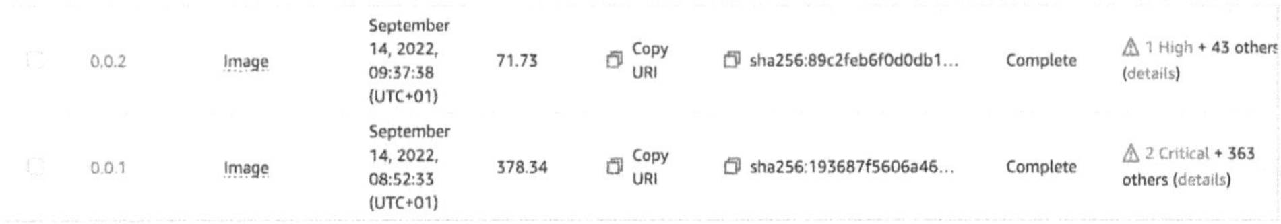

	0.0.2	Image	September 14, 2022, 09:37:38 (UTC+01)	71.73	🗐 Copy URI	🗐 sha256:89c2feb6f0d0db1...	Complete	⚠ 1 High + 43 others (details)
	0.0.1	Image	September 14, 2022, 08:52:33 (UTC+01)	378.34	🗐 Copy URI	🗐 sha256:193687f5606a46...	Complete	⚠ 2 Critical + 363 others (details)

Figure 11.3 – Improved container security posture and size

So, we have our image uploaded into ECR, the **CRITICAL** vulnerabilities have been remediated, and the size has been optimized. Next, let's look at some more advanced features of ECR before we demonstrate using that image in EKS.

Using advanced ECR features

ECR has two advanced features that are useful when you are managing a large EKS environment: **pull through cache**, which allows a private repository to cache public images, and **cross-region replication**, where you replicate images to another region for use. Let's explore both options.

Pull-through-cache explained

Pull-through-cache allows a private repository to cache images from either the public ECR repositories or from Quay (please note that Docker Hub is not currently supported). We will use the public ECR repositories in this example, and this allows us to offer public images without giving public internet access to our worker nodes.

Let's configure a rule in ECR using the following Terraform code; please note it's done at the registry level, not at the repository level:

```
resource "aws_ecr_pull_through_cache_rule" "example" {
  ecr_repository_prefix = "ecr-public"
  upstream_registry_url = "public.ecr.aws"
}
```

Once this is deployed, we can log in and use the ecr-public prefix to pull images. The following example pulls the latest Alpine image:

```
$ aws ecr get-login-password --region eu-central-1 | docker
login --username AWS --password-stdin 1122334.dkr.ecr.
eu-central-1.amazonaws.com/ecr-public
WARNING! Your password will be stored unencrypted in /home/
ec2-user/.docker/config.json.
.......
```

```
$ docker pull  1122334.dkr.ecr.eu-central-1.amazonaws.com/
ecr-public/docker/library/alpine:latest
latest: Pulling from ecr-public/docker/library/alpine
Digest: sha256:bc41182d7ef5ffc53a40b044e725193bc10142a1243f395
ee852a8d9730fc2ad
Status: Downloaded newer image for 1122334.dkr.ecr.
eu-central-1.amazonaws.com/ecr-public/docker/library/
alpine:latest
1122334.dkr.ecr.eu-central-1.amazonaws.com/ecr-public/docker/
library/alpine:latest
```

A corresponding private repository has now been created (see the following screenshot), with the pull-through cache enabled:

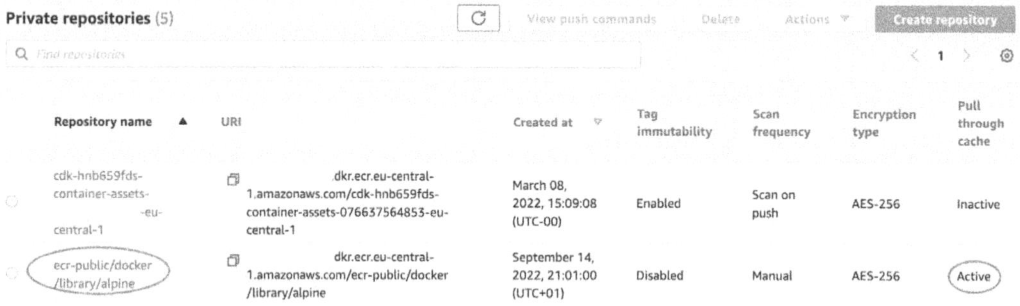
Private repositories (5)
View push commands
Delete
Actions
Create repository
Repository name
URI
Created at
Tag immutability
Scan frequency
Encryption type
Pull through cache
cdk-hnb659fds-container-assets- -eu-central-1
.dkr.ecr.eu-central-1.amazonaws.com/cdk-hnb659fds-container-assets-076637564853-eu-central-1
March 08, 2022, 15:09:08 (UTC-00)
Enabled
Scan on push
AES-256
Inactive
ecr-public/docker/library/alpine
dkr.ecr.eu-central-1.amazonaws.com/ecr-public/docker/library/alpine
September 14, 2022, 21:01:00 (UTC+01)
Disabled
Manual
AES-256
Active

Figure 11.4 – Pull-through-cache-enabled repository

Now we understand how we work with repositories in a single region, let's look at how we can work across different AWS regions.

Cross-region replication

You may want to deploy your application in multiple regions for **disaster recovery** (**DR**) reasons or for global reach. You can use cross-region replication to copy one, many, or all images from one region to another, or to multiple regions. You can do this in the same account or across different accounts, but bear in mind you need to set up a cross-account role if you want to replicate from one account to another.

Looking at the Terraform configuration shown next, we can see it consists of two parts. The first is a `destination` rule that states which region and account will be the target for the replication. Please note you can have multiple destination rules. The second part is optional and specifies a `filter` rule to select the repositories to replicate.

In the example shown next, we will use the `myapp` prefix. If this is not used, all images are replicated:

```
data "aws_caller_identity" "current" {}

resource "aws_ecr_replication_configuration" "euwest1" {
  replication_configuration {
    rule {
      destination {
        region      = "eu-west-1"
        registry_id = data.aws_caller_identity.current.account_
id
      }
      repository_filter {
        filter      = "myapp"
        filter_type = "PREFIX_MATCH"
      }
    }
  }
}
```

As only repository content pushed to a repository after replication is configured is replicated, we now need to push a new tag in order to see the image replicated to `eu-west-1`.

If you follow the commands shown in the *Building and pushing a container image to ECR* section, you can create a new image for the `myapp` repository and push it to ECR.

You will see it replicated to the region. If you use the AWS console and go to the relevant `repo/tag`, you can see the replication status. In the example shown next, `myapp:0.0.3` has been successfully replicated to `eu-west-1`:

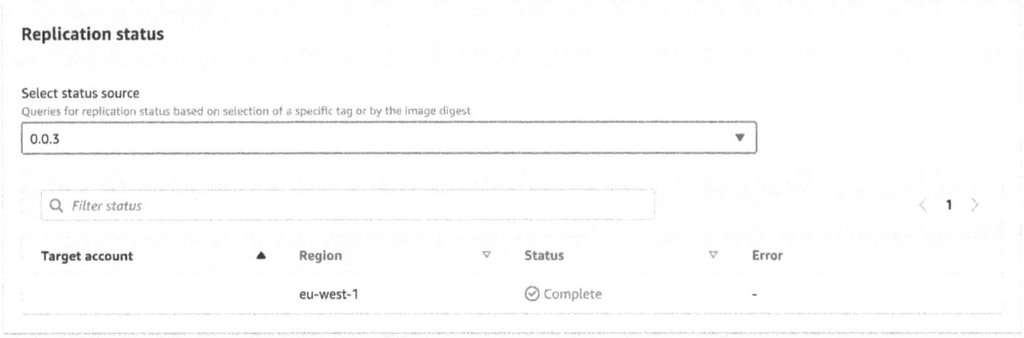

Replication status

Select status source
Queries for replication status based on selection of a specific tag or by the image digest

| 0.0.3 | ▼ |

| Q Filter status | ‹ 1 › |

Target account	▲	Region	▽	Status	▽	Error
		eu-west-1		⊘ Complete		-

Figure 11.5 – Replication status for new image tag

With this, we have explored the features and capabilities of ECR. Let's look at the final section and see how we use ECR images in EKS.

Using an ECR image in your EKS cluster

EKS worker nodes can pull images from ECR as they should have the `AmazonEC2ContainerRegistryReadOnly` managed role applied to the worker nodes.

So, the only thing that needs to be done is to specify the full `<aws_account_id>.dkr.ecr.aws_region.amazonaws.com/<image-name>:<tag>` ECR path in your Kubernetes manifest or Helm chart.

Building on *Chapter 4, Running Your First Application on EKS*, we create a deployment that uses our `myapp` container and a `NodePort` service that exposes that service outside the cluster. The only real difference is in the Pod spec, we reference the fully qualified image name. This is illustrated next. The first section defines the Kubernetes Deployment:

```
---
apiVersion: apps/v1
kind: Deployment
metadata:
  name: my-deployment
spec:
  selector:
    matchLabels:
      app: fastapi
  replicas: 1
  template:
    metadata:
      labels:
        app: fastapi
    spec:
      containers:
      - name: fastapi
        image: "1122334.dkr.ecr.eu-central-1.amazonaws.com/
myapp:0.0.2"
```

Now, we define the services:

```
---
apiVersion: v1
kind: Service
metadata:
  name: fastapi-dev
spec:
  type: NodePort
  selector:
    app: fastapi
  ports:
  - nodePort: 32410
    protocol: TCP
    port: 8080
    targetPort: 8080
```

As this is a `NodePort` service, we can get the IP address of the host the Pod is running on by running the following command:

```
$ kubectl get pod <podname> -o jsonpath={.status.hostIP}
```

We can then curl `http://<hostIP>:32410`, and we will see the FastAPI response message.

> **Important note**
> Please make sure the correct routing and security group rules are set up to allow your client to connect to the worker node IP address on port `32410`.

In this section, we have looked at how you can host your private images and deploy them into EKS with minimal changes to your manifests. We'll now revisit the key learning points from this chapter.

Summary

In this chapter, we explored how we can use ECR to store, cache, and replicate container images. Using ECR comes at a cost, which is made up of the total size of all images in your repository and egress costs, but by using the scan-on-push capability of ECR we can identify and resolve critical dependencies as well as optimize the size of the image, supporting a better security posture and more cost-effective images.

There are also more advanced features of ECR that allow us to support a DR strategy or deploy applications across multiple regions using cross-region replication as well as caching public images from the ECR public repositories or Quay. Finally, we looked at how you can configure IAM and repository policies to control access to the images inside and pull those images into EKS.

In the next chapter, we will look at how you can use the AWS storage driver to provide stateful storage to Pods as a source of your applications and Pods.

Further reading

- How the AWS Signature V4 signing process works: `https://docs.aws.amazon.com/general/latest/gr/signature-version-4.html`

- Using the ECR Public Gallery: `https://docs.aws.amazon.com/AmazonECR/latest/public/public-gallery.html`

- Using Clair to scan your containers: `https://github.com/quay/clair`

12

Deploying Pods with Amazon Storage

A guiding principle in most distributed or cloud-native applications is to limit the state where you can, and so far we have deployed Pods that are stateless, which means that when they are destroyed and recreated, any data they had is lost. In some cases, you might want to share data between containers in the Pod, maintain the state or content between reboots/re-deployments/crashes, or share data between Pods, in which case you need some sort of persistent storage.

This chapter looks at how you can use **Elastic Block Storage** (**EBS**) and **Elastic File System** (**EFS**) to persist the container state or content across multiple containers, Pods, or deployments. Specifically, we will cover the following key topics:

- Understanding Kubernetes volumes, the **Container Storage Interface** (**CSI**) driver, and storage on AWS

- Installing and configuring the AWS CSI drivers in your cluster

- Using EBS volumes with your application

- Using EFS volumes with your application

Technical requirements

You should be familiar with YAML, basic networking, and **Elastic Kubernetes Service** (**EKS**) architecture. Before getting started with this chapter, please ensure that you have the following:

- Network connectivity to your EKS cluster API endpoint

- The AWS **command-line interface** (**CLI**), Docker, and kubectl binary installed on your workstation

- A basic understanding of block and file storage systems

Understanding Kubernetes volumes, the CSI driver, and storage on AWS

The basic storage object within Kubernetes is a **volume**, which represents a directory (with or without data) that can be accessed by containers in a Pod. You can have ephemeral volumes that persist over container restarts but are aligned to the lifetime of the Pod and are destroyed by the Kubernetes scheduler when the Pod is destroyed. Persistent volumes are not destroyed by Kubernetes and exist separately from the Pod or Pods that use them.

The simplest example of an ephemeral volume is an `emptyDir` volume type. An example is shown next, which mounts host storage inside the containers using the `mountPath` key. As both containers use the same volume, they see the same data despite the fact it's mounted onto different mount points. When a Pod dies, crashes, or is removed from a node, the data in the `emptyDir` volume is deleted and lost:

```
apiVersion: v1
kind: Pod
metadata:
  name: empty-dir-example
spec:
  volumes:
  - name: shared-data
    emptyDir: {}
  containers:
  - name: nginx-container
    image: nginx
    volumeMounts:
    - name: shared-data
      mountPath: /usr/share/nginx/html
  - name: debian-container
    image: debian
    volumeMounts:
    - name: shared-data
      mountPath: /pod-data
    command: ["/bin/sh"]
    args: ["-c", "echo Hello from Debian > /pod-data/index.
html"]
```

> **Important note**
> The Pod will crash after it has run the `echo` command, but this is expected, so rest assured.

You can also create a persistent host volume using the `hostPath` type shown next. In this example, a volume is created and mapped to the host `/data` directory, which in turn, is mounted in the nginx container using the `mountPath` key. The main difference between this configuration and the previous `emptyDir` volume type is that any data stored on the volume will be persisted in the `/data` directory on the host even if the Pod is deleted:

```
apiVersion: v1
kind: Pod
metadata:
  name: host-path-example
spec:
  containers:
  - image: nginx
    name: test
    volumeMounts:
    - mountPath: /usr/share/nginx/html
      name: shared-data
  volumes:
  - name: shared-data
    hostPath:
            path: /data
```

The main challenge to these types of volumes is they are host-specific and so if there are any issues with the hosts, or if the Pod is scheduled on another host, the data is lost or not reachable.

Kubernetes started with more volume types, such as `awsElasticBlockStore`, which uses an external/non-host AWS resource and removes some of these constraints. The plugins that supported these external volume types were known as *in-tree*, as they were developed by the Kubernetes community. However, the effort required to support changes in the volume configuration and different volume types became too much, so the CSI was made generally available in Kubernetes 1.13.

The CSI specification acts as a way to expose block and file-based storage consistently, irrespective of the storage type or vendor. The CSI allows AWS (and other vendors) to develop and support storage drivers for its storage services, namely EBS and EFS.

Let's take a deeper look at these storage systems on AWS.

EBS

EBS is block-based storage that is typically attached to a single **Elastic Compute Cloud** (**EC2**) instance or Pod in a single **availability zone** (**AZ**). It comes in a variety of performance flavors from general-purpose (gp3 and gp2) and high-performance (io1 and io2) as well as SSD and HDD (magnetic) types. Amazon EBS volumes are billed by the **gigabyte-month** (**GB-month**), a measure of how many gigabytes of EBS storage are provisioned in your account and the length of time it is used for.

> **Important note**
> While EBS now supports attaching up to 16 nitro-based EC2 instances, in the same AZ, to a single EBS volume, this is a relatively new configuration option.

EFS

EFS is file-based storage based on NFS (NFSv4.1 and NFSv4.0), which allows multiple EC2 instances or Pods to access shared storage across multiple AZs. The storage provided by EFS can be regional (multi-AZ) or span a single AZ and can support both standard and infrequently accessed data patterns. Billing for Amazon EFS is based on the amount of storage used per month, measured in GB-months, as well as the storage class used and the duration of storage usage within your account.

The criteria used to choose between EBS and EFS vary but, generally, if you want a shared storage solution that can be used across multiple AZs, then EFS is a good candidate. EBS is normally used to provide persistent volumes within a single AZ with high throughput.

Let's look at how we install and configure the different CSI drivers for EBS and EFS in our cluster.

Installing and configuring the AWS CSI drivers in your cluster

We will install both the EBS and EFS drivers in this section. You will need a similar process for both, detailed next:

1. Create an **Identity and Access Management** (**IAM**) policy that will allow the plugin to perform AWS API calls for either EBS or EFS.
2. Create and map an IAM role to an EKS service account (this is discussed in detail in *Chapter 1)3*.
3. Deploy the plugin and configure it to use the service account created in *step 2*.

Installing and configuring the EBS CSI driver

The driver can be found at `https://github.com/kubernetes-sigs/aws-ebs-csi-driver`. Let's get down to installing it!

1. You can create the IAM policy from scratch or you can use the `AmazonEBSCSIDriverPolicy` AWS-managed policy.

2. We can now create the role. We will use the `–role-only` command-line switch, so we don't create the EKS service account. Using the following `eksctl` command, adjust the command line parameters as necessary:

```
$ eksctl create iamserviceaccount  --name ebs-csi-
controller-sa --namespace kube-system --cluster
myipv4cluster   --override-existing-serviceaccounts
--attach-policy-arn arn:aws:iam::aws:policy/service-
role/AmazonEBSCSIDriverPolicy  --approve --role-name
AmazonEKS_EBS_CSI_DriverRole --role-only
```

> **Important note**
>
> In the preceding example, we used the cluster we created in *Chapter 9*. If you use a different cluster, you will need to change the `--cluster` parameter to reflect your cluster name.

3. You can create an add-on for the EBS CSI controller using the following `eksctl` command, which will deploy the CSI Pods and also the service accounts needed to access the AWS API using the role created in *step 2*:

```
$ eksctl create addon --name aws-ebs-csi-driver
--cluster myipv4cluster   --service-account-role-
arn arn:aws:iam::11223344:role/AmazonEKS_EBS_CSI_
DriverRole  --force
2022-09-22 19:59:19 []  Kubernetes version "1.20" in use
by cluster "myipv4cluster"
.........
2022-09-22 20:00:28 []  addon "aws-ebs-csi-driver" active
```

4. You can validate whether the controller and DaemonSets are deployed using the following commands:

```
$ kubectl get pods -n kube-system | grep ebs
ebs-csi-controller-2233-p75xg    6/6      Running   1
ebs-csi-controller-3444-rb9zg    6/6      Running   0
ebs-csi-node-94pgc               3/3      Running   0
```

```
ebs-csi-node-mwdqc                    3/3      Running   0
ebs-csi-node-t9h77                    3/3      Running   0
$ kubectl logs deployment/ebs-csi-controller -n kube-
system -c csi-provisioner
.........
I0922 19:59:53.169651          1 leaderelection.go:258]
successfully acquired lease kube-system/ebs-csi-aws-com
.........
```

In the *Using EBS volumes with your application* section, we will see how you can attach EBS volumes directly to Pods, but before that, let's install the EFS driver.

Installing and configuring the EFS CSI driver

The driver can be found at `https://github.com/kubernetes-sigs/aws-efs-csi-driver`. Let's get down to installing it!

1. You can create the IAM policy from scratch or you can use the example policy found here: `https://raw.githubusercontent.com/kubernetes-sigs/aws-efs-csi-driver/master/docs/iam-policy-example.json`. The following commands can be used to download and create the IAM policy:

    ```
    $ curl -o iam-policy-example.json https://raw.
    githubusercontent.com/kubernetes-sigs/aws-efs-csi-driver/
    master/docs/iam-policy-example.json
    $ aws iam create-policy --policy-name AmazonEKS_EFS_
    CSI_Driver_Policy --policy-document file://iam-policy-
    example.json
    ```

2. We can now create the role and associated EKS service account using the following `eksctl` command and adjust the command line parameters as necessary (you will need to specify the **Amazon Resource Name** (**ARN**) of the policy created in *step 1*, as well as the cluster name and Region). The most important aspect to verify is that the new service account has an annotation for the new IAM role:

    ```
    $ eksctl create iamserviceaccount   --cluster
    myipv4cluster      --namespace kube-system   --name
    efs-csi-controller-sa --attach-policy-arn
    arn:aws:iam::11223344:policy/AmazonEKS_EFS_CSI_Driver_
    Policy      --approve   --region eu-central-1
    2022-09-22 20:32:29 []   3 existing iamserviceaccount(s)
    (kube-system/ebs-csi-controller-sa,kube-system/
    eni-allocator,kube-system/multus) will be exclude
    ```

```
.........
022-09-22 20:32:59 []   created serviceaccount "kube-
system/efs-csi-controller-sa"
$ kubectl describe sa efs-csi-controller-sa -n kube-
system
Name:                   efs-csi-controller-sa
.......
Annotations:            eks.amazonaws.com/role-arn:
arn:aws:iam::076637564853:role/eksctl-myipv4cluster-
addon-iamserviceaccount-Role1-P08589EN3NY7
...••
```

3. We will use Helm to install this EFS CSI driver as, unlike the EBS driver, at the time of writing, the EFS driver is not supported as an add-on. The following command will add the EFS repository to Helm and deploy the Helm chart, re-using the EKS service account that was created in *step 2*:

> **Important note**
>
> Image.repository is Region-specific, and the relevant repositories can be found at https://docs.aws.amazon.com/eks/latest/userguide/add-ons-images.html.

```
$ helm repo add aws-efs-csi-driver https://kubernetes-
sigs.github.io/aws-efs-csi-driver/
$ helm repo update
$ helm search repo aws-efs-csi-driver
NAME CHART VERSION   APP VERSION     DESCRIPTION
aws-efs-csi-driver/aws-efs-csi-driver   2.2.7 1.4.0 A
Helm chart for AWS EFS CSI Driver
$ helm upgrade -i aws-efs-csi-driver aws-efs-csi-
driver/aws-efs-csi-driver --namespace kube-system --set
image.repository=602401143452.dkr.ecr.eu-central-1.
amazonaws.com/eks/aws-efs-csi-driver --set controller.
serviceAccount.create=false --set controller.
serviceAccount.name=efs-csi-controller-sa
$ kubectl get pod -n kube-system -l "app.kubernetes.io/
name=aws-efs-csi-driver,app.kubernetes.io/instance=aws-
efs-csi-driver"
NAME                      READY   STATUS    RESTARTS   AGE
efs-csi-controller-122-hrzfg        3/3     Running   0
efs-csi-controller-1234-q8wpt       3/3     Running   0
efs-csi-node-2g46k                  3/3     Running   0
```

```
efs-csi-node-59rsx                          3/3      Running   0
efs-csi-node-ncsk8                          3/3      Running   0
$ kubectl logs deployment/efs-csi-controller -n kube-
system -c csi-provisioner
.........
I0922 20:51:53.306805        1 leaderelection.go:253]
successfully acquired lease kube-system/efs-csi-aws-com
......
```

> **Important note**
> The EFS plugin will require a pre-configured EFS cluster to be available; we will discuss how this can be created in the *Using EFS volumes with your application* section.

Now we have both drivers installed and running, we can look at how they can be used by Pods to store data.

Using EBS volumes with your application

Kubernetes has three main `kinds` that are used for persistent storage. The **PersistentVolume** (**PV**) represents the actual storage in the attached storage system, in our case, an EBS volume. The other components are a **StorageClass** (**SC**), which defines the characteristics of the storage, and a **PersistentVolumeClaim** (**PVC**), which represents a request for storage that is fulfilled by a PV based on an SC.

The reason a PVC exists is that different Pods may require different types of storage, for example, storage shared between many Pods or dedicated to just one. The PVC provides an abstraction between what a developer or DevOps engineer needs for their application and the type of storage provided by the cluster administrator.

The following diagram illustrates the relationship between an EBS volume, PV, PVC, and a Pod:

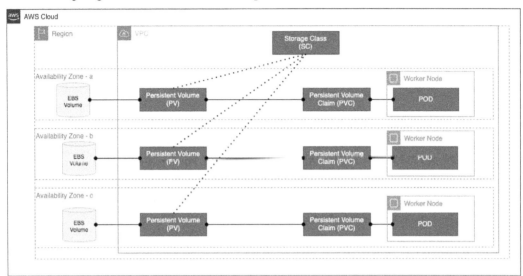

Figure 12.1 – EBS volumes

It's important to know that an EBS volume is specific to a Region and an AZ; you can't move EBS volumes between AZs. Instead, you need to create a snapshot and then create a new volume in the new AZ. A PV (EBS volume) can be created statically by an AWS administrator or dynamically as you consume a PVC, but it can only be consumed by worker nodes in the same AZ as the volume itself.

We will focus on the dynamic creation of the volumes, as this is the simplest method to implement. The latest EBS CSI driver automatically creates a gp2 SC and this can be viewed by using the following commands:

```
$ kubectl get storageclass
NAME    PROVISIONER    RECLAIMPOLICY    VOLUMEBINDINGMODE
ALLOWVOLUMEEXPANSION    AGE
gp2 (default)    kubernetes.io/aws-ebs    Delete
WaitForFirstConsumer    false    50d
```

We want to use gp3, which is a more cost-effective form of storage and performant type on AWS, so let's create a new SC using the following manifest and deploy it using the $ kubectl create -f SC-config.yaml command:

```
kind: StorageClass
apiVersion: storage.k8s.io/v1
metadata:
```

```
  name: gp3
provisioner: ebs.csi.aws.com # Amazon EBS CSI driver
parameters:
  type: gp3
  encrypted: 'true'
volumeBindingMode: WaitForFirstConsumer
reclaimPolicy: Delete
```

We can now create a PVC that will leverage the new SC. As we are using dynamic provisioning, we don't have to create a PV, as this will be created once we deploy a Pod that references the new PVC.

The following manifest will create the PVC and it can be deployed using the `$ kubectl create -f VC-config.yaml` command. The manifest contains the SC that will be used, in our case gp3, as well as the size of the volume to create 4 Gi. We don't specify any encryption requirements in the PVC, but as that is set in the SC, the volume will be encrypted; we could create a non-encrypted gp3 SC as well if we wanted to allow developers to choose an unencrypted volume:

```
apiVersion: v1
kind: PersistentVolumeClaim
metadata:
  name: ebs-claim
spec:
  accessModes:
    - ReadWriteOnce
  storageClassName: gp3
  resources:
    requests:
      storage: 4Gi
```

`accessModes` defines how the volume can be attached, and these are listed next; however, EBS will only support `ReadWriteOnce`:

- `ReadWriteOnce (RWO)`: This volume can be mounted as read-write by a single node.

- `ReadOnlyMany (ROX)`: This volume can be mounted read-only by many nodes.

- `ReadWriteMany (RWX)`: This volume can be mounted as read-write by many nodes.

- `ReadWriteOncePod (RWOP)`: This volume can be mounted as read-write by a single Pod.

The following commands show the PVC being created in a pending state (as no Pod has made a claim against it), and no associated EBS volume (PV) has been created, as the PVC is still in a pending state:

```
$ kubectl create -f ebs-pvc.yaml
persistentvolumeclaim/ebs-claim created
$ kubectl get pvc
NAME STATUS VOLUME CAPACITYACCESS MODES STORAGECLASS     AGE
ebs-claim    Pending               gp3               10s
$ kubectl get pv
No resources found
```

We can now deploy a Pod that uses this PVC, which, in turn, will, using the EBS CSI driver, create a new EBS volume (dynamic provisioning) and attach it to the Pod as specified by mountPath in the Pod specification.

> **Important note**
> It's worth noting that the Pod deployment time will take longer as the EBS volume needs to be created first. If a quicker startup time is needed, then static provisioning can be used and the PV can be created before the Pod.

The following manifest will create the Pod and references the PVC created previously. It can be deployed using the $ kubectl create -f ebs-pod.yaml command:

```
apiVersion: v1
kind: Pod
metadata:
  name: app
spec:
  containers:
  - name: app
    image: debian
    command: ["/bin/sh"]
    args: ["-c", "while true; do echo $(date -u) >> /data/out.
txt; sleep 5; done"]
    volumeMounts:
    - name: persistent-storage
```

```
        mountPath: /data
    volumes:
    - name: persistent-storage
      persistentVolumeClaim:
        claimName: ebs-claim
```

We use the following commands to verify the successful deployment of the Pod and the creation of the EBS volume. Once the Pod is created, we can see the PVC is now in a Bound state and a new PV is created also in a Bound state:

```
$ kubectl create -f ebs-pod.yaml
pod/app created
$ kubectl get pvc
NAME STATUS VOLUME CAPACITY ACCESS MODES STORAGECLASS AGE
ebs-claim    Bound    pvc-18661cce-cda5-4779-86b4-
21cb76a5ecc0    4Gi        RWO        gp3        30m
$ kubectl get pv
NAME CAPACITY    ACCESS MODES    RECLAIM POLICY    STATUS    CLAIM
pvc-1 4Gi RWO Delete    Bound    default/ebs-claim    gp3    17s
```

If we look in detail at the PV, we can see the ID of the volume created in AWS by looking at the VolumeHandle key:

```
$ kubectl describe pv pvc-1
Name:            pvc-1
Labels:          <none>
...
StorageClass:    gp3
Status:          Bound
Claim:           default/ebs-claim
Reclaim Policy:  Delete
Access Modes:    RWO
VolumeMode:      Filesystem
Capacity:        4Gi
Node Affinity:
  Required Terms:
    Term 0: topology.ebs.csi.aws.com/zone in [eu-central-1b]
Message:
Source:
```

```
Type:   CSI ( (CSI) volume source)
Driver:            ebs.csi.aws.com
FSType:            ext4
VolumeHandle:      vol-00f7c5d865ef5c14f
ReadOnly:          false
...
```

When the PVC is removed, the reclaim policy (defaulting to what is defined in the SC for dynamic provisioning) dictates what happens. In the previous example, Reclaim Policy is Delete, which means the Kubernetes resources (the PV and PVC) will be deleted, along with the associated EBS volume. If you want to preserve the EBS volume, then the Retain value should be set in the SC.

Now, go into the AWS console and search for the volume ID. The example shown next illustrates the volume, the provisioned size, and the type, along with the **Key Management Service (KMS)** details and throughput:

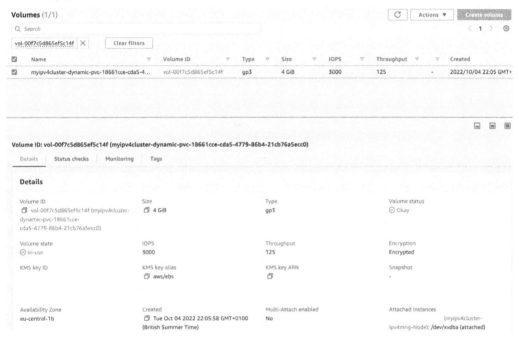

Figure 12.2 – The AWS console EBS volumes

Now we have set up block-based storage using EBS, let's look at how we can use filesystem-based storage shared between multiple Pods using EFS.

Using EFS volumes with your application

EFS is a shared storage platform unlike EBS, so while at the Kubernetes level, you have the same objects, SC, PV, and PVCs, the way you access the storage and how the storage is created are quite different.

The following diagram illustrates the relationship between an EFS instance/volume and the Kubernetes PV, PVC, and Pod:

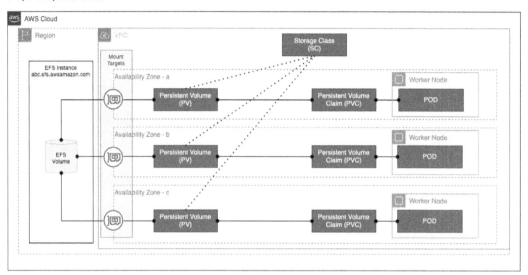

Figure 12.3 – EFS volumes

Although we have installed the CSI driver, we can't provision volumes without an EFS instance and mount targets in the required subnets. Let's look at how we can create them next.

Creating the EFS instance and mount targets

You can do this in a variety of ways, but we will use the AWS CLI. Let's start by creating the EFS filesystem and retrieving the filesystem ID. The following command will create the EFS instance and filter the response to only return `FileSystemId`. Please adjust the `-region` parameter to account for the Region you're using:

```
$ aws efs create-file-system --region
eu-central-1  --performance-mode generalPurpose --query
'FileSystemId' --output text
fs-078166286587fc22
```

The next step is to identify the subnets we want to use for our mount targets. Ideally, we place the mount targets in the same subnets as the worker nodes. The following commands will list all the subnets for a given **virtual private cloud** (VPC) (you will need to supply the correct VPC-ID) and then list which subnets and security groups are being used by your managed node group:

```
$ aws ec2 describe-subnets  --filters "Name=vpc-
id,Values=vpc-123" --query 'Subnets[*].{SubnetId:
SubnetId,AvailabilityZone: AvailabilityZone,CidrBlock:
CidrBlock}'  --output table
+-------------------+--------------------+------------------+
| AvailabilityZone  |      CidrBlock      |     SubnetId      |
+-------------------+--------------------+------------------+
|   eu-central-1a   |  192.168.96.0/19   |    subnet-1      |
|   eu-central-1b   |  192.168.32.0/19   |    subnet-2      |
|   eu-central-1a   |  192.168.0.0/19    |    subnet-3      |
|   eu-central-1c   |  192.168.160.0/19  |    subnet-4      |
|   eu-central-1c   |  192.168.64.0/19   |    subnet-5      |
+-------------------+--------------------+------------------+
$ aws ec2 describe-instances --filters
"Name=tag:aws:eks:cluster-name,Values=myipv4cluster"  --query
"Reservations[*].Instances[*].
{Instance:InstanceId,Subnet:SubnetId,
PrivateIP:PrivateIpAddress}"  --output table
+--------------------+--------------------+------------------+
|     Instance       |     PrivateIP      |     Subnet        |
+--------------------+--------------------+------- -------+
|  i-01437f1b219217d8a|  192.168.12.212   |   subnet-3      |
|  i-0f74d4d5b7e5dc146|  192.168.70.114   |   subnet-5      |
|  i-04c48cc4d2ac11ca6|  192.168.63.61    |   subnet-2      |
+--------------------+--------------------+------------------+
```

We can see from the previous output that we should create mount points in subnets 3, 5, and 2, as this is where our worker nodes that belong to myipv4cluster are placed.

> **Important note**
> These subnets also cover the three AZs for high-availability reasons.

We can now identify what security groups are being used by these instances using the next command. In our case, the instances are all part of the same security group, as they belong to the same managed node group. We will use this for the EFS mount targets for simplicity, but you may want to create a separate security group for EFS. However, ensure that any security group you use allows the TCP/2049 port between the Pods and the EFS mount targets:

```
$ aws ec2 describe-instances --filters
"Name=tag:aws:eks:cluster-name,Values=myipv4cluster"    --query
"Reservations[*].Instances[*].SecurityGroups[*]"   --output
table
|GroupId  |                      GroupName                    |
+---------------------------+-------------------------------+
|   sg-123  |    eks-cluster-sg-myipv4cluster-940370103  |
|   sg-123  |    eks-cluster-sg-myipv4cluster-940370103  |
|   sg-123  |    eks-cluster-sg-myipv4cluster-940370103  |
+---------------------------+-------------------------------+
```

We can now create and verify the mount points, one per subnet/AZ, using the following commands. When we verify the mount targets, you will see the IP address assigned to the **Elastic Network Interface** (**ENI**) placed in the subnet, which will be used by the Pods:

```
$ aws efs create-mount-target --file-system-id
fs-078166286587fc22--security-groups sg-123 --subnet-id
subnet-3
<repeat for remaining subnets>
$ aws efs describe-mount-targets --file-system-id
fs-078166286587fc22 --query "MountTargets[*].
{id:MountTargetId,az:AvailabilityZoneName,
subnet:SubnetId,EFSIP:IpAddress}" --output

+----------------+-----------------+-------------+-----------+
| EFSIP          |       az        |     id      |  subnet   |
+----------------+-----------------+-------------+-----------+
|   192.168.10.59 |  eu-central-1a  |   fsmt-22   |  subnet-3  |
|   192.168.66.201|  eu-central-1c  |   fsmt-33   |  subnet-4  |
|   192.168.34.140|  eu-central-1b  |   fsmt-44   |  subnet-5  |
+----------------+-----------------+-------------+-----------+
```

We have now set up EFS and made it available to the Pods; the next steps are almost identical to EBS and involve setting up the Kubernetes object to use EFS.

Creating your EFS cluster objects

We need to create the SC and example manifest as shown in the following code snippet. You will need to replace the fileSystemId key and then deploy it using the $ kubectl create -f SC-config.yaml command:

```
kind: StorageClass
apiVersion: storage.k8s.io/v1
metadata:
  name: efs-sc
provisioner: efs.csi.aws.com
parameters:
  provisioningMode: efs-ap
  fileSystemId: fs-078166286587fc22
  directoryPerms: "700"
```

We can now create the PVC that consumes the SC using the following manifest, and then deploy it using the $ kubectl create -f pvc.yaml command. Please note that accessMode is now set to ReadWriteMany, as this is shared storage:

```
apiVersion: v1
kind: PersistentVolumeClaim
metadata:
  name: efs-claim
spec:
  accessModes:
    - ReadWriteMany
  storageClassName: efs-sc
  resources:
    requests:
      storage: 5Gi
```

If we review the PVC and PV that get created using the commands shown next, we can see the new PVC and the PV are created and bound, as again, we are using dynamic provisioning. This is different from EBS where it's only when the PVC is *used* that the PV gets created. With EFS, you are charged only for what you use, unlike an EBS volume, which you get charged for as soon as it is created, so there are no issues with creating the PVC/PV combination as soon as the PVC is created:

```
$ kubectl get pvc
NAME STATUS VOLUME CAPACITY ACCESS MODES   STORAGECLASS   AGE
```

```
ebs-claim Bound   pvc-1    4Gi     RWO      gp3               14h
efs-claim Bound   pvc-2    5Gi     RWX      efs-sc            4s
$kubectl get pv
NAME CAPACITY ACCESS MODES RECLAIM STATUS CLAIM SC REASON AGE
pvc-1 4Gi RWO Delete Bound default/ebs-claim gp3 16h
pvc-2 5Gi RWX Delete Bound default/efs-claim efs-sc  2m1s
```

If you look in the controller logs (an example is shown next), you can see the CSI driver making a call to create the volume:

```
$ kubectl logs efs-csi-controller-xx -n kube-system  -c
csi-provisioner   --tail 10
..........
I1005 10:55:45.301869   1 event.go:282] Event (v1.
ObjectReference {Kind:"PersistentVolumeClaim",
Namespace:"default", Name:"efs-claim", UID:"323",
APIVersion:"v1", ResourceVersion:"15905560", FieldPath:""}):
type: 'Normal' reason: 'Provisioning' External provisioner is
provisioning volume for claim "default/efs-claim"
I1005 10:55:46.515609         1 controller.go:838] successfully
created PV pvc-2 for PVC efs-claim and csi volume name
fs-078166286587fc22::fsap-013a6156108263624
```

The final step is to provision the Pod to use the PVC and attach the EFS volume to a mount point within the container. The manifest shown next will create a single CentOS-based container and mount the volume under /data, which can be deployed using the $ kubectl create -f pod2. yaml command:

```
apiVersion: v1
kind: Pod
metadata:
  name: efs-app
spec:
  containers:
    - name: app
      image: centos
      command: ["/bin/sh"]
      args: ["-c", "while true; do echo $(date -u) >> /data/
out; sleep 5; done"]
      volumeMounts:
```

```
      - name: persistent-storage
        mountPath: /data
  volumes:
    - name: persistent-storage
      persistentVolumeClaim:
        claimName: efs-claim
```

You can validate whether data is being produced and stored in EFS using the following command. If you delete and recreate the Pod, the previous Pod's data will be persisted:

```
$ kubectl exec -it efs-app -- tail /data/out
Wed Oct 5 20:56:03 UTC 2022
Wed Oct 5 20:56:08 UTC 2022
```

As `Reclaim Policy` is set to `Delete` (by default), if you delete the PVC, you will remove the PV and corresponding EFS data. To sum up, in this section, we have looked at how to install and configure the EBS and EFS CSI drivers and how we use them to create persistent storage for your Pods. We'll now revisit the key learning points from this chapter.

Summary

In this chapter, we explored how EBS (block) differs from EFS (filesystem) storage. We identified that EBS is normally used where you need to provide dedicated volumes per Pod, is fixed in size, and is charged as soon as you provision it. Meanwhile, EFS is shared storage and can therefore be mounted across multiple Pods, can scale as needed, and you are only charged for what you use.

We also discussed how EFS requires more setup than EBS, as the EBS filesystem and mount targets need to be deployed prior to it being used in EKS. EFS can be viewed as more complex to set up as it's a shared storage platform, whereas EBS is just network-attached storage for a single node. EBS is generally cheaper to provision and use but it is mostly only used for columns attached to a single instance (EC2).

We then reviewed how to install the CSI drivers, creating an add-on for the EBS CSI driver and Helm for the EFS CSI driver. Once the drivers were installed, we explored the Kubernetes objects (SC, PVC, and PV) and how we can use dynamic provisioning to create the volumes in EBS and EFS from Kubernetes rather than having an administrator provision the volumes for us.

In the next chapter, we will look at how you can grant IAM permissions to your applications/Pods, allowing them to use AWS services.

Further reading

- EBS volume types: `https://docs.aws.amazon.com/AWSEC2/latest/UserGuide/ebs-volume-types.html`

- EFS SC: `https://docs.aws.amazon.com/efs/latest/ug/storage-classes.html`

- When to use EFS: `https://aws.amazon.com/efs/when-to-choose-efs/`

- EBS multi-attach versus EFS: `https://www.youtube.com/watch?v=3ORzqOjtsmE`

- Troubleshooting EFS: `https://docs.aws.amazon.com/efs/latest/ug/troubleshooting-efs-general.html`

13

Using IAM for Granting Access to Applications

AWS has over 200 services available, from SQL/NoSQL databases to machine learning and quantum computing. It's likely that at some point you will want to use one of these services from within your application deployed on EKS.

This chapter looks at how you can grant IAM permissions to Pods, how you use the associated credentials in your application to connect to an AWS service, and how to troubleshoot issues with the overall process. Specifically, we will cover the following:

- Understanding what **IAM Roles for Service Accounts (IRSA)** is and what problems it solves
- Using IRSA in your application
- How to troubleshoot IAM issues on EKS

Technical requirements

The reader should be familiar with YAML, AWS IAM, and EKS architecture. Before getting started with this chapter, please ensure the following:

- You have network connectivity to your EKS cluster API endpoint
- The AWS CLI, Docker, and the kubectl binaries are installed on your workstation
- You have a basic understanding of AWS IAM

Understanding IRSA

Firstly, let's look at how IAM role assignment works for standard EC2 instances. In AWS IAM, roles are used to allocate permissions (using one or more policies). A role can be assigned to an EC2 instance using an instance profile, which is simply a container for the IAM role that's attached to a specific EC2 instance.

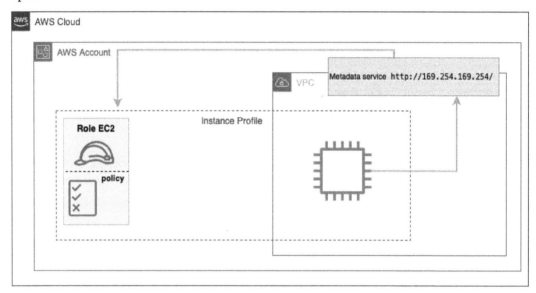

Figure 13.1 – EC2 role assignment

When an EC2 instance is created and assigned a role, the AWS platform will automatically create an instance profile. When that instance boots up, it will make a network call to the **instance metadata service** (**IMDS**), which runs in the VPC at the well-known address, 169.254.169.254, and query what (if any) instance profile (or role) is assigned to that instance. If one has been assigned, it can retrieve the access credentials, an example of which is shown next. These credentials consist of the access and secret keys, which are used for all AWS API calls and identify the role and therefore the permissions granted to the role:

```
{ "Code" : "Success",
  "LastUpdated" : "2022-04-26T16:39:16Z",
  "Type" : "AWS-HMAC",
  "AccessKeyId" : "ASIAIOSFODNN7EXAMPLE",
  "SecretAccessKey" : "bPxRfiCYEXAMPLEKEY",
  "Token" : "token",
  "Expiration" : "2022-05-17T15:09:54Z"}
```

If you log in to an EC2 instance, you can review the instance profile attached to a running instance using the `aws sts` command, which is shown next:

```
$ aws sts get-caller-identity
{
  "UserId": "hdghd78898:i-014",
  "Account": "11223344,
  "Arn": "arn:aws:sts::11223344:assumed-role/<IPROFILE>/i-014"
}
```

AWS introduced IMDSv2 to provide some security controls on container platforms, so let's review the main changes.

Introducing IMDSv2

As we have discussed, the instance profile information is retrieved through the EC2 IMDS, which runs at address `169.254.169.254` in every VPC. This service is critical to the operation of EC2 instances and should not be blocked for the worker nodes, but it should be restricted for Pods. The original IMDS version, version 1, doesn't allow any restrictions to be placed on who can use it.

IMDSv2 is an enhancement to IMDSv1 that uses session-oriented requests to add security controls to the service. IMDSv2 returns a token, which is used to make requests for metadata and credentials. As the token is never stored in IMDSv2, when the process or application using the token ends, the token is lost. The metadata service uses the TTL hop count in the IPv4/IPv6 packet to allow requests. By default, it is set to 1, which means requests can only come directly from the EC2. Any Pods running on the host will increment the hop count to 2 (as they use the bridge network inside the hots), which prevents them from using the IMDSv2 service directly and retrieving host instance profile credentials.

To force the use of IMDSv2 and restrict the hop count, you can run the following command on all the worker nodes or add the configuration into your **infrastructure-as-code** (**IaC**) definition for the launch template used for the worker nodes:

```
$ aws ec2 modify-instance-metadata-options --instance-id
i-1122233 --http-tokens required --http-put-response-hop-limit
1
{
    "InstanceId": "i-112233",
    "InstanceMetadataOptions": {
        "State": "pending",
        "HttpEndpoint": "enabled",
        "HttpTokens": "required",
        "HttpPutResponseHopLimit": 1
```

```
    }
  }
```

This only works, however, if the Pod uses IMDSv2. In most cases, the Pod uses the AWS SDK to make AWS API calls, which defaults to IMDSv2 to retrieve the credentials. These will have the hop limit applied. However, if the Pod uses IMDSv1, it can still retrieve the host credentials. In this case, the best practice is only to give the worker nodes minimal permissions (to pull ECR containers, for example) or limit access to IMDSv1 using Calico network policies or `iptables` rules.

Now, we've looked at the underlying mechanism of how instances and Pods can use IMDS to retrieve credentials (and how we can restrict them from doing so). Let's look at how we can assign specific roles directly to Pods using IRSA.

How IRSA works

IRSA allows you to assign specific privileges to a specific Pod by associating a Kubernetes **service account (SA)** with an IAM role, shown in *Figure 13.2* as step **1**. When the Pod makes an API call, it will try to use the SA credentials, which have an annotation mapping to an IAM role (step **2**). This call is translated into an `AssumeRoleWithWebIdentity` API call to the AWS **Security Token Service (STS)**, which will exchange the Kubernetes-generated credentials for AWS IAM-generated credentials. It does this by using the OIDC provider for a specific EKS cluster as the principal and assuming the role that is defined in the SA annotation (step **3**).

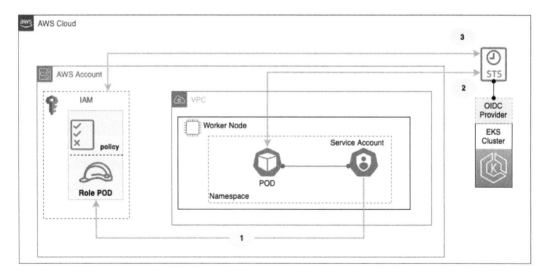

Figure 13.2 – How IRSA works

Now we understand at a high level how IRSA will work, let's look at what we need to configure so that a Pod can use IRSA.

Using IRSA in your application

Now that you understand the basic concepts behind IRSA, let's look at how you can configure and use it in your applications. We will look at how to deploy a Pod manually and configure it to use IRSA and then we will look at how you can really simplify the process using `eksctl`.

How to deploy a Pod and use IRSA credentials

The first step is to make sure you have an OIDC provider configured for your cluster. If you used `eksctl`, this will be configured already:

```
$ aws eks describe-cluster --name myipv4cluster --query
"cluster.identity.oidc.issuer" --output text
https://oidc.eks.eu-central-1.amazonaws.com/id/763683678
```

If you haven't enabled it, you can use the following `eksctl` command:

```
$ eksctl utils associate-iam-oidc-provider --cluster cluster_
name –approve
```

Now that we have an identity for our cluster that we can use, in IAM, we can create the relevant policies and roles. Let's assume we want to give our Pod access to all S3 buckets and objects in the account. So, we will use the following policy to provide S3 access:

```
{ "Version": "2012-10-17",
    "Statement": [
        {
            "Effect": "Allow",
            "Action": [
                "s3:GetAccountPublicAccessBlock",
                "s3:GetBucketAcl",
                "s3:GetBucketLocation",
                "s3:GetBucketPolicyStatus",
                "s3:GetBucketPublicAccessBlock",
                "s3:ListAccessPoints",
                "s3:ListAllMyBuckets"
            ],
            "Resource": "*"
        }
    ]
}
```

We will then create the policy in our AWS account using the following command:

```
$ aws iam create-policy --policy-name bespoke-pod-policy
--policy-document file://s3-policy.json
{
    "Policy": {
        "PolicyName": "bespoke-pod-policy",
        "PermissionsBoundaryUsageCount": 0,
        "CreateDate": "2022-11-09T15:03:58Z",
        "AttachmentCount": 0,
        "IsAttachable": true,
        "PolicyId": "ANPARDV7UN626ZCPMFH4X",
        "DefaultVersionId": "v1",
        "Path": "/",
        "Arn": "arn:aws:iam::112233444:policy/bespoke-pod-
policy",
        "UpdateDate": "2022-11-09T15:03:58Z"
    }
}
```

Now, we have the policy we need to create the role and allow the EKS cluster OIDC provider and Kubernetes SA combination to assume that role. The following commands will allow you to do this. Let's initially set up some environment variables for the AWS account, the EKS OIDC provider, the Kubernetes namespace, and SA:

```
$ export account_id=$(aws sts get-caller-identity --query
"Account" --output text)
$ export oidc_provider=$(aws eks describe-cluster --name
myipv4cluster --region eu-central-1 --query "cluster.identity.
oidc.issuer" --output text | sed -e "s/^https:\/\///")
$ export namespace=default
$ export service_account=s3-access
```

We can now create the trust relationship for the role that the Pod will assume using the following command:

```
cat >trust-relationship.json <<EOF
{
    "Version": "2012-10-17",
    "Statement": [
```

```
    {
        "Effect": "Allow",
        "Principal": {
           "Federated": "arn:aws:iam::$account_id:oidc-
provider/$oidc_provider"
        },
        "Action": "sts:AssumeRoleWithWebIdentity",
        "Condition": {
           "StringEquals": {
              "$oidc_provider:aud": "sts.amazonaws.com",
              "$oidc_provider:sub":
"system:serviceaccount:$namespace:$service_account"
           }
        }
     }
   ]
}
EOF
```

All this is doing is defining the mapping for the EKS OIDC provider and Kubernetes namespace and SA, so we need to create the role with this trust relationship and attach the policy we created previously to allow S3 access using the following commands:

```
$ aws iam create-role --role-name s3-access-default --assume-
role-policy-document file://trust-relationship.json
--description "s3 access role for pod SA s3-access/default"
{
    "Role": {
        .........
        "Arn": "arn:aws:iam::11223344:role/s3-access-default"
    }
}
$ aws iam attach-role-policy --role-name s3-access-default
--policy-arn=arn:aws:iam::$account_id:policy/bespoke-pod-policy
```

We have now set up everything that's needed in the AWS IAM, so now we just need to configure a Pod to use the SA in the namespace defined here. Let's start by configuring the SA in the `default` namespace:

```
$ cat >my-service-account.yaml <<EOF
apiVersion: v1
kind: ServiceAccount
metadata:
  name: s3-access
  namespace: default
EOF
$ kubectl apply -f my-service-account.yaml
$ kubectl annotate serviceaccount -n $namespace $service_
account eks.amazonaws.com/role-arn=arn:aws:iam::$account_
id:role/s3-access-default
serviceaccount/s3-access annotated
$ kubectl describe sa $service_account
Name:                s3-access
Namespace:           default
Labels:              <none>
Annotations:         eks.amazonaws.com/role-arn:
arn:aws:iam::11223344:role/s3-access-default
Image pull secrets:  <none>
Mountable secrets:   s3-access-token-9z6
Tokens:              s3-access-token-9z6
Events:              <none>
```

We can now run a Pod using the SA with the following commands. This will use the `aws-cli` image and run the `aws s3 ls` command, which should be able to list the buckets, as the assigned SA has the necessary permissions exposed through the role:

```
$ kubectl run -rm -ti cli  --image=amazon/aws-cli -overrides="{
'spec': { 'serviceAccount': 's3-access' }  }" s3 ls
2022-09-29 09:26:05 ingress-123-bb
2022-03-29 17:49:50 servicecatalog456643
.......
```

If you change the `serviceAccount` value to `default`, you will see the command fail, as the default SA has no annotation and therefore no mapping to a valid IAM role. Now, let's look at how we can make this process easier using IaC.

How to create an IRSA role programmatically

We have used the `eksctl create iamserviceaccount` command from the previous chapter to allow the Pods hosting the storage controllers to communicate with the AWS storage APIs.

If we look at the generic command, we can see we have associated a Kubernetes SA in a specific namespace with a specific IAM policy. The policy defines what API action can be performed and the association of an SA to a Pod allows that Pod to perform that action:

```
$ eksctl create iamserviceaccount
--cluster=<clusterName> --name=<serviceAccountName>
--namespace=<serviceAccountNamespace> --attach-policy-
arn=<policyARN>
```

So, in comparison to the previous section, the only thing we need to pre-provision is the policy with the relevant permissions, so we can provide `policyARN`. The `eksctl` tool will do the following:

1. Determine the EKS cluster OIDC provider.

2. Create the role with a trust policy using the derived OIDC details and the Kubernetes SA name and namespace provided.

3. Attach the pre-created policy to the IAM role.

4. Create the Kubernetes SA with the right annotations in the right namespace.

You can now run the `kubectl run` command we used previously in the namespace and then use the SA specified in the `eksctl` command, and it should all work. Let's look at how we can troubleshoot IRSA if there are any issues.

How to troubleshoot IAM issues on EKS

The first thing you need to do is determine whether this is an IAM permissions issue. If we look at the error message in the following example, we can see a very clear `AccessDenied` error message for an AWS API operation – in this case, the `ListBuckets` operations. This is a clear indicator that it's an IAM error:

```
$ kubectl run -ti cli   --image=amazon/aws-cli --overrides='{
"spec": { "serviceAccount": "default" }  }' s3 ls
If you don't see a command prompt, try pressing enter.
An error occurred (AccessDenied) when calling the ListBuckets
operation: Access Denied
```

The first step is to determine which SA is being used and work backward from there. In the example, it's pretty clear, as we have the run command. However, assuming we don't have it, we can use the next command to figure it out:

```
$ kubectl get po cli -o yaml | grep serviceAccountName
    serviceAccountName: default
```

We can then run the following command to make sure the annotation is in place and identify what role will be assumed:

```
$ kubectl describe sa default
Name:                default
Namespace:           default
Labels:              <none>
Annotations:         <none>
Image pull secrets:  <none>
Mountable secrets:   default-token-wjpnc
Tokens:              default-token-wjpnc
Events:              <none>
```

In this case, there is no annotation, so it's clear this SA has no permissions. If there was a role assigned, we could use the following commands to determine whether it was a policy or permissions issue:

```
$ kubectl describe sa default
…..
Annotations:           eks.amazonaws.com/role-arn:
arn:aws:iam::11223344:role/s3-access-default
…..
$ aws iam list-attached-role-policies --role-name s3-access-
default
{
    "AttachedPolicies": [
        {
            "PolicyName": "bespoke-pod-policy",
            "PolicyArn": "arn:aws:iam::11223344:policy/bespoke-
pod-policy"
        }
    ]
}
```

Once we can see the attached policy, in this case, just one, we can then iterate over it, but first, you must get the version of the policy using the get-policy command:

```
$ aws iam get-policy --policy-arn
arn:aws:iam::076637564853:policy/bespoke-pod-policy{
    "Policy": {
        "PolicyName": "bespoke-pod-policy",
        "Tags": [],
        "PermissionsBoundaryUsageCount": 0,
        "CreateDate": "2022-11-09T15:03:58Z",
        "AttachmentCount": 1,
        "IsAttachable": true,
        "PolicyId": "ANPARDV7UN626ZCPMFH4X",
        "DefaultVersionId": "v1",
        "Path": "/",
        "Arn": "arn:aws:iam::076637564853:policy/bespoke-pod-
policy",
        "UpdateDate": "2022-11-09T15:03:58Z"
    }
}
```

We can now extract the permissions using the get-policy-version command. In the following example, the s3:ListAllMyBuckets operation is missing, which is causing the problem:

```
$ aws iam get-policy-version     --policy-arn
arn:aws:iam::076637564853:policy/bespoke-pod-
policy    --version-id v1
{
    "PolicyVersion": {
        "CreateDate": "2022-11-09T15:03:58Z",
        "VersionId": "v1",
        "Document": {
            "Version": "2012-10-17",
            "Statement": [
                {
                    "Action": [
                        "s3:GetAccountPublicAccessBlock",
                        "s3:GetBucketAcl",
                        "s3:GetBucketLocation",
```

```
                    "s3:GetBucketPolicyStatus",
                    "s3:GetBucketPublicAccessBlock",
                    "s3:ListAccessPoints"
                ],
                "Resource": "*",
                "Effect": "Allow"
            }
        ]
    },
    "IsDefaultVersion": true
  }
}
```

There are a couple of other areas you can consider:

- You can find out whether the assigned role trusts the right EKS OIDC provider using the following command:

  ```
  $ aws iam get-role --role-name
  ```

- IRSA leverages a mutating webhook for Pod identity. You can validate that this has been deployed using the following command:

  ```
  $ kubectl get mutatingwebhookconfiguration pod-identity-
  webhook  -o yaml
  ```

Some other errors are covered in the *Further reading* section. In this section, we have looked at what IRSA is, how it works and is configured, and how you can do some basic IRSA troubleshooting. We'll now revisit the key learning points from this chapter.

Summary

In this chapter, we explored how AWS API permissions can be assigned to EC2 instances (worker nodes) and Pods using instance profiles and IMDS. We also noted that by default, EKS Pods inherit the permissions assigned to the worker nodes they run on, and how this may not be a good thing, as we are not observing a *least-privilege* model since many Pods may not need any AWS API access.

We discussed how IMDSv2 can be used to reduce the use of worker permission and should be used with IRSA to limit the worker node permission inheritance. We then worked through how to configure and use IRSA from the command line and how IaC tools such as eksctl can simplify the process significantly. Finally, we looked at how to do some basic troubleshooting of AWS IAM permission issues, working backward from the Kubernetes SA.

In the next chapter, we will look at how we can use AWS load balancers to make our Kubernetes services more resilient and scalable.

Further reading

- Understanding the EC2 metadata service: `https://docs.aws.amazon.com/AWSEC2/latest/UserGuide/ec2-instance-metadata.html`

- EKS updates to support IMDSv2: `https://aws.amazon.com/about-aws/whats-new/2020/08/amazon-eks-supports-ec2-instance-metadata-service-v2/`

- Troubleshooting IRSA errors: `https://aws.amazon.com/premiumsupport/knowledge-center/eks-troubleshoot-IRSA-errors/`

14

Setting Load Balancing for Applications on EKS

In *Chapter 4*, we looked at how you can use a NodePort, Ingress, and/or AWS **Load Balancer** (**LB**) to expose a simple application. In this chapter, we will dive into more detail on how to scale and provide greater resilience in your application using **AWS Elastic Load Balancers** (**ELBs**).

In most modern web or cloud-native applications, you want to ensure that the application is available to its client (resilient) and copes as the Kubernetes scheduler scales your application by replacing, removing, and adding Pods when necessary. Placing an LB in front of your application allows these Kubernetes actions to be hidden from the client, which has a consistent endpoint to access the application regardless of the location or number of Pods. Hence, specifically, we will cover the following topics in this chapter:

- What LBs are available in AWS, and how to choose the right one for your needs
- How EKS can create and use AWS LBs

Technical requirements

You should be familiar with YAML, AWS **Identity and Access Management** (**IAM**), and **Elastic Kubernetes Service** (**EKS**) architecture. Before getting started with this chapter, please ensure that you have the following in place:

- Network connectivity to your EKS cluster API endpoint
- The AWS **command-line interface** (**CLI**), Docker, and the kubectl binary are installed on your workstation
- A basic understanding of AWS networking

Choosing the right load balancer for your needs

One of the key characteristics of a modern, cloud-based application is to be able to scale horizontally (adding more instances to meet demand or recover from failure). In *Chapter 4*, we looked at how you can use deployments to create and manage multiple Pods, but you also need to distribute user traffic over those Pods. This is what an LB does, and we will work with two main types in EKS: the **Application Load Balancer** (**ALB**) and the **Network Load Balancer** (**NLB**), which are both types of ELB. In the next two sections, we will consider two key concepts that can be applied to any LB.

Concept 1 – understanding Layer 4 and Layer 7 load balancer networking

When we talk about layers in a networking context, we are talking about the **Open Systems Interconnection** (**OSI**) model, which was developed in the 1980s to simplify interconnection between different networks. The OSI model describes a seven-layer model in which the top layer, Layer 7 (application), describes the interface that applications use. Layer 4 (transport) describes how lower-level protocols, such as **User Datagram Protocol** (**UDP**)/**Transmission Control Protocol** (**TCP**), should behave. A complete description of the OSI model is out of the scope of this book, but it's worth noting that Layer 3 (networks) can be used to describe the underlying networks, which in 99% of cases will be either IPv4 or IPv6 (unless you are describing a **wide area network** (**WAN**)).

LBs that operate at Layer 7 have an understanding of the application protocols, such as HTTP/HTTPS, and will inspect and distribute traffic using HTTP paths/URLs and can perform actions such as redirection and health checks. It's worth noting that as HTTPS is encrypted, the LB must act as a proxy (see *Concept 2 – understanding proxy and DSR modes*) and, in most cases, will terminate traffic from the client before forwarding it to a (backend) service.

LBs that operate at Layer 3/4 have no understanding of higher-layer protocols, such as HTTP/HTTPS, and work at a lower level. That means they can support web applications and other traffic, such as **Secure Shell Protocol** (**SSH**) or **Simple Mail Transfer Protocol** (**SMTP**). As these LBs operate at a lower level, they can't inspect HTTP headers, so how they inspect and distribute network traffic is much simpler, and they tend to be faster. It also means they can operate as both a **proxy** and in **Direct Server Return** (**DSR**) mode.

The following diagram illustrates the two types of LBs. Both LBs see the client traffic (denoted by the 1.1.1.1 IP address in the diagram) and can do the following:

- Serve web traffic to the Layer 7 LB and understand the HTTP verbs (POST in the diagram) and the path or URL (/users/user in the diagram)

- Distribute traffic on them, whereas the Layer 4 LB will simply see the type of traffic (in the case of HTTP/HTTPS TCP) and the port (8080 in the diagram)

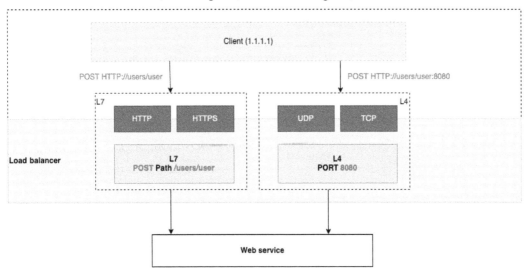

Figure 14.1 – L7 versus L4 LB

Now that we know the differences between the network layers, let's review the differences between proxy and **DSR** modes.

Concept 2 – understanding proxy and DSR modes

To inspect the HTTPS traffic (which is encrypted), the LB needs to terminate it, so this normally means it holds the encryption certificate. This model is known as a **reverse proxy mode**, as the LB will proxy the request to the backend server(s) on behalf of the client. This can be seen in the following diagram, where the source IP address of the client is replaced by the LB, which means that the request and the response traffic go through the LB:

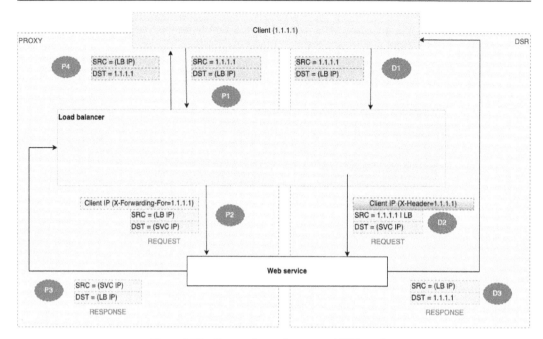

Figure 14.2 – Comparison of proxy and DSR modes

In DSR, the return/response traffic goes directly to the client. This means that the LB handles fewer requests and can theatrically scale more with less latency being introduced into the request/response traffic. It also means that the backend (web service) needs to know the client's IP address and be able to route back to it. The following table describes each of the steps in the previous diagram:

	Proxy Request–Response	DSR Request–Response
1	A **Domain Name System (DNS)** request for the service IP address resolves to the IP address of the LB, and traffic is sent to the LB IP address from the client's IP.	
2	HTTP/HTTPS traffic is inspected, and based on the protocol type/URL/port, the traffic is sent to a set of registered backend servers (targets) typically based on their health/load or on a round-robin basis. The client IP address is normally added to the X-Forwarded-For header so that the backend server can identify where the request has come from, but this is optional.	UDP/TCP traffic is inspected, and based on the protocol type/port, the traffic is sent to a set of registered backend servers (targets) typically on a round-robin basis using a Layer 2 address such as a **media access control (MAC)** address. The client IP address may be preserved in the IP packet or added as X-header, so the backend knows how to return the traffic, but the approach will vary depending on how the LB is implemented.

	Proxy Request–Response	DSR Request–Response
3	The request is handled by the backend, and the `X-Forwarded-for` header may be used to validate the request. The response is sent back to the LB.	The request is handled by the backend. The response is sent back to the client using either the preserved source IP address of `X-header` or by mimicking the LB IP.
4	The LB returns the response to the client.	This step is not needed for a DR router as the response is returned to the client in the previous step.

Table 14.1 – Request/response steps

Now we have looked at how a generic balancer works, let's look at the options available in AWS.

Which load balancers are available in AWS?

There are a number of different types of LBs available in AWS, but we will focus on the two types of ELBs commonly used with EKS: the ALB and the NLB. An ELB can be either external or internal, but not both. External means that it is accessible from the internet, and internal means it can only be accessed from the **virtual private cloud** (**VPC**) or internal addresses that have a route to the VPC hosting the ELB. The following diagram illustrates both ELB options available in AWS:

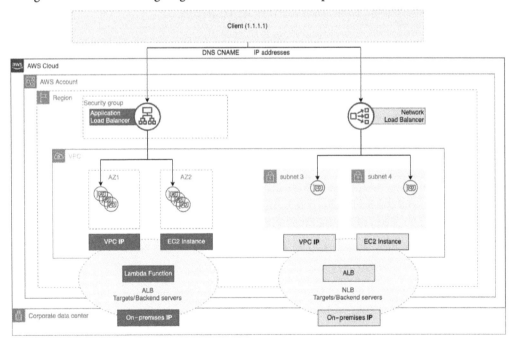

Figure 14.3 – AWS ELB

Both LBs are configured using three key concepts:

- You create an instance of an NLB or ALB and connect it to a VPC.

- You configure a listener, defining the protocol and either a port (NLB) or a URL path (ALB) that the LB will accept traffic on.

- You configure a target group, which defines the targets for the traffic sent to it from the LB listener. It also defines the health checks needed to ensure that the targets are healthy and can respond to traffic.

The ALB works as an Layer 7 proxy, so it can handle HTTP/HTTPS and HTTPv2. So if your application uses RESTful or gRPC-based APIs, an ALB will be able to support the traffic. The ALB can send traffic to targets based on *registered* IP addresses (both VPC addresses and on-premises, in the RFC 1918 address range, as long as there is a VPC route), EC2 instances, and Lambda functions. The ALB attaches to the VPC's availability zones and scales to meet traffic demands. So AWS provides a DNS **Canonical Name** (**CNAME**) record as its reference, as it may have multiple network interfaces in a VPC, and the IP addresses associated with the ALB can change. An ALB has an associated security group, meaning you can control access to either its public or private interfaces.

> **Important note**
>
> Support for gRPC is limited, so while the ALB can forward gRPC traffic, it can't make traffic distribution decisions in the same way it can with RESTful APIs.

The NLB lives in the AWS **software-defined networking** (**SDN**) fabric and so it works quite differently from the ALB. The NLB works as an Layer-4 LB, supporting both a proxy and DSR mode, depending on the type of backend servers and protocols configured. The following are examples of these:

- If the backend services are specified by the EC2 instance ID they reside on, the client IP is preserved and visible to your backend service.

- If the backend's services are specified by IP address, then we see the following:

  - If the target group protocol is TCP/**Transport Layer Security** (**TLS**), client IP preservation is disabled, and the backend service sees the LB as the source of the traffic (the client IP address can be accessed through the proxy protocol headers)

  - If the target group protocol is UDP/TCP_UDP, the client IP is preserved and is visible to your backend service

Even if the backend sees the client IP address, as the NLB is an SDN construct, return traffic is sent back through the NLB without any additional configuration. This means that the client only sees the NLB addresses, and you don't have asymmetrical routing where the response goes to one IP and the response comes back from another.

This *return traffic magic* is not explained by AWS but ensures that any traffic that is in the VPC will be routed back to the NLB even if the client IP address is the source IP; outside the VPC, you may get different, asymmetrical routing.

The NLB can send traffic to targets based on *registered* IP addresses (both VPC addresses and on-premises in the RFC 1918 address range, as long as there is a VPC route), EC2 instances, and ALBs. The NLB attaches to VPCs through fixed **Elastic Network Interfaces** (**ENIs**), so AWS provides these IP addresses (public or private), so once allocated, the IP addresses remain the same and don't change. The NLB has *no* associated security group, so external NLBs are *open* to the internet. As you can see, while there are similarities between these two ELBs, there are also differences. In the next section, let's look at how you can choose which one to use.

Choosing the right ELB

Imagine the scenario where you want to expose a simple microservice running on EKS to the outside world in a scalable and resilient manner. Which ELB would you choose? Of course, we would assume that both ELB types are available in your desired Region! Here are some questions you might want to ask to help you make your decision:

- What type of interface are you exposing? If it's not based on HTTP/HTTPS or HTTPv2, you will need to use an NLB.

- Do you want to offload encryption? If so, in most cases, you will want to use SSL/TLS, and in a lot of cases, you will offload the encryption/decryption process to the ELB. Both NLBs and ALBs support this, but if you want your Pod to do the encryption/decryption (end-to-end encryption), you will need an NLB, as it can pass the traffic through to the Pods.

- Do you need advanced web security? Only an ALB integrates with AWS **Web Application Firewall** (**WAF**) and **AWS Shield,** which acts as a **distributed denial-of-service** (**DDoS**) protection service. NLB can be protected if you have Shield Advanced but doesn't integrate with WAF and, as we mentioned, has no security group associated with it.

- Do you need static IP addresses for whitelisting? NLBs provides static IP addresses, whereas an ALB uses a DNS name, which can return different IP addresses. It is possible to put an NLB *in front* of an ALB to provide static IP addresses, but you are adding another network hop and increasing latency.

- Do you need low latency, or can you cope with large traffic bursts? As the NLB is an SDN construct, it is very low-latency and scales much faster than an ALB.

- Do I want to use a Kubernetes Ingress or Service in the deployment? Similar to an NLB, a Kubernetes service, for example, a **NodePort,** is a simple construct that distributes traffic over a set of Pods. An Ingress, on the other hand, allows much more control over routing, using different paths to distribute the load over your Pods and is analogous to an ALB. So if you want to have different Pods handling updates for users and groups, you can use path-based routing to point the user actions to one Pod and the group actions to another Pod. If you need a single Pod to handle all actions and expose a single port, you need an NLB/Service.

There are, of course, other areas you might consider, but these are the main ones I found useful when considering which ELB to use. In the next section, let's look at how we can use the **AWS Load Balancer Controller** (**ALBC**) to create and use ELBs.

Using EKS to create and use AWS LBs

We can use the ALBC, which is an open source project, to create either an ALB/NLB or use existing ones in our AWS account. Let's start with installing the controller and configuring the right privileges to access the AWS APIs.

Installing the ALBC in your cluster

The following steps should be followed in order to successfully install the ALBC:

1. The first thing you need to do is make sure your VPC is set up correctly so that, if you want to create an internal or external ELB, it is deployed into the right subnets. You do this by tagging your public subnets with kubernetes.io/role/elb and your private subnets with kubernetes.io/role/internal-elb and setting Value to 1. The following commands show you how you can tag and verify a public subnet:

    ```
    $ aws ec2 create-tags --resources "subnetid-12" --tags
    Key=kubernetes.io/role/elb,Value=1
    $ aws ec2 describe-subnets   --subnet-ids subnetid-12
    --query 'Subnets[].Tags[]'
    [{
            "Value": "myipv4cluster",
            "Key": "eksctl.cluster.k8s.io/v1alpha1/cluster-
    name"
        },
        .........
        {
            "Value": "1",
            "Key": "kubernetes.io/role/elb"
        }
    ]
    ```

2. Now you have tagged all your subnets, we can deploy the controller to your cluster. We will use eksctl and Helm. The next thing we need to do is create a role and service account for the controller to use (we will use v2.4.5, but this may change):

    ```
    $ curl -o iam-policy.json https://raw.githubusercontent.
    com/kubernetes-sigs/aws-load-balancer-controller/v2.4.5/
    docs/install/iam_policy.json
    ```

```
$ aws iam create-policy --policy-name
AWSLoadBalancerControllerIAMPolicy --policy-document
file://iam-policy.json
{ "Policy": {"PolicyName":
"AWSLoadBalancerControllerIAMPolicy",

"Arn": "arn:aws:iam::112233:policy/
AWSLoadBalancerControllerIAMPolicy",

       ..........}}
```

3. Now we have the policy, we can create the service account using the Arn that was provided in the previous command:

```
$ eksctl create iamserviceaccount    --cluster
myipv4cluster   --namespace kube-system    --name
aws-load-balancer-controller    --attach-
policy-arn arn:aws:iam::112233:policy/
AWSLoadBalancerControllerIAMPolicy    --override-existing-
serviceaccounts    --approve

..........

2022-12-12 18:46:51 [i]   created serviceaccount "kube-
system/aws-load-balancer-controller"
```

4. Now we have the service account created, we can deploy the controller and use the Kubernetes service account we just created. To do this, we use the following Helm commands with the service account created in the previous steps:

```
$ helm repo add eks https://aws.github.io/eks-charts
$ helm repo update
Hang tight while we grab the latest from your chart
repositories...

...Successfully got an update from the "eks" chart
repository

....
Update Complete.
$ helm install aws-load-balancer-controller eks/aws-load-
balancer-controller -n kube-system \
   --set clusterName=myipv4cluster \
   --set serviceAccount.create=false \
   --set serviceAccount.name=aws-load-balancer-controller \
   --set image.repository=602401143452.dkr.ecr.
eu-central-1.amazonaws.com/amazon/aws-load-balancer-
```

```
controller \
  --set region=eu-central-1 \
  --set vpcId=vpc-6575786587
```

5. Next, we verify the deployment and version using the following commands:

```
$ kubectl get deployment -n kube-system aws-load-
balancer-controller
NAME            READY   UP-TO-DATE   AVAILABLE   AGE
aws-load-balancer-controller    2/2 2      2            37s
$ kubectl describe deployment  -n kube-system  aws-load-
balancer-controller | grep Image
Image: 602401143452.dkr.ecr.eu-central-1.amazonaws.com/
amazon/aws-load-balancer-controller:v2.4.5
```

Now we have the controller deployed, let's look at how we can use it.

Using an ALB with your application

In this section, we will work through the official sample located at `https://raw.githubusercontent.com/kubernetes-sigs/aws-load-balancer-controller/v2.4.7/docs/examples/2048/2048_full.yaml`. To use an ALB with your application, please follow these steps:

1. The first thing we will do is create the namespace for the application components using the following section of the YAML file:

```
---
kind: Namespace
apiVersion: v1
metadata:
  name: game-2048
  labels:
    name: game-2048
```

2. Next, we will create a deployment of three (Pods) replicas using the official Docker image (note that your worker nodes must have internet access to pull the image) and expose port 80 on each of the Pods in the deployment using the following code snippet:

```
apiVersion: apps/v1
kind: Deployment
metadata:
```

```
    namespace: game-2048
    name: deployment-2048
  spec:
    selector:
      matchLabels:
        app.kubernetes.io/name: app-2048
    replicas: 3
    template:
      metadata:
        labels:
          app.kubernetes.io/name: app-2048
      spec:
        containers:
        - image: public.ecr.aws/l6m2t8p7/docker-2048:latest
          imagePullPolicy: Always
          name: app-2048
          ports:
          - containerPort: 80
```

3. Finally, we create a NodePort service to expose the Pod outside of the EKS cluster with the following code snippet:

```
---
apiVersion: v1
kind: Service
metadata:
  namespace: game-2048
  name: service-2048
spec:
  ports:
    - port: 80
      targetPort: 80
      protocol: TCP
  type: NodePort
  selector:
    app.kubernetes.io/name: app-2048
```

4. So far, we haven't done anything different to many of the services we have deployed throughout the book. The key difference is in the following snippet, where the Ingress uses the `alb.ingress` annotations to define the type of ALB to create, in this case, an external ALB with a target group based on IP addresses. If you remember, the ALB is a Layer 7 proxy, so we also have to define what path and port to register. In this case, we are defining `http://loadbalancername:80/`:

```
apiVersion: networking.k8s.io/v1
kind: Ingress
metadata:
  namespace: game-2048
  name: ingress-2048
  annotations:
    alb.ingress.kubernetes.io/scheme: internet-facing
    alb.ingress.kubernetes.io/target-type: ip
spec:
  ingressClassName: alb
  rules:
    - http:
        paths:
        - path: /
          pathType: Prefix
          backend:
            service:
              name: service-2048
              port:
                number: 80
```

5. The controller (ALBC) will see the annotations in the manifest and make calls to the AWS API to create an external ALB listening on port 80 and a target group with the Pod's IP addresses defined as targets, which are registered with the service we created as part of the manifest.

6. If we look at the deployed Pods using the following `kubectl` command, we can see the VPC IP addresses that have been assigned (the output has been truncated):

```
$ kubectl get po -o wide -n game-204
NAME    READY    STATUS    RESTARTS    AGE    IP
deployment-2048-7ff458c9f-fwx6h    1/1    Running    0
26m    192.168.9.154    ....
deployment-2048-7ff458c9f-k5ns5    1/1    Running    0
```

```
26m    192.168.42.16    ....
deployment-2048-7ff458c9f-v6mqw    1/1    Running    0
26m    192.168.87.245    ...
```

7. Now, if we go to the **EC2 | Load Balancers** section of the AWS Console, you will see the ALB created for the game application and the **DNS name** value associated with it (remember that IP addresses can change, so you need to always use the provided DNS name). An example is shown in the following screenshot:

EC2 > Load balancers

Load balancers (1)
Elastic Load Balancing scales your load balancer capacity automatically in response to changes in incoming traffic.

search: game X   Clear filters

Name	DNS name	State	VPC ID	Availability Zones	Type	Created
k8s-game2048-ingress2-b2967d684d	k8s-game2048-ingress2-b2967d684d-23187477.eu-central-1.elb.amazonaws.com	⊘ Active	vpc-06f8d68340929a7f 6	3 Availability Zones	application	December 20:10 (UT

Figure 14.4 – Game app ALB

8. If we look at the associated **Target groups**, we can see the spec configuration on the Kubernetes manifest: an **IP** target group listening on HTTP port 80. An example is shown in the following screenshot:

EC2 > Target groups

Target groups (1/1) Info

search: game X   Clear filters

Name	ARN	Port	Protocol	Target type	Load balancer
k8s-game2048-service2-b1df7b9df8	arn:aws:elasticloadbalancin...	80	HTTP	IP	k8s-game2048-ingress2-b2967d684d

Figure 14.5 – Game app ALB target group

9. If we open up the target group and look at **Registered targets**, we will see the IP addresses of the targets, and these should correspond to the Pod IP addresses that we listed previously using the kubectl command. An example is shown in the following screenshot:

Figure 14.6 – Registered targets for the game app

You can see that the targets are all shown with a **healthy** value in the **Health status** column. This is because, as part of the ALB creation, **Health checks** are created as part of the configuration (this is required). In the example shown in the following screenshot, the ALB will poll the path (/) using port 80 every **15 seconds** to make sure each Pod is able to receive traffic:

Figure 14.7 – Health checks for the game app

10. If you now browse to the ALB DNS name, you will be presented with the game screen and can play the game, which involves moving blocks around the screen:

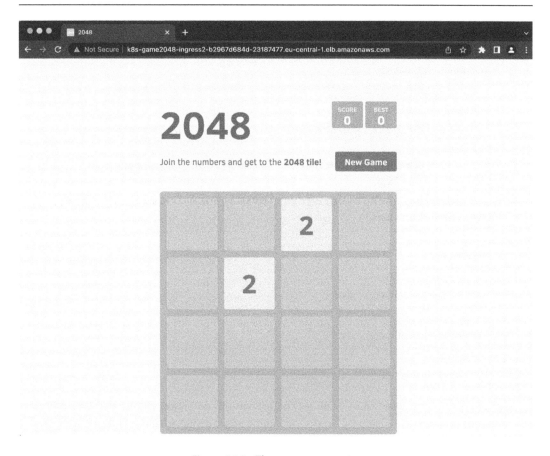

Figure 14.8 – The game app service

Let's now look at how we can modify the previous Kubernetes configuration to use an NLB instead.

Using an NLB with your application

We can reuse the namespace and Deployment specifications from the previous examples in the *Using an ALB with your application* section:

1. As the NLB is an L4 LB, we don't need the Ingress object, but we do need to modify the Service definition. The first difference is that the annotations we use define the same thing as the ALB annotations, that is, the type of NLB and target group. As this is a service, we then define the ports rather than the paths. In the example shown in the following code block, an external NLB will be created with an IP target group and expose port 80, which maps to the backend port 80:

    ```
    ---
    apiVersion: v1
    ```

```
kind: Service
metadata:
  name: nlb-service
  namespace: game-2048
  annotations:
    service.beta.kubernetes.io/aws-load-balancer-type:
external
    service.beta.kubernetes.io/aws-load-balancer-nlb-
target-type: ip
    service.beta.kubernetes.io/aws-load-balancer-scheme:
internet-facing
spec:
  ports:
    - port: 80
      targetPort: 80
      protocol: TCP
  type: LoadBalancer
  selector:
    app.kubernetes.io/name: app-2048
```

2. As before, the controller (ALBC) will see the annotations and make calls to the AWS API to create an external NLB listening on port 80 and a target group with the Pods' IP addresses defined by the `selector` statement.

3. If we look at **EC2** | **Load balancers** on the AWS Console, you will see another LB for the game application, but in this case, it's an NLB. An example is shown in the following screenshot:

Figure 14.9 – The game app NLB

> **Important note**
> While you can see the DNS name in the previous example, the NLB IP addresses are static, unlike the ALB, which can change if AWS scales the service.

4. If we review **Target groups** associated with the NLB and **Registered targets**, as shown in the following screenshot, we can see the same Pod IP addresses are associated with the NLB and in a **healthy** state:

Figure 14.10 – The game app NLB registered targets

5. Again, a health check has been automatically created, but as this is a Layer 4 LB, the health check is port-based. In the example shown in the following screenshot, a **TCP** protocol port 80 check is used to make sure each Pod is able to receive traffic:

Figure 14.11 – The game app NLB health check

6. If you browse to the DNS name of the NLB, you will see the same game screen as with the ALB (*Figure 14.8*).

Reusing an existing LB

In some cases, you might want to reuse an existing ELB. This will save you costs and also simplify your configuration. You can do this by using the `TargetGroupBinding` custom resource. This resource allows you to associate a service with an existing **TargetGroup** and by NLB.

Let's assume we have created an NLB and an associated IP-based target group but without registering any IP addresses. The following code snippet shows how we can use `TargetGroupBinding`, which allows the ALBC to register Pods associated with a Kubernetes Service with an existing NLB or ALB. The key is to specify the given ARN of `TargetGroup` in the definition:

```
---
apiVersion: elbv2.k8s.aws/v1beta1
kind: TargetGroupBinding
metadata:
  name: existing-nlb
  namespace: game-2048
spec:
  serviceRef:
    name: nlb-service
    port: 80
  targetGroupARN: arn:aws:elasticloadbalancing:eu-central-
1:112233:targetgroup/existing-target-group/234
```

> **Important note**
>
> The NLB is outside of the security group associated with the worker nodes where the Pods are running. So you will need to allow TCP:80 from the NLB ENIs to the worker nodes' security groups as the ALBC will not do this for you when you use `TargetGroupBinding`. The service referenced by `serviceRef` can be configured, as `type: ClusterIP` rather than `LoadBalancer` or `NodePort`.

In this section, we have looked at how general LBs work, what options are available in AWS, and how to configure and use the ALBC on EKS. We'll now revisit the key learning points from this chapter.

Summary

In this chapter, we explored how LBs help applications scale and provide resilience. They tend to fall into two categories, either Layer 7 or Layer 4 LBs. Layer 7 LBs, which normally work on HTTP, understand protocol-specific attributes such as paths or headers, whereas L4 LBs work at the port level and are protocol-agnostic.

We also reviewed the differences between the proxy and DSR modes; a proxy LB always sits between the client and the backend system, whereas in DSR mode, the backend can return traffic directly to the client (albeit by faking the source address to be that of the LB).

We reviewed the different types of ELBs typically used with EKS, namely the ALB and NLB, and how they differ. We then learned how to install the ALBC on an EKS cluster and then how you can use annotations and custom configuration to create either an NLB or ALB and register Pods with them so you can access the service based on the path (ALB) or ports (NLB).

Finally, we quickly reviewed how you can use `TargetGroupBinding` to register Pods with an existing NLB (or ALB). You should now be able to talk about the different options available to you in AWS and configure deployments and services in EKS to take advantage of an ALB or NLB.

In the next chapter, we will look at how you can use AWS Fargate to provide enhanced security, support small workloads, or simply not manage or pay for EC2 instances.

Further reading

- Understanding the OSI network model: `https://www.imperva.com/learn/application-security/osi-model/`

- Understanding how HTTPS works: `https://www.cloudflare.com/learning/ssl/what-is-https/`

- Understanding how `X-Forwarded-For` works: `https://en.wikipedia.org/wiki/X-Forwarded-For`

- Understanding ALB support for gRPC: `https://aws.amazon.com/blogs/aws/new-application-load-balancer-support-for-end-to-end-http-2-and-grpc/`

- Understanding NLB client IP address preservation: `https://docs.aws.amazon.com/elasticloadbalancing/latest/network/load-balancer-target-groups.html#client-ip-preservation`

- Understanding NLB proxy protocol: `https://docs.aws.amazon.com/elasticloadbalancing/latest/network/load-balancer-target-groups.html#proxy-protocol`

- Understanding AWS advanced web security features: `https://docs.aws.amazon.com/waf/latest/developerguide/what-is-aws-waf.html`

- Downloading the ALBC: `https://github.com/kubernetes-sigs/aws-load-balancer-controller`

- How to create an NLB: `https://docs.aws.amazon.com/elasticloadbalancing/latest/network/create-network-load-balancer.html`

15

Working with AWS Fargate

Throughout this book, we have used **Elastic Compute Cloud** (**EC2**) instances as worker nodes for our **Elastic Kubernetes Service** (**EKS**) cluster, but **AWS Fargate** can be used as an alternative to host Pods. As we will see later on, Fargate can be used to provide a more secure operating environment for a Pod and can also be more cost-effective (but not always).

In some cases, you want to deploy a workload/application that runs infrequently, has a small memory/CPU footprint, and/or needs enhanced security, for example, creating a regular dump of a production database. Fargate can be used to meet all of these requirements. In this chapter, we will dive into more detail on how and when you should use AWS Fargate, as well as how it works with EKS to provide an alternative to EC2-based worker nodes. Specifically, we will cover the following topics:

- What AWS Fargate is and how is it priced
- How to create a Fargate profile in EKS
- How to deploy a Pod to a Fargate instance
- How to troubleshoot common Fargate issues

Technical requirements

You should be familiar with YAML, AWS **Identity and Access Management** (**IAM**), and EKS architecture. Before getting started with this chapter, please ensure that the following is in place:

- Network connectivity to your EKS cluster API endpoint
- The AWS **Command Line Interface** (**CLI**), Docker, and the kubectl binary are installed on your workstation
- You have a basic understanding of AWS networking and EC2

What is AWS Fargate?

AWS Fargate was developed as an alternative to EC2 to provide a *serverless*, container-native compute solution with three key design tenets:

- To be as secure as possible

- To be reliable and scale to meet demand

- To be cost-efficient

If we compare the EC2-based EKS worker node and Fargate technical stacks, illustrated in *Figure 15.1*, we can see that they are very similar. They run on physical servers, with both a virtual machine operating system and a container runtime that support a containerized application. The key difference is that Fargate is serverless, which means that you don't need to care about the virtual machine operating system, container runtime, and so on, as this is all managed by AWS:

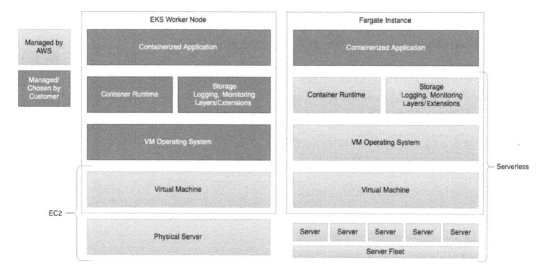

Figure 15.1 – AWS Fargate versus EC2

The other main difference is that Fargate is really designed for small, bursty, or batch workloads, unlike EC2, which is traditionally used for more stable, long-running workloads. This means that the underlying physical compute fleet is optimized to maintain a high utilization/density, which in turn means it is operationally efficient and can therefore be much cheaper to use for the consumer.

The following workloads suit the use of Fargate over a more traditional EC2 deployment:

- If your production workload is small with the occasional burst, such as sporadic web traffic during the day but low to no traffic at night
- If you have a small test/non-production environment that is used occasionally, then Fargate can be more efficient than an underutilized EC2 instance
- If your workload consists of a task that runs periodically, such as a batch or cron job

Another consideration is the use of **Firecracker,** which is a **Virtual Machine Manager** (**VMM**) developed by AWS and open source. Firecracker uses the concept of a **MicroVM** to create a small, secure, isolated environment to run containers that are very quick to create or destroy and provide fine-grained control over how **central processing unit** (**CPU**), **random access memory** (**RAM**), disk, and networking shares are allocated:

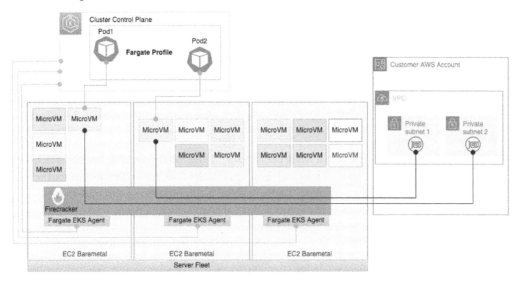

Figure 15.2 – Fargate EKS architecture

Fargate uses EC2 Baremetal instances as its fleet and Firecracker to create and manage MicroVMs on these instances for multiple tenants (customers). Firecracker ensures that while a single Fargate EC2 host can support many MicroVMs from different AWS customers, they are all isolated through different **virtual machine** (**VM**) boundary controls.

A MicroVM will host a single Pod, and these Pods don't share underlying kernels, CPU resources, memory resources, or **Elastic Network Interfaces** (**ENIs**) with another Pod. They are orchestrated through the Fargate EKS agent, which allows the K8s scheduler to schedule Pods on the Fargate fleet and connect it using the EKS AWS **virtual private cloud** (**VPC**) **Container Network Interface** (**CNI**) to private subnets (public subnets are not supported) in the customer's VPC.

The K8s scheduler uses a **Fargate profile** to determine whether a Pod specification meets the requirements to be deployed onto the Fargate fleet. We will describe this process in more detail in the subsequent section.

Now that we understand the general architecture, let's look at how Fargate is priced.

Understanding the Fargate pricing model

Fargate has a simple pricing model based on the duration for which you use the MicroVM/Pod (per-second granularity) and the vCPU/RAM and disk allocated to it.

If we first look at a 2 CPU/4 GB EC2 instance with 30 GB of disk running 100% of the time, then based on on-demand pricing using the Frankfurt Region as an example, that would cost us approximately *$21/month*.

If we use a Fargate Pod with 2 CPU/4 GB with 30 GB of disk running for 5 hours every day, based on on-demand pricing in the Frankfurt Region, that would cost us approximately *$10/month*.

At first glance, we can see that Fargate is less than half the price of an EC2 instance! However, if we just double the duration of the Pod execution time from 5 hours/day to 10 hours/day, then the cost goes up to $35/month, which is quite a bit more. Also, bear in mind that with the EC2 instance, we could run multiple Pods on an instance without incurring any additional costs, whereas with Fargate, every Pod would be an additional $10 or $35 (assuming they are configured the same and run for the same amount of time).

What you can see from this example is that while the Fargate pricing model is easy to understand, from a pure cost perspective, using Fargate for long-running workloads is not very effective, but for bursty, short-lived workloads, it will be cost-efficient. However, if you factor in the total cost of managing and operating EC2 instances, as opposed to the fact that AWS will manage and patch your Fargate ones, you may be able to build a business case around Fargate.

You should also bear in mind that most EC2 instances are not 100% utilized; in many cases, they barely touch 30% utilization. So, if you have an existing large EC2 estate (of more than 100 instances), Fargate may save you a lot of money as you can reduce the impact of higher Fargate costs with a reduction in costs in your EC2 estate. Now that we've looked at the Fargate pricing model, let's consider how we can configure EKS to use Fargate.

Creating an AWS Fargate profile in EKS

Understanding the AWS Fargate service is interesting, but we only covered it in this book to really give you some background. As Fargate is serverless, you really only need to understand how to get the Kubernetes scheduler to talk to the Fargate service and create the MicroVM, attach it to the network, and deploy the Pod. This is all done through the Fargate Profile, which will be discussed in detail in the following section.

Understanding how the AWS Fargate profile works

When considering how to integrate the Fargate service with EKS, the AWS team made a conscious decision not to make users update their existing K8s manifests to support Fargate. Instead, the **profile** identifies which namespaces and/or labels will be used to host Pods on Fargate, and no changes are required in the Pod definition. The following diagram illustrates how this process works:

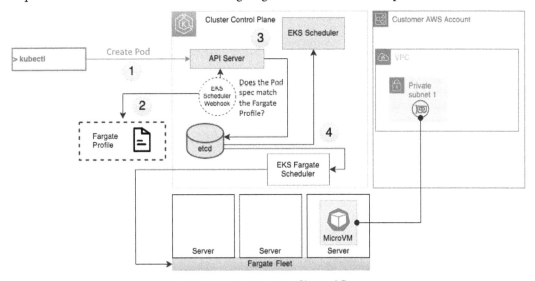

Figure 15.3 – Fargate profile workflow

The steps shown in the previous diagram are detailed as follows:

1. When a `Pod Create` API request is received by the API server (this could be an individual Pod spec, part of a deployment, or any other), it triggers an event that is captured by a custom webhook that is installed and managed by AWS in the EKS control plane.

2. This webhook looks at the Fargate profile to determine whether the namespace or labels being used are serviced by the Fargate service. If it matches, it will change the scheduler name to use the **Fargate Scheduler** instead of the standard K8s scheduler.

3. The API server now writes the *intent* with the appropriate scheduler name to `etcd` to wait to be scheduled.

4. If the scheduler name has been changed to the Fargate scheduler, then it will eventually be picked up by that scheduler, which takes care of requesting the compute resources from the AWS Fargate fleet and orchestrating the creation of the MicroVM and attaching it to the customer VPC. The Fargate Scheduler is another component that is created and managed by AWS in the EKS control plane.

As you can see, the Fargate profile controls how everything works. So now, let's create one and see how it works.

Creating and adjusting the Fargate profile

The easiest way to create a Fargate profile is to use `eksctl`. Let's first create a new namespace to host the workload using the following command:

```
$ kubectl create namespace fargate-workload
namespace/fargate-workload created
```

We can then use `eksctl` to create (and verify) the Fargate profile and specify the new namespace as a target for Fargate (by default, you can have up to 10 profiles per cluster):

```
$ eksctl create fargateprofile --cluster myipv4cluster --name fargate
--namespace fargate-workload
2022-12-16 10:42:23deploying stack "eksctl-myipv4cluster-fargate"
...
2022-12-16 10:47:12 created Fargate profile "fargate" on EKS cluster
"myipv4cluster"
$ eksctl get fargateprofile --cluster myipv4cluster -o yaml
- name: fargate
  podExecutionRoleARN: arn:aws:iam::112233:role/eksctl-myipv4cluster-
farga-FargatePodExecutionRole-1CD7AYHOTBDYO
  selectors:
  - namespace: fargate-workload
  status: ACTIVE
  subnets:
  - subnet-privat1
  - subnet-private2
  - subnet-private3
```

Now the profile is configured, let's look at how we can use it.

Deploying a Pod to a Fargate instance

You can see from the previous output `eksctl` has created not only the profile but also an execution role to allow Fargate Pods to use the AWS services and automatically assign the private subnets in the VPC.

If we now take one of the manifests previously used in this book and simply change the namespace to the `fargate-workload` namespace and deploy it, we will see the Pod is deployed on a Fargate instance rather than on EC2 workers:

```
apiVersion: apps/v1
kind: Deployment
```

```
metadata:
  name: simple-web
  namespace: fargate-workload
spec:
  replicas: 1
  selector:
    matchLabels:
      app: simple-nginx-app
  template:
    metadata:
      labels:
        app. simple-nginx-app
    spec:
      containers:
        - name: nginx
          image: nginx
```

If we look at the Pod that was deployed using the following commands, we can see it's running on Fargate:

```
$ kubectl get po -n fargate-workload -o wide
NAME    READY    STATUS    RESTARTS    AGE    IP    NODE ..
simple-web-12-    1/1    Running    0    11m    192.168.179.65
    fargate-ip-192-168-179-65.eu-central-1.compute.internal
```

We can also verify in the Pod specification whether the scheduler has been set correctly and that the MicroVM is now registered as a node with our cluster using the following commands:

```
$ kubectl get pods -o yaml -n fargate-workload  simple-web-12 | grep
schedulerName.
    schedulerName: fargate-scheduler
$ kubectl get node
......
fargate-ip-192-168-179-65.eu-central-1.compute.
internal    Ready    <none>    18m    v1.20.15-eks-14c7a48
ip-192-168-12-212.eu-central-1.compute.
internal              Ready    <none>    96d    v1.20.15-eks-ba74326
ip-192-168-63-61.eu-central-1.compute.
internal              Ready    <none>    96d    v1.20.15-eks-ba74326
ip-192-168-70-114.eu-central-1.compute.
internal              Ready    <none>    96d    v1.20.15-eks-ba74326
```

While the Pod has been created, it is only accessible from inside the VPC (it will use the same security group as the EC2 base worker node) so we can add an NLB or ALB, as described in *Chapter 14*. A quick way to test connectivity to your Pod running on Fargate is to **Secure Shell Protocol** (**SSH**) onto an existing EC2 worker node in your cluster (if you have EC2 worker nodes) and run a `curl` command, an example of which is as follows:

```
$ curl 192.168.179.65
<!DOCTYPE html>
<html>
<head>
<title>Welcome to nginx!</title>
…..
</html>
$
```

Fargate has a number of preconfigured vCPU and memory sizes; if you don't specify a vCPU and memory combination, then the smallest available combination is used (0.25 vCPU and 0.5 GB memory). This can be validated using the `kubectl describe po` command, an example of which is as follows:

```
$ kubectl describe po simple-web-12 -n fargate-workload
Name:                simple-web-99b67d675-24ptk
Namespace:           fargate-workload
Priority:            2000001000
Priority Class Name: system-node-critical
Node:                fargate-ip-1.1.1.1.eu-central-1.compute.
internal/192.168.179.65
Start Time:          Fri, 16 Dec 2022 11:46:40 +0000
Labels:              app=simple-nginx-app
                     eks.amazonaws.com/fargate-profile=fargate
                     pod-template-hash=99b67d675
Annotations:         CapacityProvisioned: 0.25vCPU 0.5GB
                     …….
```

If we adjust the Pod spec in our initial deployment and set some limits, it will then change the size of the Fargate instance. An example of a K8s manifest is shown in the following code snippet, which uses memory and CPU limits:

```
containers:
        - name: nginx
          image: nginx
          resources:
            limits:
                memory: "2Gi"
                cpu: "2000m"
```

If we rerun the `describe` command after we update the deployment, we can see the provisioned capacity has increased:

```
$ kubectl describe po simple-web-688f85f87d-gtxkb -n fargate-workload
Name:                  simple-web-688f85f87d-gtxkb
Namespace:             fargate-workload
Priority:              2000001000
Priority Class Name:   system-node-critical
Node:                  <none>
Labels:                app=simple-nginx-app
                       eks.amazonaws.com/fargate-profile=fargate
                       pod-template-hash=688f05f87d
Annotations:           CapacityProvisioned: 2vCPU 4GB
```

You can see that the limits and the Fargate annotation/size don't exactly align! This is because there is 2 GiB set for memory in the manifest but 4 GB is assigned. This is because Fargate tries to match the manifest configuration to the set CPU/memory configurations that have been defined, and it will add some overhead (246 MB RAM) to support the required Kubernetes components (`kubelet`, `kube-proxy`, and `containerd`). Each Pod will also receive 20 GB of ephemeral storage that can be used to cache data, but this will be deleted when the Pod is deleted.

It's worth noting that if you run your Pod for an extended period of time, there is a possibility that AWS will patch your Pod, and this could lead to it being evicted and deleted. In order to mitigate this, you should use **Pod Disruption Budgets** (**PDBs**) to maintain a certain number of Pods and prevent eviction, as shown in the following code snippet:

```
apiVersion: policy/v1
kind: PodDisruptionBudget
metadata:
  name: fg-pdb
spec:
  minAvailable: 1
  selector:
    matchLabels:
      app: simple-ninx-app
```

> **Important note**
> Depending on your K8s version, you may need to use the `apiVersion policy/v1beta1` beta policy.

You can validate that the PDB is in place using the following command:

```
$ kubectl get pod disruptionbudgets -n fargate-workload
NAME MIN AVAILABLE   MAX UNAVAILABLE   ALLOWED DISRUPTIONS    AGE
fg-pdb   1               N/A                  0               43s
```

While a PDB cannot guarantee your application resilience, it can go a certain way toward making sure operational issues don't impact it. As AWS operates Fargate for you, most things happen seamlessly, but sometimes issues do occur. In the next section, let's look at some common issues and how we can troubleshoot them.

Troubleshooting common issues on Fargate

The most common issue related to capacity is that occasionally, there will not be enough platform resources, and/or the CPU/RAM combination you want will not be supported. This results in the Pod status always being **PENDING**. If it is a platform issue, simply waiting and trying later (after 15/20 minutes) may resolve the issue; otherwise, adjust your Pod spec to support a different CPU/RAM combination.

If your Fargate nodes are shown as `Not Ready` when you run the `$ kubectl get nodes` command, ensure that the execution role they are using is also configured in the `aws-auth` ConfigMap, an example of which is shown as follows:

```
mapRoles: |
    - groups:
      - system:bootstrappers
      - system:nodes
      - system:node-proxier
      rolearn: <Pod_execution_role_ARN>
      username: system:node:{{SessionName}}
```

You may have issues with CoreDNS Pods staying in a PENDING state; this is normally due to the VPC DNS not being configured. The solution is to ensure you have `enableDNSHostnames` and `enableDNSSupport` set to `True` for your VPC.

If you have issues with the Fargate profile, make sure the target namespaces and labels are correctly configured in your cluster and Pod spec. There are some common processing rules that need to be considered:

- The Fargate Scheduler matches all conditions, so if namespaces and labels are used in the profile, then they must both be used in the manifest in order to be scheduled on a Fargate instance

- If multiple Fargate profiles exist and a Pod matches multiple profiles, it is scheduled using a random Fargate profile

In this section, we have looked at what Fargate is, how it works and is configured, and how you can do some basic troubleshooting. We'll now revisit the key learning points from this chapter.

Summary

In this chapter, we explored what Fargate is and how it works. You learned that Fargate is an AWS-managed service, so you really only need to focus on the Fargate profile and make sure that VPC networking and, optionally, load balancers are set up correctly for it all to work.

We also explored the technology and discovered that under the hood, Fargate uses a Firecracker MicroVM to provide complete isolation between your Pod and other Pods even if these are in the same cluster.

We reviewed how the Fargate profile is used to match Pod spec labels and namespaces in the profile and assign them to the Fargate scheduler, which handles the orchestration with the AWS Fargate service to provision your Pod on a Fargate MicroVM and connect it to your VPC.

We then looked at how you can use a Pod or deployment manifest unchanged by just matching the namespace and/or labels defined in the Fargate profile namespace. We also learned that adjusting the `Limits` or `Requests` resources in the manifest will change the size of the MicroVM (providing it matches one of the pre-defined CPU/RAM combinations).

Finally, we reviewed some common issues with Fargate and how to fix them. You should now be able to describe when to use Fargate for an EKS workload and be able to configure a Fargate profile to allow developers to deploy Pods on a Fargate instance.

In the next chapter, we will look at how you can use a service mesh to provide greater security or better telemetry/logging.

Further reading

- Understanding the Firecracker design: `https://github.com/firecracker-microvm/firecracker/blob/main/docs/design.md`

- Understanding how Fargate is priced: `https://aws.amazon.com/fargate/pricing/`

- Understanding Fargate Pod configurations: `https://docs.aws.amazon.com/eks/latest/userguide/fargate-pod-configuration.html`

16

Working with a Service Mesh

So far in this book, we have looked at how we can use AWS and K8s network controls such as security groups and network policies to control access to and from applications. A **service mesh** allows you to control application-to-application traffic communication in a more granular and consistent way as well as providing better visibility of that traffic and providing additional capabilities such as encryption.

As teams build larger, microservices-based ecosystems consisting of tens or thousands of services in EKS, controlling and instrumenting these services becomes a full-time job. Using a service mesh simplifies this and means that all services can be managed in a consistent way without the need for each development team to modify their code. In this chapter, we will dive into more details on how a service mesh works, using **AWS App Mesh** as an example. Specifically, we will cover the following:

- Exploring a service mesh and its benefits
- Installing AWS App Mesh Controller in a cluster
- How to integrate your application with App Mesh
- Using AWS Cloud Map with EKS
- Troubleshooting the Envoy proxy

Technical requirements

You should have a familiarity with YAML, AWS IAM, and EKS architecture. Before getting started with this chapter, please ensure the following:

- You have network connectivity to your EKS cluster API endpoint
- The AWS CLI, Docker, and `kubectl` binary is installed on your workstation
- You have a basic understanding of AWS and K8s networking

This chapter builds on a lot of the concepts already discussed in this book, so you are advised to read the previous chapters first.

Exploring a service mesh and its benefits

In *Chapter 7*, we reviewed what a security group is and how it can be used to control access to worker nodes (and the Pods running on them) using simple P-based rules (source/destination IP address, source/destination ports, and protocol type) in the VPC. In *Chapter 9*, we looked at using K8s network policies to control intra-cluster traffic using K8s namespaces and labels.

The challenge with both these approaches is they are relatively static, so as the application topology changes, the applications scale in or out. For example, IP addresses can change and this means changes to the configuration are needed. Also, as you deploy more services, the operational burden of ensuring the configurations are correct, deploying them across multiple clusters, and monitoring their operation becomes increasingly complex and difficult.

A service mesh resolves these issues by replacing multiple control points and configurations with a control plane, which can deploy policy changes in a consistent manner across different namespaces/Pods (the data plane), dynamically respond to changes in the application topology, and collect and expose network traffic telemetry. Most service meshes will also expose their capabilities through an API. The following diagram illustrates the general architecture of a service mesh:

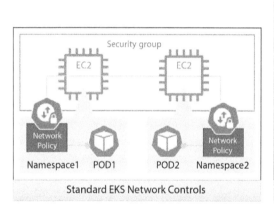
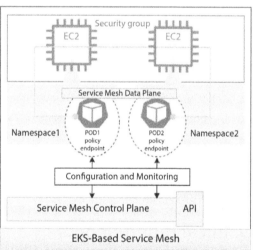

Figure 16.1 – General service mesh architecture

Now let's explore some of the different data plane options you can choose.

Understanding different data plane solution options

There are several options you can choose when selecting how you implement the service mesh data plane, which provides consistent control across different namespaces, Pods, and so on. These are as follows:

- Use an external DNS service to provide service discovery only

- Use Linux kernel technology such as **enhanced Berkeley packet filter** (**eBFP**) to provide traffic control and visibility

- Use a sidecar container that controls all the network traffic and provides telemetry data

These different data plane options are illustrated in the following diagram.

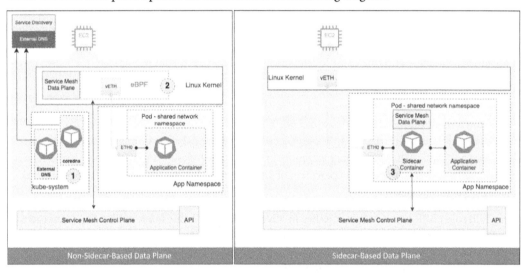

Figure 16.2 – Service mesh data plane options

Let's look at each of these data plane options in more detail.

Exploring service discovery with DNS

The simplest type of mesh simply provides service discovery. This allows Pods running on an EKS cluster to locate external services running on other clusters, in other AWS accounts/VPCs, or on-premises. This is typically achieved using coredns and configuring it to forward to an external DNS service. The external DNS service can also be used to register cluster services so that external users can locate a K8s cluster. This can be achieved using external-dns, a K8s add-on that can synchronize Kubernetes resources with an external DNS service. This add-on integrates with both **Route 53**, which is a standard AWS DNS service, and **Cloud Map**, which is a cloud service discovery tool. Later on, in the *Using AWS Cloud Map with EKS* section, we will look at how we can integrate

Cloud Map with EKS to provide a simple service discovery solution. This kind of mesh doesn't support any kind of traffic control or telemetry but is useful when you need to connect the K8s service with AWS or on-premises services.

Exploring kernel-based service meshes

The key to providing traffic control or telemetry is to implement network filters, which can control and log traffic flows. In K8s today, this is typically done using `iptables` controlled through `kube-proxy`. As K8s resources are deployed (Pods, Deployments, and Services), `kube-proxy` will write the necessary `iptables` (or IPVS) to allow traffic to flow in and out of the cluster and rewrite the packets with the correct NAT (translated) addresses.

The challenge with `iptables` is that they were designed when network speeds were relatively slow. So they can be slow if you implement a large ruleset as they need recreating when changes are made and need linear evaluation. In a large EKS cluster, you might have 5000+ standard `iptables` rules that are mostly the same and this can add latency. If you then add in complex application rules, you can seriously impact the network stack.

Berkeley Packet Filters (**BPF**) or **enhanced BPF** (**eBPF**) can be used as a replacement for `iptables`, which is much more performant and flexible. eBPF allows you to run user code in the Linux kernel without changing kernel parameters and is used a lot for firewalls and deep packet inspection appliances. As it is more performant, it is used more and more in service mesh design and with newer Kubernetes CNI implementations to support the deployment of filtering rules that support an application's network connectivity requirements.

We won't discuss eBPF-based service meshes in any more detail in this book as it's still an emergent area, but it's worth considering when assessing service meshes.

Exploring sidecar-based service meshes

The most common service mesh data plane pattern is the use of a sidecar container, which is deployed in the same Pod as the application container and acts as a proxy controlling inbound and outbound traffic under the supervision of the service mesh control plane. The advantage of this approach is that application network rules are localized to the Pod and don't have an impact on the kernel and the sidecar can be used to support enhanced capabilities such as traffic encryption (mutual TLS).

The sidecar proxy can be a custom image but most service meshes use a common proxy. **Envoy** (`https://www.envoyproxy.io/`) is a very common choice and supports HTTP/HTTPv2 proxies, TLS encryption, load-balancing, and observability (traffic telemetry). Let's look at this pattern in more detail in the next section by examining AWS App Mesh.

Understanding AWS App Mesh

There are many different service mesh implementations. We will focus on AWS App Mesh as it is a fully managed service, but bear in mind other meshes such as Istio, Linkerd, and Gloo are available (take a look at `https://layer5.io/service-mesh-landscape` if you want a community view). AWS App Mesh provides consistent network controls across Amazon EKS, AWS Fargate, Amazon ECS, Amazon EC2, and Kubernetes on EC2 using a sidecar data plane based on the Envoy proxy. We will focus on the EKS usage but bear in mind one of the major reasons for using AWS App Mesh is its ability to provide traffic control and visibility across applications deployed across a variety of different compute services in AWS.

AWS App Mesh implements a number of different constructs to control and monitor application traffic. The main one is the mesh itself. You can have multiple meshes in an account and each represents a logical network boundary for all the applications/services to reside within. Generally, you would use a single mesh to *group* lots of related services that make calls on one another and act as a single ecosystem. The mesh construct is the first thing that needs to be created. The following diagram illustrates the main constructs in AWS App Mesh:

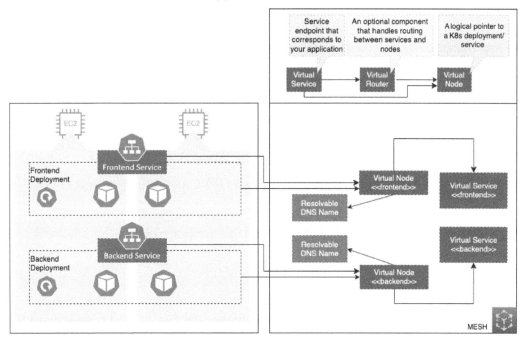

Figure 16.3 – AWS App Mesh virtual constructs

Once a mesh is created, you will need to create at least two more constructs per K8s Deployment:

- A **virtual Node** is required and represents an abstraction of your K8s Deployment/Service. It is used to link your K8s resources and the mesh constructs using the service discovery method used in your definition.

- A **virtual Service** is required and can point to either a virtual node or a virtual router and is used by other services in the mesh to connect to the K8s service.

> **Important note**
>
> A really important point to note is that any consumers of the service mesh will use the virtual service to access the underlying K8s Service and so the name defined in the virtual service awsName key has to be resolvable to an IP address (it doesn't matter what IP address it is). If all your services run in the cluster, then you can create a dummy service so the native CoreDNS service will return a cluster service IP address, which will then be translated by the Envoy sidecar when the client/consumer makes an IP request. If you services that run on other compute platforms in AWS (EC2, for example), then you will need to integrate into a common external DNS in order to locate the EKS services.

AWS App Mesh also supports two more optional constructs:

- A **virtual router**, which can be used to route traffic between servicesand is useful for things such as blue/green deployments. This type of construct will be discussed when we start deploying services.

- A **virtual gateway**, which can be used like a K8s Ingress to route and control north/south traffic. This type of construct will be discussed when we start deploying services.

Now that we understand the basic constructs, let's look at how we configure a cluster to work with AWS App Mesh.

Installing AWS App Mesh Controller in a cluster

We will use AWS App Mesh Controller for K8s (https://github.com/aws/aws-app-mesh-controller-for-k8s), which allows us to create App Mesh resources through a **K8s manifest**, as well as to automatically inject the Envoy proxy container into a Pod. The starting point is to create the namespace, IAM role, and service account needed for the controller Pods. The commands are as follows:

```
$ kubectl create ns appmesh-system
$ eksctl create iamserviceaccount --cluster myipv4cluster
--namespace appmesh-system --name appmesh-controller
--attach-policy-arn  arn:aws:iam::aws:policy/
AWSCloudMapFullAccess,arn:aws:iam::aws:policy/
```

```
AWSAppMeshFullAccess --override-existing-serviceaccounts
--approve
…. .
454 created serviceaccount "appmesh-system/appmesh-controller"
```

You will notice that as well as providing the `AWSAppMeshFullAccess` role, we also provide `AWSCloudMapFullAccess`, which will be discussed in the *Using AWS Cloud Map with EKS* section. Now we have the prerequisites in place, we can install the controller and verify it's running using the following commands:

```
$ helm install appmesh-controller eks/appmesh-controller
--namespace appmesh-system --set region=eu-central-1 --set
serviceAccount.create=false --set serviceAccount.name=appmesh-
controller
…. .
AWS App Mesh controller installed!
$ kubectl -n appmesh-system get all
NAME    READY    STATUS    RESTARTS    AGE
pod/appmesh-controller-xx    1/1    Running    0    105s
NAME TYPE    CLUSTER-IP    EXTERNAL-IP    PORT(S)    AGE
service/appmesh-controller-webhook-
service    ClusterIP    10.100.20.50    <none>    443/
TCP    105s
NAME    READY    UP-TO-DATE    AVAILABLE    AGE
deployment.apps/appmesh-controller    1/1    1  1    105s
NAME    DESIRED CURRENT    READY    AGE
replicaset.apps/appmesh-controller-xx    1    1 1    105s
$ kubectl get crds | grep appmesh
…. .
virtualgateways.appmesh.k8s.aws 2022-12-20T21:45:42Z
virtualnodes.appmesh.k8s.aws    2022-12-20T21:45:42Z
virtualrouters.appmesh.k8s.aws  2022-12-20T21:45:42Z
virtualservices.appmesh.k8s.aws 2022-12-20T21:45:42Z
```

We should now create the mesh, which will act as the logical boundary for the network traffic for any services contained in the mesh. The following K8s manifest will create a simple mesh called `webapp` in the current cluster region:

```
apiVersion: appmesh.k8s.aws/v1beta2
kind: Mesh
```

```
metadata:
  name: webapp
spec:
  namespaceSelector:
    matchLabels:
      mesh: webapp
```

The final step is to attach the `AWSAppMeshEnvoyAccess` policy to the worker node's role so that all Envoy containers can make calls to the App Mesh API. You can do this for each deployment and create an IRSA for each namespace. But in this book, we will just update the nodes.

Now that we have the mesh and worker nodes configured, let's see how we can deploy our services and configure the relevant App Mesh constructs.

Integrating your application with AWS App Mesh

In this section, we will build on a lot of the details shown in the previous chapters to build and deploy an application using standard Kubernetes resources and then modify it to use AWS App Mesh constructs to control and monitor traffic. This application traffic can be considered in two dimensions: traffic coming from the consumers/users/internet, sometimes referred to as north/south traffic, and traffic coming from other services/applications in the cluster or ecosystem, referred to as east/west traffic. The following diagram illustrates these concepts:

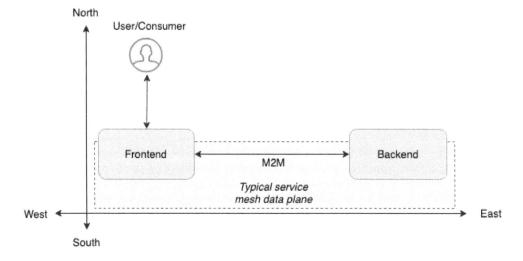

Figure 16.4 – Typical service mesh control

North/south traffic will normally need some sort of authentication/authorization. The endpoints for this traffic will normally be handled by *frontend* services, which provide a lot of the presentation logic and will aggregate or orchestrate requests across multiple backend services. East/west traffic normally comes from other systems (machine-to-machine) and endpoints are provided by *backend* services, which will tend to authorize requests and provide business data for a specific domain such as orders, accounts, and so on.

Most service meshes focus on securing, controlling, and monitoring east/west traffic, with north/west traffic being handled by standard K8s services such as a K8s Ingress. However, as these meshes have evolved, they have also begun to handle more north/west traffic replacing these services.

In the following section, we will deploy a simple frontend/backend application with a K8s Ingress (an AWS ALB) and then modify the backend to use AWS App Mesh (east/west traffic), replace the frontend with a virtual gateway (north/south), and take a high-level look at traffic monitoring and observability.

Deploying our standard application

We are going to use two Pods based on **Python** and **FastAPI**, but you can use any framework to act as your HTTP services. We will also use a third Pod, which will act as our service consumer (east/ west traffic) and can make API requests (using `curl`) to our HTTP services. The application design and Python snippets are shown in the following figure. In the initial deployment, we will just assume blue and green represent different services:

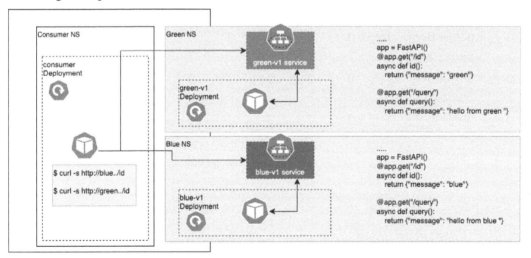

Figure 16.5 – Sample application

We will start by deploying the green service.

Deploying the green service

The service consists of a deployment of two Python/FastAPI Pods, which expose two paths on port 8081; a GET /id path, which simply returns an {"id" : "green"} message; and a GET /query path, which will simply return a {"message" : "hello from green"} message:

1. Let's first create the namespace for these resources. The following manifest will create the resources shown in *Figure 16.5* in a separate namespace, green, which doesn't have the mesh labels applied:

```
---
kind: Namespace
apiVersion: v1
metadata:
  name: green
  labels:
    name: green
```

2. Now we create a Deployment that uses the frontend code that has been containerized and pushed to a private ECR repository (please review the relevant instructions and artifacts in *Chapter 11*):

```
---
apiVersion: apps/v1
kind: Deployment
metadata:
  namespace: green
  name: green-v1
spec:
  selector:
    matchLabels:
      app.kubernetes.io/name: green-v1
  replicas: 2
  template:
    metadata:
      labels:
        app.kubernetes.io/name: green-v1
    spec:
      containers:
        - image: 112233.dkr.ecr…/green:0.0.1
```

```
        imagePullPolicy: Always
        name: backend
        ports:
        - containerPort: 8081
```

> **Important note**
>
> The Python/FastAPI code used in the green and blue container images is shown in *Figure 16.5* but any web server will do for the purposes of this exercise.

3. Next, we create a `ClusterIP` service, which will be used to access the green service inside the cluster:

```
---
apiVersion: v1
kind: Service
metadata:
  namespace: green
  name: green-v1
  labels:
    version: v1
spec:
  ports:
    - port: 8081
      protocol: TCP
  selector:
    app.kubernetes.io/name: green-v1
```

4. Now, using the following command, we can see that we have a K8s service so that other K8s Pods or Services can locate and use it:

```
$ kubectl get svc -n green
NAME     TYPE      CLUSTER-IP        EXTERNAL-IP   PORT(S)
AGE
green-v1 ClusterIP 10.100.192.178    <none>        8081/
TCP     8h
```

Now that we have a green service, let's deploy the blue service in the following section.

Deploying the blue service

The blue service follows a model similar to that of the green service and consists of a deployment of two Python/FastAPI containers that expose two paths on port 8080; a GET /id path, which simply returns an {"id" : "blue"} message; and a GET /query path, which will respond with a {"message" : "hello from blue"} message. The service has a ClusterIP service, which is available only inside the cluster:

1. Let's create the blue namespace for our application using the following manifest, which doesn't have the mesh labels applied:

    ```
    ---
    kind: Namespace
    apiVersion: v1
    metadata:
      name: blue
      labels:
        name: blue
    ```

2. Now we create the Deployment that references the backend container on ECR:

    ```
    ---
    apiVersion: apps/v1
    kind: Deployment
    metadata:
      namespace: blue
      name: blue-v1
    spec:
      selector:
        matchLabels:
          app.kubernetes.io/name: blue-v1
      replicas: 2
      template:
        metadata:
          labels:
            app.kubernetes.io/name: blue-v1
        spec:
          containers:
          - image: 112233.dkr.ecr…blue:0.0.1
    ```

```
        imagePullPolicy: Always
        name: blue-v1
        ports:
        - containerPort: 8080
```

> **Important note**
>
> The Python/FastAPI code used in the green and blue container images is shown in *Figure 16.5* but any web server will do for the purposes of this exercise.

3. Finally, we create the service, `ClusterIP`, which will create the necessary cluster DNS entry to access the Service from within the cluster:

```
    ---
    apiVersion: v1
    kind: Service
    metadata:
      namespace: blue
      name: blue-v1
      labels:
        version: v1
    spec:
      ports:
        - port: 8080
          protocol: TCP
      selector:
        app.kubernetes.io/name: blue-v1
```

4. Using the following command, we can see that we have a K8s service so that other K8s services/Pods can locate and use it:

```
$ kubectl get svc -n blue
NAME     TYPE      CLUSTER-IP      EXTERNAL-IP   PORT(S)    AGE
blue-v1    ClusterIP    10.100.223.120    <none> 8080/
TCP    8h
```

Finally, we will deploy the consumer service and test our connectivity to the blue and green services using all native, non-mesh resources.

Deploying the consumer service

Finally, we will deploy the consumer service, which consists of a single Pod that supports the `curl` command:

1. Using the following manifest will create the resources shown in *Figure 16.5* in a separate namespace, `consumer`, which doesn't have the mesh labels applied:

    ```
    kind: Namespace
    apiVersion: v1
    metadata:
      name: consumer
      labels:
        name: consumer
    ```

2. Now we create the `Deployment` that references the `alpine/curl` container pulled from a public Docker Hub repo:

    ```
    apiVersion: apps/v1
    kind: Deployment
    metadata:
      namespace: consumer
      name: consumer
    spec:
      selector:
        matchLabels:
          app.kubernetes.io/name: consumer
      replicas: 1
      template:
        metadata:
          labels:
            app.kubernetes.io/name: consumer
        spec:
          containers:
          - image: alpine/curl
            command:
            - sleep
            - "36000"
            imagePullPolicy: IfNotPresent
    ```

```
          ports:
          - containerPort: 22
            name: consumer
          restartPolicy: Always
```

3. We can check whether the Pod is deployed with the following command:

```
$ kubectl get po -n consumer
NAME                    READY   STATUS    RESTARTS    AGE
consumer-123    1/1     Running   0           13s
```

4. All done! We can now connect to our consumer Pod and test whether we can connect to the relevant K8s services using the following commands:

```
$ kubectl exec -it -n consumer consumer-123 - sh
/ # curl http://green-v1.green:8081/id
{"id":"green"}
/ # curl http://green-v1.green:8081/query
{"message":"hello from green"}
/ # curl http://blue-v1.blue:8080/id
{"id":"blue"}
/ # curl http://blue-v1.blue:8080/query
{"message":"hello from blue"}
```

> **Important note**
> Please note we have used the shortened service notation, `<scv-name>.namespace`, to call the K8s services we created in each namespace.

Now we have a working set of services, we will add the basic mesh components and test again but this time using the service mesh virtual services.

Adding the basic AWS App Mesh components

The first thing we need to do is label the `blue`, `green`, and `consumer` namespaces to identify which mesh to use and confirm we want to inject the Envoy sidecar container into all the Pods that get deployed into those namespaces automatically. The following commands illustrate how we do this for the sample application:

```
$ kubectl label namespace consumer mesh=webapp
$ kubectl label namespace consumer appmesh.k8s.aws/
```

```
sidecarInjectorWebhook=enabled
$ kubectl label namespace blue mesh=webapp
$ kubectl label namespace blue appmesh.k8s.aws/
sidecarInjectorWebhook=enabled
$ kubectl label namespace green mesh=webapp
$ kubectl label namespace green appmesh.k8s.aws/
sidecarInjectorWebhook=enabled
```

> **Important note**
> Typically, the namespace label will be created when the namespace is created; we are only doing it now to illustrate these concepts in the book.

The next step is to deploy the App Mesh `VirtualNode`, which is required for us to redeploy the application. This must be done for every K8s deployment that needs to use the mesh as it will allow the Envoy proxy to configure itself correctly. In this section, we first show the configuration for the green and blue services; the consumer service will be configured last as it references both services.

The green `VirtualNode` manifest is shown in the following snippet and references the `green-v1` K8s service we created as part of the basic application deployment. It also creates a basic health check using the `/id` path, defines DNS as the service discovery protocol for the underlying resources, and uses the fully qualified name of the K8s service:

```
---
apiVersion: appmesh.k8s.aws/v1beta2
kind: VirtualNode
metadata:
  name: green-v1
  namespace: green
spec:
  podSelector:
    matchLabels:
      app.kubernetes.io/name: green-v1
  listeners:
    - portMapping:
        port: 8081
        protocol: http
      healthCheck:
        protocol: http
```

```
          path: '/id'
          healthyThreshold: 2
          unhealthyThreshold: 2
          timeoutMillis: 2000
          intervalMillis: 5000
    serviceDiscovery:
      dns:
        hostname: green-v1.green.svc.cluster.local
```

The blue VirtualNode manifest is shown in the following snippet and references the blue-v1 K8s service but is configured in the same way as the green VirtualNode:

```
---
apiVersion: appmesh.k8s.aws/v1beta2
kind: VirtualNode
metadata:
  name: blue-v1
  namespace: blue
spec:
  podSelector:
    matchLabels:
      app.kubernetes.io/name: blue-v1
  listeners:
    - portMapping:
        port: 8080
        protocol: http
      healthCheck:
        protocol: http
        path: '/id'
        healthyThreshold: 2
        unhealthyThreshold: 2
        timeoutMillis: 2000
        intervalMillis: 5000
    serviceDiscovery:
      dns:
        hostname: blue-v1.blue.svc.cluster.local
```

We can now check whether the virtual nodes are deployed in your cluster and have also been registered in the AWS App Mesh API using the following commands:

```
$ kubectl get virtualnode --all-namespaces
NAMESPACE    NAME    ARN                    AGE
blue   blue-v1     arn:aws:appmesh:eu-central-1:112233:mesh/
webapp/virtualNode/blue-v1_blue       2m50s
green         green-v1    arn:aws:appmesh:eu-central-
1:112233:mesh/webapp/virtualNode/green-v1_green    103s
$ aws appmesh list-virtual-nodes --mesh-name webapp
{
    "virtualNodes": [
        {
....
            "virtualNodeName": "blue-v1_blue",
....
        },
        {
....
            "virtualNodeName": "green-v1_green",
.....}]}
```

> **Note**
> It's always worth checking the resources are fully deployed into the mesh using the AWS CLI as sometimes the resource is deployed in K8s but is not correctly configured so it isn't present in the mesh API.

The actual Deployment and Pods haven't changed yet, so if you list the Pods in either of the namespaces, you will see the original Pods. We can now restart the Deployment using the kubectl rollout command and we will see the container count increase for the Pods in the blue and green namespaces. An example of the commands used for the blue namespace is as follows:

```
$ kubectl get po -n blue
NAME                        READY    STATUS    RESTARTS    AGE
blue-v1-684cc59d8-5kczs     1/1      Running   0           23h
blue-v1-684cc59d8-nfvf9     1/1      Running   0           23h
$ kubectl rollout restart deployment blue-v1 -n blue
```

```
deployment.apps/blue-v1 restarted
$ kubectl get po -n blue
NAME                        READY    STATUS     RESTARTS    AGE
blue-v1-6bdfb49995-8789s    2/2      Running    0           8s
blue-v1-6bdfb49995-zzsw4    2/2      Running    0           10s
```

The final step is to add the VirtualService resources for blue and green Pods as, currently, while the Envoy proxy has been injected and configured with the VirtualNode configuration, the service is not resolvable in the mesh. As shown in the following manifest, VirtualService for the blue service uses the service name blue but will map directly to the blue-v1 virtualNode we created previously in the blue namespace:

```
---
apiVersion: appmesh.k8s.aws/v1beta2
kind: VirtualService
metadata:
  name: blue
  namespace: blue
spec:
  awsName: blue.blue.svc.cluster.local
  provider:
    virtualNode:
      virtualNodeRef:
        name: blue-v1
        namespace: blue
```

If you remember, in the *Understanding AWS App Mesh* section, we said that the awsName needed to be resolvable through DNS. As this service runs fully in K8s, we can add a dummy K8s Service called blue in the blue namespace to be able to resolve the blue.blue.svc.cluster.local service name using the following manifest:

```
---
apiVersion: v1
kind: Service
metadata:
  name: blue
  namespace: blue
  labels:
    app.kubernetes.io/name: blue
```

```
spec:
  ports:
  - port: 8080
    name: http
```

> `Note
>
> Remember, while the DNS lookup will return the cluster IP address associated with the blue service, the Envoy proxy will modify the traffic to allow it to communicate with the underlying blue-v1 service.

Once we have deployed the VirtualServices and dummy K8s services to both namespaces, we can review the configuration using the following commands:

```
$ kubectl get virtualservice --all-namespaces
NAMESPACE    NAME    ARN                                    AGE
blue    blue    arn:aws:appmesh:eu-central-1:112233:mesh/webapp/
virtualService/blue.blue.svc.cluster.local    37s
green        green    arn:aws:appmesh:eu-central-1:112233:mesh/
webapp/virtualService/green.green.svc.cluster.local    25s
$ kubectl get svc --all-namespaces
NAMESPACE    NAME      TYPE    CLUSTER-IP          ..
blue    blue       ClusterIP    10.100.217.243    <none>    8080/TCP .
blue    blue-v1    ClusterIP    10.100.50.46      <none>    8080/TCP .
green    green      ClusterIP    10.100.100.13    <none>    8081/TCP .
green    green-v1 ClusterIP    10.100.51.214    <none>    8081/TCP .
....
```

We can also view the virtual services that have been created using the aws appmesh list-virtual-services command or the console, an example of which is shown in the following figure:

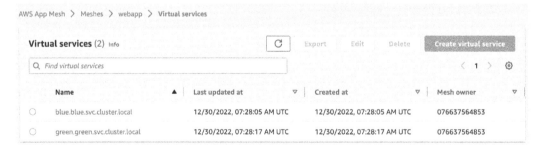

Figure 16.6 – Console view of mesh virtual services for K8s services

We have all the resources defined now for the blue and green services. We can now add the `VirtualNode` for the consumer and test connectivity to the mesh services. The manifest for the consumer `VirtualNode` is shown in the following snippet and is similar to the definitions used for the blue and green services; however, it contains a backend key that allows it to communicate with the `blue` and `green` services we created in the *Deploying a standard application* section (which is why we do this last):

```
---
apiVersion: appmesh.k8s.aws/v1beta2
kind: VirtualNode
metadata:
  name: consumer
  namespace: consumer
spec:
  podSelector:
    matchLabels:
      app.kubernetes.io/name: consumer
  listeners:
    - portMapping:
        port: 8082
        protocol: http
  backends:
    - virtualService:
        virtualServiceRef:
          namespace: blue
                name: blue
    - virtualService:
        virtualServiceRef:
                  namespace: green
              name: green
  serviceDiscovery:
    dns:
      hostname: consumer.consumer.svc.cluster.local
```

Once we have deployed the `VirtualNode` configuration, we can redeploy the consumer deployment and check the resulting resources using the following commands:

```
$ kubectl rollout restart deployment consumer  -n consumer
deployment.apps/consumer restarted
```

```
$ kubectl get po -n consumer
NAME              READY    STATUS      RESTARTS     AGE
consumer-1122. 2/2        Running     0            105s
$ aws appmesh describe-virtual-node --virtual-node-name
consumer_consumer --mesh-name webapp
{
    "virtualNode": {
        "status": {
            "status": "ACTIVE"
....}
```

We can now exec into our consumer Pod and test our App Mesh services using the following commands:

```
$ kubectl exec -it -n consumer consumer-1122  -- sh
Defaulted container "consumer" out of: consumer, envoy,
proxyinit (init)
/ # curl -s http://blue.blue.svc.cluster.local:8080/id
{"id":"blue"}
/ # curl -s http://green.green.svc.cluster.local:8081/id
{"id":"green"}
```

You may notice that as this is now a multi-container Pod, the exec command has defaulted to the app container, in this case, consumer, but you also see the envoy and the init containers (proxyinit) that were injected into the original Pod definition. We also now use the fully qualified App Mesh service names, for example, blue.blue.svc.cluster.local rather than the K8s service names, such as blue-v1.

We have now deployed the mesh and integrated it into our application. The only thing that changed from an application perspective was the service name we used in the curl command. It's still quite a bit of work, so in the next section, we will look at how a virtual router can simplify blue/green deployments.

Using a virtual router in AWS App Mesh

In this example, we are now going to assume that the blue and green services are now different versions of the same service (blue/green deployment). We will create a new service, myapp, which represents the application, and then put a virtual router in between the existing two virtual nodes and initially just send all the traffic to the green version. The following diagram illustrates this:

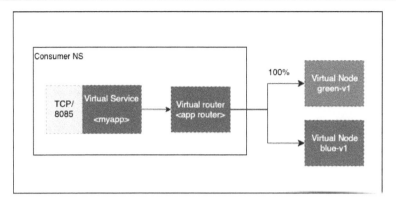

Figure 16.7 – Adding a virtual router to our service

The first thing we need to do is create the new VirtualRouter. The following manifest creates a router and a single route to map against the /id path and listen on TCP port 8085. The weight key is used to define the weight/percentage of traffic that flows to a given VirtualNode. In the following example, we send everything to the green-v1 VirtualNode:

```
---
apiVersion: appmesh.k8s.aws/v1beta2
kind: VirtualRouter
metadata:
  name: app-router
  namespace: consumer
spec:
  listeners:
    - portMapping:
        port: 8085
        protocol: http
  routes:
    - name: app-route
      httpRoute:
        match:
          prefix: /id
        action:
          weightedTargets:
            - virtualNodeRef:
                name: green-v1
                namespace: green
```

```
                    weight: 100
                    port: 8081
                  - virtualNodeRef:
                       name: blue-v1
                       namespace: blue
                    weight: 0
                    port: 8080
```

We also need to add the myapp virtual service and dummy K8s service (for DNS resolution); the following sample manifest creates both and references the VirtualRouter we created previously instead of a VirtualNode:

```
---
apiVersion: appmesh.k8s.aws/v1beta2
kind: VirtualService
metadata:
  name: myapp
  namespace: consumer
spec:
  awsName: myapp.consumer.svc.cluster.local
  provider:
    virtualRouter:
      virtualRouterRef:
        name: app-router
---
apiVersion: v1
kind: Service
metadata:
  name: myapp
  namespace: consumer
  labels:
    app.kubernetes.io/name: consumer
spec:
  ports:
  - port: 8085
    name: http
```

Once we have deployed these resources, we need to adjust the consumer `VirtualNode` specification to allow access to this new service by adding a new backend configuration, as shown in the following:

```
backends:
    - virtualService:
        virtualServiceRef:
            namespace: blue
            name: blue
    - virtualService:
        virtualServiceRef:
            namespace: green
            name: green
    - virtualService:
        virtualServiceRef:
            name: myapp
```

> **Important note**
> As the myapp service is in the same namespace as the consumer, we don't need to add the namespace key, but you might want to add it for clarity.

With all this deployed, we can now `exec` into our `consumer` and test our new services using the following commands:

```
$ kubectl exec -it -n consumer consumer-1122   -- sh
Defaulted container "consumer" out of: consumer, envoy,
proxyinit (init)
/ # curl -s http://myapp.consumer.svc.cluster.local:8085/id
{"id":"green"}
/ # curl -s http://myapp.consumer.svc.cluster.local:8085/id
{"id":"green"}
```

If we now adjust the weights in our `VirtualRouter routes` configuration, to distribute evenly over the `blue` and `green` services, we can shift traffic from the `green` service to the `blue` service, as shown in the following snippet:

```
routes:
    - name: app-route
      httpRoute:
        match:
```

```
            prefix: /id
        action:
        weightedTargets:
          - virtualNodeRef:
              name: green-v1
              namespace: green
            weight: 50
            port: 8081
          - virtualNodeRef:
              name: blue-v1
              namespace: blue
            weight: 50
            port: 8080
```

Running the same `curl` command will now result in responses from both the `blue` and `green` services:

```
/ # curl -s http://myapp.consumer.svc.cluster.local:8085/id
{"id":"green"}
/ # curl -s http://myapp.consumer.svc.cluster.local:8085/id
{"id":"blue"}
/ # curl -s http://myapp.consumer.svc.cluster.local:8085/id
{"id":"green"}
/ # curl -s http://myapp.consumer.svc.cluster.local:8085/id
{"id":"blue"}
```

Again, the only change to the application here is the URL/service being used, and Envoy and AWS App Mesh take care of all the *magic*. We have focused only on east/west traffic so far; in the next section, we will look at how we can expose this service through a virtual gateway outside the cluster.

Using a virtual gateway in AWS App Mesh

`VirtualGateway` is used to expose services running inside the mesh, and accessible to services outside the mesh that don't have access to the App Mesh control plane using a configured Envoy proxy. It does this by deploying standalone Envoy proxies and an AWS **network load balancer** (**NLB**). The standalone proxies terminate the NLB traffic and then use *Gateway Routes* to pass traffic to the relevant `VirtualService`, which in turn then passes traffic to either a `VirtualRouter` or directly to a `VirtualNode`. We will extend our `myapp` service to be accessible via the internet via a `VirtualGateway`. The following diagram illustrates this:

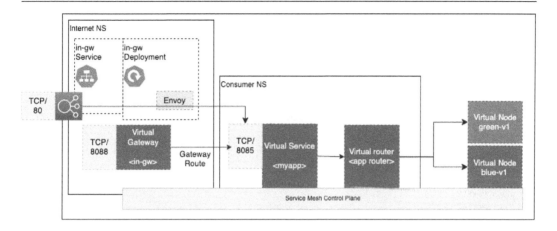

Figure 16.8 – Virtual gateway deployment

The first thing we need to do is create and label the `internet` namespace, which will host our Ingress gateway and load balancer. We do this as we are hosting the Envoy proxy in standalone mode so we don't want to use a namespace that will try and inject an Envoy proxy on top of a standalone Envoy proxy. The following commands illustrate how you can do this:

```
$ kubectl create namespace internet
$ kubectl label namespace internet gateway=in-gw
$ kubectl label namespace internet mesh=webapp
```

We can then go ahead and create the `VirtualGateway` that listens on port `8088` in the internet namespace we just created using the following manifest:

```
---
apiVersion: appmesh.k8s.aws/v1beta2
kind: VirtualGateway
metadata:
  name: in-gw
  namespace: internet
spec:
  namespaceSelector:
    matchLabels:
      gateway: in-gw
  podSelector:
    matchLabels:
      app: in-gw
```

```
listeners:
  - portMapping:
      port: 8088
      protocol: http
```

We can now create a **gateway route** pointing to our myapp VirtualService in the consumer namespace using the following manifest:

```
---
apiVersion: appmesh.k8s.aws/v1beta2
kind: GatewayRoute
metadata:
  name: myapp-route
  namespace: internet
spec:
  httpRoute:
    match:
      prefix: "/"
    action:
      target:
        virtualService:
          virtualServiceRef:
            name: myapp
            port: 8085
            namespace: consumer
```

> **Important note**
> We will use the default prefix, /, which captures all traffic and sends it to the myapp VirtualService.

Using the following commands, we can now get the ARN of the VirtualGateway we created as we need this information when we deploy the standalone Envoy proxies:

```
$ kubectl get virtualgateway --all-namespaces
NAMESPACE    NAME      ARN                             AGE
internet     in-gw     arn:aws:appmesh:eu-central-1:112233:mesh/
webapp/virtualGateway/in-gw_internet    7m37s
```

We can now deploy the standalone Envoy proxies into the `internet` namespace. In the following sample manifest, we create two replicas using the AWS Envoy image and inject the ARN of the `VirtualGateway` that we listed in the previous step, using the `APPMESH_RESOURCE_ARN` environment variable:

```yaml
---
apiVersion: apps/v1
kind: Deployment
metadata:
  name: in-gw
  namespace: internet
spec:
  replicas: 2
  selector:
    matchLabels:
      app: in-gw
  template:
    metadata:
      labels:
        app: in-gw
    spec:
      containers:
        - name: envoy
          image: 840364872350.dkr.ecr.eu-central-1.amazonaws.com/aws-appmesh-envoy:v1.24.0.0-prod
          env:
          - name: APPMESH_RESOURCE_ARN
            value: "arn:aws:appmesh:eu-central-1:112233:mesh/webapp/virtualGateway/in-gw_internet"
          - name: ENVOY_LOG_LEVEL
            value: "debug"
          ports:
            - containerPort: 8088
```

> **Important note**
>
> We set the Envoy logging level to `debug` for information only; this should not be left for any production workloads as it results in very large logs and should be reset to `info` once any troubleshooting is complete. The image used comes from the public `appmesh` repository, which you can access at `https://gallery.ecr.aws/appmesh/aws-appmesh-envoy`.

Finally, we create an NLB-based service to expose the Envoy proxies to the internet. This will use an IP-based scheme and expose port `80` on the load balancer, which will map to port `8088` using the IP addresses of the Pods in the target group to route traffic to each Envoy Pod:

```yaml
---
apiVersion: v1
kind: Service
metadata:
  name: in-gw
  namespace: internet
  annotations:
    service.beta.kubernetes.io/aws-load-balancer-type: external
    service.beta.kubernetes.io/aws-load-balancer-nlb-target-type: ip
    service.beta.kubernetes.io/aws-load-balancer-scheme: internet-facing

spec:
  ports:
    - port: 80
      targetPort: 8088
      protocol: TCP
  type: LoadBalancer
  loadBalancerClass: service.k8s.aws/nlb
  selector:
    app: in-gw
```

> **Important note**
>
> While this service exposes the Envoy proxies to the internet, we could have also configured the service to use an internal NLB (or ALB if it's an HTTP/HTTPS service), which means that other non-mesh resources could access the mesh services but only on the AWS network or a connected private network.

We can now test that our `myapp` service is exposed through the `VirtualGateway` by retrieving the URL of the NLB we just created using the `kubectl get svc` command and then using `curl` to get the K8s service ID using the following commands:

```
$ kubectl get svc -n internet
NAME TYPE  CLUSTER-IP      EXTERNAL-IP      PORT(S)         AGE
in-gw   LoadBalancer    10.100.12.98    k8s-internet-ingw-1122.
elb.eu-central-1.amazonaws.com    80:30644/TCP    53m
$ curl -s http://k8s-internet-ingw-1122.elb.eu-central-1.
amazonaws.com/id
{"id":"blue"}
$ curl -s http://k8s-internet-ingw-1122.elb.eu-central-1.
amazonaws.com/id
{"id":"green"}
```

Now we have seen how to expose our AWS App Mesh `VirtualService` to the internet using a `VirtualGateway` resource. Next, we will review how we can use AWS Cloud Map, an external DNS service, to perform service discovery with AWS App Mesh.

Using AWS Cloud Map with EKS

AWS Cloud Map is a cloud resource discovery tool so, unlike App Mesh, it has no traffic control or observability features. It simply allows consumers to discover cloud services (not just EKS-based ones).

Cloud Map operates in namespaces so the first thing we will do is create a new namespace called `myapp.prod.eu`, which we will use later. We can use the following AWS CLI commands to register and validate whether we have created the namespace:

```
$ aws servicediscovery create-private-dns-namespace --name
prod.eu --description 'european production private DNS
namespace' --vpc vpc-0614a71963e68bc86
{
    "OperationId": "pqrexzv7e5tn7wq64wiph6ztyb4c5ut3-5k7jsu2f"
}
$ aws servicediscovery get-operation  --operation-id
pqrexzv7e5tn7wq64wiph6ztyb4c5ut3-5k7jsu2f
{
    "Operation": {
        "Status": "SUCCESS",
        "CreateDate": 1672566290.293,
        "Id": "pqrexzv7e5tn7wq64wiph6ztyb4c5ut3-5k7jsu2f",
```

```
            "UpdateDate": 1672566327.657,
            "Type": "CREATE_NAMESPACE",
            "Targets": {
                "NAMESPACE": "ns-pj3fxdidxmcgax7e"
            }
        }
    }}
```

We can now create the myapp service using the following command:

```
$ aws servicediscovery create-service    --name myapp
--description 'Discovery service for the myapp service'
--namespace-id ns-pj3fxdidxmcgax7e    --dns-config
'RoutingPolicy=MULTIVALUE,DnsRecords=[{Type=A,TTL=300}]'
--health-check-custom-config FailureThreshold=1
{"Service": {
        "Description": "Discovery service for the myapp
service",
        ........
        "NamespaceId": "ns-pj3fxdidxmcgax7e",
        "Arn": "arn:aws:servicediscovery:eu-central-
1:076637564853:service/srv-kc6c4f2mqt2buibx",
        "Name": "myapp"
    }
```

To register our Pods, we now need to adjust our VirtualNode definition to use Cloud Map. In the previous blue-v1 service, we used the K8s DNS name and had to create a K8s service to register the domain; refer to the following snippet:

```
serviceDiscovery:
    dns:
        hostname: blue-v1.blue.svc.cluster.local
```

We can now adjust this to reference the Cloud Map namespace and service as shown in the following snippet and redeploy the virtual node:

```
serviceDiscovery:
    awsCloudMap:
        namespaceName: prod.eu
        serviceName: myapp
```

We can now validate that the `blue-v1` Pods have registered their IPs with our Cloud Map `myapp` service using the following commands:

```
$ kubectl get po -n blue -o wide
NAME     READY    STATUS    RESTARTS   AGE     IP          .....
blue-v1-12   2/2      Running   0    7m35s   192.168.88.141   ...
blue-v1-22   2/2      Running   0    7m35s   192.168.42.137   ...
$ $ aws servicediscovery list-instances --service-id
srv-kc6c4f2mqt2buibx
{
    "Instances": [
        {
            "Attributes": {
                "AWS_INSTANCE_IPV4": "192.168.42.137",
                "AWS_INIT_HEALTH_STATUS": "HEALTHY",
                ....},
        {
            "Attributes": {
                "AWS_INSTANCE_IPV4": "192.168.88.141",
                "AWS_INIT_HEALTH_STATUS": "HEALTHY",
                ....}]}
```

As we have connected our `prod.eu` namespace to our VPC, any node that has access to the VPC resolver can also resolve this name, as shown in the following sample from one of the EC2 worker nodes:

```
sh-4.2$ dig myapp.prod.eu
<<>> DiG 9.11.4-P2-RedHat-9.11.4-26.P2.amzn2.5.2 <<>> myapp.
prod.eu
.........
;myapp.prod.eu.              IN     A
;; ANSWER SECTION:
myapp.prod.eu.      300     IN     A     192.168.88.141
myapp.prod.eu.      300     IN     A     192.168.42.137
.....
```

> **Important note**
>
> As we now are no longer using CoreDNS in K8s, anything that references the `VirtualNode` must now be modified to use the Cloud Map DNS entry. This includes any `VirtualRouter` and/or `VirtualService`.

Now that we have reviewed how to use Cloud Map with App Mesh, let's round the chapter off with a quick look at how you troubleshoot the Envoy proxy.

Troubleshooting the Envoy proxy

As you can see, the Envoy proxy plays an integral role in AWS App Mesh. So being able to troubleshoot it is a critical skill. By default, Envoy logging is set to informational and while we are debugging, the first thing to do is to increase this logging level.

If you have control over the Pod, then you can adjust the `ENVOY_LOG_LEVEL` variable as we did when we deployed the `VirtualGateway` for the *myapp* services, as shown in the following manifest snippet:

```
env:
- name: ENVOY_LOG_LEVEL
  value: "debug"
```

Those Pods that are injected into a namespace come with the Envoy admin port `9901` enabled so we can use the `kubectl port-forward` command to map a local port to the admin port. The following command is an example of connecting to a Pod in the `green` namespace:

```
$ kubectl port-forward -n green green-v1-cf45dcc99-
fbdh7    8080:9901
```

We will use **Cloud9**, which is an integrated AWS development environment to connect the web browser to the **Envoy Proxy admin**. The following screenshot shows the home screen:

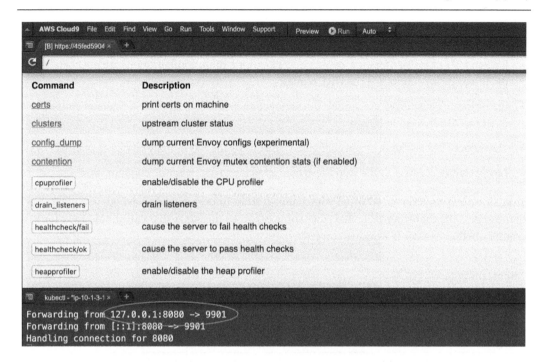

Figure 16.9 – Envoy admin home page in the Cloud9 IDE

While there is a lot of interesting data on the home page, we want to change the logging level so we get more detailed logging. We can do this through the port-forwarding connection we just set up using the following commands and then use the kubectl logs command to get or –follow the logs as they get written:

```
$ curl -X POST http://localhost:8080/logging
active loggers:
  admin: info
  alternate_protocols_cache: info
$ curl -X POST http://localhost:8080/logging?level=debug
active loggers:
  admin: debug
  alternate_protocols_cache: debug
....
$ kubectl logs -n green green-v1-cf45dcc99-fbdh7 envoy
```

> **Important note**
> Remember to specify the envoy container in the preceding command.

Typical Envoy proxy problems include the following:

- Backend, `VirtualGateway`, or `VirtualRouter` route configurations are not correct so the Envoy proxy cannot see the URL request

- Envoy doesn't have AWS credentials or cannot connect to AWS App Mesh regional endpoints due to VPC networking issues

- The service DNS resolution is not configured either using the K8s dummy service or external DNS

- Envoy cannot connect to the App Mesh control plane to get dynamic configuration

Logging in `envoy` is verbose, so when you change it from informational to debug, you will see a lot of messages. The following table describes some expected messages that you should look for to determine whether `envoy` is working correctly.

> **Important note**
> This is not an exhaustive list but just common problems you'll encounter with App Mesh.

Message	Description
[2023-x][34][debug][router] [source/common/router/router. cc:470] [C1988][S225897133909764297] cluster 'cds_ingress_ webapp_green-v1_green_http_8081' match for URL '/id' [2023-x][34][debug][router] [source/common/router/router. cc:673] [C1988][S225897133909764297] router decoding headers: ':authority', 'green-v1.green.svc.cluster.local:8081' ':path', '/id'	This message shows Envoy is receiving a request to the /id path on the green-v1 service port 8081.
[2023-x][17][debug][config] [./source/common/config/ grpc_stream.h:62] Establishing new gRPC bidi stream to appmesh-envoy-management.eu-central-1.amazonaws. com:443 for rpc StreamAggregatedResources(stream .envoy.service.discovery.v3.DiscoveryRequest) returns (stream .envoy.service.discovery.v3.DiscoveryResponse);	This message shows the Envoy proxy connecting to the appmesh regional endpoints.
2023-x][25][debug][aws] [source/extensions/ common/aws/credentials_provider_impl.cc:161] Obtained following AWS credentials from the EC2MetadataService: AWS_ACCESS_KEY_ID=****, AWS_SECRET_ACCESS_KEY=*****, AWS_SESSION_TOKEN=*****	This message shows the Pod getting its credentials to interact with the AWS API.

Message	Description
[2023-x][17][debug][dns] [source/extensions/network/dns_resolver/cares/dns_impl.cc:275] dns resolution for green-v1.green.svc.cluster.local completed with status 0	This message shows the Envoy proxy successfully resolving the DNS name of the local K8s service.
[2023-x][1][debug] [AppNet Agent] Envoy connectivity check status 200, {"stats":[{"name":"control_plane.connected_state","value":1}]} [2023-01-01 12:21:35.455][1][debug] [AppNet Agent] Control Plane connection state changed to: CONNECTED	This shows the Envoy proxy connecting to the appmesh control plane to get the dynamic configuration.

Table 14.1 – Useful Envoy proxy debug messages

Let's now revisit the key learning points from this chapter.

Summary

In this chapter, we learned what a service mesh is and how it works and then we explored the details of what AWS App Mesh is and looked at some of the services it provides. We initially focused on how we can manage east/west traffic using a simple consumer and two web services in our example. After we deployed the application using native K8s services, we then configured our mesh and added `VirtualNode` and `VirtualService`, which allowed traffic to be managed by Envoy sidecar containers that were automatically injected and configured into our application Pods.

We then used `VirtualRouter` to load-balance between green and blue services representing different versions of the same service supporting a blue/green deployment strategy and minimizing rollout disruption. We added `VirtualGateway`, which allowed us to expose our application outside of the EKS cluster using an NLB and standalone Envoy proxies.

Finally, we looked at how you can integrate AWS Cloud Map, an external DNS service, into App Mesh to allow service discovery outside of the cluster and remove the need to use K8s dummy services. We also looked at how to troubleshoot Envoy proxies by increasing the logging level and looked at common issues and messages you should look for. You should now be able to describe some of the features of AWS App Mesh and configure it to work with your existing K8s and AWS CloudMap.

In the next chapter, we will look at how you can monitor your EKS cluster using AWS and third-party and open source tools.

Further reading

- Understanding how external DNS works with AWS Cloud Map: `https://github.com/kubernetes-sigs/external-dns/blob/master/docs/tutorials/aws-sd.md`

- Understanding Envoy and how it's used: `https://www.envoyproxy.io/`

- Understanding the service mesh landscape: `https://layer5.io/service-mesh-landscape`

- Troubleshooting AWS App Mesh: `https://docs.aws.amazon.com/app-mesh/latest/userguide/troubleshooting.html`

Part 4:
Advanced EKS Service Mesh and Scaling

Congratulations! Now you are in the final stretch of your journey to mastering EKS. In the second last part, we will introduce the service mesh and how it can be integrated into EKS. Additionally, we will further explore advanced practices, covering observability, monitoring, and scaling strategies for your workload, Pods, and node groups. Finally, by the end of this part, you will have gained knowledge of automation tools and learned how to implement CI/CD practices to streamline your deployment activities on EKS.

This section contains the following chapters:

17

EKS Observability

Throughout the book, we've looked at how you build EKS clusters and deploy workloads. However, a critical part of any EKS deployment is observability. Observability is the ability to interpret logs and metrics from your cluster/workloads without which you can't troubleshoot/resolve issues or understand capacity or performance. Observability also includes tracing, which allows you to follow a request as it moves through different EKS workloads (microservices), simplifying troubleshooting in a distributed system.

In this chapter, we are going to discuss the tools and techniques you can use to monitor your clusters and workloads natively on AWS or using third-party tools. We will cover the following topics:

- Monitoring clusters and Pods using native AWS tools
- Building dashboards with Managed Service for Prometheus and Grafana
- Tracing with OpenTelemetry
- Using machine learning with DevOps Guru

Technical requirements

You should have a familiarity with YAML, AWS IAM, and EKS architecture. Before getting started with this chapter, please ensure the following:

- You have network connectivity to your EKS cluster API endpoint
- The AWS CLI, Docker, and `kubectl` binary are installed on your workstation and you have administrator access

Monitoring clusters and Pods using native AWS tools

One of the key advantages of an AWS deployment of Kubernetes (EKS) over an on-premises deployment of Kubernetes is it comes pre-integrated into CloudWatch, which is the main logging and monitoring platform for AWS. With a standard EKS cluster, you will automatically get control plane logs, EC2 worker node and load balancer (Network or Application Load Balancer) logs and metrics, along with metrics and logs from other AWS services such as databases, message queues, and so on.

Let's look at how we can create a basic CloudWatch dashboard using standard EC2 metrics to understand the work nodes for our cluster.

Creating a basic CloudWatch dashboard

We'll use Terraform to create a simple dashboard that shows an aggregated view of all instances that are tagged with a specific cluster name, and a second one that shows each individual node. The code snippet shown next illustrates the basic structure, a `data` object (which retrieves all the current AWS credential data) and an `aws_cloudwatch_dashboard` object that consists of two objects (shown further down):

```
data "aws_caller_identity" "current" {}
resource "aws_cloudwatch_dashboard" "simple_Dashboard" {
  dashboard_name = "EKS-Dashboard"
  dashboard_body = <<EOF
{"widgets": [{widget1},{widget2}]}
EOF }
```

> **Important note**
> You need to replace the {widget1|2} markers with the actual code shown next.

For the first widget, we will collect two metrics (CPU and network traffic out) and aggregate them based on the node group name, and use the `eks:cluster-name` tag to select nodes that are part of our `myipv4cluster` cluster:

```
{ "type": "explorer",
  "width": 24,
   "height": 2,
   "x": 0,
   "y": 0,
            "properties": {
                "metrics": [
                    { "metricName": "CPUUtilization",
                        "resourceType": "AWS::EC2::Instance",
                        "stat": "Average"
```

```
        },
        {. "metricName": "NetworkOut",
            "resourceType": "AWS::EC2::Instance",
            "stat": "Average"
        }],
    "region":"eu-central-1",
    "aggregateBy": {
        "key": "eks:nodegroup-name",
        "func": "MAX"
    },
    "labels": [
        {
            "key": "eks:cluster-name",
            "value": "myipv4cluster"
        }
    ],
    "widgetOptions": {
        "legend": {
            "position": "bottom"
        },
        "view": "timeSeries",
        "rowsPerPage": 1,
        "widgetsPerRow": 2
    },
    "period": 60,
    "title": "Cluster EC2 Instances (aggregated)"
}}
```

The following figure shows the widget in the AWS dashboard with two metrics aggregated per node group; `ipv4mng` is the only node group in this cluster.

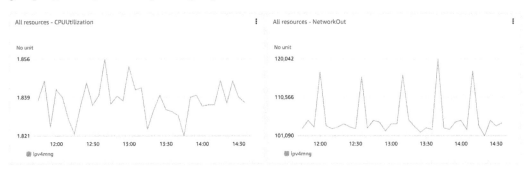

Figure 17.1 – Aggregated CloudWatch dashboard widget

The second widget is exactly the same but doesn't contain the `aggregateBy` key in the widget definition and so generates the following visualization, which shows the same data but also shows the individual instances.

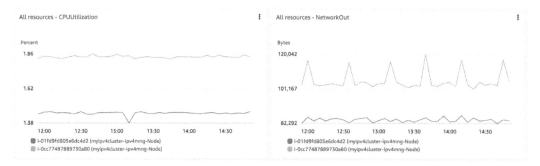

Figure 17.2 – CloudWatch instance dashboard widget

As AWS manages the EKS control plane, we won't see Kubernetes control plane metrics by default. Let's see how we can look at control plane metrics and add them to our dashboard.

Looking at the control plane logs

An EKS cluster generates the following cluster control plane log. Each log corresponds to a specific component of the EKS control plane:

- **Audit Logs**: These logs contain a set of records that describe the users' or systems' actions when using the K8s API. They are a very valuable source of data when you want to understand what happened on your cluster, when it happened, and who made it happen.

- **Authenticator Logs**: These logs contain a set of records that describe the authentication of users and systems using IAM credentials and are useful in understanding who authenticated and uses the cluster in more detail.

- **API Server Logs**: These logs contain a set of records that describe the flags being used on the different components and are useful for understanding how the cluster is being used and configured.

- **Controller Logs**: These logs contain a set of records that describe the control loops used by the cluster to perform actions such as scheduling, and are useful in understanding how the control plane is operating.

- **Scheduler Logs**: These logs contain a set of records that describe the actions taken by the scheduler to deploy, replace, and delete Pods and K8s resources, and are useful in understanding how this critical component is working.

More details can be found in the main debugging and logging section of the K8s documentation found at `https://kubernetes.io/docs/tasks/debug/`.

A typical best practice would be to enable audit and authenticator logs for all clusters and, by default, these would be sent to CloudWatch logs, which can be used for debugging, incident investigation, and forensics. The easiest way to check what logs are enabled for a cluster is to use the AWS console and browse to your cluster under the Amazon EKS. An example of a **Logging** screen with no API logging enabled is shown next:

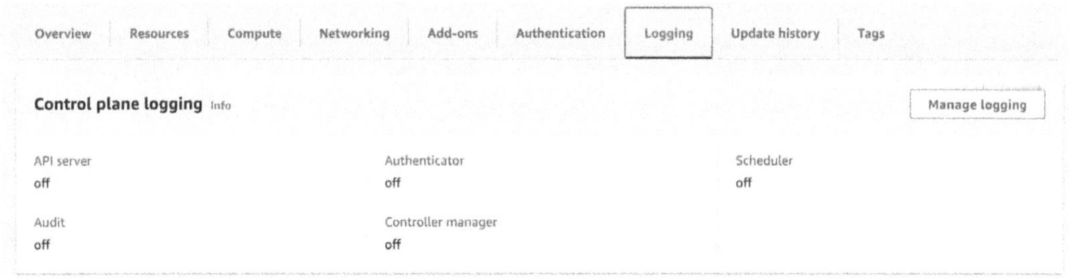

| Overview | Resources | Compute | Networking | Add-ons | Authentication | Logging | Update history | Tags |

Control plane logging Info   Manage logging

| API server | Authenticator | Scheduler |
| off | off | off |

| Audit | Controller manager |
| off | off |

Figure 17.3 – Verifying EKS cluster logging in the AWS console

We can modify the cluster configuration to allow audit and authenticator logging with the following command:

```
$ aws eks update-cluster-config --region eu-central-1 --name
myipv4cluster --logging
'{"clusterLogging":[{"types":["audit","authenticator"],
"enabled":true}]}'
{
    "update": {
        "status": "InProgress",
        "errors": [],
......

        "type": "LoggingUpdate",
        "id": "223148bb-8ec1-4e58-8b0e-b1c681c765a3",
        "createdAt": 1679304779.614}}
```

We can verify the update was successful using the following command:

```
$ aws eks describe-update --region eu-central-1 --name myipv4cluster \
    --update-id 223148bb-8ec1-4e58-8b0e-b1c681c765a3
{
    "update": {
        "status": "Successful",
        "errors": [],
... . .
```

```
      "type": "LoggingUpdate",
      "id": "223148bb-8ec1-4e58-8b0e-b1c681c765a3",
      "createdAt": 1679304779.614
  }}
```

If we now look at the CloudWatch service, in the AWS console, we will see a new log group has been created for our cluster, which we can use as a data source for queries and other CloudWatch functions. An illustration of the log group for `myipv4cluster` is shown next.

Figure 17.4 – CloudWatch cluster log groups

Now we have a data source, EKS control plane logs, we can use **Log Insights** to generate visualizations and metrics off that data without any more configuration. The following example will look in the audit logs for records that refer to updates or read the `aws-auth` ConfigMap, which controls access to the EKS cluster. We can also add this to our simple dashboard using the **Add to dashboard** button on the **Log Insights** screen:

Figure 17.5 – Using Log Insights to generate insights into EKS audit data

> **Important note**
>
> Because the control plane logging is relying on the Amazon CloudWatch log to store the data streams, visualization, and insights, additional costs will apply. To get more details, please refer to the CloudWatch pricing page: `https://aws.amazon.com/cloudwatch/pricing/`.

By default, CloudWatch keeps your logs indefinitely and they never expire. It means that they won't be deleted unless you manually clean them up. This can potentially increase your data storage cost if the CloudWatch log group keeps the old control plane logs that you don't want to save.

To optimize the storage cost, there is a little tip to save your money by configuring the retention policy for each CloudWatch log group. By setting the log group retention period, any log streams within this log group older than the retention settings will be deleted automatically. You can choose a retention period for your EKS control plane log from 1 day to 10 years.

You can follow these steps to configure the log retention policy for your CloudWatch log group:

1. To find the CloudWatch log group for your cluster, go to **CloudWatch | Log groups** and search for your cluster name.

2. In the **Actions** drop-down menu, select **Edit retention setting** (a sample is shown in the following figure):

Figure 17.6 – Edit retention setting of your log group

3. Select the log retention value in the drop-down menu and save the setting. A typical value would be keeping logs for *30 days/1 month* and deleting them after that, but it will depend on what you need the logs for, as some logs may need to be stored for regulatory or security purposes.

Shrinking the old log streams can make sure it only keeps the data you really care about. This is another useful tip to help you reduce the storage cost for storing EKS control plane logs in Amazon CloudWatch log groups.

Now we've looked at what we get "out of the box" with EKS, let's look at what we need to add to enhance the overall observability experience, starting with the control plane and Pod metrics and logs.

Exploring control plane and Pod metrics

Kubernetes control plane components expose metrics on the `/metrics` endpoints in the Prometheus Metrics format. You can access these metrics using `kubectl` or by *scraping* the `/metrics` endpoint. An example is using `kubectl` to extract node data and using the `jq` utility to format the data and filter it to the first (0) node. At the end of the output, you can see node `usage` data for CPU and RAM:

```
$ kubectl get --raw "/apis/metrics.k8s.io/v1beta1/nodes" | jq
'.items[0]'
{"metadata": {
    "name": "ip-1.2.3.4.eu-central-1.compute.internal",
    "creationTimestamp": "2023-03-18T15:23:51Z",
    "labels": {
      ….
      "failure-domain.beta.kubernetes.io/region": "..1",
    }
  },
  "timestamp": "2023-03-18T15:23:40Z",
  "window": "20.029s",
  "usage": {
    "cpu": "48636622n",
    "memory": "1562400Ki"
}}
```

We will now install AWS **Container Insights** (**CI**), which can transport `/metrics` data to CloudWatch as well as application logs. It does this by installing two agents, the CloudWatch agent (metrics) and either Fluent Bit or FluentD for logs. We will use the QuickStart guide, which uses Fluent Bit (which is a more efficient agent).

The first thing to do is grant the worker permission to access the CloudWatch API. We will add `CloudWatchAgentServerPolicy` to the worker node IAM policy. An example is shown next. This will allow any of the CloudWatch agent or FluentBit Pods to communicate with the CloudWatch API.

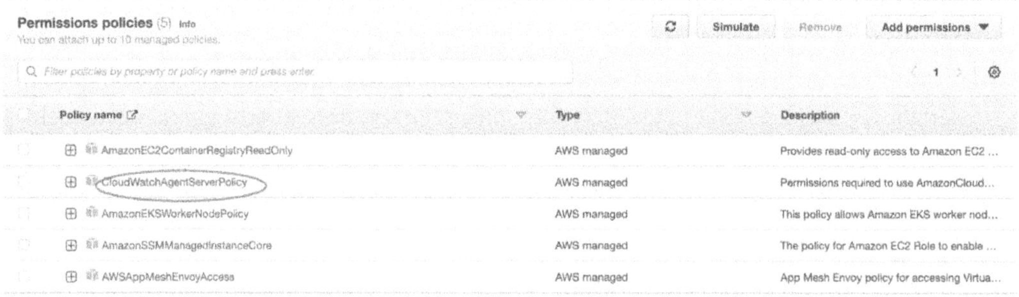

Figure 17.7 – Additional permissions needed for CI

Once we have the permissions applied, we can install the two agents (CW and FluentBit).

We can now install the agents using the instructions shown at this URL: `https://docs.aws.amazon.com/AmazonCloudWatch/latest/monitoring/Container-Insights-setup-EKS-quickstart.html`. The configuration and output are shown next, and we've modified `ClusterName` and `RegionName` to match our cluster configuration. When we execute, the CloudWatch and FluentBit agents are installed:

```
$ ClusterName=myipv4cluster
$ RegionName=eu-central-1
$ FluentBitHttpPort='2020'
$ FluentBitReadFromHead='Off'
$ [[ ${FluentBitReadFromHead} = 'On' ]] &&
FluentBitReadFromTail='Off'|| FluentBitReadFromTail='On'
[$ [ -z ${FluentBitHttpPort} ]] && FluentBitHttpServer='Off' ||
FluentBitHttpServer='On'
$ curl https://raw.githubusercontent.com/aws-samples/amazon-
cloudwatch-container-insights/latest/k8s-deployment-manifest-
templates/deployment-mode/daemonset/container-insights-monitoring/
quickstart/cwagent-fluent-bit-quickstart.yaml | sed 's/{{cluster_
name}}/'${ClusterName}'/;s/{{region_name}}/'${RegionName}'/;s/
{{http_server_toggle}}/"'${FluentBitHttpServer}'"/;s/
{{http_server_port}}/"'${FluentBitHttpPort}'"/;s/{{read_
from_head}}/"'${FluentBitReadFromHead}'"/;s/{{read_from_
tail}}/"'${FluentBitReadFromTail}'"/' | kubectl apply -f -
% Total%Received%Xferd Average Speed Time Time Time  Current
100 16784  100 16784    0     0  95087      0 ... 95363
...

daemonset.apps/fluent-bit created
```

We can verify the deployment of the agents using the following command:

```
$ kubectl get po -n amazon-cloudwatch
NAME                      READY   STATUS    RESTARTS   AGE
cloudwatch-agent-6z16c    1/1     Running   0          3m32s
cloudwatch-agent-xp45k    1/1     Running   0          3m32s
fluent-bit-vl29d          1/1     Running   0          3m32s
fluent-bit-vpswx          1/1     Running   0          3m32s
```

Logging with FluentBit

Now that we have the agents running, we can look in CloudWatch to see the logs and metrics being generated. Firstly, if we look at CloudWatch logs and filter on `containerinsights`, we see four new log groups. An example is shown next:

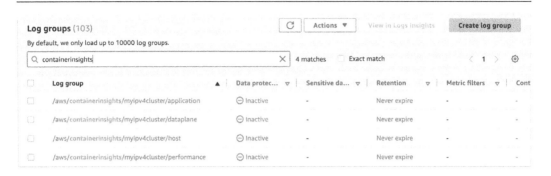

Figure 17.8 – New log groups created by CI

These logs extract data from the node logs. The following table shows which node logs and journal files are used on each host. The `application` log group contains logs written to `stdout` from the containers.

`/aws/ containerinsights/ Cluster_Name/ application`	All log files in `/var/log/containers`

`/aws/ containerinsights/ Cluster_Name/ host`	All log files in
	
	`/var/log/dmesg,`
	
	`/var/log/secure,` and `/var/log/messages`

`/aws/ containerinsights/ Cluster_Name/ dataplane`	The logs in `/var/log/journal` for
	
	`kubelet.service`
	
	`kubeproxy.service`
	
	`docker.service`

`/aws/ containerinsights/ Cluster_Name/ performance`	Contains K8s performance events detailed at `https:// docs.aws.amazon.com/AmazonCloudWatch/ latest/monitoring/Container-Insights- reference-performance-logs-EKS.html`

Table 17.1 – CI log group configuration

We use the following manifest to create a Pod that generates log messages and then terminates itself:

```
apiVersion: v1
kind: Pod
metadata:
```

```
    name: logger
    namespace: logger-app
spec:
  containers:
  - image: busybox
    command: ["/bin/sh"]
    args: ["-c", "for i in `seq 4`; do echo 'Logging Message';done"]
    imagePullPolicy: IfNotPresent
    name: busybox
  restartPolicy: Never
```

We can use the following commands to create the namespace, deploy the Pod, and validate that it generates the log messages:

```
$ kubectl create namespace logger-app
$ kubectl create -f logger.yaml
$ kubectl logs logger -n logger-app
Logging Message
Logging Message
Logging Message
Logging Message
```

If we now look at the application log group, you will see a log entry for the logger Pod, in the logger-app namespace running on one of your hosts. In the example shown next, it is host 192.168.32.216:

Figure 17.9 – CloudWatch container logging output

From this point on, you can visualize your logs as we did in the *Looking at the control plane logs* section. You can also turn the logs into metrics and visualize them in the dashboard we created previously or you could forward them to another logging service such as OpenSearch, Loki, or Splunk.

Metrics with CloudWatch

CloudWatch CI uses a combination of metrics and logs to create different views and dashboards using the data from FluentBit and the CloudWatch agents. One of the most useful views is the map view, which provides a graphical view of the resources deployed in your cluster on top of which you can overlay CPU or memory heat maps. An example is shown next for our cluster, which shows the `logger` Pod we deployed previously and has a green status for all CPU stats.

Figure 17.10 – CI map view

We can change the view from a map to a performance dashboard to deep dive into any issue with CPU/ RAM, and so on. The following example shows a breakdown of CPU, RAM, and so on segregated by namespace (each of the lines):

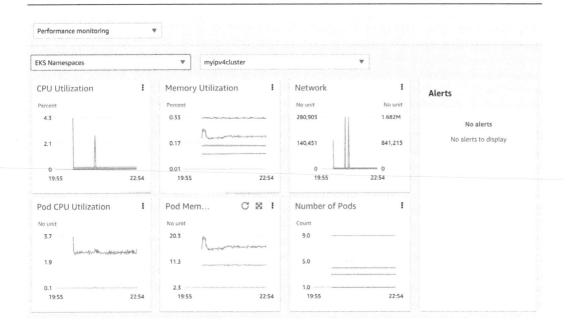

Figure 17.11 – CI performance per namespace

> **Important note**
> CloudWatch CI is charged, with log storage charges and CloudWatch custom metrics: `https://aws.amazon.com/cloudwatch/pricing/`.

Now we've seen how we can use native AWS tools, let's look at using some standard K8s third-party tools.

Building dashboards with Managed Service for Prometheus and Grafana

Prometheus and Grafana are the de facto monitoring tools for K8s. Prometheus is a graduated project from the **Cloud Native Computing Foundation (CNCF)**, which "scrapes" time series data from an endpoint (in the case of K8s, it's the `/metrics` endpoint) and can generate alerts and store/forward the data. Grafana is an open source tool that can visualize metrics (time series), and log and trace data (discussed in the *Tracing with OpenTelemetry* section). Together, Prometheus and Grafana provide equivalent functionality to CloudWatch, so why use them?

As Grafana is open source, it has wide community adoption, which means it has lots of reusable dashboards created for it, is integrated into a variety of data sources (not just AWS), and arguably, has a more complete set of visualizations than CloudWatch. Prometheus supports any sort of health endpoint and so can be used easily for your applications as well as the general Pod/cluster metrics. So, Grafana and Prometheus provide a flexible solution for which, if running on EKS or EC2, you will only pay the running costs. The main challenge with these tools is you need to manage the infrastructure and, in some cases, use additional products for managing long-term storage of metric or log data. This is where **AWS Managed Prometheus** (**AMP**) and **AWS Managed Grafana** (**AMG**) come in, offering flexibility without the management overhead.

Setting up AMP and AWS Distro for OpenTelemetry (ADOT)

The first thing we will do is create an AMP to capture our metrics; AWS will create an area to store and query metrics (time series data). The Terraform code shown next will create a `myamp` workspace:

```
resource "aws_prometheus_workspace" "myamp" {
  alias = "myamp"
}
```

The following AWS SDK commands can be used to describe the workspace and get the endpoint for the workspace:

```
$ aws amp list-workspaces
{    "workspaces": [{..
             "alias": "myamp",
             "workspaceId": "ws-503025bc-01d5-463c-9157-11",
             "createdAt": 1679741187.4,
             "arn": "arn:aws:aps:eu-central-1:22:workspace/
ws-503025bc-..}]
$ aws amp describe-workspace --workspace-id ws-503025bc-01d5-
463c-9157-11
{..
        "prometheusEndpoint": "https://aps-workspaces.eu-central-1.
amazonaws.com/workspaces/ws-503025bc-01d5-463c-9157-11/",
        "alias": "myamp",
        "workspaceId": "ws-503025bc-01d5-463c-9157-11",
        "arn": "arn:aws:aps:eu-central-1:22:workspace/ws-503025bc-
01d5-463c-9157-11",
        "createdAt": 1679741187.4
}}}
```

AMP can ingest metrics from two main sources, which, in turn, "scrape" metrics from Prometheus-enabled endpoints such as the K8s `/metrics` endpoint. You can use either existing Prometheus servers or **ADOT** to remotely write metrics to the AMP workspace.

We will use ADOT, as it will be used later for tracing:

1. The first thing we need to do is create the `prometheus` namespace to host ADOT and create a service account with IAM mappings (IRSA). Example commands are shown next:

```
$ kubectl create ns prometheus
namespace/prometheus created
$ eksctl create iamserviceaccount --name amp-iamproxy-ingest-role \
--namespace prometheus --cluster myipv4cluster \
--attach-policy-arn arn:aws:iam::aws:policy/
AmazonPrometheusRemoteWriteAccess \
--approve --override-existing-serviceaccounts
....
2023-03-25 16:02:19 created serviceaccount "prometheus/
amp-iamproxy-ingest-role"
```

2. We need to install `cert-manager` (if it's not already installed) as ADOT will use it during operations such as sidecar injection. The commands needed are shown next:

```
$ kubectl apply -f https://github.com/cert-manager/cert-manager/
releases/download/v1.8.2
....
validatingwebhookconfiguration.admissionregistration.k8s.io/
cert-manager-webhook created
$ kubectl get po -n cert-manager
NAME                     READY   STATUS    RESTARTS   AGE
cert-manager-12-5k4kx     1/1    Running   0          47s
cert-manager-cainjector-12-kj8w5   1/1   Running     47s
cert-manager-webhook-12-bptdx      1/1   Running     47s
```

3. We will install ADOT as an add-on to allow simpler upgrades and management, so we now need to give permission to EKS add-ons to install ADOT using the following commands:

```
$ kubectl apply -f https://amazon-eks.s3.amazonaws.com/docs/
addons-otel-permissions.yaml
namespace/opentelemetry-operator-system created
clusterrole.rbac.authorization.k8s.io/eks:addon-manager-otel
created
clusterrolebinding.rbac.authorization.k8s.io/eks:addon-manager-
otel created
role.rbac.authorization.k8s.io/eks:addon-manager created
rolebinding.rbac.authorization.k8s.io/eks:addon-manager created
```

4. We will now deploy and verify the ADOT deployment using the following commands:

```
$ CLUSTER_NAME=myipv4cluster
$ aws eks create-addon --addon-name adot --addon-version
v0.51.0-eksbuild.1 --cluster-name $CLUSTER_NAME
{"addon": {
       "status": "CREATING",
 . .
       "createdAt": 1679761283.129}}
$ aws eks describe-addon --addon-name adot --cluster-name
$CLUSTER_NAME | jq .addon.status
"ACTIVE"
```

5. We can now download and configure the ADOT deployment using the following commands, modifying REGION and prometheusEndpoint:

```
$ AMP_REMOTE_WRITE_URL=https://aps-workspaces.eu-central-1.
amazonaws.com/workspaces/ws-503025bc-01d5-463c-9157-11/api/v1/
remote_write
$ AWS_REGION=eu-central-1
$ curl -O https://raw.githubusercontent.com/aws-samples/
one-observability-demo/main/PetAdoptions/cdk/pet_stack/
resources/otel-collector-prometheus.yaml
  % Total     % Received % Xferd  Average Speed    …
100 12480  100 12480     0        0  …
$ sed -i -e s/AWS_REGION/$AWS_REGION/g otel-collector-
prometheus.yaml
$ sed -i -e s^AMP_WORKSPACE_URL^$AMP_REMOTE_WRITE_URL^g otel-
collector-prometheus.yamls
```

6. Finally, we can install and verify ADOT using the otel-collector-prometheus.yaml manifest we downloaded and modified using the following commands:

```
$ kubectl apply -f ./otel-collector-prometheus.yaml
opentelemetrycollector.opentelemetry.io/observability created
clusterrole.rbac.authorization.k8s.io/otel-prometheus-role
created
clusterrolebinding.rbac.authorization.k8s.io/otel-prometheus-
role-binding created
$ kubectl get all -n prometheus
NAME       READY    STATUS     RESTARTS    AGE
pod/observability-collector-123    1/1      Running      110s
NAME  TYPE  CLUSTER-IP  EXTERNAL-IP   PORT(S)    AGE
service/observability-collector-
monitoring   ClusterIP   10.100.154.149   <none>      8888/
TCP    110s
NAME   READY   UP-TO-DATE   AVAILABLE    AGE
deployment.apps/observability-collector   1/1 110s
```

```
NAME             DESIRED   CURRENT   READY    AGE
replicaset.apps/observability-collector-123   1    1 110s
```

7. We now have ADOT set up and configured to send metrics to our AMP. We can query this
    directly through the AMS Prometheus API or by using Grafana. As a quick check, let's install
    and use `awscurl` (which allows us to use the AWS credentials to curl APIs directly) to test
    whether metrics are being received by AMP:

```
$ pip3 install awscurl
Defaulting to user installation because normal site-packages is
not writeable
Collecting awscurl
  Downloading awscurl-0.26-py3-none
....
$ export AMP_QUERY_ENDPOINT=https://aps-workspaces.eu-central-1.
amazonaws.com/workspaces/ws-503025bc-01d5-463c-9157-11/api/v1/
query
$ awscurl -X POST --region eu-central-1  --service aps "$AMP_
QUERY_ENDPOINT?query=up"  | jq .
{"status": "success",
  "data": {
    "resultType": "vector",
    "result": [
      {
        "metric": {
          "__name__": "up",
          "app": "cert-manager",
          "app_kubernetes_io_component": "controller",
          "app_kubernetes_io_instance": "cert-manager",
          "app_kubernetes_io_name": "cert-manager",
          "app_kubernetes_io_version": "v1.8.2",
          "instance": "192.168.68.6:9402",
          "job": "kubernetes-pods",
          "kubernetes_namespace": "cert-manager",
          "kubernetes_pod_name": "cert-manager-12-5k4kx",
          "pod_template_hash": "66b646d76"},
        "value": [
        1679763539.307,
        "1"]},
      {
        "metric": {
          "__name__": "up",
...
      ]}]}}
```

> **Important note**
>
> To access the Prometheus API, either to send metrics or make queries, we need network access to the public AWS Prometheus API, through a NAT or internet gateway, or using a VPC endpoint.

Now we have installed ADOT and verified that metrics are being sent and stored in Prometheus, we can look at how we can visualize them graphically using AMG.

Setting up AMG and creating a dashboard

AMG needs to have a user identity store, which is different from AWS IAM. It will integrate through AWS Identity Center (the successor to AWS Single Sign-On) or through SAML. **Security Assertion Markup Language** (**SAML**) is an open standard used for authentication, which will transfer authentication data between two parties: the **identity provider** (**IdP**) and the **service provider** (**SP**). We will use **AWS Identity Center** (**AIC**) as it's simpler to set up. Through the AWS console, select the Identity Center service and click on the **Enable** button. The console splash screen is shown next:

Figure 17.12 – AWS Identity Center splash screen

> **Important note**
>
> You will be asked to create an organization, which is used to group and control multiple accounts. Accept this action and you will also be sent an email, which you will need to verify in order for the organization and, ultimately, Identity Center to be created.

Once AIC is enabled, you will be able to add a user through the console by clicking on the **Add user** button and entering some general information such as name and email. Once you have verified your user email and set a password, you will be able to log in through the AIC console.

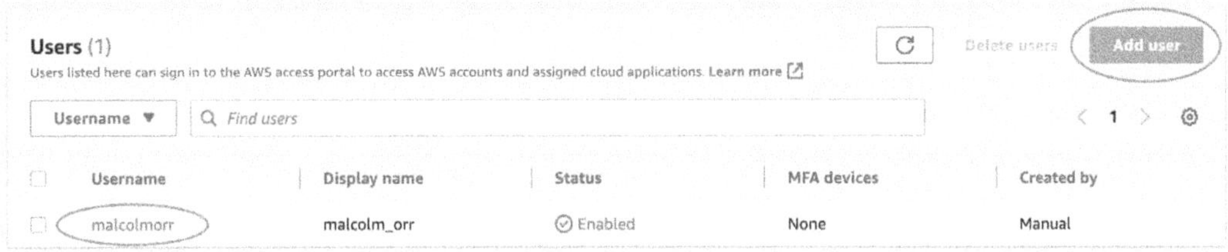

Figure 17.13 – Example AIC Users admin screen

If we click on the user shown in the preceding figure, we can get the unique user identity (**User ID**). This is shown in the following screenshot as **73847832-1031-70a6-d142-6fbb72a512f0**. We will use this later on in this example when we configure AMG.

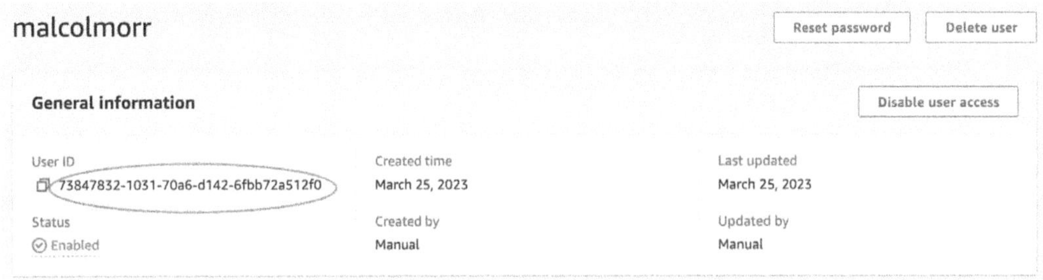

Figure 17.14 – AIC user details

Like AMP, AMG is organized around a workspace. The first thing we need to do is set up the IAM policies for the workspace to be able to communicate with the data sources (in our case, AMP). We will create a role that can be assumed by AMG and attach the Prometheus permission to it. An example using Terraform is shown next:

```
resource "aws_iam_role" "assume" {
  name = "grafana-assume"
  assume_role_policy = jsonencode({
    Version = "2012-10-17"
    Statement = [
      { Action = "sts:AssumeRole"
        Effect = "Allow"
        Sid    = ""
        Principal = {
```

```
                    Service = "grafana.amazonaws.com"
            }
        },
    ]
  })
}
resource "aws_iam_policy" "policy" {
  name        = "amgadditional"
  path        = "/"
  description = "additional policies"
  policy = jsonencode({
    Version = "2012-10-17"
    Statement = [
      {
        Action = [
          "aps:ListWorkspaces",
          "aps:DescribeWorkspace",
          "aps:QueryMetrics",
          "aps:GetLabels",
          "aps:GetSeries",
          "aps:GetMetricMetadata"
        ]
        Effect   = "Allow"
        Resource = "*"
      },]})}

resource "aws_iam_role_policy_attachment" "amgattachement" {
  role       = aws_iam_role.assume.name
  policy_arn = aws_iam_policy.policy.arn
}
```

Now that we have the right IAM permissions for AMG to query Prometheus, we can create the workspace and assign the user we created previously (AIC) as an admin user. We will set the authentication provider to AWS_SSO, and also configure Prometheus and CloudWatch references. An example using Terraform is shown next:

```
resource "aws_grafana_workspace" "myamg" {
  account_access_type       = "CURRENT_ACCOUNT"
  authentication_providers  = ["AWS_SSO"]
  permission_type           = "SERVICE_MANAGED"
  role_arn                  = aws_iam_role.assume.arn
  data_sources              = ["PROMETHEUS","CLOUDWATCH"]
}
```

```
resource "aws_grafana_role_association" "admin" {
  role          = "ADMIN"
  user_ids      = ["73847832-1031-70a6-d142-6fbb72a512f0"]
  workspace_id = aws_grafana_workspace.myamg.id
}
```

> **Important note**
> This can take several minutes to provision, and you will need to change `user_ids` to one you created in your AIC.

If we now go to the AMG service in AWS, we will see the new workspace, and clicking on the URL under **Grafana workspace URL** will launch the Grafana splash page, which we can log in to using the AIC credentials we created and associated in the previous steps. An example is shown next:

Figure 17.15 – Grafana workspace launch screen

While we have configured the Grafana service to support both Prometheus and CloudWatch, we need to configure the data source inside Grafana before we can see any metrics. The first step is to click on the AWS icon on the left-hand sidebar and click on the **Data sources** link. An example is shown next:

Figure 17.16 – Selecting AWS data sources

Next, select **Amazon Managed Service for Prometheus** from the dropdown, choose your Region, select the Prometheus instance we created, and click on the **Add 1 data source** button. In the example shown next, we use the **eu-central-1** Region and the myapm instance we created with Terraform in the *Setting up AMP and ADOT* section:

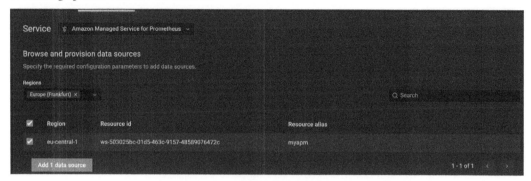

Figure 17.17 – Adding an AMP data source

As we now have a data source, we can now use an open source dashboard; we will use Kubernetes cluster monitoring (via Prometheus), which has an ID of 3119. If you click the **Create** or + button and select **Import**, you can simply type 3119 in the ID and then load and save the dashboards. An example is shown next:

Figure 17.18 – Importing open source dashboards from Grafana.com

One of the great advantages of Grafana is we can easily consume work from the community. The dashboard we just imported, in the example shown next, gives a comprehensive view of the cluster, and we can even drill down into individual nodes if we want to.

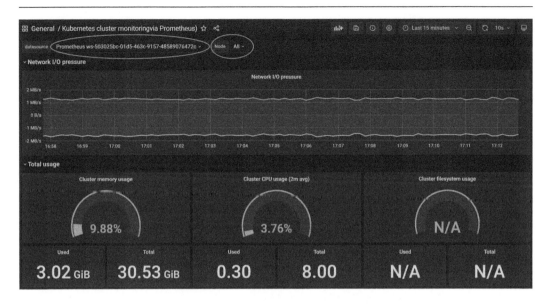

Figure 17.19 – Kubernetes cluster dashboard

> **Important note**
> Please make sure you have selected the data source for the AMP instance we added previously in this section.

Now we've seen how to visualize these metrics with AMG with a community dashboard, let's look at how we can use ADOT to send application trace information.

Tracing with OpenTelemetry

OpenTelemetry (**OTel**) is a CNCF project that provides a standard way to send application trace information. Traces become important as you begin to build a distributed system as you need to be able to trace a request and response through multiple systems. OTel provides a vendor-agnostic instrumentation library that can be used to forward trace data to a backend to visualize or analyze the data.

In this book, we will use ADOT as the trace forwarder and AWS X-Ray to analyze and visualize the trace data.

Modifying our ADOT configuration

As X-Ray is an AWS service, we first need to modify the service account permissions to allow it to send traces to X-Ray, as currently it only has AMP permissions. If we view the current `ServiceAccount`, we can get the IAM role, `arn`, as shown next:

```
$ kubectl get sa amp-iamproxy-ingest-role -n prometheus -o json
{
    "apiVersion": "v1",
    "kind": "ServiceAccount",
    "metadata": {
        "annotations": {
            "eks.amazonaws.com/role-arn": "arn:aws:iam::112233:role/
eksctl-myipv4cluster-addon-iamserviceaccount-Role1-1V5TZL1L6J58X"
....
}
```

We can then add X-Ray permission directly to the IAM role, as shown in the next figure. We will add the `AWSXRayDaemonWriteAccess` managed policy to allow ADOT to write traces and segments.

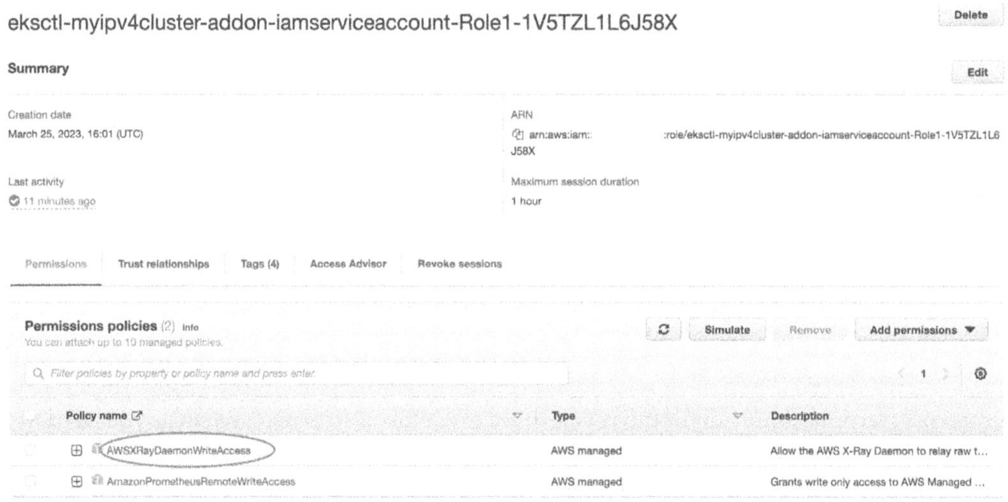

Figure 17.20 – Adding X-Ray permissions to ADOT IRSA

We now need to modify the ADOT configuration to support OTel and X-Ray. A full configuration can be found at `https://raw.githubusercontent.com/aws-observability/aws-otel-community/master/sample-configs/operator/collector-config-xray.yaml`, with the new receivers, processors, exporters, and pipelines added to the `otel-collector-prometheus.yaml` file in the *Setting up AMP and ADOT* section:

```
receivers:
    otlp:
```

```
        protocols:
          grpc:
            endpoint: 0.0.0.0:4317
          http:
            endpoint: 0.0.0.0:4318
  processors:
      batch/traces:
        timeout: 1s
        send_batch_size: 50
  exporters:
      awsxray:
        region: eu-central-1
  pipelines:
      traces:
        receivers: [otlp]
        processors: [batch/traces]
        exporters: [awsxray]
```

We can now redeploy the ADOT collector or simply delete it and recreate it, but if we check the logs, we can see the new elements have successfully started and we will see an `Everything is ready` message. The command and some sample output texts are shown next:

```
$ kubectl logs observability-collector-11 -n prometheus
2023/03/26 17:05:54 AWS OTel Collector version: v0.20.0
....
2023-03-26T17:05:54.973Z          info    pipelines/pipelines.
go:82        Exporter started.      {"kind": "exporter", "data_type":
"traces", "name": "awsxray"}

...
2023-03-26T17:05:54.973Z          info    pipelines/pipelines.
go:82        Exporter started.
2023-03-26T17:05:54.974Z          info    pipelines/pipelines.
go:102       Receiver is starting... {"kind": "receiver", "name":
"otlp", "pipeline": "traces"}
2023-03-26T17:05:54.974Z          info    otlpreceiver/otlp.go:70
Starting GRPC server on endpoint 0.0.0.0:4317   {"kind": "receiver",
"name": "otlp", "pipeline": "traces"}
2023-03-26T17:05:54.974Z          info    otlpreceiver/otlp.go:88
Starting HTTP server on endpoint 0.0.0.0:4318   {"kind": "receiver",
"name": "otlp", "pipeline": "traces"}

....
2023-03-26T17:05:54.975Z          info    service/collector.
go:128       Everything is ready. Begin running and processing data.
```

Instrumenting your applications to send OTel-based traces can be a complex task and as such, is outside the scope of this book. Instead, we will use a simple trace emitter provided by OTel to explore what you can do with X-Ray.

The first step is to create a K8s namespace to host our emitter; an example is shown next:

```
$ kubectl create ns adot
namespace/adot created
```

Next, we will download, modify, and deploy the sample applications (emitter) from https://raw. githubusercontent.com/aws-observability/aws-otel-community/master/sample-configs/sample-app.yaml. You will need to change the elements in the manifest shown next:

```
... .
---
apiVersion: apps/v1
kind: Deployment
...
    spec:
      containers:
        - env:
          - name: AWS_REGION
            value: eu-central-1
          - name: LISTEN_ADDRESS
            value: 0.0.0.0:4567
          - name: OTEL_EXPORTER_OTLP_ENDPOINT
            value: http://observability-collector.prometheus:4317
          - name: OTEL_RESOURCE_ATTRIBUTES
            value: service.namespace=adot,service.name=emitter
        image: public.ecr.aws/aws-otel-test/aws-otel-java-
spark:1.17.0
... . .
```

Once we've made the changes to the AWS_REGION, OTEL_EXPORTER_OTLP_ENDPOINT, and OTEL_RESOURCE_ATTRIBUTES environment variables to point to our modified ADOT instance, we can deploy the manifest and validate it is running using the commands shown next:

```
$ kubectl create -f sample-app-modified.yaml -n adot
service/sample-app created
deployment.apps/sample-app created
$ kubectl get po -n adot
NAME                      READY   STATUS    RESTARTS   AGE
sample-app-7cbb94b84-ckhdc   1/1     Running   0          8s
```

We now need to generate some traffic. Handily, OTel also provides a traffic generator, which is a Pod that runs in the same namespace as the sample application and will make queries to the application API, which, in turn, makes calls out to amazon.com. The command used in the traffic generator Pod is shown next, and the full manifest can be downloaded from https://raw.githubusercontent.com/aws-observability/aws-otel-community/master/sample-configs/traffic-generator.yaml:

```
....
 - args:
                - /bin/bash
                - -c
                - sleep 10; while :; do curl sample-app:4567/outgoing-
 http-call > /dev/null 1>&1; sleep 2; curl ot-sample-app:4567/aws-sdk-
 call > /dev/null 2>&1; sleep 5; done
```

We can run this unchanged as long as we haven't changed the name of the sample application service. The commands shown next will deploy the traffic generator and start making calls to the sample application API:

```
$ kubectl create  -f traffic-generator.yaml -n adot
service/traffic-generator created
deployment.apps/traffic-generator created
$ kubectl get all  -n adot
NAME                          READY   STATUS    RESTARTS   AGE
pod/sample-app-7cbb94b84-ckhdc    1/1     Running   0        18m
pod/traffic-generator-123-ch4x2   1/1     Running   0        10m
```

If we now go to the X-Ray service in the AWS console, we will be presented with a service map that shows our client (the traffic generator Pod) making calls to the emitter service, which, in turn, makes calls to the remote aws.amazon.com service. The service map can have telemetry for health with health (latency) applied on top, which will adjust the size and color of the individual rings. The service map gives a very easy way to visualize your services. An example is shown next for our emitter/traffic generator deployments:

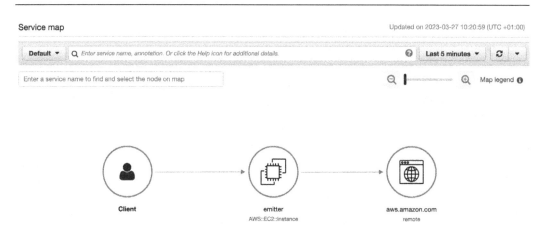

Figure 17.21 – X-Ray service map

> **Important note**
> As the client (traffic generator) code is not instrumented with OTel, we don't have any visibility of its latency, so our trace starts when it reaches the emitter service.

We can drill down into individual traces to see the different segments to troubleshoot or understand the traffic flows in more detail. In the example shown next, we can see the two requests/responses – the initial request from the traffic request, GET /outgoing-http-call, and the time taken for the aws.amazon.com response:

Figure 17.22 – X-Ray trace details

Now we have explored tracing using OTel and X-Ray, we can look at one of the more advanced services, DevOps Guru, which uses machine learning models to drive into EKS node-level issues.

Using machine learning with DevOps Guru

DevOps Guru is a fully managed service that uses pre-trained machine learning models to baseline resources and gains insights into their use. As it's fully managed, you just need to set it up and allow it to run. To do this, choose the **Amazon DevOps Guru** service and click the **Get Started** button. We will choose the option to monitor the current account and analyze all the resources and enable the service. The screen shown next illustrates the options that were chosen:

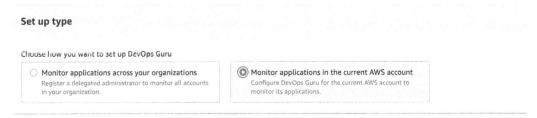

Figure 17.23 – DevOps Guru options

We also need to tell DevOps Guru what resources are in scope, as shown in the next figure:

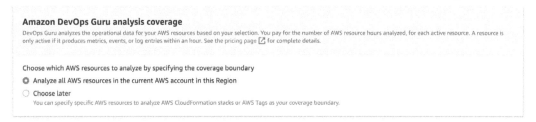

Figure 17.24 – DevOps Guru setup options

> **Important note**
> You may need to wait anywhere between 20 and 90 minutes for DevOps Guru to collect and review the data.

Once the analysis is complete, the dashboard will be updated with any findings. In the example shown next, you can see a service view that shows our EKS cluster as healthy.

It's hard to generate resource issues but DevOps Guru will detect EKS hosts that have high memory, CPU, or filesystem utilization, as well as Pod-level metrics such as CPU/RAM Pod limit issues, identifying resources that are at risk of producing errors due to resource exhaustion. Amazon DevOps Guru also tracks container restarts, issues with pulling images, or issues with application startup, which can help identify poor code or manifest configurations.

Amazon DevOps Guru has very low operational overhead as you simply enable it and let it run, and AWS continues to enhance the underlying ML models to provide greater insights, but it does cost, so please review https://aws.amazon.com/devops-guru/pricing/ before using it.

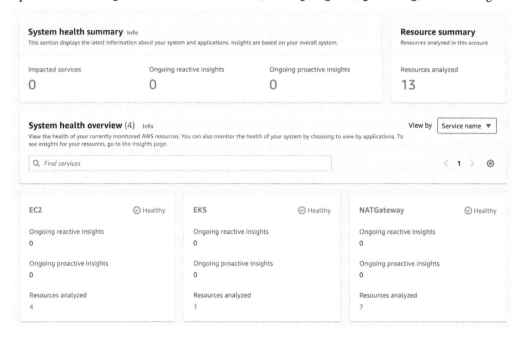

Figure 17.25 – DevOps Guru summary dashboard

In this section, we have looked at EKS observability, and how you can use a variety of AWS services and open source tools to get better insights into your clusters, nodes, and applications. We'll now revisit the key learning points from this chapter.

Summary

In this chapter, we looked at the different ways to collect and analyze EKS logs, metrics, and traces, commonly known as observability. We initially looked at how we can install logging and metric agents (fluentBit and CloudWatch, respectively) that can easily integrate with the AWS CloudWatch service and Container Insights to provide a detailed analysis of this data without deploying any monitoring servers or software licenses.

While CloudWatch provides a complete monitoring platform, we also discussed how some people want to use open source or non-AWS services for greater flexibility and less platform lock-in. Prometheus and Grafana are open source projects that offer similar functionality to CloudWatch, and have the advantage of being supported by a large community as well, but need to be installed and managed.

Next, we reviewed how we can deploy and configure AMP and AMG to get the flexibility of these services but without the operational overhead, and how we can deploy ADOT into our cluster to forward K8s /metrics data to AMP. We also deployed a community-developed K8s monitoring dashboard from `Grafana.com` that can visualize standard K8s metrics, demonstrating how easy it can be to build complex visualizations.

We then extended the ADOT configuration to support the collection of OTel traces and the forwarding of these to the AWS X-Ray service. We deployed a simple trace emitter and traffic generator service in EKS and reviewed the service map and segment information in X-Ray to allow us to understand the traffic flow through our small microservice architecture from a traffic volume, latency, and error perspective.

Finally, we enabled Amazon DevOps Guru to provide better analysis, with zero operational overhead, in our cluster and nodes within our cluster.

In the next chapter, we will look at how you can increase resilience and performance with cluster scaling tools and approaches.

Further reading

- EKS observability tools: `https://docs.aws.amazon.com/eks/latest/userguide/eks-observe.html`

- Prometheus metrics format: `https://prometheus.io/docs/instrumenting/exposition_formats/`

- More information on Prometheus: `https://prometheus.io/`

- OpenTelemetry in Python: `https://opentelemetry.io/docs/instrumentation/python/`

18

Scaling Your EKS Cluster

Capacity planning on EKS (and K8s generally) can be hard! If you under- or overestimate your cluster resources, you may not meet your application's demand or end up paying more than you need. One of the reasons it's hard is that it can be difficult to know what the expected load will be for your application. With a web application, for example, the load is normally non-deterministic and a successful marketing campaign or an event similar to Amazon Prime Day may see your load triple or quadruple. Some form of cluster/pod scaling strategy is needed to cope with the peaks and troughs of load placed on a modern application.

In this chapter, we will walk through several common strategies and tools that can be used with Amazon EKS and help you understand how to optimize your EKS cluster for load and cost. Specifically, this chapter covers the following topics:

- Understanding scaling in EKS
- Scaling EC2 ASGs with Cluster Autoscaler
- Scaling worker nodes with Karpenter
- Scaling applications with Horizontal Pod Autoscaler
- Scaling applications with custom metrics
- Scaling with KEDA

Technical requirements

The reader should have familiarity with YAML, AWS IAM, and EKS architecture. Before getting started with this chapter, please ensure the following:

- You have network connectivity to your EKS cluster API endpoint
- The AWS CLI, Docker, and the kubectl binary are installed on your workstation with administrator access

Understanding scaling in EKS

When we consider scaling in any system or cluster, we tend to think in terms of two dimensions:

- Increasing the size of a system or instance, known as vertical scaling
- Increasing the number of systems or instances, known as horizontal scaling

The following diagram illustrates these options.

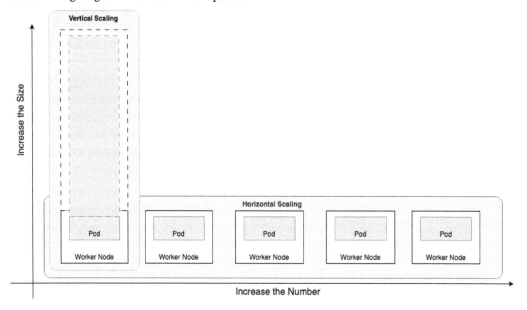

Figure 18.1 – General scaling strategies

The scaling strategy is closely linked with the resilience model, where you have a traditional master/standby or N+1 resilience architecture, such as a relational database. Then, when you increase capacity, you normally need to scale *up* (i.e., vertically) by increasing the size of your database instances. This is due to the limitations of the system architecture.

In K8s, the resilience model is based on multiple worker nodes hosting multiple pods with an ingress/load balancer providing a consistent entry point. This means that a node failure should have little impact. The scaling strategy is therefore predominantly to scale *out* (horizontally) and while you can do things such as vertically scale pods to cope with increases in demand, we will focus on horizontal scaling.

As AWS manages the EKS control plane (scaling and resilience), we will focus mainly on the data plane (worker nodes) and application resources (pods/containers). Let's begin with a high-level examination of the technology that supports scaling the data plane on EKS.

EKS scaling technology

There are three layers of technology involved in supporting EKS scaling:

1. AWS technology that supports scaling the data plane, such as EC2 **Autoscaling Groups (ASGs)** and the AWS APIs that allow systems to interact these ASGs.

2. The K8s objects (Kinds) that support scaling and deploying pods, such as Deployments.

3. The K8s scheduler and controllers that provide the link between the K8s objects (2) and the AWS technology (1) to support horizontal scaling at the pod and cluster levels.

The following diagram illustrates these three layers.

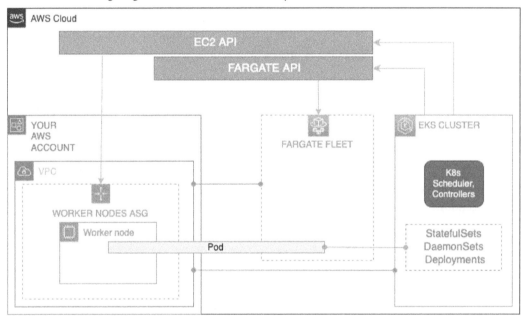

Figure 18.2 – EKS scaling technology

Let's look at these layers in detail.

AWS technology

In *Chapter 8, Managing Worker Nodes on EKS*, we discussed the use of EC2 ASGs for resilience. When you create an ASG, you specify the minimum number of EC2 instances in the group, along with the maximum number and your desired number, and the group will scale within those limits. Calls to the EC2 API will allow the group to scale up and down (within a set of cool-down limits) based on these calls. The entity calling the EC2 ASG API must make the decisions to scale in and out.

In *Chapter 15, Working with AWS Fargate*, we discussed how pods could be created on a Fargate instance using the Fargate profile. In this case, AWS handles the deployment and placement of pods on the Fargate fleet and the Fargate service handles scaling decisions, while the calling entity just requests the deployment of one or more pods.

K8s objects

Throughout the book, we've used K8s deployments to deploy and scale our pods. Under the covers, this uses **deployments**, which in turn use **ReplicaSets** to add/remove new pods as needed and also to support deployment strategies such as rolling updates. K8s also supports StatefulSets and DaemonSets for pod deployments.

A **StatefulSet** is a K8s controller that deploys pods, but will guarantee a specific order or deployment and that Pod names are unique, as well as providing storage. A **DaemonSet** is also a controller that ensures that the pod runs on all the nodes of the cluster.

Both ReplicaSets and StatefulSets create pods with the expectation that the K8s scheduler will be able to deploy them. If the scheduler determines that it doesn't have enough resources – typically, worker node CPU/RAM or network ports (**NodePort** services) – then the pod stays in the *Pending* state.

K8s scheduler and controller

K8s was designed to be extensible and can be extended using controllers. With autoscaling, we can extend EKS using the controllers in the following list, which we will examine in more detail in the following sections:

- **K8s Cluster Autoscaler** (**CA**) can scale AWS ASGs based on K8s scheduler requirements
- **Karpenter** can scale EC2 instances based on K8s scheduler requirements
- **K8s Horizontal Pod Autoscaler** (**HPA**) can scale deployments based on custom metrics or CPU utilization across EC2 or Fargate instances
- Use KEDA to integrate different event sources to trigger scaling actions controlled through HPA

Now that we've looked at the three technology layers, let's deep dive into how we install and configure the different controllers and services to scale our EKS clusters.

Scaling EC2 ASGs with Cluster Autoscaler

Kubernetes CA is a core part of the K8s ecosystem and is used to scale worker nodes in or out based on two main conditions:

- If there is a Pod in the Kubernetes cluster in the Pending state due to an insufficient resources error
- If there is a worker node in the Kubernetes cluster that is identified as underutilized by Kubernetes CA

The following diagram illustrates the basic flow of a scale-out operation to support a single pod being placed in the `Pending` state and not being scheduled.

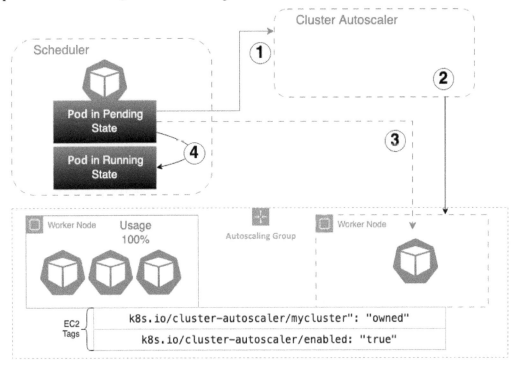

Figure 18.3 – High-level Cluster AutoScaler flow

In the preceding diagram, we can see the following:

1. The CA is actively looking for pods that cannot be scheduled for resource reasons and are in the `Pending` state.

2. The CA makes calls to the EC2 ASG API to increase the desired capacity, which in turn will add a new node to the ASG. A key aspect to note is that the nodes need tagging with `k8s.io/cluster-autoscaler/` so that the CA can discover them and their instance types.

3. Once the node has registered with the cluster, the scheduler will schedule the pod on that node.

4. Once the pod is deployed and assuming there are no issues with the pod itself, the state is changed to `Running`.

Now we've looked at the concepts behind the CA, let's install it.

Installing the CA in your EKS cluster

As the CA will interact with the AWS EC2 API, the first thing we need to do is make sure that the subnets used by the autoscaler have been tagged correctly. This should be done automatically if you're using **eksctl** to provision node groups. We can check whether the two tags, k8s.io/cluster-autoscaler/enabled and k8s.io/cluster-autoscaler/myipv4cluster, have been applied to the subnets:

```
$ aws ec2 describe-subnets --filters "Name=tag:k8s.io/cluster-
autoscaler/enabled,Values=true" | jq -r '.Subnets[].SubnetId'
subnet-05d5323d274c6d67e
subnet-087e0a21855f08fd3
subnet-0dbed7d2f514d8897
$ aws ec2 describe-subnets --filters "Name=tag:k8s.io/cluster-
autoscaler/myipv4cluster,Values=owned" | jq -r '.Subnets[].SubnetId'
subnet-05d5323d274c6d67e
subnet-087e0a21855f08fd3
subnet-0dbed7d2f514d8897
```

> **Note**
>
> myipv4cluster is the name of the cluster in my example, but yours may vary.

Now we have confirmed that the subnets have the correct tags applied, we can set up the AWS IAM policy to be associated with the K8s service account that the CA pods will use.

> **Note**
>
> It is a best practice to add a condition to limit the policy to those resources owned by the cluster it is deployed on. In our case, we will use the tags we created/verified in the previous step.

The following is the autoscaling policy that you are recommended to create:

```
{"Version": "2012-10-17",
    "Statement": [ {
            "Effect": "Allow",
            "Action": [
                "autoscaling:SetDesiredCapacity",
                "autoscaling:TerminateInstanceInAutoScalingGroup"
            ],
            "Resource": "*",
            "Condition": {
                "StringEquals": {
                    "autoscaling:ResourceTag/k8s.io/cluster-
```

```
autoscaler/enabled": "true",
                   "aws:ResourceTag/k8s.io/cluster-
autoscaler/myipv4cluster": "owned"
                }}},
        { "Effect": "Allow",
            "Action": [
                "autoscaling:DescribeAutoScalingInstances",
                "autoscaling:DescribeAutoScalingGroups",
                "autoscaling:DescribeScalingActivities",
                "ec2:DescribeLaunchTemplateVersions",
                "autoscaling:DescribeTags",
                "autoscaling:DescribeLaunchConfigurations",
                "ec2:DescribeInstanceTypes"
            ],
            "Resource": "*"
        }]}
```

We can create the policy and associate it with an EKS service account using the following commands. Also, take note of the current EKS cluster version:

```
$ aws iam create-policy --policy-name AmazonEKSClusterAutoscalerPolicy
\
--policy-document file://autoscaler_policy.json
{
    "Policy": {
        "......}}
$ eksctl create iamserviceaccount  --cluster=myipv4cluster
--namespace=kube-system --name=cluster-autoscaler  --attach-policy-
arn=arn:aws:iam::112233:policy/AmazonEKSClusterAutoscalerPolicy
--override-existing-serviceaccounts --approve
......
2023-05-02 19:31:55 []  created serviceaccount "kube-system/cluster-
autoscaler"
$ kubectl version
Client Version: version.Info{Major:"1",
Minor:"22+", GitVersion:"v1.22.6-eks-7d68063",
GitCommit:"f24e667e49fb137336f7b064dba897beed639bad",
GitTreeState:"clean", BuildDate:"2022-02-23T19:32:14Z",
GoVersion:"go1.16.12", Compiler:"gc", Platform:"linux/amd64"}
Server Version: version.Info{Major:"1",
Minor:"22+", GitVersion:"v1.22.17-eks-ec5523e",
GitCommit:"49675beb7b1c90389418d067d37024616a313555",
GitTreeState:"clean", BuildDate:"2023-03-20T18:44:58Z",
GoVersion:"go1.16.15", Compiler:"gc", Platform:"linux/amd64"}
```

You can now download the `https://raw.githubusercontent.com/kubernetes/autoscaler/master/cluster-autoscaler/cloudprovider/aws/examples/cluster-autoscaler-autodiscover.yaml` installation manifest and modify the following lines (line numbers may vary).

Modify the autodiscovery tag (line 165)

This will configure the autoscaler to use the specific cluster tag we (or `eksctl`) created:

```
node-group-auto-discovery=asg:tag=k8s.io/cluster-autoscaler/
enabled,k8s.io/cluster-autoscaler/myipv4cluster
```

Add command switches under the autodiscovery tag line (line 165)

These switches allow the autoscaler to balance more effectively across availability zones and scale autoscaling node groups to zero:

```
- --balance-similar-node-groups
- --skip-nodes-with-system-pods=false
```

Modify the container image to align with your K8s server version (line 149)

This will use the same autoscaler version as the cluster itself. Although newer versions exist, it's best practice to use the same version as your cluster:

```
image: registry.k8s.io/autoscaling/cluster-autoscaler:v1.22.2
```

> **Note**
> The page at `https://github.com/kubernetes/autoscaler/releases` can be used to look up the required release.

Now we have a modified manifest, we can deploy the autoscaler, patch the service account, and verify it is running using the following commands:

```
$ kubectl create -f cluster-autoscaler-autodiscover.yaml
....
deployment.apps/cluster-autoscaler created
Error from server (AlreadyExists): error when creating "cluster-
autoscaler-autodiscover.yaml": serviceaccounts "cluster-autoscaler"
already exists
$ kubectl patch deployment cluster-autoscaler -n kube-system -p
'{"spec":{"template":{"metadata":{"annotations":{"cluster-autoscaler.
kubernetes.io/safe-to-evict": "false"}}}}'
$ kubectl get po -n kube-system
```

```
NAME                    READY   STATUS    RESTARTS   AGE
aws-node-2wrq6            1/1    Running   0          3d7h
aws-node-b1f12           1/1    Running   0          3d7h
cluster-autoscaler-577  1/1     Running   0          12s
......
```

> **Note**
>
> The deployment returns an error as the service account already exists. This will not affect the deployment or running of the autoscaler pod, but does mean that if you delete the manifest, the SA will also be deleted.

Now we have CA installed, let's test whether it is working.

Testing Cluster Autoscaler

If we look at the ASG created by `eksctl` for the node group created with the cluster, we can see the desired, minimum, and maximum capacities are set to **2**. As there are two nodes already provisioned and the maximum is **2**, autoscaling will never happen. So, we need to edit the ASG using the **Edit** button, and increase the maximum capacity to 5.

Figure 18.4 – eksctl node group ASG capacity

If we look at the cluster, we can see we have two nodes deployed and registered. Changing the ASG's maximum capacity has no effect on the current nodes as nothing has yet triggered any rescaling:

```
$ kubectl get node
NAME              STATUS    ROLES     AGE       VERSION
ip-192-168-18-136.eu-central-1.compute.
internal    Ready     <none>    3d8h      v1.22.17-eks-a59e1f0
ip-192-168-43-219.eu-central-1.compute.
internal    Ready     <none>    3d8h      v1.22.17-eks-a59e1f0
```

If we now deploy a manifest with a lot of replicas, we will see the autoscaler scale out the ASG to support the pods. The following manifest will cause more nodes to be provisioned as it requests 150 replicas/pods:

```
apiVersion: apps/v1
kind: Deployment
metadata:
  name: nginx-deployment
spec:
  selector:
    matchLabels:
      app: nginx
  replicas: 150
  template:
    metadata:
      labels:
        app: nginx
    spec:
      containers:
      - name: nginx
        image: nginx
        ports:
        - containerPort: 80
```

If we deploy this manifest and monitor the nodes and autoscaler using the following command, we can see the pods transition from `Pending` to the `Running` state as the ASG scales:

```
$ kubectl create -f tester.yaml
$ kubectl get po
NAME              READY   STATUS    RESTARTS   AGE
nginx-deployment-12   0/1     Pending   0          18m
nginx-deployment-13   0/1     Pending   0          18m
….
WAIT 10 MINUTES
$ kubectl get node
NAME            STATUS   ROLES    AGE    VERSION
ip-192-168-18-136.eu-central-1.compute.
internal    Ready    <none>   3d8h   v1.22.17-eks-a59e1f0
ip-192-168-34-4.eu-central-1.compute.
internal      Ready    <none>   18m    v1.22.17-eks-a59e1f0
ip-192-168-43-219.eu-central-1.compute.
internal    Ready    <none>   3d8h   v1.22.17-eks-a59e1f0
ip-192-168-77-75.eu-central-1.compute.
internal      Ready    <none>   18m    v1.22.17-eks-a59e1f0
```

```
ip-192-168-85-131.eu-central-1.compute.
internal    Ready      <none>    18m    v1.22.17-eks-a59e1f0
```

We can see the nodes have scaled up to 5 (the maximum set in the ASG configuration) to support the increased number of pods, but some pods will remain Pending as there are not enough nodes to support them and the autoscaler won't violate the ASG capacity limits to create more nodes. If we now delete the manifest using the following commands, we can see the ASG scale back to 2 (desired capacity) after nodes have not been needed for at least 10 minutes (this is the default – you can adjust the scan time for CA, but this will introduce more load onto your cluster, and as we will see later, Karpenter is much more suited for faster scaling):

```
$ kubectl delete -f tester.yaml
deployment.apps "nginx-deployment" deleted
WAIT AT LEAST 10 MINUTES
$ kubectl get node
NAME                STATUS    ROLES    AGE      VERSION
ip-192-168-34-4.eu-central-1.compute.
internal    Ready      <none>    47m    v1.22.17-eks-a59e1f0
ip-192-168-77-75.eu-central-1.compute.
internal    Ready      <none>    47m    v1.22.17-eks-a59e1f0
```

> **Note**
>
> The original, older nodes were removed and two of the newer nodes remain.

If you want to monitor the autoscaler's actions, you can use the following command:

```
$ kubectl -n kube-system logs -f deployment.apps/cluster-autoscaler
I0502 21:22:59.599092        1 scale_down.go:829] ip-192-168-18-136.
eu-central-1.compute.internal was unneeded for 7m2.220392583s
```

Using ASGs has its advantages but when you want to use lots of different instance types or scale up/down quickly, then Karpenter may provide more flexibility. Let's look at how we can deploy and use Karpenter.

Scaling worker nodes with Karpenter

Karpenter (https://karpenter.sh) is an open source autoscaling solution built for Kubernetes and is designed to build and remove capacity to cope with fluctuating demand without the need for node or ASGs. The following diagram illustrates the general flow:

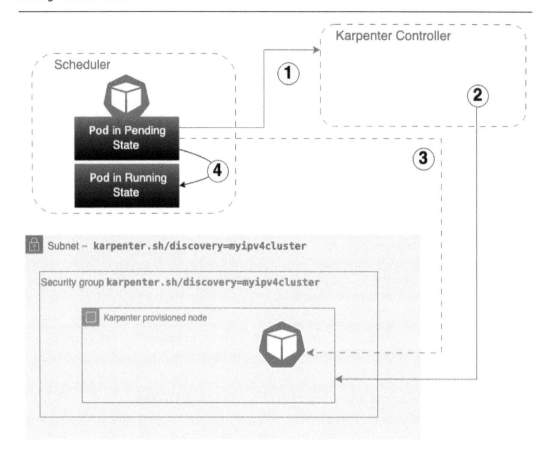

Figure 18.5 – High-level Karpenter flow

In the preceding diagram, we can see the following:

1. Karpenter is actively looking for pods in the Pending state that cannot be scheduled due to insufficient resources.

2. The Karpenter controller will review **resource requests**, **node selectors**, **affinities**, and **tolerations** for these pending pods, and provision nodes that meet the requirements of the pods.

3. Once the node has registered with the cluster, the scheduler will schedule the pod on that node.

4. Once the pod has been deployed and assuming there are no issues with the pod itself, the state is changed to **Running**.

Now that we've looked at the concepts behind Karpenter, let's install and test it.

Installing Karpenter in your EKS cluster

We will create the Karpenter controller on the existing managed node group (ASG) but use it to schedule workloads on additional worker nodes:

1. In order for our installation to be successful, we need to first set up a few environment variables. We can do this as follows:

```
$ export CLUSTER_NAME=myipv4cluster
 export AWS_PARTITION="aws"
 export AWS_REGION="$(aws configure list | grep region | tr -s "
" | cut -d" " -f3)"
 export OIDC_ENDPOINT="$(aws eks describe-cluster --name
${CLUSTER_NAME} --query "cluster.identity.oidc.issuer" --output
text)"
 export AWS_ACCOUNT_ID=$(aws sts get-caller-identity --query
'Account' --output text)
$ printenv
.....
AWS_PARTITION=aws
CLUSTER_NAME=myipv4cluster
AWS_REGION=eu-central-1
AWS_ACCOUNT_ID=111222333
OIDC_ENDPOINT=https://oidc.eks.eu-central-1.amazonaws.com/
id/123455
```

> **Note**
>
> Modify the cluster name to align with your cluster.

2. Next, we need to create the AWS IAM policy that will be associated with the nodes created by Karpenter. This will ensure they have the right EKS, ECR, and SSM permissions. We start with a trust policy that allows the EC2 instances to assume a role, as follows:

```
{ "Version": "2012-10-17",
  "Statement": [
    {
      "Sid": "",
      "Effect": "Allow",
      "Principal": {
        "Service": "ec2.amazonaws.com"
      },
      "Action": "sts:AssumeRole"
    }] }
```

3. We can then create a role, `KarpenterInstanceNodeRole`, which is used by the nodes created by Karpenter and references this trust policy as shown here:

    ```
    $ aws iam create-role --role-name
    KarpenterInstanceNodeRole    --assume-role-policy-document
    file://"trust_policy.json"
    ```

4. We can then attach the four required managed polices to this role using the following commands:

    ```
    $ aws iam attach-role-policy --policy-arn
    arn:aws:iam::aws:policy/AmazonEKSWorkerNodePolicy --role-name
    KarpenterInstanceNodeRole
    $ aws iam attach-role-policy --policy-arn
    arn:aws:iam::aws:policy/AmazonEKS_CNI_Policy --role-name
    KarpenterInstanceNodeRole
    $ aws iam attach-role-policy --policy-arn
    arn:aws:iam::aws:policy/AmazonEC2ContainerRegistryReadOnly
    --role-name KarpenterInstanceNodeRole
    $ aws iam attach-role-policy --policy-
    arn  arn:aws:iam::aws:policy/AmazonSSMManagedInstanceCore
    --role-name KarpenterInstanceNodeRole
    ```

5. We now create the instance profile used for the nodes:

    ```
    $ aws iam create-instance-profile --instance-profile-name
    "KarpenterNodeInstanceProfile-${CLUSTER_NAME}"
    {
        "InstanceProfile": {
            "Path": "/",
            "InstanceProfileName": "KarpenterNodeInstanceProfile-
    myipv4cluster",
            "InstanceProfileId": "AIPARDV7UN62ZBGEB7AV4",
            "Arn": "arn:aws:iam::111222333:instance-profile/
    KarpenterNodeInstanceProfile-myipv4cluster",
            "CreateDate": "2023-05-03T06:55:12+00:00",
            "Roles": []
        }
    }
    ```

6. Then we assign the role created previously to the instance profile:

    ```
    $ aws iam add-role-to-instance-profile --instance-profile-name
    "KarpenterNodeInstanceProfile-${CLUSTER_NAME}" --role-name
    "KarpenterInstanceNodeRole"
    ```

7. Now we have the instance profile for the EC2 nodes to use. The next task is to create the AWS IAM policy to be associated with the Karpenter pods. We will go through a similar process as we did for the instance profile. First, we create the trust policy, which allows the cluster's OIDC

endpoint to assume a role. This uses the `OIDC_ENDPOINT` and `AWS_ACCOUNT` environment variables we set up previously:

```
$ cat << EOF > controller-trust-policy.json
{
    "Version": "2012-10-17",
    "Statement": [
        {
            "Effect": "Allow",
            "Principal": {
                "Federated": "arn:aws:iam::${AWS_ACCOUNT_
ID}:oidc-provider/${OIDC_ENDPOINT#*//}"
            },
            "Action": "sts:AssumeRoleWithWebIdentity",
            "Condition": {
                "StringEquals": {
                    "${OIDC_ENDPOINT#*//}:aud": "sts.amazonaws.
com",
                    "${OIDC_ENDPOINT#*//}:sub":
"system:serviceaccount:karpenter:karpenter"
                }
            }
        }
    ]
}
EOF
```

8. Then we create the role for the Karpenter controller using the trust policy with the following command:

```
$ aws iam create-role --role-name KarpenterControllerRole-
${CLUSTER_NAME} --assume-role-policy-document file://controller-
trust-policy.json
{"Role": {
        "Path": "/",
        "RoleName": "KarpenterControllerRole-myipv4cluster",
.....
```

9. The following command is used to create the policy needed for the controller and again relies on the environment variables we set earlier:

```
cat << EOF > controller-policy.json
{
    "Statement": [
        {
            "Action": [
```

```
                    "ssm:GetParameter",
                    "ec2:DescribeImages",
                    "ec2:RunInstances",
                    "ec2:DescribeSubnets",
                    "ec2:DescribeSecurityGroups",
                    "ec2:DescribeLaunchTemplates",
                    "ec2:DescribeInstances",
                    "ec2:DescribeInstanceTypes",
                    "ec2:DescribeInstanceTypeOfferings",
                    "ec2:DescribeAvailabilityZones",
                    "ec2:DeleteLaunchTemplate",
                    "ec2:CreateTags",
                    "ec2:CreateLaunchTemplate",
                    "ec2:CreateFleet",
                    "ec2:DescribeSpotPriceHistory",
                    "pricing:GetProducts"
                ],
                "Effect": "Allow",
                "Resource": "*",
                "Sid": "Karpenter"
            },
            {
                "Action": "ec2:TerminateInstances",
                "Condition": {
                    "StringLike": {
                        "ec2:ResourceTag/karpenter.sh/provisioner-
name": "*"
                    }
                },
                "Effect": "Allow",
                "Resource": "*",
                "Sid": "ConditionalEC2Termination"
            },
            {
                "Effect": "Allow",
                "Action": "iam:PassRole",
                "Resource": "arn:${AWS_PARTITION}:iam::${AWS_
ACCOUNT_ID}:role/KarpenterInstanceNodeRole",
                "Sid": "PassNodeIAMRole"
            },
            {
                "Effect": "Allow",
                "Action": "eks:DescribeCluster",
                "Resource": "arn:${AWS_PARTITION}:eks:${AWS_
```

```
REGION}:${AWS_ACCOUNT_ID}:cluster/${CLUSTER_NAME}",
        "Sid": "EKSClusterEndpointLookup"
    }
],
    "Version": "2012-10-17"
}
EOF
```

10. We create the IAM role that will be used by the Karpenter controller using the policy created in the previous step:

```
$ aws iam put-role-policy --role-name KarpenterControllerRole-
${CLUSTER_NAME} --policy-name KarpenterControllerPolicy-
${CLUSTER_NAME} --policy-document file://controller-policy.json
```

11. We now need to tag the subnets we want Karpenter to use when it adds nodes by adding the `karpenter.sh/discovery=myipv4cluster` tag. We can use the `describe-subnets` command to identify which subnets have been tagged. The following is an example of this usage:

```
$ aws ec2 describe-subnets --filters "Name=tag:karpenter.sh
/discovery,Values=myipv4cluster" | jq -r '.Subnets[].SubnetId'
subnet-05d5323d274c6d67e
subnet-087e0a21855f08fd3
subnet-0dbed7d2f514d8897
```

> **Note**
> We've used the same subnets as the autoscaler, but you could use different ones.

12. We also need to tag the security group with the same discovery tag, `karpenter.sh/discovery=myipv4cluster`, so that Karpenter nodes will be able to communicate with the control plan and other nodes. We will use the cluster security group, which can be located in the **Networking** section:

Figure 18.6 – Locating the cluster security group

We can tag the security group with the following command:

```
$ aws ec2 create-tags --tags "Key=karpenter.sh/
discovery,Value=${CLUSTER_NAME}" --resources
sg-0222247264816d807
$ aws ec2 describe-security-groups --filters
"Name=tag:karpenter.sh/discovery,Values=myipv4cluster" | jq -r
'.SecurityGroups[].GroupId'
sg-0222247264816d807
```

13. Finally, we need to edit the aws-auth ConfigMap to allow the Karpenter node role to authenticate with the API servers. We need to add a new group with the following configuration to the ConfigMap:

```
mapRoles: |
    - groups:
    - system:bootstrappers
    - system:nodes
    rolearn: arn:aws:iam::123:role/eksctl-myipv4cluster-node
    username: system:node:{{EC2PrivateDNSName}}
    - groups:
    - system:bootstrappers
    - system:nodes
    rolearn: arn:aws:iam::123:role/KarpenterInstanceNodeRole
    username: system:node:{{EC2PrivateDNSName}}
```

You can use the $ kubectl edit configmap aws-auth -n kube-system command to make the changes.

All this preparation work now means we can download and customize the Karpenter Helm chart. We will use version *0.27.3*, which is the latest at the time of writing. The following command can be used set the Karpenter version and customize the Helm chart based on the environment variables and IAM policies created in the previous steps, saving it to the karpenter.yaml manifest:

```
$ export KARPENTER_VERSION=v0.27.3
$ helm template karpenter oci://public.ecr.aws/karpenter/karpenter
--version ${KARPENTER_VERSION} --namespace karpenter     --set
settings.aws.defaultInstanceProfile=KarpenterInstanceNodeRole  --set
settings.aws.clusterName=${CLUSTER_NAME}     --set serviceAccount.
annotations."eks\.amazonaws\.com/role-arn"="arn:${AWS_
PARTITION}:iam::${AWS_ACCOUNT_ID}:role/KarpenterControllerRole-
${CLUSTER_NAME}"     --set controller.resources.requests.
cpu=1     --set controller.resources.requests.memory=1Gi     --set
controller.resources.limits.cpu=1     --set controller.resources.
limits.memory=1Gi > karpenter.yaml
```

We now need to add some additional configuration to the karpenter.yaml file.

> **Note**
>
> The line numbers may be different for you.

Modify the affinity rules (line 482)

This will deploy Karpenter on the existing node group:

```
- matchExpressions:
            - key: eks.amazonaws.com/nodegroup
              operator: In
              values:
              - ipv4mng
```

We then create the namespace and add the Karpenter custom resources using the following commands:

```
$ kubectl create namespace karpenter
namespace/karpenter created
$ kubectl create -f https://raw.githubusercontent.com/aws/
karpenter/${KARPENTER_VERSION}/pkg/apis/crds/karpenter.sh_
provisioners.yaml
customresourcedefinition.apiextensions.k8s.io/provisioners.karpenter.
sh created
$ kubectl create -f https://raw.githubusercontent.com/aws/
karpenter/${KARPENTER_VERSION}/pkg/apis/crds/karpenter.k8s.aws_
awsnodetemplates.yaml
customresourcedefinition.apiextensions.k8s.io/awsnodetemplates.
karpenter.k8s.aws created
```

And finally, we can deploy the Helm chart and verify the deployment using the following commands:

```
$ kubectl apply -f karpenter.yaml
poddisruptionbudget.policy/karpenter created
serviceaccount/karpenter created
secret/karpenter-cert created
configmap/config-logging created
......
validatingwebhookconfiguration.admissionregistration.k8s.io/
validation.webhook.karpenter.k8s.aws created
$ kubectl get all  -n karpenter
NAME                READY    STATUS    RESTARTS    AGE
pod/karpenter-fcd8f5df6-12h6k    1/1      Running   0      43s
pod/karpenter-fcd8f5df6-r2vzw    1/1      Running          43s


NAME    TYPE    CLUSTER-IP   ..
service/karpenter    ClusterIP   10.100.76.202   ..
```

```
NAME     READY    UP-TO-DATE    AVAILABLE    AGE
deployment.apps/karpenter    2/2    2            2              43s

NAME             DESIRED    CURRENT    READY    AGE
replicaset.apps/karpenter-fcd8f5df6    2    2    2        43s
```

> **Note**
> If you've followed this entire chapter from the start, you will have both CA and Karpenter controllers deployed. You can disable CA by scaling down to zero using the following command: `kubectl scale deploy/cluster-autoscaler -n kube-system --replicas=0`.

Now we have Karpenter installed, let's test whether it is working.

Testing Karpenter autoscaling

The first thing we need to do is create a **Provisioner** and its associated **AWSNodeTemplate**. A **Provisioner** creates the rules used by Karpenter to create nodes and defines the pod selection rules. At least one provisioner must exist for Karpenter to work. In our next example, we will allow Karpenter to handle the following:

- Creating on-demand EC2 instances
- Choosing an instance type of either `c5.large`, `m5.large`, or `m5.xlarge`
- Labeling any new nodes with the `type=karpenter` label
- De-provisioning the node once it is empty of pods for 30 seconds

Karpenter will also be limited from creating additional nodes once the CPU and memory limits have been reached.

AWSNodeTemplate is used to describe elements of the AWS-specific configuration, such as the subnet and security groups. You can manually configure these details, but we will use the discovery tags we created in the previous sections.

The following example manifest can be deployed using the `$ kubectl create -f provisioner.yaml` command:

```
apiVersion: karpenter.sh/v1alpha5
kind: Provisioner
metadata:
  name: default
spec:
  labels:
    type: karpenter
```

```
    requirements:
      - key: karpenter.sh/capacity-type
        operator: In
        values: ["on-demand"]
      - key: "node.kubernetes.io/instance-type"
        operator: In
        values: ["c5.large", "m5.large", "m5.xlarge"]
    limits:
      resources:
        cpu: 1000
        memory: 1000Gi
    providerRef:
      name: default
    ttlSecondsAfterEmpty: 30
---
apiVersion: karpenter.k8s.aws/v1alpha1
kind: AWSNodeTemplate
metadata:
  name: default
spec:
  subnetSelector:
    karpenter.sh/discovery: myipv4cluster
  securityGroupSelector:
    karpenter.sh/discovery: myipv4cluster
```

Once we have successfully deployed the **Provisioner** and **AWSNodeTemplate**, we can move on to deploy the following manifest, which will create a namespace and a deployment with zero replicas to be scheduled on a node with a `type=karpenter` label:

```
apiVersion: v1
kind: Namespace
metadata:
  name: other
---
apiVersion: apps/v1
kind: Deployment
metadata:
  name: inflate
  namespace: other
spec:
  replicas: 0
  selector:
    matchLabels:
      app: inflate
```

```
    template:
      metadata:
        labels:
          app: inflate
      spec:
        nodeSelector:
          type: karpenter
        terminationGracePeriodSeconds: 0
        containers:
          - name: inflate
            image: public.ecr.aws/eks-distro/kubernetes/pause:3.2
            resources:
              requests:
                memory: 1Gi
```

Using the following commands, we can deploy the previous manifest, validate that no replicas exist, and also check that no nodes exist with the `type=karpenter` label:

```
$ kubectl create -f deployment.yaml
namespace/other created
deployment.apps/inflate created
$ kubectl get all -n other
NAME              READY    UP-TO-DATE    AVAILABLE    AGE
deployment.apps/inflate    0/0       0            0           11s


NAME              DESIRED    CURRENT    READY    AGE
replicaset.apps/inflate-11    0                 0          0        11s
$ kubectl get node -l type=karpenter
No resources found
```

Now if we scale the deployment, we will see pods get created in the `Pending` state as there is no EKS node satisfying **NodeSelector**. Karpenter will then create the node and the pods will be deployed and move to the `Running` state. The following commands illustrate this flow:

```
$ kubectl scale -n other deployment/inflate --replicas 5
deployment.apps/inflate scaled
$ kubectl get po -n other
NAME                        READY    STATUS    RESTARTS    AGE
inflate-6cc55bfc74-4rfts    0/1      Pending   0           10s
inflate-6cc55bfc74-9kl5n    0/1      Pending   0           10s
inflate-6cc55bfc74-nspbf    0/1      Pending   0           10s
inflate-6cc55bfc74-rq4cn    0/1      Pending   0           10s
inflate-6cc55bfc74-swtmv    0/1      Pending   0           10s
$ kubectl get node -l type=karpenter
```

```
NAME        STATUS    ROLES     AGE    VERSION
ip-192-168-55-119.eu-central-1.compute.
internal    Ready     <none>    99s    v1.22.17-eks-a59e1f0
$ kubectl get po -n other
NAME                        READY   STATUS    RESTARTS    AGE
inflate-6cc55bfc74-4rfts    1/1     Running   0           2m36s
inflate-6cc55bfc74-9k15n    1/1     Running   0           2m36s
inflate-6cc55bfc74-nspbf    1/1     Running   0           2m36s
inflate-6cc55bfc74-rq4cn    1/1     Running   0           2m36s
inflate-6cc55bfc74-swtmv    1/1     Running   0           2m36s
```

If we now delete the deployment , we will see the node is de-provisioned:

```
$ kubectl delete -f deployment.yaml
namespace "other" deleted
deployment.apps "inflate" deleted
$ kubectl get node -l type=karpenter
NAME             STATUS    ROLES     AGE      VERSION
ip-192-168-55-119.eu-central-1.compute.
internal    Ready     <none>    5m57s    v1.22.17-eks-a59e1f0
$ kubectl get node -l type=karpenter
No resources found
```

> **Note**
>
> The scale-in/out process is much faster than with CA, which is one of the key advantages of Karpenter.

We have focused on scaling the underlying EKS compute node using CA or Karpenter. Both of these controllers look for pods in the `Pending` state due to resource issues, and up to now we have been creating and scaling pods manually. We will now look at how we can scale pods automatically using HPA.

Scaling applications with Horizontal Pod Autoscaler

HPA is a component of Kubernetes that allows you to scale pods (through a **Deployment/ReplicaSet**) based on metrics rather than manual scaling commands. The metrics are collected by the K8s metrics server, so you will need to have this deployed in your cluster. The following diagram illustrates the general flow.

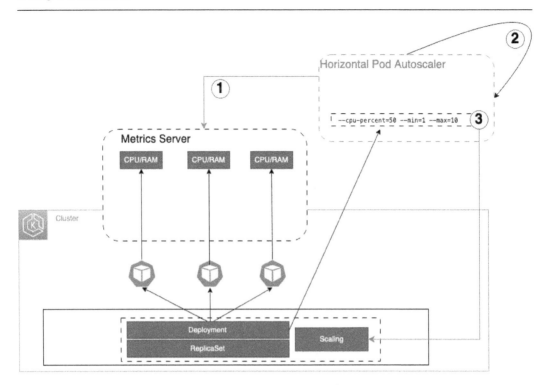

Figure 18.7 – High-level HPA flow

In the preceding diagram, we can see the following:

1. HPA reads metrics from the metrics server.

2. There is a control loop that triggers HPA to read the metrics every 15 seconds.

3. HPA assesses these metrics against the desired state of the autoscaling configuration and will scale the deployment if needed.

Now we've looked at the concepts behind the HPA, let's configure and test it.

Installing HPA in your EKS cluster

As we've discussed, HPA is a feature of K8s, so no installation is necessary; however, it does depend on K8s Metrics Server. To check whether Metrics Server is installed and providing data, the following commands can be used:

```
$ kubectl -n kube-system get deployment/metrics-server
NAME                 READY   UP-TO-DATE   AVAILABLE   AGE
metrics-server       1/1     1            1           34h
$ kubectl top pod -n kube-system
NAME                                  CPU(cores)    MEMORY(bytes)
```

```
aws-node-2tx2g              3m      38Mi
aws-node-9rhjs              3m      38Mi
coredns-7b6fd76bcb-6h9b6    1m      12Mi
coredns-7b6fd76bcb-vsvv8    1m      12Mi
kube-proxy-rn96m            1m      11Mi
kube-proxy-tf8d9            1m      10Mi
metrics-server-68c56b9d8c-24mng  3m  17Mi
```

if you don't have Metrics Server installed, you can use the following command to install the latest version:

```
$ kubectl apply -f https://github.com/kubernetes-sigs/metrics-server/
releases/latest/download/components.yaml
```

Now we have HPA's prerequisites installed, let's test whether it is working.

Testing HPA autoscaling

To test this, we will just use the K8s example to deploy a standard web server based on the php-apache container image. We then add the HPA autoscaling configuration and then use a load generator to generate load and push the metrics higher to trigger HPA to scale out the deployment. The K8s manifest file used is as follows:

```
apiVersion: apps/v1
kind: Deployment
metadata:
  name: php-apache
spec:
  selector:
    matchLabels:
      run: php-apache
  template:
    metadata:
      labels:
        run: php-apache
    spec:
      containers:
      - name: php-apache
        image: registry.k8s.io/hpa-example
        ports:
        - containerPort: 80
        resources:
          limits:
            cpu: 500m
          requests:
```

```
            cpu: 200m
---
apiVersion: v1
kind: Service
metadata:
  name: php-apache
  labels:
    run: php-apache
spec:
  ports:
  - port: 80
  selector:
    run: php-apache
```

We can now deploy this manifest and add the autoscaling configuration to maintain CPU utilization at around 50% across 1-10 pods using the following commands:

```
$ kubectl create -f hpa-deployment.yaml
deployment.apps/php-apache created
service/php-apache created
$ kubectl get all
NAME           READY   STATUS     RESTARTS    AGE
pod/php-apache-11-22   1/1    Running   0           57s
NAME      TYPE          CLUSTER-IP     EXTERNAL-IP   PORT(S)   AGE
service/php-apache   ClusterIP    10.1.2.1 <none>   80/TCP    57s
NAME            READY   UP-TO-DATE   AVAILABLE   AGE
deployment.apps/php-apache   1/1    1                     1      58s
NAME            DESIRED   CURRENT   READY    AGE
replicaset.apps/php-apache-1122   1          1              1      58s
$ kubectl autoscale deployment php-apache --cpu-percent=50 --min=1
--max=10
horizontalpodautoscaler.autoscaling/php-apache autoscaled
$ kubectl get hpa
NAME      REFERENCE    TARGETS   MINPODS    MAXPODS REPLICAS   AGE
php-apache Deployment/php-apache   0%/50% 1   10   1            19s
```

Now that we've added the autoscaling configuration, we can generate some load. As the CPU utilization of the pods will increase under the load, HPA will modify the deployment, scaling in and out in an effort to maintain the CPU utilization at 50%.

> **Note**
>
> You will need several terminal sessions for this exercise.

In the first terminal session, run the following command to generate the additional load:

```
$ kubectl run -i --tty load-generator --rm --image=busybox:1.28
--restart=Never -- /bin/sh -c "while sleep 0.01; do wget -q -O-
http://php-apache; done"
If you don't see a command prompt, try pressing enter.
OK!OK!OK!OK!OK!OK!OK!OK!OK!OK!OK!OK!OK!OK!OK!OK!OK!OK!OK!OK!OK!OK!O
K!OK!OK!OK!OK!OK!OK!OK!OK!OK!OK!OK!OK!OK!OK!OK!OK!.
```

In the second terminal, we can look at the HPA stats and will see the number of replicas gradually increase as HPA scales the deployment to cope with the increased load.

You can see that TARGETS (the third column in the following output) is initially higher than the 50% target as the load increases, and then as HPA adds more replicas the values come down, until it reaches under the 50% target with 5 replicas. This means HPA should not add any further replicas:

```
$ kubectl get hpa php-apache --watch
NAME       REFERENCE             TARGETS  MINPODS  MAXPODS  REPLICAS  AGE
php-apache Deployment/php-apache 119%/50%  1       10       1         10m
php-apache Deployment/php-apache 119%/50%  1       10       3         10m
php-apache Deployment/php-apache 188%/50%  1       10       3         10m
php-apache Deployment/php-apache 88%/50%   1       10       4         11m
php-apache Deployment/php-apache 77%/50%   1       10       4         11m
php-apache Deployment/php-apache 48%/50%   1       10       5         11m
```

If you now terminate the container running in the first session, you will see HPA scale back the deployment. The output of the kubectl get hpa php-apache --watch command is shown next, demonstrating the current load value dropping to 0 and HPA scaling back to 1 replica:

```
NAME       REFERENCE             TARGETS   MINPODS  MAXPODS  REPLICAS  AGE
php-apache Deployment/php-apache 119%/50%  1        10       1         10m
php-apache Deployment/php-apache 119%/50%  1        10       3         10m
........................................
php-apache Deployment/php-apache 0%/50%    1        10       5         16m
php-apache Deployment/php-apache 0%/50%    1        10       1         16m
```

HPA can query core metrics through the metrics.k8s.io K8s API endpoint, and can also query custom metrics using the external.metrics.k8s.io or custom.metrics.k8s.io API endpoints. With more complex applications, you need to monitor more than just **CPU** and **memory**, so let's look at how we can use custom metrics to scale our application.

Autoscaling applications with custom metrics

In order for you to use custom metrics, the following must be fulfilled:

1. Your application needs to be instrumented to produce metrics.

2. These metrics need to be exposed through the `custom.metrics.k8s.io` endpoint.

The application developer or dev team is responsible for point 1, and we will install and use Prometheus and the Prometheus adapter to satisfy point 2. The following diagram illustrates the high-level flow of this solution.

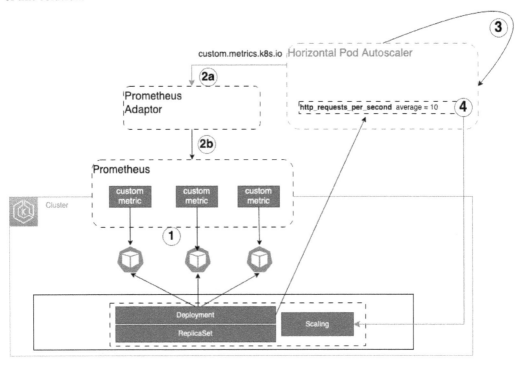

Figure 18.8 – HPA custom metrics high-level flow

Let's look at the flow in brief.

1. The Prometheus server installed in your cluster will "scrape" custom metrics from your pods.

2. HPA will do the following:

   A. Read metrics from the `custom.metrics.k8s.io` custom endpoint, hosted on the Prometheus adapter.

   B. The Prometheus adapter will pull data from the Prometheus server.

3. HPA assesses these metrics against the desired state of the autoscaling configuration. This assessment will reference custom metrics such as the average number of HTTP requests/second, and HPA will scale the deployment if needed.

Now we've looked at the concepts behind HPA custom metrics, let's install the prerequisites and test it.

Installing the Prometheus components in your EKS cluster

We will first install a local Prometheus server in the cluster using Helm. The first set of commands shown in the following code are used to get the latest Prometheus server chart:

```
$ kubectl create namespace prometheus
namespace/prometheus created
$ helm repo add prometheus-community https://prometheus-community.
github.io/helm-charts
"prometheus-community" has been added to your repositories
$ helm repo update
Hang tight while we grab the latest from your chart repositories...
... . . . .
...Successfully got an update from the "prometheus-community" chart
repository
...Successfully got an update from the "stable" chart repository
Update Complete. Happy Helming
```

> **Note**
> You can use AWS Managed Service for Prometheus instead if you so desire.

We can now install the chart and verify the pods all start using the following commands:

```
$ helm upgrade -i prometheus prometheus-community/
prometheus      --namespace prometheus      --set alertmanager.
persistentVolume.storageClass="gp2",server.persistentVolume.
storageClass="gp2"
Release "prometheus" does not exist. Installing it now.
NAME: prometheus
LAST DEPLOYED: Sun May  7 13:16:28 2023
NAMESPACE: prometheus
STATUS: deployed
REVISION: 1
TEST SUITE: None
......... .
For more information on running Prometheus, visit:
https://prometheus.io/
$ kubectl get po -n prometheus
```

```
NAME                              READY    STATUS      RESTARTS    AGE
prometheus-alertmanager-0    1/1        Running     0           19m
prometheus-kube-state-metrics-12    1/1   Running    0  19m
prometheus-prometheus-node-exporter-12  1/1  Running    0      19m
prometheus-prometheus-node-exporter-12   1/1  Running    0      19m
prometheus-prometheus-pushgateway-13     1/1   Running  0      19m
prometheus-server-677fbf6f-14             2/2         Running   0      19m
```

To verify that Prometheus is working, we can use the port forward command shown next and then use a local browser to navigate to `http://localhost:8080`:

```
$ kubectl --namespace=prometheus port-forward deploy/prometheus-server
8080:9090
Forwarding from 127.0.0.1:8080 -> 9090
Forwarding from [::1]:8080 -> 9090
```

We can then use the metrics explorer (the icon is highlighted in the following screenshot) to get data in table or graph formats. The example in the following screenshot is for the `container_memory_usage_bytes` metric.

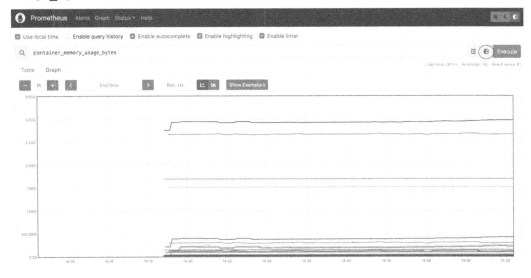

Figure 18.9 – Prometheus server displaying metric data

Now we have a Prometheus server instance installed and working, we can install the **podinfo** application. This is a small microservice often used for testing and exposes a number of metrics and health APIs.

> **Note**
> `podinfo` requires at least Kubernetes 1.23, so please make sure your cluster is running the correct version. We will also install an HPA configuration that we will replace later on.

Using the following command we can deploy the pod, its service, and the HPA configuration:

```
$ kubectl version help
...
Server Version: version.Info{Major:"1",
Minor:"23+", GitVersion:"v1.23.17-eks-0a21954",
GitCommit:"cd5c12c51b0899612375453f7a7c2e7b6563f5e9",
GitTreeState:"clean", BuildDate:"2023-04-15T00:32:27Z",
GoVersion:"go1.19.6", Compiler:"gc", Platform:"linux/amd64"}
$ kubectl create ns podinfo
namespace/podinfo created
$ kubectl apply -k github.com/stefanprodan/podinfo/kustomize -n
podinfo
service/podinfo created
deployment.apps/podinfo created
horizontalpodautoscaler.autoscaling/podinfo created
$ kubectl get hpa -n podinfo
NAME     REFERENCE          TARGETS   MINPODS   MAXPODS   REPLICAS   AGE
podinfo  Deployment/podinfo  2%/99%    2         4         2          13m
$ kubectl get po -n podinfo
NAME                      READY   STATUS    RESTARTS   AGE
podinfo-78989955bc-12     1/1     Running   0          35m
podinfo-78989955bc-13     1/1     Running   0          13m
```

if we look at the `deployment.yaml` file in the `podinfo` GitHub repository, we can see the following two annotations:

```
prometheus.io/scrape: "true"
prometheus.io/port: "9797"
```

This means that Prometheus can automatically scrape the `/metrics` endpoint on port 9797, so if we look in the Prometheus server (using port forwarding) we can see that one of the metrics being collected from the `podinfo` pods is `http_requests_total`, which we will use as our custom metric. This is illustrated in the following screenshot.

Figure 18.10 – Reviewing podinfo custom metric data in Prometheus

As we now have a working Prometheus server collecting custom metrics from our application (podinfo deployment), we next have to connect these metrics to the `custom.metrics.k8s.io` endpoint by installing the Prometheus adapter using the following commands.

The adapter will be installed in the Prometheus namespace and will point to the local Prometheus server and port. The adapter will have the default set of metrics configured to start, which we can see by querying the `custom.metrics.k8s.io` endpoint using the `$ kubectl get --raw` command as follows:

```
$ helm install prometheus-adapter prometheus-community/prometheus-
adapter  --set prometheus.url="http://prometheus-server.prometheus.
svc",prometheus.port="80" --set image.tag="v0.10.0" --set rbac.
create="true" --namespace prometheusNAME: prometheus-adapter
....

$ kubectl get po -n prometheus
NAME             READY    STATUS    RESTARTS    AGE
prometheus-adapter-123-chsmv  1/1       Running   0       92s
....

$ kubectl get --raw /apis/custom.metrics.k8s.io/v1beta1 | jq .
{
   "kind": "APIResourceList",
   "apiVersion": "v1",
   "groupVersion": "custom.metrics.k8s.io/v1beta1",
   "resources": [
     {
        "name": "nodes/node_vmstat_pgpgin",
....
```

The easiest way to configure our metrics is to replace the default `prometheus-adapter` ConfigMap with the configuration shown next, which only contains the rules for the `http_requests_total` metric exported from the `podinfo` application using the `/metrics` endpoint:

```
---
apiVersion: v1
kind: ConfigMap
metadata:
  name: prometheus-adapter
  namespace: prometheus
data:
  config.yaml: |
    rules:
    - seriesQuery: 'http_requests_total'
      resources:
        overrides:
          namespace:
```

```
            resource: "namespace"
        pod:
            resource: "pod"
    name:
      matches: "^(.*)_total"
      as: "${1}_per_second"
    metricsQuery: 'rate(http_requests
total{namespace="podinfo",app="podinfo"}[2m])'
```

We can now replace the ConfigMap with the configuration shown previously, restart the **Deployment** to re-read the new ConfigMap, and query the metrics through the custom endpoint using the following commands:

```
$ kubectl replace cm prometheus-adapter -n prometheus -f cm-adapter.
yaml
configmap/prometheus-adapter replaced
$ kubectl rollout restart deployment prometheus-adapter -n prometheus
deployment.apps/prometheus-adapter restarted
$ kubectl get po -n prometheus
NAME          READY    STATUS     RESTARTS    AGE
prometheus-adapter-123-h7ztg  1/1      Running   0     60s
......
$ kubectl get --raw /apis/custom.metrics.k8s.io/v1beta1 | jq .
{
  "kind": "APIResourceList",
  "apiVersion": "v1",
  "groupVersion": "custom.metrics.k8s.io/v1beta1",
  "resources": [
    {
      "name": "pods/http_requests_per_second",
      "singularName": "",
      "namespaced": true,
      "kind": "MetricValueList",
      "verbs": [
        "get"
      ]
    },
    {
      "name": "namespaces/http_requests_per_second",
      "singularName": "",
      "namespaced": false,
      "kind": "MetricValueList",
      "verbs": [
        "get"
```

```
      ]}]}
$ kubectl get --raw "/apis/custom.metrics.k8s.io/v1beta1/namespaces/
podinfo/pods/*/http_requests_per_second" | jq .
{
  "kind": "MetricValueList",
  "apiVersion": "custom.metrics.k8s.io/v1beta1",
  "metadata": {},
  "items": [
    {
      "describedObject": {
        "kind": "Pod",
        "namespace": "podinfo",
        "name": "podinfo-78989955bc-89n8m",
        "apiVersion": "/v1"
      },
      "metricName": "http_requests_per_second",
      "timestamp": "2023-05-08T22:42:11Z",
      "value": "200m",
      "selector": null
    },
    {
      "describedObject": {
        "kind": "Pod",
        "namespace": "podinfo",
        "name": "podinfo-78989955bc-rnr9c",
        "apiVersion": "/v1"
      },
      "metricName": "http_requests_per_second",
      "timestamp": "2023-05-08T22:42:11Z",
      "value": "200m",
      "selector": null
    }]}
```

Now we have the podinfo metrics being exposed through the custom metric endpoint, we can replace the HPA configuration with one that uses the custom metrics rather than the standard CPU one it was deployed with. To do this, we use the following configuration:

```
---
apiVersion: autoscaling/v2beta1
kind: HorizontalPodAutoscaler
metadata:
  name: podinfo
  namespace: podinfo
spec:
```

```
scaleTargetRef:
  apiVersion: apps/v1
  kind: Deployment
  name: podinfo
minReplicas: 1
maxReplicas: 10
metrics:
  - type: Pods
    pods:
      metricName: http_requests_per_second
      targetAverageValue: 10
```

We can use the following commands to replace the HPA configuration and validate it:

```
$ kubectl replace -f hpa-requests.yaml
Warning: autoscaling/v2beta1 HorizontalPodAutoscaler is
deprecated in v1.22+, unavailable in v1.25+; use autoscaling/v2
HorizontalPodAutoscaler
horizontalpodautoscaler.autoscaling/podinfo replaced
$ kubectl describe hpa podinfo -n podinfo
Warning: autoscaling/v2beta2 HorizontalPodAutoscaler is
deprecated in v1.23+, unavailable in v1.26+; use autoscaling/v2
HorizontalPodAutoscaler
Name:                                 podinfo
Namespace:                            podinfo
Labels:                               <none>
Annotations:                          <none>
CreationTimestamp:                    Sun, 07 May 2023 15:30:19 +0000
Reference:                            Deployment/podinfo
Metrics:                              ( current / target )
  "http_requests_per_second" on pods: 200m / 10
Min replicas:                         1
Max replicas:                         10
Deployment pods:                      1 current / 1 desired
...... .
```

Now we have HPA's prerequisites installed, let's test whether it is working.

Testing HPA autoscaling with custom metrics

To test this, we will just use a simple image with `curl` installed and call the `podinfo` API repeatedly, increasing the request count.

> **Note**
> You will need several terminal sessions for this exercise.

In the first terminal session, run the following command to generate load:

```
$ kubectl run -it load-test --rm --image=nginx -n prometheus - bash

root@load-test:/# curl http://podinfo.podinfo.svc.cluster.local:9898
{
"hostname": "podinfo-78989955bc-zfwdj",
  "version": "6.3.6",
  "revision": "073f1ec5aff930bd3411d33534e91cbe23302324",
  "color": "#34577c",
  "logo": "https://raw.githubusercontent.com/stefanprodan/podinfo/
gh-pages/cuddle_clap.gif",
  "message": "greetings from podinfo v6.3.6",
  "goos": "linux",
  "goarch": "amd64",
  "runtime": "go1.20.4",
  "num_goroutine": "9",
  "num_cpu": "2"
}
root@load-test:/# while sleep 0.01; do curl http://podinfo.podinfo.
svc.cluster.local:9898; done
........
```

In the second terminal session, we can look at the HPA stats and see the number of replicas gradually increase as HPA scales the deployment to cope with the increased load.

The third column in the following output, TARGETS, is initially low but gradually increases as more requests are responded to. Once the threshold has been exceeded, then more replicas are added:

```
$ kubectl get hpa -n podinfo --watch
NAME     REFERENCE TARGETS    MINPODS    MAXPODS    REPLICAS   AGE
podinfo Deployment/podinfo    200m/10      1 10   1    31h
podinfo  Deployment/podinfo   216m/10      1 10   1    31h
podinfo  Deployment/podinfo   19200m/10    1 10   1    31h
podinfo  Deployment/podinfo   19200m/10    1 10   2    31h
podinfo  Deployment/podinfo   20483m/10    1 10   2    31h
podinfo  Deployment/podinfo   14868m/10    1 10   2    31h
podinfo  Deployment/podinfo   15744m/10    1 10   3    31h
```

> **Note**
>
> The m character shown in the output represents milli-units, which means 0.1 req/sec.

If you exit the loop and container in the first terminal session, HPA will gradually scale down back to a single replica. While this solution works, it is not designed for large production environments. In the final section of this chapter, we will look at using **Kubernetes Event-Driven Autoscaling (KEDA)** for pod autoscaling, which supports large environments and can also use events or metrics from external sources.

Scaling with Kubernetes Event-Driven Autoscaling

KEDA is an open source framework that allows you to scale K8s workloads based on metrics or events. We do this by deploying the KEDA operator, which manages all the required components, broadly consisting of the following:

- An agent, responsible for scaling the deployment up or down depending on events.

- A metrics server that exposes metrics from applications or external sources.

- A **ScaledObject** custom resource that maintains the mapping between the external source or metric and the K8s deployment, as well as the scaling rules. This effectively creates a corresponding HPA *Kind*.

- Internal and external event sources that are used to trigger a KEDA action.

The following diagram illustrates the main KEDA components.

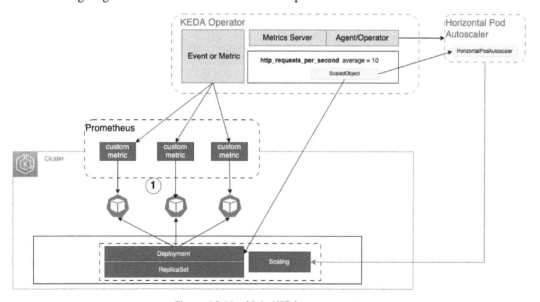

Figure 18.11 – Main KEDA components

Now we've looked at the concepts behind the KEDA custom metrics, let's install and test it.

Installing the KEDA components in your EKS cluster

We will use the existing Prometheus and podinfo deployments we created in the previous exercise, but I do suggest first removing the Prometheus adapter using the following command so there are no conflcts to scheduling:

```
$ helm delete prometheus-adapter  --namespace prometheus
release "prometheus-adapter" uninstalled
```

Now we can deploy the KEDA operator using the following commands:

```
helm repo add kedacore https://kedacore.github.io/charts
helm repo update
kubectl create namespace keda
helm install keda kedacore/keda --namespace keda –version 2.9.4
$ kubectl get po -n keda
NAME                              READY   STATUS    RESTARTS   AGE
keda-operator-123-5cv     1/1     Running   0            7m49s
keda-operator-metrics-apiserver-123   1/1     Running     7m49s
```

> **Note**
>
> As we are using K8s version 1.23, we need to install a 2.9 release. At the time of writing, 2.9.4 is the latest of these. You can use the `helm search repo kedacore  -l` command to get the latest chart versions.

We now need to deploy `ScaledObject` to tell KEDA what to monitor (metric name), what the external source is (Prometheus), what to scale (the podinfo deployment), and what the threshold is (10). Please note that in the example configuration shown here, we have set `minReplicaCount` to 2, but the default is 0:

```
---
apiVersion: keda.sh/v1alpha1
kind: ScaledObject
metadata:
  name: prometheus-scaledobject
  namespace: podinfo
spec:
  scaleTargetRef:
    name: podinfo
  minReplicaCount:   2
  maxReplicaCount:   10
```

```
    pollingInterval: 10
    cooldownPeriod:   30
    fallback:
      failureThreshold: 3
      replicas: 2
    triggers:
    - type: prometheus
      metadata:
        serverAddress: http://prometheus-server.prometheus.svc.cluster.
  local:80
        metricName: http_requests_total
        threshold: '10'
        query: sum(rate(http_requests_
  total{namespace="podinfo",app="podinfo"}[2m]))
```

We can use the following commands to deploy and verify this configuration. Looking at the HPA configuration, we can see two configurations – the one managed by KEDA, `keda-hpa-prometheus-scaledobject`, and the one deployed with the original HPA-based scheduling:

```
$ kubectl create -f scaledobject.yaml
scaledobject.keda.sh/prometheus-scaledobject created
$ kubectl get ScaledObject -n podinfo
AME                          SCALETARGETKIND        SCALETARGETNAME
    MIN    MAX    TRIGGERS        AUTHENTICATION    READY
ACTIVE    FALLBACK    AGE
prometheus-scaledobject      apps/
v1.Deployment    podinfo                  2      10      prometheus
     True      True      True       4m25s
  False    False    False
$ kubectl get hpa -n podinfo
NAME      REFERENCE    TARGETS    MINPODS    MAXPODS    REPLICAS    AGE
keda-hpa-prometheus-scaledobject    Deployment/podinfo    200m/10
  (avg)    2            10         2          4m42s
podinfo                            Deployment/
podinfo    2%/99%    2             4          2            84m
```

Now we have KEDA installed and an `ACTIVE` scaling configuration deployed, so let's test that it is working.

Testing KEDA autoscaling

To test this, we will just use a simple image with curl installed and will call the podinfo API repeatedly, increasing the request count.

> **Note**
> You will need several terminal sessions for this exercise.

In the first terminal session, run the following command to generate load:

```
$ kubectl run -it load-test --rm --image=nginx -n prometheus -- bash
root@load-test:/# while sleep 0.01; do curl http://podinfo.podinfo.
svc.cluster.local:9898; done
.......
```

In the second terminal session, you can look at the HPA stats and see the number of replicas gradually increase as HPA scales the deployment to cope with the increased load.

The third column in the following output, TARGETS, is initially low and increases as more requests are responded to. Once the threshold has been exceeded then more replicas are added. You will notice that the number of replicas fluctuates, which is because, unlike native HPA, KEDA dynamically adjusts the replica count to meet the incoming demand.

If we had left minReplicaCount at 0, we would have seen greater fluctuation.

> **Note**
> This highlights a key consideration for using KEDA: if you need to cope with fluctuating, non-deterministic demand, then KEDA is an ideal choice.

The following commands will show HPA scaling in and out the pods:

```
$ kubectl get hpa keda-hpa-prometheus-scaledobject -n podinfo --watch
NAME      REFERENCE   TARGETS   MINPODS   MAXPODS   REPLICAS   AGE
keda-hpa-prometheus-scaledobject      Deployment/podinfo   16742m/10
(avg)     2           10        2         16m
keda-hpa-prometheus-scaledobject      Deployment/podinfo   8371m/10
(avg)     2           10        4         16m
keda-hpa-prometheus-scaledobject      Deployment/podinfo   16742m/10
(avg)     2           10        2         16m
keda-hpa-prometheus-scaledobject      Deployment/podinfo   8371m/10
(avg)     2           10        4         16m
keda-hpa-prometheus-scaledobject      Deployment/podinfo   4961m/10
(avg)     2           10        3         17m
```

If you exit the loop and container in the first terminal session, KEDA will quickly scale back down to the value set in minReplicaCount.

In this section, we have looked at different ways to scale sour clusters and their workloads. We'll now revisit the key learning points from this chapter.

Summary

In this chapter, we looked at the different ways to scale EKS compute nodes (EC2) to increase resilience and/or performance. We reviewed the different scaling dimensions for our clusters and then set up node group/ASG scaling using the standard K8s CA. We then discussed how CA can take some time to operate and is restricted to ASGs, and how Karpenter can be used to scale much more quickly without the need for node groups, which means you can configure lots of different instance types. We deployed Karpenter and then showed how it can be used to scale EC2-based worker nodes up and down more quickly than CA using different instance types to the existing node groups.

Once we reviewed how to scale worker nodes, we discussed how we can use HPA to scale pods across our worker nodes. We first looked at basic HPA functionality, which uses K8s Metrics Server to monitor pod CPU and memory statistics to add or remove pods from a deployment as required. We then considered that complex applications usually need to scale based on different, specific metrics and examined how we could deploy a local Prometheus server and the Prometheus adapter to take custom application metrics and expose them through the K8s custom metrics endpoint and scale our deployment based on these custom metrics.

Finally, we reviewed how we can use KEDA to employ custom metrics or external data sources to cope with fluctuating demand and scale pods up and down very quickly based on these events.

In the next chapter, we will look at how we can develop on EKS, covering AWS tools such as Cloud9 and CI/CD tools such as Argo CD.

Further reading

- EKS observability tools:

  `https://docs.aws.amazon.com/eks/latest/userguide/eks-observe.html`

- Getting to know podinfo:

  `https://github.com/stefanprodan/podinfo`

- Using Managed Service for Prometheus with a Prometheus adapter:

  `https://aws.amazon.com/blogs/mt/automated-scaling-of-applications-running-on-eks-using-custom-metric-collected-by-amazon-prometheus-using-prometheus-adapter/`

- Getting to know KEDA:

  `https://keda.sh/docs/2.10/concepts/`

- Which KEDA version supports which K8s versions?:

  `https://keda.sh/docs/2.10/operate/cluster/`

19

Developing on EKS

Throughout the book, we've looked at how to build EKS clusters and deploy workloads. In this chapter, we will look at some ways you can make these activities more efficient if you're a developer or DevOps engineer using automation and CI/CD.

In this chapter, we will discuss the tools and techniques you can use to deploy and test clusters and workloads natively on AWS, or by using third-party tools. We will cover the following:

- Different IT personas
- Using Cloud9 as your integrated development environment
- Building clusters with EKS Blueprints and Terraform
- Using CodePipeline and CodeBuild to build clusters
- Using Argo CD, Crossplane, and GitOps to deploy workloads

Technical requirements

You should have a familiarity with YAML, AWS IAM, and EKS architecture. Before getting started with this chapter, please ensure the following:

- You have network connectivity to your EKS cluster API endpoint
- The AWS CLI, Docker, and `kubectl` binaries are installed on your workstation and have administrator access

Different IT personas

Before we look at the technology that supports development, it's important to consider who in your organization or team will deploy your EKS clusters or applications/workloads. The following diagram illustrates IT functional groups you might find in a typical enterprise; this is often referred to as the cloud operating model and consists of the following:

- Application engineers that build applications

- Application operations that operate and support applications

- Platform engineers that build middleware, networks, databases, and so on

- Platform operations that operate and support infrastructure and middleware

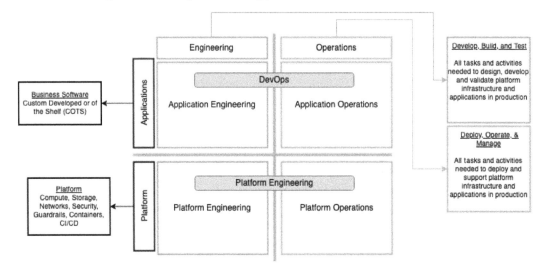

Figure 19.1 – Cloud operating model functional architecture

Many organizations now use a DevOps model, where they combine **Application Engineering** and **Application Operations** in the developer team, using the mantra "*you build it, you run it.*" This can also include platform engineering but often traditional IT operational teams for network and databases exist, and they must work with the application teams.

In recent years, platform engineering teams have also started appearing to being engineering and supporting parts of the infrastructure used by developers/DevOps engineers, such as EKS, databases, messaging, and APIs. This team's mantra is "*you code and test and we'll do all the rest.*"

Which specific model is used and which teams do what is really down to your organization. However, for the rest of this section, we will use the term *DevOps engineers* to refer to roles that are responsible for application engineering/operations, and *platform engineers* for roles that are responsible for the EKS cluster and support infrastructure, such as databases or networking.

Let's explore how we can interact with the AWS environment to build, deploy, and test platform and application services.

Using Cloud9 as your integrated development environment

Cloud9 is a simple **integrated development environment** (IDE) that runs on top of EC2 and is similar in nature to other IDEs, such as Microsoft's Visual Studio Code, Eclipse, or PyCharm. It can be used by platform engineers or developers alike. While Cloud9 isn't as extensible as those IDEs, it does have several advantages, such as the following:

- It runs on EC2 inside your account/s, which will allow you to communicate with private resources, such as private EKS clusters, without network access

- You can use AWS Systems Manager Session Manager to connect to your instance, which only needs IAM permissions and access to the AWS console

- As it's an EC2 instance, you can assign a role to your instance with the permissions required, and these credentials are automatically refreshed and don't expire (which is useful when you're provisioning clusters, as this can take some time)

- It provides an integrated AWS toolkit to simplify your interaction with resources such as S3 and Lambda

- You can run Docker containers on your instance and preview HTTP if your container or code uses a localhost address on port 8080, 8081, or 8082

- Most recently, it has been integrated with Amazon CodeWhisperer, which uses machine learning and can generate code for languages such as Python and Java

I've used Cloud9 extensively throughout this book's development, as it is simple and secure to use, but you can, of course, use any IDE. In the rest of this section, we will look at how you can set up and use Cloud9 to develop for EKS.

Creating and configuring your Cloud9 instance

We will use the following Terraform code to create a Cloud9 instance, allow the user defined within the `myuser_arn` local to use it, and connect it to the subnet defined in `subnet_id`. As we have defined the connection type as `CONNECT_SSM`, this subnet can be private as long as it has connectivity to the AWS SSM API, either through a private endpoint or a NAT gateway:

```
data "aws_region" "current" {}
locals {
  myuser_arn = "arn:aws:sts::123:myuser"
}
resource "aws_cloud9_environment_ec2" "k8sdev" {
```

```
  name = "k8sdev"
  instance_type = "t3.medium"
  connection_type = "CONNECT_SSM"
  description = "cloud9 K8s development environment"
  subnet_id = "subnet-123"
  owner_arn = local.myuser_arn
}
data "aws_instance" "cloud9_instance" {
  filter {
    name = "tag:aws:cloud9:environment"
    values = [
    aws_cloud9_environment_ec2.k8sdev.id]
}}
```

> **Note**
>
> Please note that can you modify `instance_type` to whatever you are comfortable paying for because, although there is no charge for Cloud9, there is a charge for the EC2 instance hosting it.

Once the Terraform code has completed, you can use the AWS console, browse to the **Cloud9 | Environments** tab, and use the **Open** link to start up your EC2 instance and launch the IDE in your browser, using an SSM session. This is illustrated in the following screenshot.

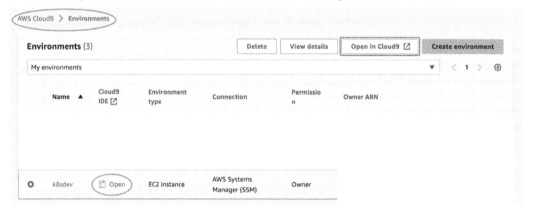

Figure 19.2 – Launching a Cloud9 SSM session

By default, Cloud9 will use AWS managed temporary credentials, which have limited permissions and can be found at the following link: `https://docs.aws.amazon.com/cloud9/latest/user-guide/security-iam.html#auth-and-access-control-temporary-managed-credentials-supported`. They won't allow you to fully interact with the AWS platform. We will create a role with `AdministratorAccess`, turn off managed temporary credentials in our Cloud9 instance, and then associate this new role with the EC2 instance hosting the Cloud9 IDE.

The role description is shown next, and it has an explicit trust with the `ec2.amazonaws.com` service. You can follow the process described in the following link to configure your Cloud9 instance: `https://catalog.us-east-1.prod.workshops.aws/workshops/c15012ac-d05d-46b1-8a4a-205e7c9d93c9/en-US/15-aws-event/cloud9`.

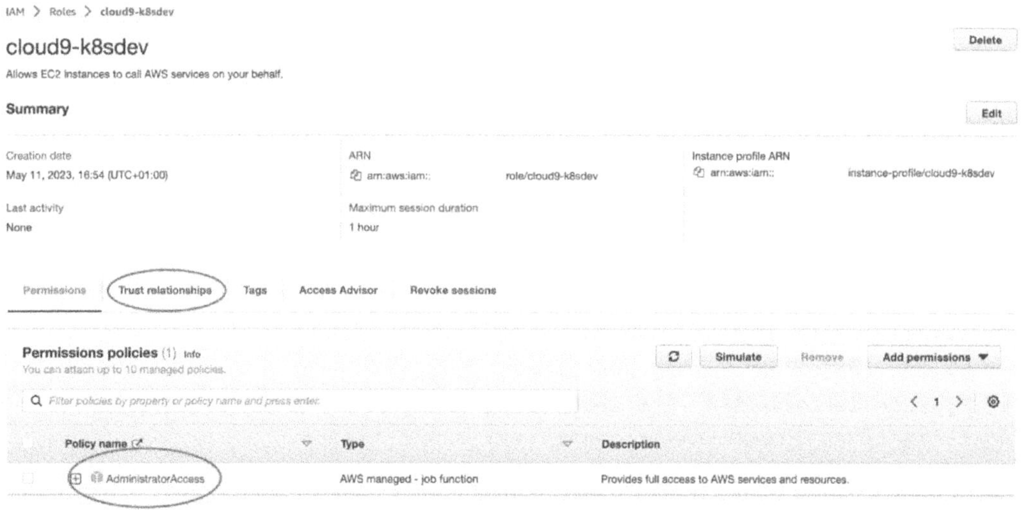

Figure 19.3 – An example IAM role

> **Note**
>
> We only add the `AdministratorAccess` policy for simplicity. Ideally, you would tailor the Cloud9 permissions to support the least amount of privilege needed.

We can verify the role is attached using the following command in a Cloud9 terminal session:

```
$ aws sts get-caller-identity
{"UserId": "343242342:i-12",
    "Account": "1122334455",
    "Arn": "arn:aws:sts::1234:assumed-role/cloud9-k8sdev/i-12" }
```

We now need to install the necessary tools; as Cloud9 comes with the AWS CLI, Python, and Docker, we still need to install `kubectl` and so on. You can install these components manually, but AWS provides a handy script as part of its Cloud9 workshop (in the URL shown previously), so we will use this to install the necessary tools, including `kubectl` and AWS **Cloud Development Kit** (**CDK**). The commands are shown here:

```
$ wget https://jiwony-seoul-public.s3.ap-northeast-2.amazonaws.com/cloud9-prereq.sh
--2023-05-11 16:12:15--  https://jiwony-seoul-public.s3.ap-northeast-2.amazonaws.com/cloud9-prereq.sh
...... .
```

```
$ sh cloud9-prereq.sh
Upgrading awscli
Requirement already up-to-date: awscli in
Complete!
----------------------------
You successfully installed all the required tools to your workspace
$  kubectl version --short
Flag --short has been deprecated, and will be removed in the future.
The --short output will become the default.
Client Version: v1.27.1
Kustomize Version: v5.0.1
The connection to the server localhost:8080 was refused - did you
specify the right host or port?
$ cdk version
2.78.0 (build 8e95c37)
******************************************************
*** Newer version of CDK is available [2.79.1]   ***
*** Upgrade recommended (npm install -g aws-cdk) ***
******************************************************
```

We will also install/upgrade `terraform`, as we will use this later on in this section, using the following commands:

```
$ sudo yum install -y yum-utils
$ sudo yum-config-manager --add-repo https://rpm.releases.hashicorp.
com/RHEL/hashicorp.repo
$ sudo yum -y install terraform
```

We can also add `eksctl`, which was used in the earlier sections of the book, using these commands:

```
$ ARCH=amd64
$ PLATFORM=$(uname -s)_$ARCH
$ curl -sLO "https://github.com/weaveworks/eksctl/releases/latest/
download/eksctl_$PLATFORM.tar.gz"
$ tar -xzf eksctl_$PLATFORM.tar.gz -C /tmp && rm eksctl_$PLATFORM.tar.
gz
$ sudo mv /tmp/eksctl /usr/local/bin
$ eksctl version
0.140.0
```

Finally, we will just set the default region so that all tools that use the SDK will use the region we specify:

```
$ aws configure
AWS Access Key ID [None]:
AWS Secret Access Key [None]:
Default region name [None]: eu-central-1
Default output format [None]:
```

Now, we have our Cloud9 instance configured. We will now use it to deploy clusters using EKS Blueprints.

Building clusters with EKS Blueprints and Terraform

In this book, we mainly used `eksctl` to build our clusters and leverage add-ons to support simpler upgrades of standard components, such as the VPC CNI plugin or kube-proxy. We also deployed additional software such as Prometheus and KEDA (*Chapter 18*). EKS blueprints provides you with a way to build an opinionated cluster, with this operational software already deployed. This simplifies the job of the platform of DevOps engineers, and they can use blueprints to repeatedly build clusters for different environments and/or teams with very little effort.

EKS Blueprint Clusters are built using AWS CDK, which is a set of libraries and constructs that allow you to create and deploy complex CloudFormation templates, using standard programming languages such as TypeScript or Python. Recently, AWS has released EKS Blueprints for Terraform, and this is what we will use in the rest of the section to create a cluster that can be used by our developers to deploy their applications.

You can follow a phased approach to developing your cluster configuration. The following diagram shows the suggested approach.

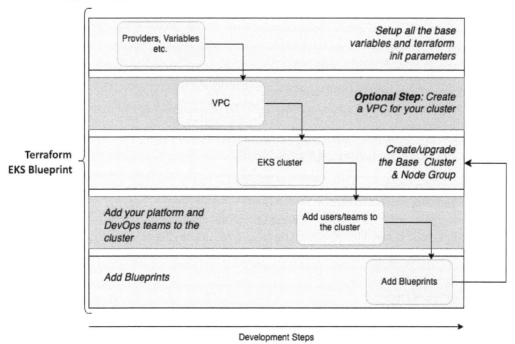

Figure 19.4 – The EKS blueprints development life cycle

In the next section, we will step through each phase of the development life cycle as we download, version, and customize our blueprint code.

Customizing and versioning EKS Blueprints for Terraform

The first thing we're going to do is use our Cloud9 instance to create a Git-compliant repository in CodeCommit to store our version of the Terraform code. The following commands can be used to create the repository, clone it, and create a new branch for our work:

```
$ aws codecommit create-repository --repository-name cluster-tf
--repository-description "repository for TF Blueprint" --tags
Team=devops --region eu-central-1
{
      "........
        "cloneUrlHttp": "https://git-codecommit.eu-central-1.
amazonaws.com/v1/repos/cluster-tf",
...}}
$ git clone https://git-codecommit.eu-central-1.amazonaws.com/v1/
repos/cluster-tf
Cloning into 'cluster-tf'...
warning: You appear to have cloned an empty repository.
$ cd cluster-tf
(master) $ git checkout -b initial
Switched to a new branch 'initial'
```

In our `cluster-tf` directory, we will create a new `.gitignore` file based on the template found at `https://github.com/github/gitignore/blob/main/Terraform.gitignore` (you can create your own).

Setting up the base variables and providers

To use the Terraform blueprint modules, we need to configure key Terraform resources such as the providers and data sources to use. Let's start with the providers, which are the base "engines" of Terraform, and translate the Terraform resources into actual deployed objects in AWS or K8s. The following configuration is saved in the `providers.tf` file in our cloned repository directory:

```
terraform {
  required_version = ">= 1.0.1"
  required_providers {
    aws = {
      source  = "hashicorp/aws"
      version = ">= 4.47"
    }
```

```
    kubernetes = {
      source  = "hashicorp/kubernetes"
      version = ">= 2.10"
    }
    helm = {
      source  = "hashicorp/helm"
      version = ">= 2.4.1"
    }
    kubectl = {
      source  = "gavinbunney/kubectl"
      version = ">= 1.14"
    }
  }
}
```

We will also create a `data.tf` file that will get the current AWS credentials, Region, and Availability Zones for that Region:

```
data "aws_caller_identity" "current" {}
data "aws_region" "current" {}
data "aws_availability_zones" "available" {
  state = "available"}
```

We will also create a `local.tf` file that maintains the base configuration, including the cluster name and version. The cluster name is derived from the repository path, but for production usage, you will want to use the `locals int` variables and then populate them at build time:

```
locals {
  name            = basename(path.cwd)
  region          = data.aws_region.current.name
  cluster_version = "1.24"
  vpc_cidr = "172.31.0.0/16"
  azs        = slice(data.aws_availability_zones.available.names, 0, 3)
  node_group_name = "mgmt-nodegroup"
  tags = {
    Blueprint  = local.name
    GithubRepo = "github.com/aws-ia/terraform-aws-eks-blueprints"
  }
}
```

We can now run the following commands to initialize Terraform with the providers and push the initial code to our **CodeCommit** repository:

```
(initial)$ terraform init
Initializing the backend...
Initializing provider plugins...
- Finding hashicorp/aws versions matching ">= 4.47.0"...
- Finding hashicorp/kubernetes versions matching ">= 2.10.0"...
.....
(initial)$ git add .
(initial)$ git commit -m "initial commit with providers and
configuration"
....
(initial)$ git push --set-upstream origin initial
Enumerating objects: 8, done.
Counting objects: 100% (8/8), done.
.....
branch 'initial' set up to track 'origin/initial'.
(initial)$
```

Now that we have the providers and the base configuration stored, we can use it to create a VPC and tag it for use with EKS.

Creating the EKS VPC

Your cluster needs an existing VPC for the EKS cluster. We will create a new one with the code shown next, but you can modify the code shown in the *Creating the EKS cluster* section to use a pre-existing one and skip this step:

```
module "vpc" {
    source  = "terraform-aws-modules/vpc/aws"
    version = "3.16.0"
    name = local.name
    cidr = local.vpc_cidr
    azs  = local.azs
    public_subnets  = [for k, v in local.azs : cidrsubnet(local.vpc_
cidr, 8, k)]
    private_subnets = [for k, v in local.azs : cidrsubnet(local.vpc_
cidr, 8, k + 10)]
    enable_nat_gateway   = true
    create_igw           = true
    enable_dns_hostnames = true
    single_nat_gateway   = true
    manage_default_network_acl   = true
    default_network_acl_tags     = { Name = "${local.name}-default" }
```

```
manage_default_route_table    = true
default_route_table_tags      = { Name = "${local.name}-default" }
manage_default_security_group = true
default_security_group_tags   = { Name = "${local.name}-default" }
public_subnet_tags = {
  "kubernetes.io/cluster/${local.name}" = "shared"
  "kubernetes.io/role/elb"              = "1"
}
private_subnet_tags = {
  "kubernetes.io/cluster/${local.name}" = "shared"
  "kubernetes.io/role/internal-elb"     = "1"
}
  tags = local.tags
}
```

We will also create an `outputs.tf` file that stores the newly created VPC's ID, which can be used when we create the EKS cluster using the following code:

```
output "vpc_id" {
  description = "The id of the new VPC"
  value       = module.vpc.vpc_id
}
```

We can now validate that the code is correct, create the VPC, and save the final code by using the following commands:

```
(initial)$ terraform init
Initializing the backend...
Downloading registry.terraform.io/terraform-aws-modules/vpc/aws 3.16.0
for vpc...
....
Terraform has been successfully initialized!
(initial)$ terraform plan
....
Plan: 23 to add, 0 to change, 0 to destroy.
Changes to Outputs:
  + vpc_id = (known after apply)
...
(initial)$ terraform apply --auto-approve
data.aws_region.current: Reading...
data.aws_caller_identity.current: Reading...
Apply complete! Resources: 23 added, 0 changed, 0 destroyed.
Outputs:
vpc_id = "vpc-0d5fb4e92b71eb9e6"
(initial)$ git add .
```

```
(initial)$ git commit -m "added vpc and deployed"
....
create mode 100644 vpc.tf
create mode 100644 outputs.tf
(initial) $ git push
Enumerating objects: 4, done.
...
```

> **Note**
>
> Terraform stores its state in a state file, `terraform.tfstate`. At present, this will be stored
> locally in the repository directory and ignored by Git (because of the `.gitignore` file). We
> will discuss strategies for managing this file later on in this chapter.

Now that we have a new VPC, we will use EKS Blueprints to configure and deploy an EKS cluster
referencing the new VPC.

Creating the EKS cluster

We will now create an EKS cluster using the Blueprint module; we will use 4.31.0, which is the latest
at the time of writing. An example configuration, `main.tf`, is shown in the following snippet. This
will create the cluster in the VPC we created previously with just the standard K8s services:

```
provider "aws" {
  region = "us-east-1"
  alias  = "virginia"
}
provider "kubernetes" {
  host                    = module.eks_blueprints.eks_cluster_endpoint
  cluster_ca_certificate  = base64decode(module.eks_blueprints.eks_
cluster_certificate_authority_data)
  token                   = data.aws_eks_cluster_auth.this.token
}
provider "helm" {
  kubernetes {
    host                    = module.eks_blueprints.eks_cluster_
endpoint
    cluster_ca_certificate = base64decode(module.eks_blueprints.eks_
cluster_certificate_authority_data)
    token                   = data.aws_eks_cluster_auth.this.token
  }
}
provider "kubectl" {
  apply_retry_count      = 10
```

```
  host                    = module.eks_blueprints.eks_cluster_endpoint
  cluster_ca_certificate = base64decode(module.eks_blueprints.eks_
cluster_certificate_authority_data)
  load_config_file        = false
  token                   = data.aws_eks_cluster_auth.this.token
}
module "eks_blueprints" {
  source = "github.com/aws-ia/terraform-aws-eks-
blueprints?ref=v4.31.0"
  cluster_name     = local.name
  vpc_id                  = module.vpc.vpc_id
  private_subnet_ids = module.vpc.private_subnets
  cluster_version = local.cluster_version
  managed_node_groups = {
    mg_5 = {
      node_group_name = local.node_group_name
      instance_types  = ["m5.large"]
      subnet_ids      = module.vpc.private_subnets
    }
  }
  tags = local.tags
}
```

> **Note**
>
> In the `eks blueprints` module shown previously, we use the `ref` keyword to indicate which version of the blueprint module we will call; this may change depending on the blueprints' release schedule.

We need to configure some additional data sources for our cluster deployment to work, including one in another region, `eu-east-1`. A sample configuration created in the `eks-data.tf` file is shown in the following snippet:

```
data "aws_eks_cluster" "cluster" {
  name = module.eks_blueprints.eks_cluster_id
}
data "aws_eks_cluster_auth" "this" {
  name = module.eks_blueprints.eks_cluster_id
}
# To Authenticate with ECR Public in eu-east-1
data "aws_ecrpublic_authorization_token" "token" {
  provider = aws.virginia
}
```

We also need to configure an additional output in the eks-output.tf file, shown next, so that we can interact manually with the cluster using our Cloud9 instance:

```
output "configure_kubectl" {
  description = "run the following command to update your kubeconfig"
  value       = module.eks_blueprints.configure_kubectl }
```

Now we have all the configurations in place, we can validate whether the code is correct, create the EKS cluster, and save the code by using the following commands:

```
(initial)$ terraform init
Initializing the backend...
Initializing modules...
Downloading git::https://github.com/aws-ia/terraform-aws-eks-
blueprints.git?ref=v4.31.0 for eks_blueprints...
- eks_blueprints in .terraform/modules/eks_blueprints
....
Terraform has been successfully initialized!
(initial)$ terraform plan
....
Plan: 32 to add, 0 to change, 0 to destroy.
Changes to Outputs:
  + vpc_id = (known after apply)
  + configure_kubectl = (known after apply)
(initial)$ terraform apply --auto-approve
data.aws_region.current: Reading...
data.aws_caller_identity.current: Reading...
...
Apply complete! Resources: 32 added, 0 changed, 0 destroyed.
...
Outputs:
configure_kubectl = "aws eks --region eu-central-1 update-kubeconfig
--name cluster-tf"
vpc_id = "vpc-0d5fb4e92b71eb9e6"
(initial) $ aws eks --region eu-central-1 update-kubeconfig --name
cluster-tf
Added new context arn:aws:eks:eu-central-1:123:cluster/cluster-tf to /
home/ec2-user/.kube/config
(initial) $ kubectl get node
NAME    STATUS   ROLES    AGE      VERSION
ip-172-31-10-122.eu-central-1.compute.
internal   Ready    <none>   2m52s   v1.24.11-eks-a59e1f0
ip-172-31-11-172.eu-central-1.compute.
internal   Ready    <none>   2m48s   v1.24.11-eks-a59e1f0
ip-172-31-12-210.eu-central-1.compute.
internal   Ready    <none>   2m49s   v1.24.11-eks-a59e1f0
```

```
(initial) $ git add .
(initial) $ git commit -m "deployed working cluster"
[initial dbf80aa] deployed working cluster
 5 files changed, 182 insertions(+)
 create mode 100644 README.md
 create mode 100644 eks-data.tf
 create mode 100644 eks-ouputs.tf
 create mode 100644 main.tf
 (initial) $ git push
Enumerating objects: 9, done.
....
To https://git-codecommit.eu-central-1.amazonaws.com/v1/repos/
cluster-tf
   c5319f4..dbf80aa  initial -> initial
```

> **Note**
>
> Please note that it can take up to 15 minutes to deploy your cluster.

Now that we have a working cluster, we can allow access to different users, roles, or teams.

Adding users/teams to your cluster

At present, only the role/identity associated with the credentials you've used to run the terraform will have access to your clusters. So, we will add a new administrator to the cluster and then add a tenant.

In the main.tf file, you can add a map roles section, which will add a single role as an administrator for the cluster:

```
 map_roles = [
    {
      rolearn  = "arn:aws:iam::${data.aws_caller_identity.current.
account_id}:role/Admin"
      username = "admin-role"
      groups   = ["system:masters"]
    }
  ]
```

> **Note**
>
> You will need to replace the role/admin with an appropriate role in your account. Remember that if the IAM credentials used by Terraform are not included in the configuration after its application, Terraform may lose access to the cluster to perform K8s API actions, such as modifying the aws-auth config map.

For the tenants/users, we will create a new `locals` file, `locals-team.tf`, but again, you will probably want to use a variable. An example is shown next for two teams, a platform team and an application team:

```
locals {
platform_admins = ["arn:aws:iam::123:role/plat1"]
app_team_1 = ["arn:aws:iam::123:role/dev1"]
}
```

> **Note**
> You will need to use valid user account ARNs or `[data.aws_caller_identity.current.arn]`.

We now need to modify our `main.tf` file for the cluster and add the following code snippet, `platform_teams`, to provide cluster admin access to a list of platform team users. This will create a new IAM role with cluster access and allow the list of users assigned to the platform teams to assume that role and get admin access:

```
platform_teams = {
  admin = {
    users = local.platform_admins
}}
```

And in the `main.tf` file, we can add also add a tenant DevOps or application team with limits, which will also create a namespace:

```
application_teams = {
  alpha = {
    "labels" = {
      "appName"     = "alpha",
      "projectName" = "project-alpha",
      "environment" = "dev"
    }
    "quota" = {
      "pods"                = "15",
      "services"            = "10"
    }
    users        = [local.app_team_alpha]
  }}
```

We can now do the regular Terraform `plan` and `apply` commands to deploy these changes, grant access to the ARNs listed in the local file, and use our standard Git commands to commit the changes to our repository. Examples of the main commands are shown here:

```
(initial) $ terraform plan
module.eks_blueprints.module.aws_eks.module.kms.data.aws_partition.
current: Reading...
module.eks_blueprints.data.aws_region.current: Reading...
....
Plan: 9 to add, 3 to change, 0 to destroy..
(initial) $ terraform apply --auto-approve
odule.eks_blueprints.module.aws_eks.module.kms.data.aws_partition.
current: Reading...
Note: Objects have changed outside of Terraform
...
Apply complete! Resources: 2 added, 1 changed, 0 destroyed.
Outputs:
configure_kubectl = "aws eks --region eu-central-1 update-kubeconfig
--name cluster-tf"
vpc_id = "vpc-0d5fb4e92b71eb9e6"
(initial) $ kubectl get ns
NAME                STATUS    AGE
alpha               Active    10m
..
(initial) $ kubectl get ResourceQuota -n alpha
NAME      AGE    REQUEST                      LIMIT
quotas    10m    pods: 0/15, services: 0/10
```

If you want to see the `kubectl` commands that each team needs to configure, you can add the following configuration to the `outputs.tf` file:

```
output "platform_team_configure_kubectl" {
  description = "Configure kubectl for Platform Team"
  value       = try(module.eks_blueprints.teams[0].platform_teams_
configure_kubectl["admin"], null) }
output "alpha_team_configure_kubectl" {
  description = "Configure kubectl for each Application Team "
  value       = try(module.eks_blueprints.teams[0].application_teams_
configure_kubectl["alpha"], null) }
```

Now that we've set up our cluster with the right access for both the platform engineering teams, as well as the application development teams, we can deploy a number of add-ons.

Adding blueprints to your cluster

As we saw in previous chapters, deploying tools such as the AWS Load Balancer Controller or Karpenter can take quite a bit of work. Blueprints extend the EKs add-on concepts to other tools and can leverage the EKS add-on or ArgoCD to deploy this software. The currently supported add-ons can be found at `https://aws-ia.github.io/terraform-aws-eks-blueprints/add-ons`.

We will deploy ArgoCD, which is a GitOps deployment tool (discussed in more detail in the *Using ArgoCD, Crossplane, and GitOps to deploy workloads* section), and then ArgoCD will deploy (most of the) other add-ons.

The first thing we will do is create a `locals-blueprints.tf` file in our repository, with the contents shown next. This will tell ArgoCD where to look for the different helm charts to deploy the add-ons:

```
locals {
  addon_application = {
    path                 = "chart"
    repo_url             = "https://github.com/aws-samples/eks-
blueprints-add-ons.git"
    add_on_application = true }}
```

The next step is to deploy `argodCD` and tell it which add-ons to deploy. Note that the blueprint add-on module is opinionated, so some of the add-ons, such as the AWS CSI driver, will be deployed directly as EKS add-ons (and will appear as add-ons), whereas others will be handled by `argoCD`.

We will deploy `argoCD` and the AWS EBS CSI driver directly, and then Argo CD (`argoCD`) will deploy the following:

- The AWS Load Balancer Controller
- Fluent Bit for logging
- The metrics server for standard metrics
- Karpenter for autoscaling
- Crossplane (discussed later) for infrastructure as code

The following code snippet will be used as `blueprints.tf`:

```
module "kubernetes_addons" {
  source = "github.com/aws-ia/terraform-aws-eks-
blueprints?ref=v4.31.0/modules/kubernetes-addons"
  eks_cluster_id       = module.eks_blueprints.eks_cluster_id
  enable_argocd            = true
  argocd_manage_add_ons = true
  argocd_applications = {
    addons     = local.addon_application}
```

```
argocd_helm_config = {
  set = [{ name  = "server.service.type"
      value = "LoadBalancer" }]}
enable_aws_load_balancer_controller  = true
enable_amazon_eks_aws_ebs_csi_driver = true
enable_aws_for_fluentbit             = true
enable_metrics_server                = true
enable_Crossplane                    = true
enable_karpenter                     = true }
```

The following commands can be used to do the following:

- Deploy the Terraform updates

- Validate that the add-ons in EKS have all been deployed successfully:

```
(initial) $ terraform init
Downloading git::https://github.com/aws-ia/terraform-aws-eks-
blueprints.git?ref=v4.31.0 for kubernetes_addons...
....
(initial) $ terraform plan module.eks_blueprints.module.aws_eks.
module.kms.data.aws_partition.current: Reading...
module.eks_blueprints.data.aws_region.current: Reading...
....
Plan: 29 to add, 0 to change, 0 to destroy.
(initial) $ terraform apply --auto-approve
odule.eks_blueprints.module.aws_eks.module.kms.data.aws_partition.
current: Reading...
Note: Objects have changed outside of Terraform
...
Apply complete! Resources: 29 added, 0 changed, 0 destroyed.
Outputs:
configure_kubectl = "aws eks --region eu-central-1 update-kubeconfig
--name cluster-tf"
vpc_id = "vpc-0d5fb4e92b71eb9e6"
(initial) $ aws eks list-addons --cluster-name cluster-tf
{"addons": [
        "aws-ebs-csi-driver"]}
```

We can now get the ArgoCD details and access them to review the details of the other add-ons, by using the following commands:

```
(initial) $ kubectl get deploy -n argocd
NAME                               READY   UP-TO-DATE   AVAILABLE   AGE
argo-cd-argocd-applicationset-controller   1/1   1 1 82m
argo-cd-argocd-dex-server                  1/1   1 1 82m
```

```
argo-cd-argocd-notifications-controller      1/1   1 1 82m
argo-cd-argocd-repo-server                   2/2   2 2 82m
argo-cd-argocd-server                        2/2   2 2 82m
argo-cd-redis-ha-haproxy                     3/3   3 3 82m
(initial) $ export ARGOCD_SERVER=`kubectl get svc argo-cd-argocd-
server -n argocd -o json | jq --raw-output '.status.loadBalancer.
ingress[0].hostname'`
(initial) $ echo https://$ARGOCD_SERVER
https://1234-453293485.eu-central-1.elb.amazonaws.com
(initial) $ kubectl -n argocd get secret argocd-initial-admin-secret
-o jsonpath="{.data.password}" | base64 -d
Myinteretsingp355word
```

We can now browse to the ArgoCD URL and log in with the details shown previously to see the status of the other add-ons:

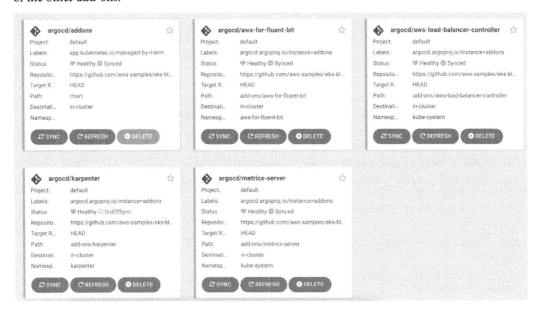

Figure 19.5 – The argoCD applications/add-ons status

> **Note**
>
> Please make sure you have pushed all changes to the CodeCommit repository and have also destroyed the cluster using the terraform destroy command. It can take some time to destroy the VPC and the networking components.

Modification and upgrades follow a similar pattern; the Terraform code is modified, and then the Terraform `plan` and `apply` commands are used to upgrade or reconfigure the cluster, node groups, access permission, and blueprints.

Now that we have created (and destroyed) our resources manually using Terraform, let's look at how we can use AWS CI/CD tools to automate the testing and deployment of your cluster.

Using CodePipeline and CodeBuild to build clusters

We have done the deployment manually so far by running the Terraform `plan` and `apply` commands. CodeBuild is an AWS service that acts as a CI build server but also deploys our Terraform configuration. CodePipeline automates the end-to-end release pipeline and sequences build, test, and deploy phases, based on commits to a repository such as CodeCommit.

The first thing we need to do is adjust our Terraform code to support the storage of state in an S3 bucket. This is necessary, as by default, Terraform will use local storage for its state, and as CodeBuild is a transient environment, that state will be lost between builds. Terraform relies on a state file to determine what needs adding, changing, or removing. We will simply add the backend configuration code shown next to the `providers.tf` file we created previously. We don't need to specify any details, as this will be configured dynamically during the Terraform `init` phase:

```
terraform {
...
  backend "s3" {}
```

> **Note**
> Once you've modified the code, commit the changes to your repository.

The next thing we need to do is add a `buildspec.yml` file to the `root` directory of our repository. This file is used by CodeBuild to run the build/deploy commands. The `buildspec` file is a specific format and consists of a number of phases:

- In the *install* phase, install the latest version of **Terraform** and **jq**

- In the *pre-build* phase, run `terraform init` and configure it to use an S3 bucket and prefix in a specific region, using environment variables, and also run the Terraform `validate` command as a basic test

- In the *build* phase, a Terraform `plan`, `apply`, or `destroy` command can be run based on the action specified in an environment variable

An example of the `buildspec.yml` file is shown next:

```
version: 0.2
env:
  exported-variables:
    - BuildID
    - BuildTag
phases:
  install:
    commands:
      - yum update -y
      - yum install -y yum-utils
      - yum-config-manager --add-repo https://rpm.releases.hashicorp.
com/AmazonLinux/hashicorp.repo
      - yum -y install terraform jq
      - terraform version
  pre_build:
    commands:
      - echo creating S3 backend for bucket ${TFSTATE_BUCKET} region
${TFSTATE_REGION} prefix ${TFSTATE_KEY}
      - cd "$CODEBUILD_SRC_DIR"
      - terraform init -input=false -backend-config="bucket=${TFSTATE_
BUCKET}" -backend-config="key=${TFSTATE_KEY}" -backend-
config="region=${TFSTATE_REGION}"
      - terraform validate
  build:
    commands:
      - echo running command terraform ${TF_ACTION}
      - cd "$CODEBUILD_SRC_DIR"
      - terraform ${TF_ACTION} -input=false
```

Once you've modified the code, commit the changes to your repository.

As we now have the Terraform backend configured and a `buildspec` file that CodeBuild will use to build/deploy the resources, we need to create and configure the build project.

Setting up the CodeBuild project

Using the AWS console, navigate to the AWS CodeBuild Service and add a new build project. Fill in the **Project name** and **Description** fields, as shown in the following figure:

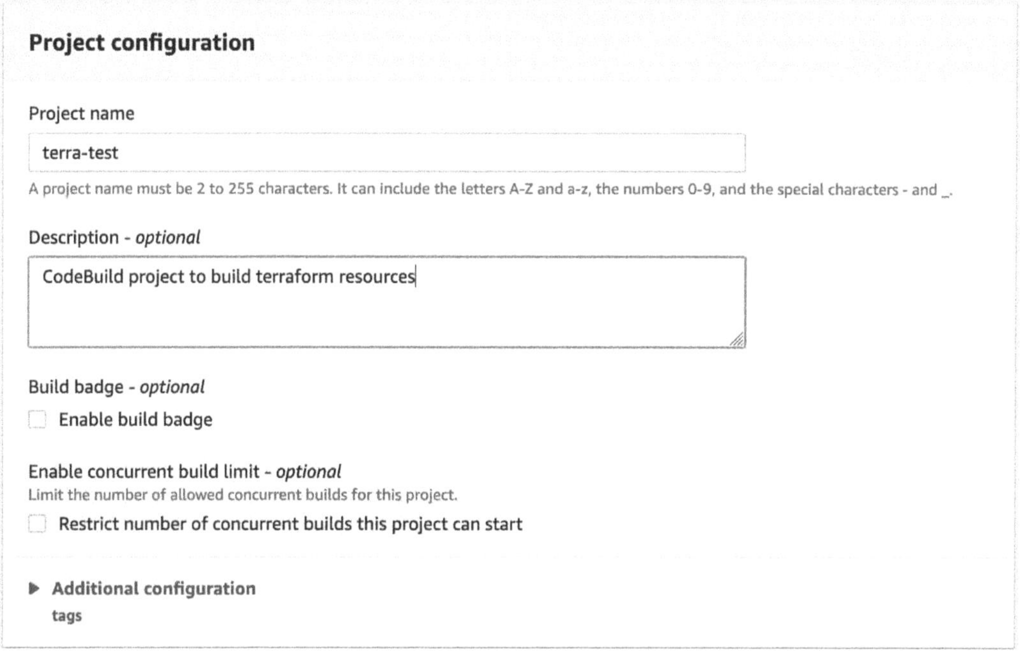

Project configuration

Project name

> terra-test

A project name must be 2 to 255 characters. It can include the letters A-Z and a-z, the numbers 0-9, and the special characters - and _.

Description - *optional*

> CodeBuild project to build terraform resources

Build badge - *optional*
☐ Enable build badge

Enable concurrent build limit - *optional*
Limit the number of allowed concurrent builds for this project.
☐ Restrict number of concurrent builds this project can start

▶ **Additional configuration**
   tags

Figure 19.6 – CodeBuild project configuration

In the **Source** panel, configure the `CodeCommit` repository and branch where the Terraform code and `buildspec` files are located, as shown in the following figure:

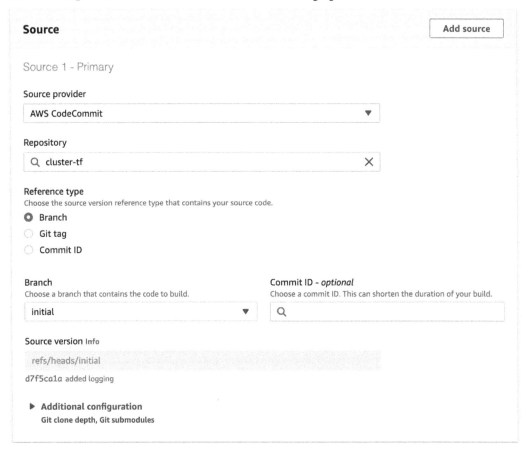

Figure 19.7 – CodeBuild source configuration

In the first part of the **Environment** panel, define the build environment as a standard Linux environment, as shown in the following figure:

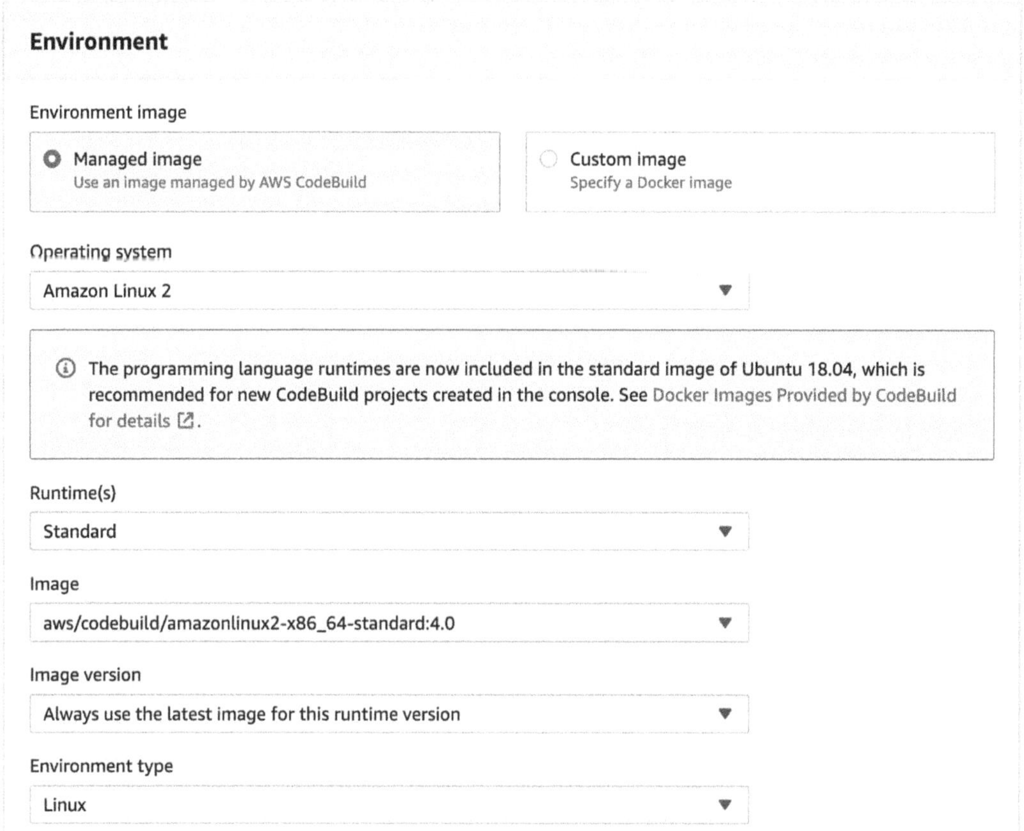

Figure 19.8 – CodeBuild environment configuration

Leave the service role to create a new service role and the **Buildspec** panel as is (shown next). Then, click on **Create Build Project** at the bottom of the screen (not shown):

Buildspec

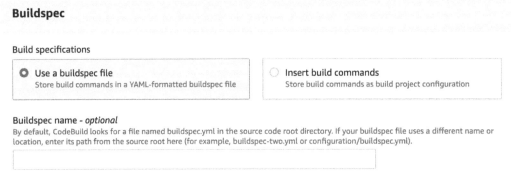

Figure 19.9 – CodeBuild buildspec configuration

You will need to configure the following environment variables, which are used by the `buildspec` file:

- **TFSTATE_BUCKET** points to an existing S3 bucket name

- **TF_ACTION** will perform and **apply -auto-approve**, but this could be changed to a **destroy** or **plan** action

- **TFSTATE_KEY** defines the prefix and file; in the example shown next, we will use the `cluster/ cluster-tf/terraform.tfstate` value

- **TFSTATE_REGION** points to the correct region

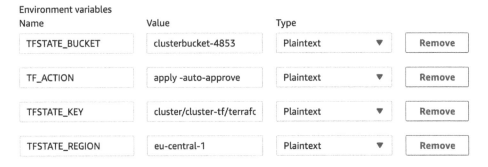

Figure 19.10 – CodeBuild environment variables

Once you have configured the environment variables, click on **Create Build Project**.

> **Note**
> The build project service role created for the project will need to have the relevant IAM permissions added to it to allow the Terraform code to create the resources.

We should also add the service role used explicitly by the code build to the `map_role` section in our `main.tf` code, as shown next:

```
{rolearn  = "arn:aws:iam::${data.aws_caller_identity.current.account_
id}:role/service-role/codebuild-terra-test-service-role"
        username = "admin-role"
        groups   = ["system:masters"] }
```

> **Note**
> Replace the `service-role` name with the one your CodeBuild project uses, and commit your changes to the repository.

Now, we have built a project pointing to our repository and branch with a specific `buildspec.yml` file, which provides the commands we need to deploy the Terraform configuration.

Figure 19.11 – The CodeBuild Start build dropdown

Once the build starts, you can look at the logs and see any errors, but it will eventually be complete, and then you can review the build history. If you look at the example shown next, you can see it took just over 30 minutes to deploy Terraform, and it completed successfully.

	Build run	Status	Build number	Source version	Submitter	Duration	Completed
	terra-test:7fff1c1c-e0b9-4832-9b77-7e98fa7ac80a	⊘ Succeeded	9	refs/heads/initial	Admin/ormalcol-Isengard	30 minutes 34 seconds	3 hours ago

Figure 19.12 – The CodeBuild Build history screen

If we look in the S3 bucket, we can see the prefix we defined in the `TFSTATE_KEY` environment variable and the `terraform.tfstate` file.

Figure 19.13 – The S3 Terraform state file

In order to trigger the build job, we need to either click on the **Start build** button or use the CodeBuild API. Next, we will look at how we can use CodePipeline to trigger the build on a code change.

> **Note**
>
> You should delete the Terraform-created resource before progressing, either manually or by changing the build job TF_ACTION to destroy -auto-approve and rerunning the build job.

Setting up CodePipeline

When we set up CodePipeline, we will configure two stages – a *source* stage that references our CodeCommit repository with the Terraform and buildspec files, and a *build* stage that references our CodeBuild project. An example is shown in the following screenshot:

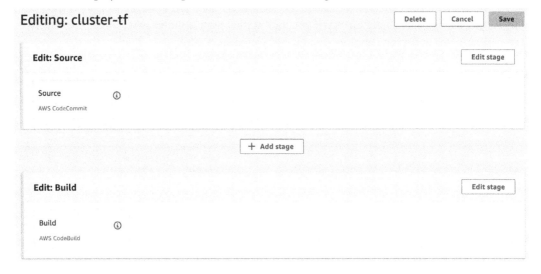

Figure 19.14 – The CodePipeline stages

We will configure our source stage with the CodeCommit repository and the branch details we will use for our code, and we will leave the default change detection and output artifacts. This means that when we make a change (commit), we will trigger a CloudWatch event that will be used in the next stage. An example of the CodeCommit configuration is shown next:

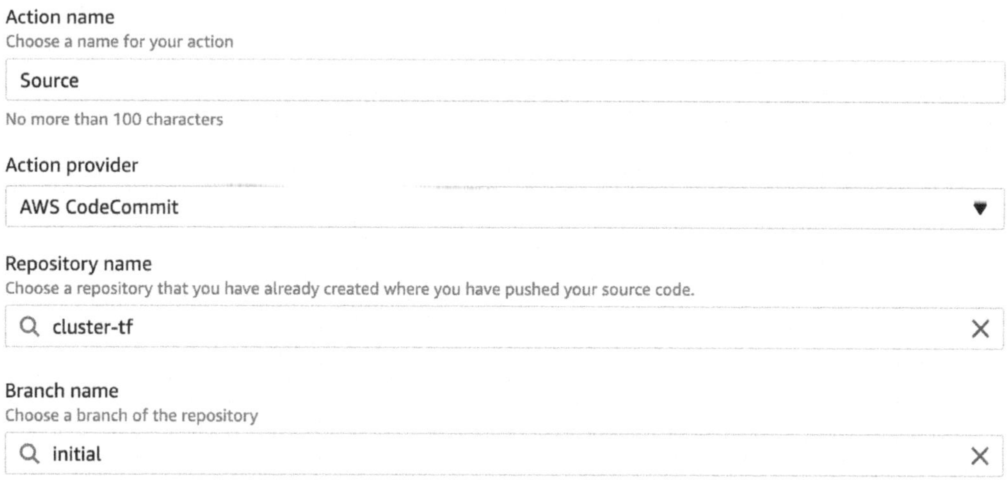

Figure 19.15 – A CodePipeline source stage configuration snippet

We then need to configure our build stage to point to our existing CodeBuild project in the correct region. An example of the CodeBuild configuration is shown next:

Figure 19.16 – A CodePipeline build stage configuration snippet

Now when we make a commit, CodePipeline detects it and triggers CodeBuild to run the build project we created previously. We can see in the example next that the commit ID and message are shown as the trigger:

Figure 19.17 – A successful pipeline run

> **Note**
>
> As the source code is now generated by CodePipeline and in the Terraform code, we will use the filepath of the repository and see a cluster built with the name of src (which is the name of the directory generated by CodePipeline). We should change the way Terraform generates the cluster name using a variable or local.

Now that we have had a quick review of using CodePipeline and CodeBuild to build our cluster based on changes to our code, let's see how we can use ArgoCD and Crossplane to deploy EKS workloads in a similar manner.

Using ArgoCD, Crossplane, and GitOps to deploy workloads

In the previous section, we used CodePipline to deploy changes to our AWS environment based on a commit and a CodePipeline configuration.

GitOps is a way of implementing **continuous deployment** (**CD**) to deploy both a containerized application and infrastructure but with a focus on self-service and developer experience. This means that the developer can use the Git repository to not only store, version, test, and build their code but also do the same for their infrastructure as code, deploying both things together.

We will use two open source projects in this chapter – **ArgoCD**, which is a deployment tool that will continually poll our application repository to look for changes, and the **K8s API** to deploy them. Crossplane allows us to use a custom Kubernetes resource to build infrastructure resources that support our application like a database. ArgoCD can use Helm to deploy and modify (patch) K8s resources or Kustomize. **Kustomize** allows you to easily customize K8s manifest files and can also be used directly by the **kubectl** tool. The architecture used is shown next.

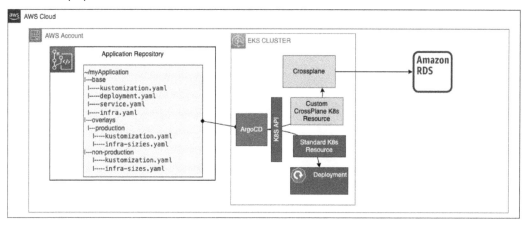

Figure 19.18 – GitOps architecture

We will use the cluster we created using the Terraform BluePrint, which already has ArgoCD installed and running, so we will start with the ArgoCD repository configuration.

Setting up our application repository

We will create and clone a new CodeCommit repository called myapp, using the same commands shown in the *Customizing and versioning EKS Blueprints for Terraform* section, to create and clone the repository into our Cloud9 instance.

We also should install Kustomize locally in our environment for local testing, using the following commands:

```
(master) $ curl -s "https://raw.githubusercontent.com/kubernetes-
sigs/kustomize/master/hack/install_kustomize.sh"  | bash
kustomize installed to /..
(master) $ kustomize version
v5.0.3
```

Now that we have the repository and the **Kustomize** tool installed, we can set up the general structure. We will use the pause container image and adjust the namespace, replica count, and memory request size based on the environment.

We will use two manifest files, which, once created, should only be changed when resources are added or deleted. The namespace.yaml file will define the namespace; an example is shown here:

```
apiVersion: v1
kind: Namespace
metadata:
  name: app
```

The deployment.yaml file will define the deployment for the pause container. An example is shown here:

```
apiVersion: apps/v1
kind: Deployment
metadata:
  name: inflate
  namespace: app
spec:
  replicas: 0
  selector:
    matchLabels:
      app: inflate
  template:
    metadata:
      labels:
        app: inflate
    spec:
      containers:
        - name: inflate
          image: public.ecr.aws/eks-distro/kubernetes/pause:3.2
          resources:
            requests:
              memory: 1Gi
```

We will now create the `base` directory and `kustomise.yaml` file that will reference the preceding templates, and also do a dry run of the deployment using the `kubectl create -k` command. These commands are shown here:

```
(master) $ mkdir base
(master) $ cd base
(master) $ touch namespace.yaml
(master) $ touch deployment.yaml
(master) $ touch kustomization.yaml
(master) $ kubectl create -k . --dry-run=client
namespace/app created (dry run)
deployment.apps/inflate created (dry run)
```

We've discussed the namespace and deployment file, but the `kustomize.yaml` file is also used by Kustomize to understand what resources it needs to deploy or modify (patch). An example is shown next:

```
apiVersion: kustomize.config.k8s.io/v1beta1
kind: Kustomization
resources:
  - namespace.yaml
  - deployment.yaml
```

As this file is created in the base directory, it simply references the two manifest files with no amendments. We will now create two overlays that adjust the values of these files for the non-production and production environments:

```
(master) $ mkdir -p ../overlays/production
(master) $ mkdir -p ../overlays/non-production
(master) $ touch ../overlays/production/kustomization.yaml
(master) $ touch ../overlays/non-production/kustomization.yaml
(master) $ touch ../overlays/non-production/deployment.yaml
master) $ touch ../overlays/production/deployment.yaml
```

The `kustomize.yaml` file for non-production is shown next and will adjust the namespace and `non-production-` prefix to all the resources:

```
resources:
- ../../base
apiVersion: kustomize.config.k8s.io/v1beta1
kind: Kustomization
namespace: non-production
namePrefix: non-production-
patches:
- path: deployment.yaml
```

It also references a `deployment.yaml` file in the local directory, which is shown next, increases the replica count in the base template to 1, and also adds new limits and requests:

```
apiVersion: apps/v1
kind: Deployment
....
spec:
  replicas: 1
.......
      containers:
        - name: inflate
.......
          resources:
            limits:
              memory: 1250Mi
            requests:
              memory: 1250Mi
```

When we run the `kubectl create -k` command, these changes will be merged with the base manifests and deployed. The following commands will deploy and verify our customizations for non-production:

```
(master) $ pwd
../myapp/overlays/non-production
(master) $ kubectl create -k .
namespace/non-production created
deployment.apps/non-production-inflate created
(master) $ kubectl get all -n non-production
NAME        READY    STATUS      RESTARTS    AGE
pod/non-production-inflate-123    1/1      Running    0    13s

NAME    READY    UP-TO-DATE    AVAILABLE    AGE
deployment.apps/non-production-inflate    1/1      1      1 13s

NAME      DESIRED    CURRENT    READY    AGE
replicaset.apps/non-production-inflate-12    1 1 1 13s
(master) $ kubectl get po non-production-inflate-123 -n non-production
-o json | jq -r '.spec.containers[].resources'
{
  "limits": {
    "memory": "1250Mi"
  },
  "requests": {
    "memory": "1250Mi"
  }
```

We can now replicate the configuration into the `./overlays/production` directory, changing the prefix and namespace to `production`, the limits and request to `2Gi`, and the number of replicas to 3. We can now commit these changes to our repository, and we know that if we run the `Kustomize` command from either the production or non-production `overlays` directories, we will get slightly different configurations for each environment.

The next step is to configure ArgoCD to deploy these resources.

Setting up the ArgoCD application

ArgoCD uses the *application* concept, which represents a Git repository. Depending on the configuration of the application, ArgoCD will poll that repository and, in our case, use Kustomize to add, change, or delete resources.

ArgoCD doesn't support AWS IAM roles, so it will use SSH credentials to poll the repository. So, we need to configure SSH credentials for a CI/CD user that has permission to access the `codecommit` repository. We will use the instructions shown at this link: `https://docs.aws.amazon.com/codecommit/latest/userguide/setting-up-ssh-unixes.html` to create an SSH key, and add it to a user with CodeCommit privileges. Once we have the SSH key ID, we can do the following:

- Install and configure the ArgoCD client

- Add a secret for ArgoCD to use to connect to the repository

- Add our application and check the deployment

The following commands will install the ArgoCD client:

```
(master) $ sudo install -m 555 argocd-linux-amd64 /usr/local/bin/
argocd
(master) $ rm argocd-linux-amd64
(master) $ argocd version
argocd: v2.7.2+cbee7e6
  BuildDate: 2023-05-12T14:06:49Z
  GitCommit: cbee7e6011407ed2d1066c482db74e97e0cc6bdb
  GitTreeState: clean
  GoVersion: go1.19.9
  Compiler: gc
  Platform: linux/amd64
FATA[0000] Argo CD server address unspecified
```

Next, we will configure the necessary environment variables to connect to our environment; examples are shown next, but you should add details relevant to your environment:

```
ARGOCD_SERVER=$(kubectl get svc argo-cd-argocd-server -n argocd -o
json | jq --raw-output '.status.loadBalancer.ingress[0].hostname')
```

```
(master) $ ARGOCD_PWD=$(kubectl -n argocd get secret argocd-initial-
admin-secret -o jsonpath="{.data.password}" | base64 - (master) $
GITOPS_IAM_SSH_KEY_ID=APKARDV7UN6242ZX
(master) $ AWS_DEFAULT_REGION=eu-central-1
Admin:~/environment/myapp (master) $ APP_REPO_NAME=myapp
(master) $ GITOPS_REPO_URL=ssh://${GITOPS_IAM_SSH_KEY_ID}@
git-codecommit.${AWS_DEFAULT_REGION}.amazonaws.com/v1/repos/${APP_
REPO_NAME}
(master) $ echo $GITOPS_REPO_URL > ./argocd_repo_url
(master) $ cat ./argocd_repo_url
ssh://APKARDV7UN6242ZX@git-codecommit.eu-central-1.amazonaws.com/v1/
repos/myapp
(master) $ argocd login $ARGOCD_SERVER --username admin --password
$ARGOCD_PWD --insecure
'admin:login' logged in successfully
Context 'a4e22bc700a154a13af063e8abe72c22-1646159678.eu-central-1.elb.
amazonaws.com' updated
```

We can now add our repository and SSH keys to ArgoCD using the following command:

```
(master) $ argocd repo add $(cat ./argocd_repo_url) --ssh-private-key-
path ${HOME}/.ssh/argocd --insecure-ignore-host-key --upsert --name
myapp
Repository 'ssh://APKARDV7UN6242ZX@git-codecommit.eu-central-1.
amazonaws.com/v1/repos/myapp' added
(master) $ argocd repo list
TYPE  NAME  INSECURE  OCI LFS  CREDS  STATUS  MESSAGE  PROJECT
git   myapp  ssh://APKARDV7UN6242ZX@git-codecommit.
eu-central-1.amazonaws.com/v1/repos/
myapp  true      false false  false  Successful
```

We can set up our application to use the repository and private key to deploy the resources. We will point it to the non-production overlay so that it will use the Kustomize configuration located there:

```
(master) $ argocd app create myapp --repo $(cat ./argocd_repo_url)
--path overlays/non-production --dest-server https://kubernetes.
default.svc --sync-policy automated --self-heal --auto-prune
application 'myapp' created
(master) $ argocd app list | grep myapp
argocd/myapp  https://kubernetes.default.
svc    default Synced      Healthy  Auto-Prune  <none>      ssh://
APKARDV7UN6242ZX@git-codecommit.eu-central-1.amazonaws.com/v1/repos/
myapp  overlays/non-production
(master) $ kubectl get all -n non-production
NAME      READY   STATUS    RESTARTS   AGE
pod/non-production-inflate-22    1/1      Running   0    24s
NAME       READY   UP-TO-DATE   AVAILABLE   AGE
deployment.apps/non-production-inflate   1/1  1  1    25s
```

```
NAME     DESIRED   CURRENT   READY   AGE
replicaset.apps/non-production-inflate-22   1   1   1     25s
```

If we look at the Argo CD UI, we can see the app is healthy and the components have been deployed, and ArgoCD will continue to keep them in sync as we make changes to the underlying CodeCommit repository.

Figure 19.19 – The myapp application status in ArgoCD

Now, we have a working application that will be continually deployed by Argo CD. We can see how we add infrastructure resources to the same repository and have them provisioned by Crossplane.

Adding AWS infrastructure with Crossplane

Throughout this book, we saw how we can add K8s resources and use K8s controllers, such as the AWS Load Balancer Controller, to create AWS resources such as a network or application load balancer. Crossplane can be seen as a generic controller for AWS resources.

We will use the cluster we created with Blueprints but replace the Crossplane deployment with the latest version. So, we will install helm and then use it to deploy the Crossplane charts:

```
$ curl -fsSL -o get_helm.sh https://raw.githubusercontent.com/helm/
helm/main/scripts/get-helm-3
$ chmod 700 get_helm.sh
$ ./get_helm.sh
$ helm repo add Crossplane-stable https://charts.Crossplane.io/stable
$ helm install Crossplane --create-namespace --namespace Crossplane-
system Crossplane-stable/Crossplane
```

> **Note**
> You may need to delete the Crossplane-system namespace before deploying.

Now that we have installed the latest version of Crossplane, we need to configure the provider and its associated permissions.

Setting up our Crossplane AWS providers

As Crossplane will create resources in AWS, it requires a role/permission to do this. We will start by creating an IRSA role, mapping it to our cluster, and assigning it the admin role. The commands for this are shown here:

```
$ account_id=$(aws sts get-caller-identity --query "Account" --output
text)
$ oidc_provider=$(aws eks describe-cluster --name src --region $AWS_
DEFAULT_REGION --query "cluster.identity.oidc.issuer" --output text |
sed -e "s/^https:\/\///")
$ cat > trust.yaml <<EOF
{ "Version": "2012-10-17",
  "Statement": [
    {
      "Effect": "Allow",
      "Principal": {
        "Federated": "arn:aws:iam::${account_id}:oidc-provider/${oidc_
provider}"
      },
      "Action": "sts:AssumeRoleWithWebIdentity",
      "Condition": {
        "StringLike": {
          "${oidc_provider}:sub": "system:serviceaccount:Crossplane:sy
stem:provider-aws-*"
        }}}]}
EOF
$ aws iam create-role --role-name bespoke-Crossplane --assume-role-
policy-document file://trust.json --description "Crossplane IRSA role"
{
    "Role": {
        "Path": "/",
        "RoleName": "bespoke-Crossplane",
        "RoleId": "AROARDV7UN62754DFZQBL",
        "Arn": "arn:aws:iam::112233:role/bespoke-Crossplane",
....
$ aws iam attach-role-policy --role-name bespoke-Crossplane --policy-
arn=arn:aws:iam::aws:policy/AdministratorAccess
```

Now, we have a role that trusts our cluster's OIDC provider and has permission to provision AWS resources. Next, we need to configure the Crossplane deployment to use it. This can be done using the following manifest to configure the provider and the controller:

```
apiVersion: pkg.Crossplane.io/v1alpha1
kind: ControllerConfig
metadata:
```

```
  name: aws-config
  annotations:
     eks.amazonaws.com/role-arn: arn:aws:iam::112233:role/bespoke-
Crossplane
spec:
  podSecurityContext:
     fsGroup: 2000
  args:
     - --debug
---
apiVersion: pkg.Crossplane.io/v1
kind: Provider
metadata:
  name: provider-aws
spec:
  package: xpkg.upbound.io/upbound/provider-aws:v0.27.0
  controllerConfigRef:
     name: aws-config
```

We can deploy the AWS provider using the following commands:

```
$ kubectl create -f Crossplane-provider.yaml
controllerconfig.pkg.Crossplane.io/aws-config created
provider.pkg.Crossplane.io/provider-aws created
$ kubectl get providers
NAME   INSTALLED   HEALTHY   PACKAGE              AGE
provider-aws    True        True        xpkg.upbound.io/upbound/provider-
aws:v0.27.0    52m
```

Once the provider is *healthy*, we can finish the configuration by adding a provider configuration and defining the credential insertion method as IRSA. This is one of the differences of the upbound AWS provider – it uses a different API and the IRSA source key:

```
apiVersion: aws.upbound.io/v1beta1
kind: ProviderConfig
metadata:
  name: provider-aws
spec:
  credentials:
     source: IRSA
```

We can deploy this manifest file with the following command:

```
$ kubectl create -f ub-config.yaml
providerconfig.aws.upbound.io/provider-aws created
```

As we enabled debug logging, we can look at the logs of the provider to confirm that all the configurations and AWS permissions are in place with the following commands:

```
$ kubectl get po -n Crossplane-system
NAME   READY   STATUS   RESTARTS   AGE
Crossplane-12   1/1   Running   1 (57m ago)   66m
Crossplane-rbac-manager-12   1/1   Running   0   66m
provider-aws-12   1/1   Running   1 (58m ago)   60m
$ k logs provider-aws-12 -n Crossplane-system
....
1.6848748355755348e+09   DEBUG   provider-
aws   Reconciling   {"controller": "providerconfig/providerconfig.
aws.upbound.io", "request": "/provider-aws"}
```

> **Note**
>
> For a production configuration, you should disable debug logging, as it is very verbose and generates a lot of data.

Creating infrastructure resources

Now that we have a working Crossplane AWS provider, we can actually provision an AWS resource. We will configure an S3 bucket with some basic configuration. The following manifest will create an S3 bucket called myapp-Crossplane-bucket637678 and use the AWS provider we created in the previous step:

```
apiVersion: s3.aws.upbound.io/v1beta1
kind: Bucket
metadata:
  name: myapp-Crossplane-bucket637678
spec:
  forProvider:
    region: eu-central-1
  providerConfigRef:
    name: provider-aws
```

We can deploy and verify the bucket using the following commands:

```
$ kubectl create -f Crossplane-us3.yaml
bucket.s3.aws.upbound.io/myapp-Crossplane-bucket637678 created
$ kubectl get bucket
NAME   READY   SYNCED   EXTERNAL-NAME   AGE
myapp-Crossplane-bucket637678   True   True   myapp-Crossplane-
bucket637678   15s
$ aws s3 ls | grep Crossplane
```

```
2023-05-23 20:57:39 myapp-Crossplane-bucket637678
$ kubectl get  bucket myapp-Crossplane-bucket637678 -o json | jq
.status.atProvider.arn
"arn:aws:s3:::myapp-Crossplane-bucket637678"
```

This manifest can be added to our application repository and the relevant `kustomize.yaml` files modified. This now means that, as a DevOps engineer or developer, we can configure not only an application but also any supporting infrastructure. If you want to use ArgoCD to deploy a Crossplane resource, please refer to this link: `https://docs.Crossplane.io/v1.10/guides/argo-cd-Crossplane/`.

While this is a long chapter, I have only touched the surface of developing for EKS, but hopefully, you have enough information to allow you to explore further!

In this section, we looked at how we can develop on EKS, use a variety of AWS services and open source tools to automate our cluster builds, and deploy and test our applications. We'll now revisit the key learning points from this chapter.

Summary

In this chapter, we started by considering that there are multiple personas that need to develop on EKS, from traditional developers to DevOps or platform engineers. Each of these roles needs similar but different things to do their job, so it is really important to consider your operating model when looking at EKS development.

Next, we looked at how you can use an IDE to develop your infrastructure/application code and how AWS Cloud9 provides a simple and secure interface to do this on EKS. We then built a **Cloud9** instance using Terraform and installed all the required tools on it needed for our development. Using our Cloud9 instance, we explored the EKS Terraform blueprint, creating the various configuration files, committing them to a `CodeCommit` repository, and deploying it using the Terraform commands. This created a complete EKS cluster, in a new VPC, with a set of applications and add-ons automatically configured.

We then looked at how platform/DevOps engineers can automate the deployment/testing of the EKS cluster using a **CodeBuild** job and a `buildspec.yaml` file, and we automated this process using **CodePipeline**, based on a commit to the `CodeCommit` branch. Additionally, we looked at how DevOps engineers or developers can use ArgoCD/Kustomize to automate the customization and deployment of K8s manifest files.

Finally, we looked at how we can incorporate AWS infrastructure resources into our application repository, by using Crossplane and creating an S3 bucket in AWS using a K8s manifest and custom resource.

In the final chapter, we will look at how to troubleshoot common EKS problems.

Further reading

- Using Cloud9 in headerless mode:

  `https://aws.amazon.com/blogs/devops/how-to-run-headless-front-end-tests-with-aws-cloud9-and-aws-codebuild/`

- Getting started with EKS blueprints for Terraform:

  `https://aws-ia.github.io/terraform-aws-eks-blueprints/getting-started/`

- Creating a secure AWS CI/CD pipeline:

  `https://aws.amazon.com/blogs/devops/setting-up-a-secure-ci-cd-pipeline-in-a-private-amazon-virtual-private-cloud-with-no-public-internet-access/`

- GitOps on AWS:

  `https://aws.amazon.com/blogs/containers/gitops-model-for-provisioning-and-bootstrapping-amazon-eks-clusters-using-Crossplane-and-argo-cd/`

Part 5:
Overcoming Common
EKS Challenges

The goal of this fifth section is to provide more details on troubleshooting common EKS issues.

This section has the following chapter:

20

Troubleshooting Common Issues

Throughout the book, we have created clusters and added controllers, add-ons, workloads, and so on, but not everything has gone according to plan. And while K8s does a great job of being easy to use, you will probably have at least one issue following this book or in your day job.

Understanding how to troubleshoot and what tools to use to identify root causes and hopefully fix them is an important part of using or running **Elastic Kubernetes Service** (**EKS**). In this chapter, we will look at the common techniques and tools used with EKS, as well as the frequent errors you may see when using Amazon EKS.

In this chapter, we will cover a couple of common questions when you start using Amazon EKS, walk through the details, and learn how to do troubleshooting such as the following:

- Common K8s tools/techniques for troubleshooting EKS
- Common cluster access problems
- Common Node/compute problems
- Common Pod networking problems
- Common workload problems

Let's get started!

Technical requirements

The reader should have a familiarity with YAML, AWS IAM, and EKS architecture. Before getting started with this chapter, please ensure the following:

- You have network connectivity to your EKS cluster API endpoint
- The AWS CLI, Docker, and kubectl binary is installed on your workstation and have administrator access

Common K8s tools/techniques for troubleshooting EKS

Any troubleshooting process begins with trying to understand the problem and differentiate between symptoms and the root cause of the problem. Symptoms can often be mistaken for the root cause, so the troubleshooting process tends to be iterative, with constant testing and observation as you focus on what the actual problem is and disregard the symptoms and false positives.

Once you understand the problem, it's now a case of understanding how to mitigate, solve, or ignore it. Not all problems can be solved then and there, so you may need a strategy to work around them for the time being.

The final stage will be the resolution/fixing of the problem. This might require an update to your cluster, application code, or both, and depending on the nature of the problem, the number of clusters you manage and the impact on the users/customers may be quite an involved process.

Generally, I use the following checklist when trying to understand the problem:

- *What has changed?* – The mantra for most support engineers; has there been a new deployment? A cluster or add-on upgrade? An AWS/on-premises infrastructure change? We'll look at tools next but having a record of any changes (in production at least) is a good practice to help engineers determine what has changed across these three areas.

- *Investigate the impact* – Here, you look at the symptoms. What problem is being observed? A slowdown of processing or a complete failure? What's the scope? Limited to one namespace? One cluster? One VPC? Combined with an understanding of what has changed, this normally allows an engineer to narrow down the problem to the root cause but may require you to iterate through several hypotheses. Is it the new node type added to the cluster? No, it's the new deployment on the node! Or, it's the application library in the deployment!

- *Plan your fix or mitigation* – Can you fix it easily with no impact or do you need to plan your change? Form a plan and discuss it with your team, application owner, and any customer representatives. If you can replicate the problem and the fix in a non-production environment prior to any production change, then you should, and this will help with the overall plan.

Now we've got a basic understanding of the steps you would typically go through to troubleshoot EKS problems. Next, let's look at some of the tools you might use to do so.

Common EKS troubleshooting tools

The following table provides a list of common troubleshooting tools; it's not exhaustive as the K8s ecosystem is large and has lots of contributors, but these are the ones I use or have used in the past. (Sorry if your favorite one isn't included!)

Phase	Tool	Description
What has changed?	AWS CloudTrail	CloudTrail can provide logs of every API call made in your AWS accounts; this includes AWS EKS API calls (not K8s API), API calls to load balancers, IAM, and so on.
	AWS CloudWatch	Provides dashboards and logs for the control and (optionally) data planes.
	Grafana Loki `https://grafana.com/oss/loki/`	An open source log aggregator.
	`kubectl diff`	`kubectl diff` allows you to compare a local manifest file with the running configuration to see what will change (or has changed) and is a useful tool if you have access to previous manifest files or commits.
Investigating the impact	Linux command-line tools	Any of the standard Linux tools such as `dig`, `ping`, `tcpdump`, and so on should be used to determine the scope and impact.
	kubectl	`kubectl describe`, `kubectl get events`, and `kubectl logs` are fundamental to any troubleshooting process. `kubectl top` can be used to look at Pod- and Node-level stats (as long as the metrics servers are installed)
	Ktop: `https://github.com/vladimirvivien/ktop`	A useful CLI for cluster management
	k9s: `https://github.com/derailed/k9s`	A useful CLI for cluster management
	AWS Log Collector `https://github.com/awslabs/amazon-eks-ami/tree/master/log-collector-script/linux`	AWS support script that can be used to collect OS and K8s logs.

Table 20.1 – Common EKS troubleshooting tools

> **Note**
>
> You can also now use `kubectl debug` to inject a troubleshooting container into a running pod to do live debugging of running pods in K8s 1.25 and above.

Along with technical tools/services, AWS provides a number of support services, which are listed here.

AWS Premium Support

AWS provides technical support service for all customers and offers 24/7 service 365 days a year. It is designed to give you the right mix of tools and access to AWS expertise, so you can focus on business growth while optimizing system performance, learning how to cut unnecessary infrastructure costs, and reducing the complexity for doing troubleshooting when using each AWS service.

The support plan includes different levels, such as *Developer*, *Business*, and *Enterprise*. Depending on what support plan you have, you can use email, phone calls, or even chat to reach out to AWS experts for consulting on technical or operational issues through the AWS Support case console.

> **Note**
>
> If you are interested in the AWS Premium Support plan and would like to learn more detail, you can check out their service feature page: `https://aws.amazon.com/premiumsupport/plans/`.

Part of the support model is access to Knowledge Center, which has a lot of additional information on all the AWS platform products, not just EKS.

AWS Support Knowledge Center

AWS Support Knowledge Center is maintained by AWS and comprises a centralized resource center to help you better learn how to fix operational issues or your configuration when using AWS services. It lists the most frequent questions and requests that AWS support receives from its customers. You can check more details by accessing the following link: `https://aws.amazon.com/premiumsupport/knowledge-center/`.

You can review the section on Amazon EKS to find out the common issues in Amazon EKS. Some articles also include featured videos with complete step-by-step tutorials. Now we've looked at some common tools for troubleshooting, let's look at some typical cluster access problems.

Common cluster access problems

This section lists common issues when trying to access your EKS cluster. The next few sections describe common symptoms and how to fix them.

You cannot access your cluster using kubectl

Interacting with your cluster API through **kubectl** or as part of a CI/CD pipeline or tool is a critical part of using EKS! Some common problems are listed next, along with potential solutions.

> **Note**
>
> While the errors shown next may point to a specific problem, they may also be related to an issue not documented here.

In the error message shown, the shell has no credentials configured as environment variables or as a profile in the ~/.aws directory:

```
$ kubectl get node
Unable to locate credentials. You can configure credentials by running
"aws configure".
$ aws eks update-kubeconfig --name mycluster  --region eu-central-1
Unable to locate credentials. You can configure credentials by running
"aws configure".
```

You may also get the following error message, which is different but means the same thing – the shell has no credentials configured as environment variables or as a profile in the ~/.aws directory:

```
$ kubectl get node
Unable to locate credentials. You can configure credentials by running
"aws configure".
```

In the error message shown next, the credentials configured in the shell don't have the right IAM privilege or K8s privileges:

```
$ kubectl get node
error: You must be logged in to the server (Unauthorized)
```

In this error message, the most likely issue is a network connectivity issue, with the client having restricted network access to a private EKS cluster or with an IP whitelist. This error is sometimes seen if an IAM role is used without the relevant access:

```
$ kubectl get node
Unable to connect to the server: dial tcp 3.69.90.98:443: i/o timeout
```

Now we've looked at some common cluster access problems let's look at some typical Node/compute problems.

Common Node/compute problems

This section lists common issues you might see with worker nodes in your EKS cluster, along with potential solutions.

Node/Nodes can't join the cluster

For this problem, what has changed, for example, a new node being added or an IP whitelist being changed, will determine what needs fixing. Often, the error is simply nodes being in a NotReady/ Unknown state, shown next, which has a number of different root causes:

```
$ kubectl get node
NAME    STATUS    ROLES    AGE    VERSION
ip-172-31-10-50.x.internal    NotReady    <none>    7d4h    v1.24.13-
eks-0a21954
ip-172-31-11-89.x.internal    Unknown    <none>    7d4h    v1.24.13-
eks-0a21954
```

If you're running self-managed nodes, did EC2 run the bootstrap.sh script? With a managed node, this will happen automatically, but if not, your EC2 instance will not register automatically.

If you have an IP whitelist on a public cluster, did you include the public address of your nodes or the NAT gateway to the whitelist? If not, then your nodes will not be able to communicate with the K8s cluster.

For a private or private/public cluster, was your worker node security group registered with the cluster security group? If not, then your nodes will not be able to communicate with the K8s cluster.

```
Dec 23 17:42:36 ... kubelet[92039]: E1223 17:42:36.551307 92039
kubelet.go:2240] node "XXXXXXXXX" not found
```

In the error message shown previously from the kubelet logs, the most likely issue is a VPC DNS issue where the VPC hasn't been configured with DNS hostnames or resolution.

```
Error: Kubernetes cluster unreachable: Get "https://XXXXXXXXXX.gr7.
eu-central-1.eks.amazonaws.com/version?timeout=32s": dial tcp <API_
SERVER_IP>:443: i/o timeout
```

In the error message shown previously from the kubelet logs, the most likely issue is a networking issue where a security group, NACL, NAT gateway, or endpoint is misconfigured or doesn't exist.

```
Jan 01 12:23:01 XXXXXXXXX kubelet[4445]: E1012 12:23:01.369732    4445
kubelet_node_status.go:377] Error updating node status, will retry:
error getting node "XXXXXXXXX": Unauthorized
```

In the error message shown previously from the `kubelet` logs, the most likely issue is an IAM authentication issue where the node's IAM role has not been added to the `aws-auth` config map.

```
onditions:Type    Status   LastHeartbeatTime
LastTransitionTime     Reason          Message
   MemoryPressure    False    Tue, 12 Jul 2022 03:10:33 +0000    Wed, 29
Jun 2022 13:21:17 +0000    KubeletHasSufficientMemory    kubelet has
sufficient memory available
   DiskPressure      True     Tue, 12 Jul 2022 03:10:33 +0000    Wed, 06
Jul 2022 19:46:54 +0000    KubeletHasDiskPressure        kubelet has
disk pressure
```

In the error message shown previously from the `describe node` command, the most likely issue is a disk issue due to low disk space (normally due to out-of-control logging). Now we've looked at some common cluster compute problems, let's look at some typical networking problems.

Common Pod networking problems

In previous sections, we've discussed networking problems in the context of the API/control plane and worker nodes. This section lists common issues you might see with pod networking in an EKS cluster, along with potential solutions.

```
* connect to 172.16.24.25 port 8080 failed: Connection timed out
* Closing connection 0
curl: (7) Failed to connect to 172.16.24.25 port 8080 failed:
Connection timed out
```

In the error message shown previously from the pod logs, the most likely issue is a worker (or pod) security group issue. Check that the worker security group is configured to allow all the needed ports, IP CIDR ranges, and other security groups (including itself). If you using NACLs, make sure ephemeral ports are allowed out, as well as any ingress ports.

```
Error: RequestError: send request failed caused by: Post dial tcp: i/o
timeout
```

In the error message shown previously from the pod logs, the most likely issue is a DNS issue. Make sure `clusterDNS` and `CoreDNS` are working and the VPC has been enabled with DNS resolution and hostnames.

```
Error: RequestError: send request failed caused by: Post dial tcp
172.16.24.25:443: i/o timeout
```

In the error message shown previously from the pod logs, the most likely issue is a connectivity issue.

```
Failed create pod mypod: rpc error: code = Unknown desc =
NetworkPlugin cni failed to set up pod network: add cmd: failed to
assign an IP address to container
```

The previous error message from the `pod describe` command shows the pod stuck in a `ContainerCreating` status; the most likely issue is that the VPC has no more free IP addresses. If prefix addressing is not being used, then the EC2 instance type may have exhausted the number of IP addresses it can support.

```
NAME           READY      STATUS                 RESTARTS      AGE
aws-node-bbwpq  0/1        CrashLoopBackOff       12            51m
aws-node-nw7v8  0/1        CrashLoopBackOff       12            51m
coredns-12      0/1        Pending                0             54m
coredns-13      0/1        Pending                0             54m
```

In the error message shown previously from the `get pod` command, the most likely issue is a VPC or security group issue, which has a knock-on effect for the CNI or DNS operations in the pod.

```
"msg"="Reconciler error" "error"="failed to build LoadBalancer
configuration due to retrieval of subnets failed to resolve 2
qualified subnets.
```

In the error message from the `describe deployment` command, the most likely issue is a subnet has not been tagged for an internal or external load balancer so it cannot be discovered. Now we've looked at some common pod networking problems, let's look at some typical workload problems.

Common workload problems

This section lists common issues you might see with pods and/or deployments in an EKS cluster, along with potential solutions.

```
State:  Running
Started: Sun, 16 Feb 2020 10:20:09 +0000
Last State: Terminated
Reason: OOMKilled
```

In the preceding error message from the `kubectl describe pod` command, the most likely issue is a connectivity issue or a memory issue, as `OOMKilled` means that the pod has reached its memory limit, so it restarts. You need to increase the memory setting in the deployment or pod specification.

```
NAME               READY  STATUS                 RESTARTS   AGE
myDeployment1-123... 1/1    Running                1          17m
myDeployment1-234... 0/1    CrashLoopBackOff       2          1m
```

In the error message from `kubectl get po` command, there are several possible issues, whether from a bad DockerFile, pulling the image file, and so on. Run the `kubectl logs` command to get more information about what caused the error.

```
   Warning  FailedScheduling  22s (x14 over 13m)   default-
scheduler  0/3 nodes are available: 3 Insufficient cpu.
```

The error message shown previously from the `kubectl describe po` command shows the pod in a `Pending` status. The most likely issue is insufficient CPU available in your worker nodes.

```
  Warning  FailedScheduling  80s (x14 over 15m)  default-
scheduler  0/3 nodes are available: 3 Insufficient memory.
```

The `kubectl describe po` command's error message shows the pod in a `Pending` status; the most likely issue is insufficient memory available in your worker nodes.

```
    State:          Waiting
    Reason:         ErrImagePull
```

The preceding error message from the `kubectl describe po` command shows the pod in a `Pending` status. The most likely issue is the container image is incorrect, not available, or hosted in a private repository that has not been configured in your worker nodes.

```
  Warning  FailedScheduling  77s (x3 over 79s)  default-scheduler  0/1
  nodes are available: 1 node(s) had taint {node-typee: high-memory},
  that the pod didn't tolerate.
```

The preceding error message from the `kubectl describe po` command shows the pod in a `Pending` status. The most likely issue is the pod doesn't match a corresponding node toleration. This chapter won't touch all the possible symptoms and root causes you will encounter with K8s/EKS but hopefully, you have enough information to cover the common problems you will encounter.

In this section, we looked at tools and techniques for troubleshooting EKS and common problems you may encounter. We'll now revisit the key learning points from this chapter.

Summary

In this chapter, we started by looking at a general approach to troubleshooting EKS clusters and some common tools that can be used to determine what has changed and the scope/impact of the problem.

We then moved on to common problems/symptoms you may encounter in connecting to your EKS cluster, compute nodes, pod networking, and workloads and used **kubectl** commands to identify these issues and provide some possible resolutions.

This is the final chapter and by now, you should have all the knowledge required to build and manage EKS clusters and the workloads that run on them.

Congratulations on completing this book! We hope you have found it informative and useful.

Further reading

- Debugging K8s Tools:

  `https://www.cncf.io/blog/2022/09/15/10-critical-kubernetes-tools-and-how-to-debug-them/`

- EKS official troubleshooting guide:

  `https://docs.aws.amazon.com/eks/latest/userguide/troubleshooting.html`

Index

packtpub.com

Subscribe to our online digital library for full access to over 7,000 books and videos, as well as industry leading tools to help you plan your personal development and advance your career. For more information, please visit our website.

Why subscribe?

- Spend less time learning and more time coding with practical eBooks and Videos from over 4,000 industry professionals

- Improve your learning with Skill Plans built especially for you

- Get a free eBook or video every month

- Fully searchable for easy access to vital information

- Copy and paste, print, and bookmark content

Did you know that Packt offers eBook versions of every book published, with PDF and ePub files available? You can upgrade to the eBook version at packtpub.com and as a print book customer, you are entitled to a discount on the eBook copy. Get in touch with us at customercare@packtpub.com for more details.

At www.packtpub.com, you can also read a collection of free technical articles, sign up for a range of free newsletters, and receive exclusive discounts and offers on Packt books and eBooks.

Other Books You May Enjoy

If you enjoyed this book, you may be interested in these other books by Packt:

AWS CDK in Practice

Mark Avdi, Leo Lam

ISBN: 978-1-80181-239-9

- Turn containerized web applications into fully managed solutions
- Explore the benefits of building DevOps into everyday code with AWS CDK
- Uncover the potential of AWS services with CDK
- Create a serverless-focused local development environment
- Self-assemble projects with CI/CD and automated live testing
- Build the complete path from development to production with AWS CDK
- Become well versed in dealing with production issues through best practices

AWS Cloud Computing Concepts and Tech Analogies

Ashish Prajapati, Juan Carlos Ruiz

ISBN: 978-1-80461-142-5

- Implement virtual servers in the cloud
- Identify the best cloud storage options for a specific solution
- Explore best practices for networking and databases in the cloud
- Enforce security with authentication and authorization in the cloud
- Effectively monitor applications in the cloud
- Leverage scalability and automation in the cloud
- Get the hang of decoupled and serverless architecture
- Grasp the fundamentals of containers and Blockchain in the cloud

Packt is searching for authors like you

If you're interested in becoming an author for Packt, please visit `authors.packtpub.com` and apply today. We have worked with thousands of developers and tech professionals, just like you, to help them share their insight with the global tech community. You can make a general application, apply for a specific hot topic that we are recruiting an author for, or submit your own idea.

Share Your Thoughts

Now you've finished *Mastering Elastic Kubernetes Service on AWS*, we'd love to hear your thoughts! Scan the QR code below to go straight to the Amazon review page for this book and share your feedback or leave a review on the site that you purchased it from.

`https://packt.link/r/1803231211`

Your review is important to us and the tech community and will help us make sure we're delivering excellent quality content.

Download a free PDF copy of this book

Thanks for purchasing this book!

Do you like to read on the go but are unable to carry your print books everywhere?

Is your eBook purchase not compatible with the device of your choice?

Don't worry, now with every Packt book you get a DRM-free PDF version of that book at no cost.

Read anywhere, any place, on any device. Search, copy, and paste code from your favorite technical books directly into your application.

The perks don't stop there, you can get exclusive access to discounts, newsletters, and great free content in your inbox daily

Follow these simple steps to get the benefits:

1. Scan the QR code or visit the link below

https://packt.link/free-ebook/9781803231211

2. Submit your proof of purchase
3. That's it! We'll send your free PDF and other benefits to your email directly

Milton Keynes UK
Ingram Content Group UK Ltd.
UKHW030238080324
439059UK00007B/70